The Victor Sayings in the Book of Revelation

The Victor Sayings in the Book of Revelation

MARK WILSON

Eugene, Oregon

THE VICTOR SAYINGS IN THE BOOK OF REVELATION

Copyright © 2007 Mark Wilson. All rights reserved. Except for brief quotations in critical publications or reviews, no part of this book may be reproduced in any manner without prior written permission from the publisher. Write: Permissions, Wipf and Stock, 199 W. 8th Ave., Eugene, OR 97401.

ISBN 13: 978-1-55635-146-4

Manufactured in the U.S.A.

The content of this manuscript is copyrighted by the University of South Africa © 1997 and used with permission.

All scripture quotations, unless otherwise indicated, are taken from the HOLY BIBLE, NEW INTERNATIONAL VERSION®. NIV®. Copyright © 1973, 1978, 1984 by International Bible Society. Used by permission of Zondervan. All rights reserved.

I want to dedicate this volume to my wife Dindy, a "companion in the suffering and kingdom and patient endurance" (Rev 1:19) that comes with research and publication. Without her continual encouragement and prayer support, the initial writing and later revision of this work could not have occurred. She gladly became the breadwinner during my study sabbatical and other research periods. I rather like J. M. Court's words to his wife in the introduction to *Myth and History in the Book of Revelation*: "To have lived with me and a work on the Apocalypse is more than anybody should be expected to endure." My sentiments exactly, Dindy.

Contents

Acknowledgements / ix
Introduction / xi
Abbreviations / xiv

1
The Structure of the Seven Letters and Revelation / 1

2
The Form of the Seven Letters / 31

3
The Victors and the Victor Sayings / 77

4
The Text of the Victor Sayings / 103

5
The Fulfillment of the Victor Sayings / 173

6
The Appropriation of the Victor Sayings / 231

Appendix / 257
Bibliography / 263

Acknowledgements

THE PUBLICATION of a book is a corporate one, with many individuals and institutions having a part in its completion. I would like to recognize some of these. First, I would like to thank my doctoral promoter Professor H. A. Lombard whose knowledge of apocalyptic literature has made him an invaluable resource for my research. Thanks are extended to the University of South Africa for permission to revise and publish part of my doctoral thesis originally accepted at Unisa. Professor Willie J. Wessels, although a scholar of the "other" testament, has been a valuable friend and contact at Unisa. I wish to thank the New Testament Society of South Africa for the privilege of being a member of this esteemed scholarly body, and I have enjoyed the occasional opportunities to attend its annual meetings.

During my masters program at Regent University, Professor J. Rodman Williams cemented my interest in the book of Revelation and in eschatology. His friendship, along with that of his wife Johanna, has been a special inspiration. The late Regent professor Charles H. Holman gave me a foundation in hermeneutics as well as continued support in my role as an adjunct professor at Regent. Finally, I would like to thank Dr. K. C. Hanson and Wipf and Stock for their interest in publishing this manuscript. Their friendly and efficient assistance in its publication has been greatly appreciated.

Numerous individuals have given generous financial support for the research and writing of this volume. It is impossible to name each one of them or to mention the many other friends who have prayed for and encouraged me in this project. I also wish to thank the pastoral leadership, the session, and the congregation of my home church, Kempsville Presbyterian in Virginia Beach, Virginia, for their ongoing support. They provided financial resources for trips to Turkey and South Africa, as well as monthly support during a study sabbatical.

Invaluable assistance was provided by the library at Regent University, which went out of its way to provide books and articles necessary for my research. I wish to thank the entire staff, but especially Bob Sivigny. Jim Funari has provided invaluable computer support as well as a friendly ear throughout the years.

Acknowledgements

During my midlife period of postgraduate study I have seen my four children—Leilani, Winema, Jim, and David—grow up, attend college, and leave home. Now most have married and have their own children. Hopefully they were not neglected too badly in the process, and that my accomplishment will inspire their own future endeavors! I wish to give David and his wife Heather special thanks for their work in preparing the volume for publication. Finally, I would like to thank my parents Wayne and Idella Wilson for their ongoing encouragement and support of my academic career.

Introduction

THE LETTERS to the seven churches, according to Beasley-Murray, "comprise the best known and most frequently expounded section of the book of Revelation."[1] This is undoubtedly because chapters 1–3 are the most accessible section of Revelation, which Ulfgard describes as "one of the most disputed books of the New Testament, and one of the most difficult to appreciate."[2] Whether chapters 2–3 should be called letters,[3] prophetic letters,[4] messages,[5] prophetic messages,[6] or proclamations[7] remains open to question and personal preference. Many commentators today prefer "message," although the traditional terminology "letter" continues to be commonly used. In this study I will use the traditional "letters" (*Sendschreiben*) to describe these chapters.

The form of these letters has received much scrutiny in recent years, with increasing investigation of their various sections. Such research is long overdue. The final (at least in four of the letters) and perhaps most significant section is the victor sayings. Poirier remarked a generation ago "que leur interprétation est une partie faible chez plusieurs commentateurs."[8] This remains the case despite a host of commentaries, monographs, and articles on the book of Revelation. A master's thesis done by R. R. Benedict in 1967 is the only other major study found that focuses on these promises and their place in Revelation. Thus this volume is timely and relevant in its examination of the victor sayings.

Two major studies that concentrated largely on the historical background of the letters were done in the twentieth century—W. M. Ramsay's *The Letters to the Seven Churches of Asia* (1904) and C. H. Hemer's *The*

---

1. Beasley-Murray, *Revelation*, 70.
2. Ulfgard, *Feast and Future*, 8.
3. Ramsay, *Letters to the Seven Churches*, 25–33.
4. Schüssler Fiorenza, *Book of Revelation*, 165.
5. Roberts, "Letter to Seven Churches," 22–23.
6. Bauckham, *Climax of Prophecy*, 2.
7. Aune, "Form and Function of the Proclamations," 183ff.
8. "that their interpretation is a weak part with several interpreters"; Poirier, *Les sept églises*, 42.

Introduction

Letters to the Seven Churches of Asia in their Local Setting (1986). The importance of historical-critical study for interpreting Revelation has been well stated by Mulholland: "[It] can provide an understanding of the contemporary meaning of this pool of resources upon which the account of the vision builds.... Historical-critical methods can give us the starting point of the images, myths, and symbols."[9] From this starting point recent commentators have begun to investigate the letters from newer critical perspectives such as literary criticism,[10] rhetorical criticism,[11] sociological criticism,[12] and reader-response criticism.[13] Each of these approaches has provided fresh insights into Revelation 2–3. In this study I propose to adopt an eclectic approach, utilizing insights from the aforementioned methodologies. My underlying presupposition, in the well-chosen words of R. L. Gundry, "assumes that the language of the biblical text, including its symbolic language, grows out of and speaks to the historical situation of the writer and his readers."[14]

The book begins with an examination of the structure of Revelation 2–3 within the structure of the entire book. The victor sayings functioned within a larger rhetorical unit, which in turn formed part of a complex literary document. Chiasmus is proposed as the macrostructure of Revelation, suggested in part by the promises found in chapters 2–3 and their fulfillment in chapters 19–22. A chiastic outline is evaluated according to criteria proposed by Blomberg.

Chapter 2 examines several proposals regarding the form of the seven letters. Imperial edicts, prophetic oracles, and ancient letters are given extensive analysis. Revelation 2–3 is determined to be seven prophetic letters divided into seven sayings—address, epithet, praise, blame, coming, hearing, and victor.

Chapter 3 examines the topic of victory, beginning with the biblical use of νικάω. The victors are identified as all believers, not just martyrs. Victory, an ideal in the Greco-Roman world and exemplified in the athletic games, is highlighted.

---

9. Mulholland, *Revelation*, 23.
10. Ryken, "Revelation," 302–28.
11. Kirby, "Rhetorical Situations of Revelation 1–3," 197–207.
12. McVann, ed., "Apocalypse of John in Social-Scientific Perspective."
13. Long, "Real Reader Reading Revelation," 395–411.
14. Gundry, "New Jerusalem, " 255.

Introduction

Chapter 4 is the center of the study and focuses on the victor sayings and their promises (*Siegersprüche* or *Überwindersprüchen*) that end each letter. Bauckham captures the importance of this quest:

> Thus the call to conquer . . . is a call to engage in the eschatological battle described in the central chapters of the book, in order to reach the eschatological destiny described at the end of the book. In a sense *the whole book is about the way the Christians of the seven churches may, by being victorious within the specific situations of their own churches, enter the new Jerusalem* (my emphasis—MW).[15]

Beale likewise notes their significance: "Therefore, the logical flow of each letter climaxes with the promise of inheriting eternal life with Christ, which is the main point of each letter."[16] Textual and grammatical questions related to each victor saying are first examined. Then the key images in the promises are investigated in the context of local references. Co-texts related to the images in Biblical and Extrabiblical literature are likewise discussed.

In chapter 5 a final victor saying is investigated initially. Then the fulfillments to the victor sayings are highlighted. Each image is developed as it appears throughout Revelation, particularly in chapters 19–21 where the thousand years and the new Jerusalem are introduced. The examination of the hermeneutical spiral, begun in chapter 1, is here completed.

The volume concludes in chapter 6 with a discussion of Revelation's theme and the function of the seven letters. The coming of Jesus and victory are determined to be macrodynamic themes. The letters with their victor sayings function as parenetic and prophetic wake-up calls to the seven churches. Through repentance and obedience the believers are assured of participation in the rewards promised in the eschatological kingdom to be established at Jesus' soon coming. The study thus analyzes the victor sayings in Revelation and examines how the audience in these seven representative Asian churches might have understood and responded to these promises in the midst of their social, political, and spiritual challenges.

---

15. Bauckham, *Theology of the Book of Revelation*, 14.
16. Beale, *John's Use of the Old Testament in Revelation*, 302.

Abbreviations

ALL ABBREVIATIONS used in the volume follow *The SBL Handbook of Style* (Peabody, Mass.: Hendrickson, 1999). Italicized words are part of the original quotation unless otherwise noted. Greek translations are my own, unless otherwise noted, and are based on the Rahlfs edition of the Septuagint and the UBS^4/Nestle-Aland^{27} text. All classical references are taken from their respective editions in the Loeb Classical Library except those of Philo, which are drawn from Yonge's updated Hendrickson edition. References from the Dead Sea Scrolls are taken from the updated translation by Martínez. The two-volume edition edited by J. H. Charlesworth provided references to the Pseudigrapha. Quotations from the early church fathers follow the standard edition edited by P. Schaff and A. Roberts.

1

The Structure of the Seven Letters and Revelation

Introduction

THE VICTOR sayings with their catchword νικάω are part of a larger literary unit, the seven letters, which themselves comprise a section within Revelation. To understand how these sayings function rhetorically, it is necessary to locate them first within these larger literary units. As Ulfgard has well observed, "no attempt at understanding a part of Rev can be made without having a general idea of its place within the whole book."[1] Therefore we begin our study by examining the vexing problem of Revelation's structure. In spite of a growing mass of research, little consensus exists regarding structure. Michaels in his exegetical guide to Revelation makes this pessimistic assessment that "there are as many different outlines as there are interpreters."[2] And Barr, who served for years as chairman of the Society of Biblical Literature seminar on Reading the Apocalypse, likewise states in a recent paper: "There is no consensus on how we should organize or outline the material in the book. There are almost as many outlines as there are commentators doing the organizing."[3]

The truth of these statements is clearly seen in the analysis by Lombard of structural outlines by five leading commentators. Lombard includes Kraft, Hahn, Lambrecht, Schüssler Fiorenza, and Hellholm.[4] While certain similarities are apparent, one is struck by the profound differences among the outlines of these five authors. Add the eight others whom Michaels references plus his own,[5] and it is apparent that a major interpretive problem is at work. If scholars cannot agree on a structural approach, it is understandable that the average reader has difficulty making

---

1. Ulfgard, *Feast and Future*, 1.
2. Michaels, *Interpreting the Book of Revelation*, 69.
3. Barr, "Plots and Echoes," 1.
4. Lombard, "Structure of Revelation," 154–57.
5. Michaels, *Interpreting the Book of Revelation*, 69 n. 9 and 69–71.

sense of the book's organization. Yet, as Rissi acutely observes, "In scarcely any other biblical book are the method of exposition and the understanding of the book's literary structure so thoroughly intertwined as they are in the Revelation to John. The question of construction deeply touches the highly problematic character of the book."[6]

Many commentators consider Revelation 1:19 to be a structural key to the book: "Therefore, write what you have seen, what is and what is about to happen after this." Schüssler Fiorenza affirms this observation, "The passage most generally used for dividing the book is Rev. 1:19." Whether the verse suggests a twofold or a threefold division is hotly debated, and Beale has provided a complete discussion of the options.[7]

In his widely circulated commentary Walvoord advocates a threefold division: "The things referred to as having already been seen are those contained in chapter 1 . . . . The second division, 'the things which are,' most naturally includes chapters 2 and 3 . . . . The third division, 'the things which shall be hereafter,' would naturally include the bulk of the book which was to be prophetic."[8] The futurist interpretive view, which Walvoord represents, sees the events of chapters 4–22 as occurring in the period immediately preceding the parousia. The church is seen as raptured in chapter 4 and thus out of the picture during the judgments depicted in the seals, trumpets, and bowls. Because the word "church" does not appear after chapters 1–3, Walvoord concludes "that the church may be considered as in heaven and not related to events which will take place on the earth in preparation for Christ's return in power and glory."

Discontinuity between chapters 1–3 and 4–22 is the hallmark of this interpretation, which from a literary perspective is difficult to sustain. Schüssler Fiorenza rightly points to the book's continuity: "As the seventh element of the preceding seven-series opens up a new series of visions in the plague septets of the book, so the seventh element of the letter vision opens up a new series of visions. It is therefore inappropriate to separate the letter septet from the following visions of the book." She also observes that such a division suborns authorial intent "since it separates parenesis and apocalyptic vision."[9] While 1:19 can assist in understanding the tem-

---

6. Rissi, *Time and History*, 1.
7. Beale, "Interpretative Problem," 360–87.
8. Walvoord, *Revelation*, 48j.
9. Schüssler Fiorenza, *Revelation*, 172, 173.

poral perspectives within the prophecy, it cannot provide a macrostructure for the book.[10]

The seven letters of chapters 2–3 are perhaps the most familiar section of Revelation. While many studies note the unique structure of the seven letters for rhetorical effect (this will be developed in chapter 2), few consider the macrostructure of these chapters in terms of chiasmus. Likewise, the promises in the victor sayings with their corresponding fulfillments in the book's final chapters suggest that chiasmus may be a possible macrostructure for Revelation. We will now explore whether chiasmus may be the structural key both for the seven letters as well as for the entire book.

Chiasmus as a Structural Technique in Ancient Literature

The burgeoning interest in rhetorical criticism has led to increased focus on the role of chiasmus as a structural device in ancient literature. Kennedy's favorable mention of chiasmus in his influential *New Testament Interpretation through Rhetorical Criticism* has certainly spurred interest in it.[11] The nature of chiasmus and its structural place in classical and biblical literature, particularly Revelation, are discussed next.

Chiasmus derives its name from its likeness to the Greek letter *chi* (C). Bullinger classified chiasmus under "Introverted Correspondence," declaring:

> This is where there are two series, and the first of the one series corresponds with the last of the second; the second of the first corresponds with the penultimate (or the last but one) of the second: and the third of the first corresponds with the antepenultimate of the second. That is to say, if there are six members, the first corresponds with the sixth, the second with the fifth, and third with the fourth, and so on.

Chiasmus as thus broadly defined includes direct, inverted, and antithetical parallelism. Breck, however, seeks to narrow the common definition, insisting that chiasmus can be distinguished from other parallel structures by a "pivotal theme, about which the other propositions of the literary unity are developed." Genuine chiasmus, Breck continues, has

---

10. In spite of hermeneutical evidence to the contrary, Walvoord's approach remains the prevailing one among many readers today. In my wing of Christendom, the Pentecostal/charismatic movement, this perspective is nearly the exclusive one and others are largely unknown. A recent example that adopts a futurist perspective is the 1991 commentary, *The Ultimate Victory*, by Pentecostal scholar S. M. Horton.

11. Kennedy, *New Testament Interpretation*, 11–12, 28–29.

a central focus at its "crossing point," which sets "in relief the central idea or theme the writers tries to express."[12] Chiasmus therefore has a rhetorical force distinct from other structural devices.

Kennedy notes that chiasmus is an example of a literary figure "commonly found in ancient texts and given labels by modern critics [but] not identified at all in handbooks of the classical period."[13] The importance of chiasmus has been identified by Stock as "a seriously needed element of internal organization in ancient writings, which did not make use of paragraphs, punctuation, capitalization and other such synthetic devices to communicate the conclusion of one idea and the commencement of the next."[14]

According to Parunak, chiasmus is a simple structural form "used to divide, unify, and emphasize biblical texts."[15] Modern readers, accustomed to visual interpretive aids such as punctuation, parentheses, and paragraphs, can little understand the situation of the first-century reader or listener. Speaking of Revelation, Bauckham explains, "It is important to realise that the essential structure of the book . . . must have been intended to be perceptible in oral performance."[16] For the ancient audience external structural features were necessary to introduce and close pericopes, to signal emphasis, and to define argumentation.

Since Revelation's audience was raised in a Greco-Roman literary environment, it is important to look at the rhetorical background in classical literature. Chiasmus was used in classical Greek literature as early as Homer and was very common in Latin literature, especially in poetry of the Augustan period. Classical scholars often term such structuration as "ring composition." Talbert calls this "the principle of balance," and lists a number of classical works and uses Vergil's *Aeneid* as a particular example.[17] Homer, whose home was Smyrna, used it extensively in the *Illiad*,[18] and scholars have identified chiasmus in numerous other works including Hesiod's *Theogeny*, Aeschylus' *Persae*, Thucydides' *History*, and Euripides' *Bacchae*.[19]

12. Breck, "Biblical Chiasmus," 71.
13. Kennedy, *New Testament Interpretation*, 28.
14. Stock, "Chiastic Awareness," 23.
15. Parunak, "Oral Typesetting," 168.
16. Bauckham, *Climax of Prophecy*, 1.
17. Talbert, *Literary Patterns*, 67ff.
18. Whitman, *Homer*, 249–84 passim.
19. For Hesiod see Hamilton, *Architecture*, 40; for Aeschylus see Holtsmark, "Ring Composition," passim; for Thucydides see Connor, *Thucydides*, 251ff.; for Euripides see Kernell, "Ordering Principles," passim.

The Structure of the Seven Letters and Revelation

Because of the many symbols, allusions, and possible quotations in Revelation from the Old Testament, John seemingly presumes that his audience is familiar with its books. Chiasmus, often in ABA′ form, has been identified in much Old Testament literature.[20] The use of chiasmus in prophetic literature is noteworthy, particularly the ABA′ format. The writings of the classical prophets generally fall into a threefold pattern: (1) God's threats against his people, (2) oracles against the nations, and (3) promises of restoration. Such a pattern is seen in Ezekiel:

(1) Chapters 1–24
   (2) Chapters 25–32
(3) Chapters 33–48

Wolf presents a variation of this outline in Isaiah:[21]

Judgment with Assyrian backdrop as poetry (ch. 1–35)
   Historical interlude as prose (ch. 36–39)
Comfort with Babylonian backdrop as poetry (ch. 40–66)

Goldingay has noted chiastic structure even in the languages of Daniel:[22]

Hebrew (1—2:4a)
   Aramaic (2:4b—7:28)
Hebrew (8:1—12:13)

Baldwin observes that Zechariah begins with an appeal for repentance while "the closing verses look ahead to the time when all men will worship the true God." She then notes how Daniel and Revelation follow a similar progression.[23]

---

20. The following are some of the books identified by their commentators as displaying chiastic structure–Deuteronomy: Christensen, *Deuteronomy*, xli; Ruth: Luter and Rigsby, "Adjusted Symmetrical Structuring," 15ff.; Job: Andersen, *Job*, 20–22; Clines, *Job 1–20*, xxxv–xxvii; Ecclesiastes: Fredericks, "Chiasm and Parallel Structure," 19; Isaiah: Laaton, "Composition," 212–13; Daniel: Baldwin, *Daniel*, 59–62; Goldingay, *Daniel*, 325; and Zechariah: Baldwin, *Haggai*, 75–81.

21. Wolf, *Interpreting Isaiah*, 40.

22. Goldingay, *Daniel*, 325.

23. Baldwin, *Haggai*, 74. Another remarkable feature of these prophetic books is that a structural break occurs in the middle of the prophecy. Isaiah divides into chapters 1–39 and 40–66; Daniel into chapters 1–6 and 7–12; Zechariah into chapters 1–8 and 9–14. Likewise Revelation can be divided into chapters 1–11 and 12–22.

Commentators have likewise found examples of chiasmus throughout the New Testament.[24] Brouwer has recently attempted to develop a chiastic reading for John 13–17,[25] and Thomson has suggested five examples of intermediate length chiasmus in Paul's letters.[26] Luter and Lee have recently proposed chiasmus as the macro-structure for Philippians.[27] It is evident that the New Testament authors by virtue of their background and training were also familiar with chiasmus as a rhetorical structural device.

Literary Characteristics of Chiasmus

In his seminal study of biblical chiasmus, *Chiasmus in the New Testament*, Lund notes seven "laws" of chiastic structure:[28]

1. The center, which may consist of up to four lines, is always the turning point.
2. At the center a change of thought often occurs and an antithetic idea introduced. After this the original trend is resumed and continued until the system is concluded.
3. Identical ideas often occur in the extremes and at the center and nowhere else in their respective system.
4. Ideas often occur at the center of one system and recur in the extremes of a corresponding one, with the second system evidently constructed to match the first.
5. Certain terms tend to gravitate toward certain positions within a given system, e.g., the divine names in the Psalms and quotations in the New Testament at the center.
6. Larger units are frequently introduced and concluded by frame-passages.
7. A mixture of chiastic and alternating lines often occurs within the same unit.

---

24. A representative list follows: Matthew: Gundry, *Survey*, 164–67; Anderson, "Double and Triple Stories," 75–76; Mark: Dewey, *Markan Public Debate*, passim; Luke: Bailey, *Poet and Peasant*, 63; John: Culpepper, "Pivot," 31; Acts: Wolfe, "Chiastic Structure," 60–71; 2 Corinthians: Blomberg, "Structure of 2 Corinthians," 8ff.; Ephesians: Porter, "ἴστε γινώσκοντες," 273; Galatians: Longnecker, *Galatians*, 213; James: Davids, *James*, 25–29; and Jude: Bauckham, *Jude*, 5–6; cf. Wendland, "Comparative Study," 211–12.

25. Brouwer, *Literary Development of John 13–17*.

26. Thomson, *Chiasmus in the Pauline Letters*. Other examples are identified by Scholer and Snodgrass, "Preface," xvii–xviii, and by Blomberg, "Structure of 2 Corinthians 1–7," 5–8.

27. Luter and Lee, "Philippians as Chiasmus."

28. Lund, *Chiasmus in the New Testament*, 40–41.

Breck has narrowed Lund's seven "laws" to four: (1) framing by inclusion, (2) pivoting at the middle, (3) heightening between parallel elements, and (4) spiraling from the extremities to the center.[29] Thomson has likewise reworked Lund's work, omitting 1, 3, 4, redrafting the other four "laws," and adding two characteristics: (1) balancing elements have similar length and (2) the center contains the focus of the author's thought.[30]

Because ancient writing was meant to be read aloud, rules of rhetorical discourse invaded all fields of literature. Stock identifies two primary rules. First, "a literary work should begin and end in the same way, with similar material (and so should smaller passages within the work), with the most important material in the middle." Second, "each unit begins and ends with narrative material between which discourse material will be framed."[31] Stock's first rule accords with Lund's rules 1 and 3, and his second with rule 6.

Clark identifies three types of guidelines for identifying chiasmus: (1) content, (2) form or structure, and (3) language. Two other identifiable features of pericope are setting and theology. All of these criteria, according to Clark, are "*to be seen as a cline with varying degrees of strength and persuasiveness rather than as a feature which is definitely either present or absent.*"[32] Chiastic structure, undoubtedly apparent to ancient readers, often becomes difficult for modern interpreters to delimit exactly, even in the same pericopes. An example is Mark 2:1—3:6 where differing chiastic structures are identified by Dewey and Harrington.[33]

The rising interest in chiasmus as a structural device has produced a down side. Chiasmus is now being found everywhere in Scripture, with many suggestions being improbable. Such abuse has prompted Blomberg to suggest nine criteria that must be met before hypotheses of extended chiasmus can be considered credible.[34] These criteria are summarized as follows:

1. A problem must be perceived in the structure of the text in question, which more conventional outlines fail to resolve.

---

29. J. Breck, *Shape of Biblical Language*, 31–45.
30. Thomson, *Chiasmus in the Pauline Letters*, 26–27.
31. Stock, "Chiastic Awareness and Education in Antiquity," 26.
32. Clark, "Criteria for Identifying Chiasm," 63, 65.
33. Dewey, "Literary Structure," 396, and Harrington, *Mark*, 24–25.
34. Blomberg, "Structure of 2 Corinthians 1–7," 5–7.

2. Clear examples of parallelism must be evident between the two "halves" of the hypothesized chiasmus, to which commentators call attention even when they propose quite different outlines for the text overall.
3. Verbal (grammatical) and conceptual (structural) parallelism should characterize most if not all of the corresponding pairs of subdivisions.
4. Verbal parallelism should involve central or dominant imagery or terminology, not peripheral or trivial language.
5. Both verbal and conceptual parallelism should involve words and ideas not regularly found elsewhere within the proposed chiasmus.
6. Multiple sets of correspondences between passages opposite each other in the chiasmus as well as multiple members of the chiasmus itself are desirable.
7. The outline should divide the text at natural breaks that would be agreed upon even by those proposing very different structures to account for the whole.
8. The center of the chiasmus, which forms its climax, should be a passage worthy of that position in light of its theological or ethical significance.
9. Ruptures in the outline, such as shifts between the forward and reverse parts of the structure, should be avoided if possible.

Adherence to Blomberg's sensible criteria will assist interpreters in finding valid examples of chiasmus in Scripture. Later in the chapter our proposed chiastic outline will be examined in light of each criterion.

Chiasmus in Revelation

These laws and criteria will serve as a starting point for our discussion in Revelation, where illustrations of these criteria will be pointed out. Most commentators on Revelation have largely ignored discussion of rhetorical figures such as chiasmus. The indexes of such standard commentaries as Charles, Kiddle, Tenney, Mounce, Beasley-Murray, Sweet, and Ford omit any reference to chiasmus. It is largely newer commentators who include discussions of the subject.[35]

Wall, speaking of John's rhetorical devices generally, observes: "The author often repeats similar words and phrases in inverted (ABCC'B'A') or chiastic (ABCDC'B'A') order."[36] Several examples of macro-chiasm found by interpreters in Revelation follow.

Giblin suggests a modified chiastic structure for the seven beatitudes:[37]

> A Beatitude 1 (1:3)
>   B Beatitude 2 (14:13)
>   C Beatitude 3 (16:15)
>   D' Beatitude 4 (19:9)
>   B' Beatitude 5 (20:6)
> A' Beatitude 6 (22:7)
>   C' Beatitude 7 (22:14)

Giblin explains that beatitudes 1 and 6 deal with an expected response to the reading of the book, beatitudes 2 and 5 speak of a heavenly reward prior to the general resurrection, and beatitudes 3 and 7 refer to guarding (keeping) and washing one's own clothes. Beatitude 4 highlights the invitation to the wedding supper of the Lamb and is the only beatitude with no explanation given. Though it stands alone among the seven and in the center, it does not appear to have central importance. "Nonetheless, it does stand out as a uniquely arresting statement of God's "grace" or blessing."[38] Giblin argues that beatitudes 3 and 7—those which deliberately upset the concentric order, especially 7 (C')—seem to be underscored in the progression of the series. Giblin's observations concerning structuration in the beatitudes is valid and significant. A relationship between the beatitudes and the victor sayings will be presented in the next chapter.

Mulholland, following Bornkamm, portrays the rebellion against God in the form of a chiasmus, beginning with the introduction of Death and Hades in 6:8 and concluding with their destruction in 20:14.[39] However, Death and Hades in 6:8 are named in the context of the fourth seal, and

---

35. Breck, *Shape of Biblical Language*, 232–35, provides a disappointing addendum on Revelation in his volume. He provides only three examples, with that of 9:17d–18 the most convincing.

36. Wall, *Revelation*, 15.

37. Giblin, *Book of Revelation*, 217n. 164.

38. Ibid.

39. Mulholland, *Revelation*, 38.

their mention does not appear to begin a chiastic sequence. Therefore the chiasmus proposed by Bornkamm and Mulholland seems unconvincing.

Gaechter and Strand among others have proposed another model called "the great chiastic symmetry of the second half of the Apocalypse."[40] Here the dragon, the two beasts, and Babylon are destroyed in the reverse order of their appearance. Such a model also validates that John himself saw a division in his document following chapter 11. Strand diagrams this chiasmus as follows, with only the first verse of multi-verse references given:[41]

>   A Dragon (12:3)
>   B Sea-beast (13:1)
>   C Earth-beast = false prophet (13:11)
>   D Babylon (14:8)
>   E Beast-worshipers (14:9)
>   E´ Beast-worshipers (16:2)
>   D´ Babylon (16:19)
>   C´ Earth-beast = false prophet (19:20)
>   B´ Sea-beast (19:20)
>   A´ Dragon (20:2)

One flaw in Strand's diagram is that the sea-beast is reintroduced in 19:19–20 before the false prophet, hence C´ and B´ should be switched. This chiastic anomaly is understandable because the two beasts work together so closely that they might be considered a unit. Strand demonstrates convincingly that chiasmus is used for thematic structuration in the second half of Revelation. Such an observation lends credence to the suggestion that chiasmus might likewise serve as the book's macrostructure.

Wall sees chiasmus shaping both the prologue (21:1–5a) and the main body (21:5b–22:6a) of the vision of the new Jerusalem.[42] The center of the prologue's chiasmus focuses on a bride rather than a city (21:2a), thus drawing the reader to John's real concern. Wall believes that John's emphasis here accords with 19:6, where the eschatological community is explicitly called the bride of the Lamb. The second chiasmus shapes the main body of the vision, which follows from and expands upon the prologue.

---

40. Gaechter, "Semitic Literary Forms," 559.
41. Strand, "Chiastic Structure," 403.
42. Wall, *Revelation*, 244.

> A John's recommissioning to write (21:5b)
>   B Water of life given (21:6)
>   C Inheritance of the community of overcomers (21:7)
>   D Overcomers escape the second death because not evildoers (21:8)
>   E Extended description of new Jerusalem (21:9—26)
>   D′ Impure do not inherit new order (21:27a)
>   C′ Overcomers found in Lamb's book of life (21:27b)
>   B′ Water of life in garden given to overcomers (22:1–5)
> A′ John's vision of new order called trustworthy and true (22:6a)

The center of this second chiasmus likewise equates the new Jerusalem with the bride found in the vortex of the prologue. Wall thinks John's vision here has been crafted to underscore one foundational eschatological principle—"the primary result of God's coming triumph over evil is a redeemed and transformed people, who live forever with God and God's Lamb."[43]

Wall's attempt to find John's emphasis here by using chiasmus is creatively executed, yet flawed. Without doing an in-depth analysis utilizing Blomberg's criteria, suffice it to say that Wall's proposal fails Blomberg's first criterion. Conventional outlines typically break after 21:8, with verse 9 beginning a new section. Botha notes correctly that "21:1–8 forms the link between the visions of the ultimate salvation and the foregoing visions of judgment."[44] This is the pericope's inherent structure because 21:1—22:6 is another example of a double vision, in this case of the heavenly city/bride. Vision 1 comprises 21:1–8; vision 2 consists of 21:9—22:6. The emphases of this double vision will be discussed later. Because the chiasmus does not follow the natural literary division, its elements must be forced into artificial parallelisms. Commentators have found other examples of chiasmus in Revelation: Talbert in 8:2–6[45]; Aune in 9:17b–18b[46]; Siew in 11:1—14:5[47]; Beale in 17–22[48]; Harris in the hymns of 4–5.[49]

---

43. Ibid., 245.
44. Botha, "Authorship," 135.
45. Talbert, *Apocalypse*, 38.
46. Aune, *Revelation*, 2:540.
47. Siew, *War between the Two Beasts and the Two Witnesses*.
48. Beale, *Book of Revelation*, 983.
49. Harris, "Literary Function of Hymns," 310–19.

Chiasmus in the Seven Letters

We will next discuss the heuristic value of chiasmus for exegesis by critiquing several chiastic models proposed to interpret the letters. Lund himself devoted a chapter to "The Structure of the Seven Epistles."[50] Farrer has extensively examined the literary structure in Revelation and sees chiasmus at work in the portrayal of the divine speaker from heaven to John and to the churches. He observes this as beginning in the initial vision:[51]

> A "One like a son of man . . . his eyes as flaming fire and his feet like burnished brass" (1:13–15)
> B "And out from his mouth a sharp double-edged sword proceeding" (1:16)
> C "I am the first and the last and the living, and I was dead and lo am alive" (1:17–18)
> D "The secret of the seven stars thou sawst at my right hand and the seven golden candlesticks" (1:20)

The first four letters, then, repeat and reverse the order of these statements:

> D´ To Ephesus: "Thus saith the holder of the seven stars in his right hand, who walks among the seven golden candlesticks" (2:1)
> C´ To Smyrna: "Thus saith the first and the last who was dead and lived" (2:8)
> B´ To Pergamus: "Thus saith he who hath the sharp two-edged sword" (2:12)
> A´ To Thyatira: "Thus saith the Son of God who hath his eyes as flaming fire and his feet like burnished brass" (2:18)

Welch has uncritically accepted Farrer's proposal and states that "precise inverted repetition such as this is common in the book of Revelation."[52] Upon closer examination, Farrer's neat arrangement is not so precise. What has become of the speaker in the final three letters? The Sardian portrayal dealing with the seven spirits and seven stars is drawn from 1:4, 16 (B) and 1:20 (D) above. The Philadelphian portrayal, which speaks of the key of David, echoes 1:18 (C) where the keys of death and Hades are

---

50. Lund, *Studies in the Book of Revelation*, 66–84.
51. Farrer, *Revelation of St. John the Divine*, 166.
52. Welch, "Chiasmus in the New Testament," 243.

mentioned. The final Laodicean portrayal—of Jesus as the faithful witness—first appears in 1:5. Portrayals used in the seven letters in order of appearance are:

Sardis (3:1)	1:4	Seven spirits
Laodicea (3:14)	1:5	Faithful witness
Ephesus (2:1)	1:12	Seven golden lampstands
Thyatira (2:18)	1:14	Eyes as flaming fire
Thyatira (2:18)	1:15	Feet like burnished brass
Ephesus (2:1), Sardis (3:1)	1:16	Seven stars in right hand
Pergamum (2:12)	1:16	Double-edged sword out of mouth
Smyrna (2:8)	1:17	First and the last
Smyrna (2:8)	1:18	Dead and now alive
Philadelphia (3:7)	1:18	Holds the keys

Welch concludes that, while such an example is "relatively facile, [it] shows the writer's proclivity to use chiasmus."[53]

The order proposed by Farrer and approved by Welch seems problematic given the interrelatedness of the derived texts. John seems to have borrowed freely from the imagery of the opening vision without following a structural plan. John may tend to use chiasmus but such use cannot be validated from this example. Even if it were, recognition of chiasmus gives little help in understanding why a particular identification of Jesus had relevance to the life setting of each individual church. As Kennedy states: "If rhetorical criticism is to be valid, it must be practiced with some awareness of the traditions of Jewish speech of which chiasmus is one, and if it is to be useful it must embrace more than style."[54]

In his introduction to chapters 2–3 Morris notes that a literary pattern is to be observed in the sevenfold arrangement: "Churches 1 and 7 are in grave danger, churches 2 and 6 are in excellent shape, churches 3, 4, and 5 are middling, neither very good nor very bad."[55] Wall uncritically accepts Morris's observation concerning the spiritual condition of the Ephesian church and labels the unnamed pattern as chiastic (ABCB′A′). The chiastic patterns proposed by Morris and Wall might be outlined thus:[56]

53. Ibid.
54. Kennedy, *New Testament Interpretation*, 12.
55. Morris, *Revelation*, 58.
56. Beale, *John's Use of the Old Testament*, 302, also suggests an identical chiastic struc-

Morris		Wall
1 Ephesus	Danger	A Ephesus
2 Smyrna	Excellent	B Smyrna
3 Pergamum	Middling	C Pergamum
4 Thyatira	Middling	C Thyatira
5 Sardis	Middling	C Sardis
6 Philadelphia	Excellent	B´ Philadelphia
7 Laodicea	Danger	A´ Laodicea

Wall's conclusion is quoted at length to show how he draws an application for a canonical reading: [57]

> Chiasmus calls the reader's attention to the vortex of the pattern (C), where one finds what is most important for the author: that is, John is calling our attention to those churches with a "middling" spirituality. His purpose is certainly pastoral: most congregations do not find themselves on the margins of spiritual excellence (with the congregations at Smyrna and Philadelphia) or apathy (with the congregations at Ephesus and Laodicea), but rather in the mainstream of spiritual mediocrity (with the congregations at Pergamum, Thyatira, and Sardis). This is, then, the nature of the spiritual crisis for most of John's readers, who constantly struggle against those forces and factors which might prevent the maturing of faith and keep our witness "middling."

The problem with this analysis is twofold. First, it circumvents the sevenfold pattern in these chapters (and the book) by assigning C collectively to the three middle churches rather than dealing with each church individually. Second, its approach is deductive, basing the pattern on an analysis of church A, Ephesus, and not on John's structural emphasis. Wall predicates his conclusion on the acceptance of Morris's assessment of the spiritual condition of the Ephesian church.

It is difficult, however, to see how the Ephesian church is in "grave danger" or apathetic. Bullinger cites the praise in 2:6, after the reproof of verses 4–5, as an example of palinodia—"the approval of one thing

---

ture. For him its significance is that the whole Christian church is seen as being in poor condition. The literary pattern also "points to this emphasis because the churches in the worst condition form the literary boundaries of the letters and the churches with serious problems form the very core of the presentation." My discussion that follows likewise takes issue with this analysis of the spiritual condition of the churches.

57. Wall, *Revelation*, 69.

after reproving for another thing."[58] Thus the Ephesian situation cannot be totally negative. Indeed the church is commended for its works, labor, and endurance (v. 2), the opposite of apathy which is defined as "lack of interest or concern; indifference."

The translation of ἀφῆκες in 2:4 as "you have abandoned" (NRSV) or "forsaken" (NIV) unfortunately suggests a graver situation than is the case. Both of these English verbs suggest intentional, willful desertion. Unconscious neglect seems to characterize better the Ephesian situation as the translations "left" (KJV, NASB) or "lost" (REB) suggest. Louw and Nida assign it to the semantic domain of "Cease and Stop," suggesting this translation: "you have stopped loving me (as you did) at first."[59] As Charles acutely notes, "Though the Church in Ephesus has preserved its moral and doctrinal purity and maintained an unwavering loyalty in trial, it has lost the warm love which it had at the beginning."[60] The Ephesians remain zealous, but their zeal is lacking the dimension of love.

The problem of the Laodicean church, on the other hand, is that it is a "middling" church: "because you are lukewarm, and neither cold nor hot . . ." (3:16). Apathy *may* characterize this church, but materialism and self-sufficiency better diagnose the problem: "I am rich, I have prospered, I have need of nothing" (3:17). To call the Pergamene church "middling" also is problematic. Like the Smyrnean and Laodicean churches, it had suffered for the faith. In fact, the only martyr mentioned by name in the book—Antipas—was from Pergamum (2:13). Though a minority was promulgating false teaching, the majority had remained faithful to the Lord. I would agree that "middling" is an accurate portrayal only for the Thyatiran and Sardian churches. Therefore the interpretation of the chiastic construct suggested by Morris and developed by Wall breaks down when the text is carefully examined. A better chiastic outline might be:

    A Ephesus
        B Smyrna
             C Pergamum
                  D Thyatira
            C′ Sardis
        B′ Philadelphia
    A′ Laodicea

---

58. Bullinger, *Figures of Speech*, 978.
59. Louw and Nida, *Greek–English Lexicon*, 1. §68.43.
60. Charles, *Revelation of St. John*, 1.50–51.

Since chiasmus typically focuses on the central element (D), Thyatira should be the point of emphasis among the seven. A breakdown of these letters by word count bears this out: Ephesus–147, Smyrna–98, Pergamum–147, Thyatira–230, Sardis–143, Philadelphia–196, and Laodicea–188. Kirby concurs, "Thyatira, in the central position of the list, receives the lengthiest letter."[61] Although quantity of words does not alone signify preeminence, it is an important factor. We will next discuss an important term in the letters that is highlighted semantically in the Thyatiran letter.

An interpretive problem in chapter 2 is the mention of the Nicolaitans. In the Ephesian letter John writes, "You hate the works of the Nicolaitans, which I also hate" (v. 6). No elaboration or clarification is provided; the presupposition is that this group and its activities are well known. In the Pergamene letter John writes: "You have there those who hold to the teaching of Balaam, who taught Balak to put a stumbling block before the children of Israel by eating food sacrificed to idols and to commit sexual immorality. Thus you also have those who hold to the teaching of the Nicolaitans likewise" (vv. 14–15).[62] The heteropraxy of a group within the church is first compared to the teaching of the prototypical Old Testament false prophet—Balaam (cf 2 Pt 2:15; Jude 11). His counsel to Balak was that Israel could be seduced by laying a snare involving food sacrificed to idols and sexual immorality (Nm 25:1–3). The Nicolaitans were likewise (ὁμοίως) promoting similar doctrines. Two groups are not being suggested here. Rather current false teaching is analogously compared with one of Israel's past moral failures. Nicolaitanism receives further definition here, albeit a link with sexual immorality and food sacrificed to idols.[63]

This false teaching is fully developed in the Thyatiran letter without mention of Nicolaitanism. Interestingly, in it John again uses the verb ἀφίημι (ἀφεῖς; 2:20) to begin the blame saying, albeit with a different

---

61. Kirby, "Rhetorical Situations of Revelation 1–3," 204.

62. The parallelism in the Greek text is noted below:

2:14 ἔχεις ἐκεῖ	2:15 οὕτως ἔχεις καὶ σὺ
κρατοῦντας τὴν διδαχὴν Βαλαάμ,	κρατοῦντας τὴν διδαχὴν [τῶν] Νικολαϊτῶν
ὃς ἐδίδασκεν τῷ Βαλὰκ βαλεῖν σκάνδαλον ἐνώπιον τῶν υἱῶν Ἰσραήλ,	—
φαγεῖν εἰδωλόθυτα καὶ πορνεῦσαι.	ὁμοίως.

63. The later tradition regarding Nicolaitanism is confused. Eusebius (*Hist. eccl.* 3.29) recounts, on the one hand, that the sect practices promiscuity, but his own sources depict Nicolaus and his wife as monogamous and their children as chaste.

connotation ("tolerate"; NIV, NRSV[64]). The Thyatirans had compromised spiritually and morally through the teaching of a prophetess called Jezebel, after the prototypical Old Testament false prophetess. Her teaching advocated compromise like Balaam's—to commit sexual immorality and to eat food sacrificed to idols. This inversion is perhaps related to the predominant problem in each city. That Jezebel was an actual person is evident from the seven feminine personal pronouns used in verses 20–23 to describe her. Jezebel is therefore a prophetess in the Thyatiran church who is using her authority to teach error. That the content of her teaching is exactly the same as the Nicolaitans suggests that she belongs to the same party. Watson concludes similarly that "it is probable that, although not specifically named, the Nicolaitans were present there also, and that she [Jezebel] was a Nicolaitan prophetess." [65]

The fullest explication for this false teaching threatening three Asian churches is reserved for the central church in the chiasmus. Unless the Thyatirans repent, judgment in the form of physical death is forthcoming. They will be made an example to the other six churches, particularly to those believers in them who are tempted to follow the Nicolaitan teaching (2:23; cf. Ananias and Sapphira, Acts 5:1–11). Apart from the mention of the churches in the greeting and closing of each letter, this is the only reference to the other churches in the *narratio* of the seven letters. Thyatira is to be made an example to the other churches over this issue of accommodation.

Lund perceptively observes, "It is significant that the strongest representation of idolatry . . . and the ultimate doom of that perversion of worship . . . should be found in the central epistle of the seven."[66] For unless compromise is forestalled, the Son of God knows that the very existence of the church in Asia is threatened. Lund also points out that "in no other epistle is the person who was presented in the vision in 1:14–16 identified and *named* [i. e., 'the Son of God'] . . . . In six other epistles the identification could have been introduced, but the author chose the fourth epistle, because it was the pivot in his scheme."[67] The epithet "the

---

64. The suggested translation of Louw & Nida 1.§13.140, "you let the women Jezebel . . . teach," making διδάσκει an infinitive rather than a coordinate verb, seems less satisfactory here. Incidentally, this wordplay certainly evidences John's literary skill with Greek, which is often maligned because of the book's poor grammar and syntax.

65. Watson, "Seven Churches," 4.1107; cf. Hemer, *Letters to the Seven Churches of Asia*, 91.

66. Lund, *Chiasmus in the New Testament*, 337.

67. Ibid., 337, 338.

Son of God," a familiar Johannine Christological designation (John 1:34, 49; 10:36; 11:4, 27; 20:31; 1 John 3:9; 4:15; 5:5, 20), is used only here in Revelation. Indeed John's use of chiasmus points to the Thyatiran conflict as paradigmatic for the other churches.[68]

Chiasmus and the Seven Victor Sayings

We will next discuss briefly the chiastic implications of our topic and its place in the structure of Revelation. The promises in the victor sayings and their eschatological fulfillments in the final chapters are universally noted (the text of both will be examined in depth in chapters 4 and 5). Schüssler Fiorenza observes concerning this special relationship: "The promises of the letters to the victorious one recur in 19:11—22:9. The first unit and the last unit of Rev. are thus related to each other as promise and fulfillment."[69] Wall likewise observes: "John has constructed a parallelism, vaguely chiastic, between key phrases found in Christ's exhortations to overcome . . . and John's vision of the new Jerusalem."[70] Promises with verse references and their fulfillments are shown in the following chart. Only promises with obvious fulfillments are used, but these comprise the majority. Promises whose fulfillments are debatable are excluded.

B Seven Churches (1:4—4:2)	B′ New Jerusalem (19:6—22:9)
Promise	*Fulfillment*
1. Tree of life (2:7)	Tree of life (22:2, 14, 19)
2. Exemption from second death (2:11)	Second death (20:6, 14; 21:8)
3. New name (2:17; 3;12)	New name (19:11–16)
4. Rule nations with rod of iron (2:26); Morning Star (2:27)	Judge nations, Christ holds rod of iron (20:4; cf. 19:15); Morning Star (22:16)
5. Dressed in white; Name in book of life (3:5)	Dressed in white, as a bride (19:7–8; 21:2); Names in book of life (20:15; 21:27)

---

68. See my doctoral thesis, "A Pie in a Very Bleak Sky?" 123–26, where examples of chiasmus in the Greek text of the letters are presented.

69. Schüssler Fiorenza, *Book of Revelation*, 175.

70. Wall, *Revelation*, 258, note on 21:2, 9–10.

The Structure of the Seven Letters and Revelation

B Seven Churches (1:4—4:2)	B′ New Jerusalem (19:6—22:9)
Promise	*Fulfillment*
6. New Jerusalem down from heaven (3:12)	New Jerusalem down from heaven (21:2, 10)
7. Sit on throne (3:21)	Martyrs seated on thrones (20:4)

From the chart it is apparent that the promises and their fulfillments are themselves not organized chiastically, e.g., A–G/G′–A′. Continuity between each promise in the seven letters and its fulfillment in the future eschaton can be clearly seen from this chart. The promises are given to the members of the seven Asian churches, and their fulfillments at the book's conclusion are clearly intended for the same audience. Therefore the Asian Christians are the primary recipients of the final chapters, contrary to the futurist view. The relationship between these two sections is one of the clearest and strongest pointers for chiasmus as Revelation's macrostructure.[71] The next section will explore whether that observation is viable.

Chiasmus as Revelation's Macrostructure

Chiasmus as Revelation's macrostructure has been proposed by several interpreters. In 1898 Bullinger published his major study on biblical rhetoric, *Figures of Speech Used in the Bible*, which featured a discussion of chiasmus illustrated with numerous Old and New Testament examples. His commentary on Revelation appeared in 1902, and insights gained from the study of rhetoric are apparent in his structuration of the book. His basic outline is:[72]

> A Introduction (1:1–20)
>   B The people on earth (2:1—3:22)
>   C Visions (4:1—20:15)
>   B′ The people on the new earth (21:1—22:5)
> A′ Conclusion (22:6–21)

Bullinger divides the central C section into seven visions, wherein each vision alternates between heaven and earth. Of these the middle fourth vision covers 12:1—13:18. "As to position, it occupies, literally and actually,

---

71. The sections are depicted as B and B′ in all the outlines presented below except Ellul's (Snyder's overlaps with C′ also).
72. Bullinger, *Commentary on Revelation*, 116.

the central part of the book; while as to its subject matter, we shall see ... that it is as important as its position declares it to be."[73] In this outline the seven trumpets and seven seals are paired—"the two most solemn portions of all the judgments which the book contains."[74] A major weakness of Bullinger's outline, however, is designating only the C section as "Visions." John's first vision of Christ occurs in 1:9ff. (A), and chapter 21 (B′) is likewise a vision. Thus visions are found outside the central section.

Bullinger's outline is a pioneering one for chiastic studies in Revelation. His identification of chapter 12 as the center of the book and the pairing of the trumpet and seal judgments find common ground with our proposed outline. His idiosyncratic exegesis of Revelation has undoubtedly caused many interpreters to ignore his attempt to structure the book chiastically.

The most famous exponent of chiasmus is Lund who published his outline in 1942.[75] Lund fails to cite Bullinger's work on Revelation, although he shows familiarity with two other books by Bullinger. Lund's detailed outline is later repeated in his volume *Studies in the Book of Revelation*. Both outlines generally agree; however, the earlier one projects some transposition of text based on source-critical analysis, an approach later discarded. Lund's proposed chiastic outline in simplified form is:[76]

    A Prologue (1:1–20)
        B Seven epistles (2:1—3:22)
            C Seven seals (4:1—8:5)
                D Seven trumpets (8:2, 6–11:19)
                    E The little book (10:1–11)
                        F The two witnesses (11:1–13)
                        F′ The dragon and the woman (12:1–17)
                    E′ The two beasts (13:1–18)
            C′ Seven angels (14:1—15:4)
                D′ Seven bowls (15:1, 5–16:21)
        B′ Seven angels (17:1—22:5)
    A′ Epilogue (22:6–21)

Of significance in Lund's outline are two points shared with the other outlines that follow. At B and B′ are chapters 2–3 and chapter 21 through

---

73. Ibid., *Revelation*, 119.
74. Ibid., 120.
75. Lund, *Chiasmus in the New Testament*, 325–26.
76. Lund, *Revelation*, 27.

at least 22:5. The complementarity of these two sections, no matter what form the remainder of the outline takes, is important to our discussion of the victor sayings and their fulfillment. The second observation is that chapter 12 appears at the center of each outline.

Schüssler Fiorenza likewise recognizes a concentric ABCDC′B′A′ structure, although she does not call it chiasmus. The following outline is simplified from the original, which included subpoints:[77]

> A Prologue and epistolary greeting (1:1–8)
> > B Rhetorical situation in the cities of Asia Minor (1:9—3:22)
> > > C Opening the sealed scroll: Exodus plagues (4:1—9:21; 11:15–19)
> > > > D The bitter-sweet scroll: "War" against the community (10:1—15:4)
> > > C′ Exodus from the oppression of Babylon/Rome (15:5—19:10)
> > B′ Liberation from evil and God's world-city (19:11—22:9)
> A′ Epilogue and epistolary frame (22:10–21)

In another essay, "The Composition and Structure of Revelation," Schüssler Fiorenza further simplifies her outline, providing only the letter and scripture reference. There she also includes 15:1 under C′. In the same place she argues further that "the whole book is patterned after the epistolary framework which represents an inclusion."[78] While limiting a chiastic outline to these seven elements is debatable, I nevertheless agree with her assessment that "the structure of the book underscores that the main function of Rev. *is the prophetic interpretation of the situation of the community*" (my emphasis).[79]

Barr also sees a concentric structure in the Apocalypse:[80]

> Letter frame
> > Vision report frame
> > > Letter scroll: Vision of the majestic human on Patmos
> > > > Worship scroll: Vision of the throne in heaven
> > > War scroll: Vision of the dragon's war and defeat
> > Vision report frame
> Letter frame

---

77. Schüssler Fiorenza, *Revelation*, 35–36.
78. Schüssler Fiorenza, *Book of Revelation*, 175.
79. Ibid.
80. Barr, *Tales of the End*, 149.

According to Barr, there are two implications of this structure. First, the worship scroll comprises the center of the work. "It is here that God's will is most perfectly realized . . . and the reader sees most directly the correspondence between the above and the below." Second, there is an implied correlation between the letter and the war scroll, for the stories in these scrolls call the audience to fight for victory. "The war scroll dramatizes in concrete and vivid imagery the struggles abstractly indicated in the letter scroll with its repeated promise 'to the one who conquers . . . .'" Barr believes that in both these stories "the audience is expected to conquer; in the worship scroll all conquest is attributed to the lamb."[81] Barr's structural analysis yields important conclusions related to the victory theme in the book. However, his concentric configuration leaves the book structurally unbalanced, with the war scroll section predominating. Although the dragon is not introduced until chapter 12, there is clearly a vision of his war and defeat in the seal and trumpet cycles.

Strand has also proposed a chiastic structure with a sevenfold form for Revelation's structure, although his center D has four elements.[82] This central section likewise has symmetry. Da and Da′ include the trumpet and bowl judgments, while Db and Db′ deal with the evil forces. Apart from the prologue and epilogue, the sections follow his projection of eight visions in the book.

    A Prologue (1:1–11)
        B Church militant (1:12—3:22)
            C God's salvatory work in progress (4:1—8:1)
                Da Trumpet warnings (8:2—11:18)
                Db Aggression by evil forces (11:19—14:20)
                Da′ Plague punishments (15:1—16:21)
                Db′ Judgment on evil forces (17:1—18:24)
            C′ God's salvatory work completed (19:1—21:4)
        B′ Church triumphant (21:5—22:5)
    A′ Epilogue (22:6–21)

In a later study Strand modified the names of several of the pericopes, although the blocks of text remained unchanged.[83]

Ellul has proposed an axial structure for Revelation based on theological criteria. Chapter 12 forms the main theological focus of the book

---

81. Ibid., 149.
82. Strand, "Chiastic Structure," 401.
83. Strand, "Eight Basic Visions," 108.

because the birth and exaltation of Christ are described. Ellul's outline is as follows: [84]

> A The church and her Lord (1:4—4:11)
>   B The revelation of history (5:1—7:17)
>   C Jesus Christ, the keystone (8:1—14:5)
>   B′ Judgment and destruction of evil (14:6—20:15)
> A′ The new creation (21:1—22:16)

According to Ellul, each section contains a vision of Jesus Christ; for example, a vision of the omnipotent Lord is found (1:4–20) in A while in A′ the Lord of the end time is seen (22:6–16). Ellul sees these five sections framed by eight liturgical texts; for example, a revelation on the church is found in 1:5–6 and in 4:1–11.[85] Ellul's divisions seem arbitrary from a literary perspective, but again his approach is theological. However, his axis corresponds to the center of other chiastic models, so this observation confirms the importance of chapter 12 to Revelation's structure.

Snyder has also developed a chiastic model for Revelation's macro-structure. Beale argues that her model "presents the most viable chiastic outline of the book so far attempted."[86] Snyder's proposed structure is as follows:

A Introduction: Apocalypse, Epistle, Prophecy (1:1–3, 4–8, 9–20)
  B Vision regarding Saints on Earth (2–3)
    C Heavenly Sanhedrin Convened for Judgment and Enthronement (4–5)
      D Seven Seals (6:1—8:1)
        E Seven Trumpets (8:2—9:21)
          F Theophany of the Messenger of the Lord Descending to Sea and Land (10)
            G War against the Saints on Earth (11)
            G′ War against the Dragon in Heaven (12)
          F′ Counter-Theophany of Yamm's 2 Messengers Ascending from Sea and Land (13)

---

84. Ellul, *Apocalypse*, 45–52. Since Ellul never provides a diagram of his outline, one must be assembled from the text, which is somewhat confusing to follow. Hence, my outline differs somewhat from the one suggested by du Rand, *Johannine Perspectives*, 303.

85. Ellul, *Apocalypse*, 234–55.

86. Beale, *Book of Revelation*, 143. During the course of my doctoral research I never discovered Snyder's unpublished dissertation, so am grateful for Beale mentioning it in his commentary.

E′ Unnumbered Series of 7 Proclamations (14)
D′ Seven Bowls (15–16)
C′ Heavenly Sanhedrin Convened for Judgment and Messianic Reign (17–20)
B′ Vision of Bride/Saints in Heaven (21:1—22:5)
A′ Conclusion: Apocalypse, Epistle, Prophecy (22:6–9, 10–20, 21)[87]

The strengths of Snyder's proposal are that it shows thematic correspondences, discloses natural breaks between sections, and highlights contrasting correspondences. A weakness to be noted immediately is that section E, Seven Trumpets, does not end at 9:21. Instead the seventh trumpet sounds at the end of chapter 11, which is the G, or central section of Snyder's chiasmus. Also, to characterize chapter 11 as a general war against the saints is to read beyond the text. Rather the war is against two specific witnesses who, from a literary perspective, are contrasted with the two beasts of chapter 13.

In recent years other interpreters working in Revelation have also proposed chiastic structures.[88] Lambrecht refines Vanni's structuration and presents it in a concentric framework, although he includes only 4:1—22:5.[89] Beagley has adopted a seven acts outline and combined it with chiastic structure.[90] Without mentioning chiasmus Park suggests that the letters (chs. 2–3) and the new Jerusalem section (21:1—22:5) "frame and encircle the central portion of the book."[91] This central portion—4:1—22:5—describes both what will happen before the end of time and what the church is to conquer. Park's structuration, however, is confusing because his frame section is also included as part of the center.

This author's own chiastic outline of Revelation is now offered:[92]

---

87. Snyder, "Combat Myth in the Apocalypse," 83. In footnotes to sections E and C′ Snyder notes that chapters 10–11 and 17–22 break down into further chiasms, which she discusses later.

88. The increased interest in Revelation's chiastic structure is evidenced by two papers presented at the annual meetings of the Evangelical Theological Society by Luter, "Twin Peaks" (1994, Chicago) and by Lee, "A Call to Martyrdom" (1995, Philadelphia). My proposed outline that follows was also presented initially as a paper at the 1994 ETS annual meeting.

89. Lambrecht, "Structuration of Revelation," 85–86.

90. Beagley, *'Sitz im Leben' of the Apocalypse*, 30–31, 181.

91. Park, "More than a Regained Eden," 258.

92. In an earlier version of this outline I divided sections D and D′ into two sections:
    D Seven trumpets (8:2—9:21)
        E Two witnesses (10:1—11:19)

The Structure of the Seven Letters and Revelation

A Prologue and Greeting (1:1–8)
  B Seven Churches (1:4—4:2)
    C Seven Seals (3:21—8:5)
      D Seven Trumpets-Angel-Two Witnesses (8:2—11:19)
        E Woman, Dragon, and Male Child (12:1–18)
      D′ Two Beasts-Angels-Seven Bowls (13:1—16:21)
    C′ Destruction of Babylon (16:18—19:10)
  B′ New Jerusalem the Bride (19:6—22:9)
A′ Closing and Epilogue (22:6–21)

This outline seeks to preserve several of the key structural observations that commentators have made. First, it recognizes the sevenfold structural patterns within sections B, C, D, and D′, but does not force the unnumbered sections into a similar pattern.[93] Second, the overlapping of sections avoids the rigid demarcations inherent in most proposed structures and instead suggests the fluidity of John's structuration. Bauckham makes this key observation: "To insist on assigning these verses only to one or other of these sections . . . is to misunderstand John's literary methods, among which are the overlapping and interweaving of the sections of his work."[94] Note that E—the center of the chiasmus—is the only section with a clearly defined beginning and end. This section has always proved problematic as Bauckham further notes: "Most attempts to discern the structure of Revelation have found it particularly difficult to see how chapters 12–14 fit into the overall structure. The beginning of chapter 12 seems an uncharacteristically abrupt fresh start, devoid of literary links with anything that precedes."[95] Third, these sectional overlaps allow identification of inclusios at the sectional transitions. These are either verbal or thematic or both. The eschatological earthquake with its cosmic phenomenon of

---

    F Woman, dragon, and the male child (12:1–18)
   E′ Two beasts (13:1—14:20)
  D′ Seven bowls (15:1—16:21)
Since the seventh trumpet with its inclusio is found in 11:15–19 (E), the sevenfold structuration of the trumpets was ignored in this draft. The present outline omits that defect as well as preserves the structuration of the book in seven units, apart from the prologue and epilogue.

93. Contra Yarbro Collins, *Apocalypse*, xiii.
94. Bauckham, *Climax of Prophecy*, 5.
95. Ibid., 15

thunder and lightning functions as an inclusio following the seven seals (8:5), the seven trumpets (11:19), and the seven bowls (16:18).

Evaluation Using Blomberg's Criteria

Using the criteria developed by Blomberg, we will next evaluate my proposed outline using a question-and-answer approach.

1. *Is there a problem in Revelation's structure that more conventional outlines have failed to resolve?* Yes, as noted earlier, no consensus exists among commentators regarding the structure of the book.

2. *Are clear examples of parallelism evident between the two "halves" of the hypothesized chiasmus, even to commentators who propose quite different outlines?* Yes, commentators invariably note the relationships between the prologue/epilogue (A/A'), the seven trumpets/seven bowls (D/D'), and the promises/fulfillments (B/B').

3. *Does grammatical and structural parallelism characterize most of the corresponding pairs of subdivisions?* The structural parallelism between A/A' and D/D' will be demonstrated in 4 and 6 respectively. Problematic are the unnumbered sections C' and B'. There is parallelism between C and C'. C begins with a scene depicting God sitting upon his throne surrounded by his heavenly court; C' begins with the great prostitute Babylon sitting upon many waters presiding over her earthly coterie. Although within B seven churches are enumerated, some interpreters[96] see within B' seven unnumbered scenes of final victory.

4. *Does verbal parallelism involve central imagery or terminology, not peripheral or trivial language?* The following chart shows significant verbal parallelism in the Greek text of the prologue and epilogue:

---

96. Cf. Boring, *Revelation*, 31.

The Structure of the Seven Letters and Revelation

A Prologue (1:1–8)	A´ Epilogue (22:6–21)
1:1 Ἀποκάλυψις Ἰησοῦ Χριστοῦ, ἣν ἔδωκεν αὐτῷ ὁ θεός, δεῖξαι τοῖς δούλοις αὐτοῦ ἃ δεῖ γενέσθαι ἐν τάχει, καὶ ἐσήμανεν ἀποστείλας διὰ τοῦ ἀγγέλου αὐτοῦ τῷ δούλῳ αὐτοῦ Ἰωάννῃ	22:6 καὶ ὁ κύριος, ὁ θεὸς τῶν πνευμάτων τῶν προφητῶν, ἀπέστειλεν τὸν ἄγγελον αὐτοῦ δεῖξαι τοῖς δούλοις αὐτοῦ ἃ δεῖ γενέσθαι ἐν τάχει
1:2 τὴν μαρτυριαν Ἰησοῦ	22:18, 20 Μαρτυρῶ . . . ὁ μαρτυρῶν
1:3 μακάριος ὁ ἀναγινώσκων καὶ οἱ ἀκούοντες τοὺς λόγους τῆς προφητείας καὶ τηροῦντες τὰ ἐν αὐτῇ γεγραμμένα,	22:7 μακάριος ὁ τηρῶν τοὺς λόγους τῆς προφητείας τοῦ βιβλίου τούτου.
1:3 ὁ γὰρ καιρὸς ἐγγύς.	22:10 ὁ καιρὸς γὰρ ἐγγύς ἐστιν
1:4 Ἰωάννης	22:8 Ἰωάννης
1:4 ταῖς ἑπτὰ ἐκκλησίαις ταῖς ἐν τῇ Ἀσίᾳ	22:16 Ἐγὼ Ἰησοῦς ἔπεμψα τὸν ἄγγελόν μου μαρτυρῆσαι ὑμῖν ταῦτα ἐπὶ ταῖς ἐκκλησίαις
1:5 ἀπό τῶν ἑπτὰ πνευμάτων	22:17 τὸ πνεῦμα
1:4 χάρις ὑμῖν . . . 1:5 ἀπὸ Ἰησοῦ Χριστοῦ	22:21 Ἡ χάρις τοῦ κυρίου Ἰησοῦ
1:8 Ἐγώ εἰμι τὸ Ἄλφα καὶ τὸ Ὠ	22:13 ἐγὼ τὸ Ἄλφα καὶ τὸ Ὠ

5. *Does verbal and conceptual parallelism involve words and ideas not regularly found elsewhere within the proposed chiasmus?* Yes, one example is "church" (ἐκκλησία) which appears nineteen times in chapters 1–3 and does not reappear until 22:16.

6. *Are there multiple sets of correspondences between passages opposite each other in the chiasmus as well as multiple members of the chiasmus itself?* Yes, an excellent example of such correspondences is found in D/D´, although they are not an exact match (such variations are normal in chiasmus).

D Seven Trumpets	D′ Seven Bowls
1. Fire hurled to earth which is burned up	4. Sun scorches people with fire
2. Sea turns to blood, living creatures die	2. Sea turns to blood, living creatures die
3. Rivers and springs become bitter	3. Rivers and springs become blood
4. Sun, moon, stars turn dark	5. Beast's kingdom turned to darkness
5. Locusts afflict people without mark of God on their foreheads	1. Ugly, painful sores afflict people with mark of the beast
6. Four angels released at great river Euphrates to kill 1/3 of humanity	6. Great river Euphrates dried up to gather kings for battle of Armageddon
7. Flashes of lightning, rumblings, peals of thunder, earthquake, and great hailstorm	7. Lightning, rumblings, peals of thunder, great earthquake, great plague of hail

7. *Does the outline divide the text at natural breaks which would be agreed upon even by those proposing very different structures?* Most proposed structures have breaks at or near the divisions suggested in the outline.

8. *Is the climactic center of the chiasmus worthy of that position in light of its theological or ethical significance?* The British novelist D. H. Lawrence in his idiosyncratic work *Apocalypse* identifies the myth in chapter 12 "as the centre-piece of the Apocalypse, and figures as the birth of the Messiah."[97] The literary instincts of this noted author are sustained in each of the above outlines. Certainly the Incarnation is *the* preeminent theological event of Christianity.

9. *Are there ruptures in the outline, such as shifts between the forward and reverse parts of the structure?* Ruptures involving reorganization of the text to harmonize the two halves of the outline have been avoided.

---

97. Lawrence, *Apocalypse*, 85.

The Structure of the Seven Letters and Revelation

Intentionality in Structuration

Certainly a legitimate question to ask is whether John consciously planned the various chiastic structures in Revelation. Clark suggests that the answer regarding biblical literature in general is not simply yes or no; rather "such patterns may surely be the result of subconscious effort on the part of an author or redactor."[98] Mnemonic repetition, which characterized education in antiquity, would result in assimilation of such literary configurations. Likewise today when we compose a personal or business letter, we adopt accepted stylistic forms to which we usually give little thought. Our writings simply reflect prevailing literary conventions taught through years of education. Speaking of Paul, Thomson writes that he was "involved in the matter of *persuasion* as he tries to move his readers from their present position to where he wants them to be. The use of chiasmus is one of the means to that end of persuasion."[99] John likewise had an audience to persuade. Although it cannot be proved conclusively, from the internal evidence John appears to have consciously used chiasmus to structure Revelation on a macro level. For the more stylistic chiastic examples, it is probable that John, with his mind saturated particularly in the Old Testament, simply reflects the stylistic devices of that literature.

A further question arises: would the Asian Christians have recognized chiasmus in the Apocalypse? If so, such recognition would allow the audience to develop a strategy for "hearing" the book. I agree with Mealy's observation that "the reader is being trained from the start to expect the same reality to be re-expressed under different figures and to be viewed from different aspects . . . . and is being required to pick up a piece of terminology, [e.g.], 'the second death,' which will only much later . . . be given an explicit context."[100] Thus chiasmus through repetition, analogies, and recapitulation establishes through its frame of reference in the ancient literary culture an effective rhetoric of persuasion in Revelation.[101]

As the reader proceeded through the document, the listeners could track his progress. That is why the explicit sevenfold structure predomi-

---

98. Clark, "Criteria for Identifying Chiasmus," 71.

99. Thomson, *Chiasmus in the Pauline Letters*, 39.

100. Mealy, *After the Thousand Years*, 82.

101. Thomson, *Chiasmus in the Pauline Letters*, 39, differs with this assessment: "It still remains difficult, however, to imagine how anything beyond a short chiasmus could be detected by a listener, even if the ancients could perform what seem to moderns to be prodigious feats of memory." The option most attractive to him is one suggested by Talbert, that the audience intuitively felt the structure but did not consciously perceive it until after reflection; cf. Talbert, "Artistry and Theology," 363–65.

nates in the upper half of Revelation's chiasmus. The audience would be aware of the center or pivot point at chapter 12 and then be able to follow John out of the document, especially after the seven trumpets. Revelation's verbal and grammatical repetition and structural parallelisms would facilitate understanding for ancient audiences. With the listeners tuned into chiasmus as the macrostructure, it would be easier for them to follow the rhetoric of the smaller units.

Chapter Summary

The structure of Revelation has remained problematic for interpreters, with little consensus emerging. Chiasmus has been proposed as a structural device because of its frequent usage in classical and biblical literature. A number of rules and criteria for recognizing valid chiasmus have been listed. The most obvious indicator of the book's chiastic structure is the promises in the seven victor sayings in chapters 2–3 and their fulfillments in chapters 19–22. Several examples proposing chiasmus as the macrostructure for Revelation were presented before my own outline. This outline incorporates many elements of the others while seeking to include other unique literary characteristics of the book. This outline was then evaluated for congruency with Blomberg's nine criteria. Three examples of the heuristic value of chiasmus for exegesis were discussed. Chiasmus is a viable way to view the structure of Revelation, and adoption of this perspective allows readers today to make valuable insights into the book's emphases, especially that of victory. The rhetorical form of the seven letters will be addressed next in chapter 2.

2

The Form of the Seven Letters

Introduction

IN CHAPTER 1 we examined the internal chiastic structure of chapters 2–3, noting the common structural features among the seven letters. In this chapter we will develop the external literary form of these letters, looking particularly at ancient literary antecedents. Our review begins with four suggested affinities, namely, wisdom instruction, Near East covenants, Greek rhetoric, and church liturgy. We will then examine the literary connections with imperial edicts and prophetic oracles before looking at ancient letters. Within all these categories the features shared with the seven letters will be noted, especially as we try to determine what forms John would most probably know and utilize. The observation of Bach speaks to the uniqueness of chapters 2–3: "Les critiques s'accordent à reconnaître une certaine parenté, pour ne pas dire unité, entre les sept lettres d'Ap 2–3. En effet, elles sont toutes construites selon le même plan et la symétrie est à peu près parfaite."[1] We will close with a brief discussion of the address, epithet, and hearing sayings.

Wisdom Instruction

The seven letters, according to Comblin, "ressemblent très fort, par leur object et par les thèmes qu'elles mettent en œuvre, aux instruction de la sagesse. Elles sont l'exercice de la *paideia* caractéristique des livres de la Sagesse."[2] Appearing as Wisdom, Jesus sends the letters as wisdom instruction. The intention and content of the letters is summed up in the state-

---

1. "The critics agree to recognize a certain relationship, not to say unity, between the seven letters of Revelation 2–3. Indeed, they all are constructed according to the same plan, and the symmetry is about perfect"; Bach, "La structure au service de la predication," 294.

2. ". . . resemble very much, by the object and themes that they put in the work, with wisdom instruction. They are the exercise of the *paideia* characteristic of the books of Wisdom"; Comblin, *Le Christ dans l'Apocalypse*, 120.

ment, ἐλέγχω καὶ παιδεύω (3:19). "Les lettres elles-mêmes constituent un exemple concret de cette forme d'éducation."[3] Because instruction is a central theme of the Wisdom books, the letters are an example *par excellence* of New Testament wisdom instruction.

Comblin presents a number of thematic parallels, with references, between the seven letters and Wisdom literature: (1) the attention to good works, (2) with the contrasting denunciation of evil works, (3) the appeal to conversion, (4) testing, and (5) rewards. He also shows that such Christological epithets as the "Beginning of God's creation" (3:14) is likewise an attribute of Wisdom in Proverbs 8:22. While never denying the apocalyptic or prophetic character of the letters, Comblin convincingly demonstrates their sapiental quality as well. While making this important observation, he never suggests though that wisdom literature provides the form of the letters.

A peculiar parallel is found in Proverbs 9:1: "Wisdom has built a house for herself, and she has set up seven pillars (στύλους)." Skehan has suggested that the extended wisdom discourses of Proverbs 1–9 have an architectural balance resembling chiasmus. The discourses in chapters 1 and 8–9 frame seven others in chapters 2–7, which Skehan identifies as the "seven columns" of the house of Wisdom.[4] (In 3:18 Wisdom is called a "tree of life"; cf. Rev 2:7.) Because of the subjective nature of Skehan's divisions, it is difficult to believe John would see such a sevenfold division in Proverbs. The promise that the victors would become pillars (3:12) has a more probable explanation. Wisdom sayings, as Comblin has shown, do constitute a source for the body of the letters.

Near East Covenants

Shea uses the landmark studies of G. E. Mendenhall on law and covenant to suggest the presence of covenant formulary in the letters. The form of the Israelite covenant found in Exodus parallels closely a Hittite suzerainty treaty. Because of the numerous Old Testament allusions in Revelation, Shea believes "the presence of the covenant concept is reasonably to be expected in it."[5] John's only use of διαθήκη is found in 11:19 where, following the seventh trumpet, the ark of the covenant is seen in the heavenly temple.

---

3. "The letters themselves constitute a concrete example of this form of education"; Ibid., 121.

4. Skehan, *Studies in Israelite Poetry and Wisdom*, 9–14.

5. Shea, "Covenantal Form," 71, 72.

The Form of the Seven Letters

The five elements of the treaty with the parallels Shea finds in Revelation are now outlined:[6]

Israelite/Hittite Treaty	Letters to the Seven Churches
1. Preamble (royal author of covenant identified by name, titles, attributes, and genealogy)	"The word of him who . . ." (a new and different title for Jesus follows)
2. Historical prologue (describes past relations between the two contracting parties)	"I know your works . . ." (refrain implying past relations between suzerain Jesus and his vassal the church)
3. Stipulations (detail the obligations imposed upon the vassal)	"Repent," "remember," "be faithful," etc. (instructional imperatives to rectify deficiencies previously described)
4. Witnesses (pagans invoked their god; Jews substituted other elements)	"Hear what the Spirit says to the churches" (Spirit is obvious witness)
5. Blessings and curses (occur in the case of loyalty to, or breach of, the covenant)	"To him who overcomes I will grant . . ." (blessing pronounced upon the overcomer) "If . . .," "if not . . .," or "because . . ." (curse pronounced upon disobedient)

Shea divides each of the seven letters into these five covenantal treaty elements, with the hope that "more meaningful labels can be drawn very appropriately from the designations given to the sections of the suzerainty covenant."[7] The letters to Smyrna and Philadelphia most clearly illustrate this model; within the other letters there is considerable variation between the prologue, stipulation, and curse sections. Shea acknowledges this variation, saying "this is in reality quite natural, for ancient covenant statements did not slavishly follow exactly the same order in every instance."[8]

Shea's suggestion of covenantal form is an attractive hypothesis. John uses the plagues of Exodus as a background for the seven trumpets and seven bowls, and also closes with the curse that Moses uttered when he began the covenant renewal with Israel at Beth Peor. The five parts of an ancient treaty do suggest some parallels in the seven letters. However, to find these parallels Shea ignores the address saying that opens each letter.

---

6. Shea, "Covenantal Form," 72–75, 81.

7. Ibid., 76, through page 80 for the divisions.

8. Ibid., 82–83.

This section clearly adds at least one other element to the form. To connect the blessing section with the victor sayings is also problematic, since Shea had already recognized its connection with the seven beatitudes.[9] Aune correctly makes this analysis: "Shea has forced the structure of the seven proclamations into a framework which is essentially alien to them (the seven proclamations deal primarily with a temporary situation rather than the legal establishment of a long-term relationship), and his verse-by-verse analysis reveals far too many exceptions to the overall schema."[10]

Most damaging to Shea is the lack of covenant language here. The standard Hebrew phrase כרת ברית (LXX διατίθεμαι διαθήκην) is found at the initiation of the covenant at Sinai (Exod 24:8) and at its renewal at Beth Peor (Deut 4:23; 5:2). Covenant language is an integral part of the final promise found in Revelation 21:7. But the absence of such language in chapters 2–3 suggests strongly that the seven letters do not constitute a covenant renewal.

Greek Rhetoric

Diefenbach has recently asserted that "der Seher Johannes kennt die antike Rhetoriklehre" and assumes that John wrote as a diaspora Jew who was a hellenistically trained author.[11] To prove his thesis, he enlists the seven letters as an example of Greek rhetoric. After doing a form critical analysis of the microstructure of chapters 2–3, Diefenbach observes the repeated use of anaphora (A) and epiphora (E) in them.[12] He outlines each of the letters, like the first to Ephesus, in the following way:[13]

A	2:1:	Τῷ ἀγγέλῳ τῆς ἐν Ἐφέσῳ ἐκκλησίας γράψον· Τάδε λέγει ὁ…

---

9. Ibid., 74.

10. Aune, "Form and Function," 182n. 4.

11. "… the Seer John knows the ancient rhetorical teaching"; Diefenbach, "Die 'Offenbarung des Johannes,'" 52.

12. Anaphora, from ἀνά, "again," and φέρω, "to bring or carry," is defined by Bullinger, *Figures of Speech*, 199, as "The Repetition of the same Word at the beginning of successive Sentences." Epiphora (or epistrophe), from ἐπί, "upon," and φέρω, he defines as "The Repetition of the same Word or Words at the end of successive Sentences" (p. 241). Bullinger prefers to call anaphora by the term epibole, which "differs from *Anaphora* in that it consists of the repetition of several words, whereas in *Anaphora* only one word is repeated" (p. 346).

13. Diefenbach, "Die 'Offenbarung des Johannes,'" 55–56.

	2:2:	Οἶδα τὰ ἔργα σου καὶ ...
E	2:7:	ὁ ἔχων οὖς ἀκουσάτω τί τὸ πνεῦμα λέγει ταῖς ἐκκλησίαις. τῷ νικῶντι δώσω αὐτῷ + infinitive ...

Diefenbach's analysis relates primarily to the aspect of style in ancient rhetoric (cf. Quintilian *Orat.* 3.3.1). John's adoption of such stylistic devices did not require rhetorical training, however, for numerous examples of anaphora and epiphora can be found in the Old Testament.[14] Since the Old Testament seems to have been John's predominant influence and his orientation more semitic than hellenistic, Diefenbach's thesis is overstated. His identification of anaphora and epiphora is a significant observation, however. Diefenbach importantly notes that repetition was good rhetorical style in Greek, whereas in languages such as German and English it is not.[15] Repetition likewise is important in terms of modern information theory. Anderson explains, "Verbal repetition increases predictability, creates expectations, eliminates noise, persuades, and reduces alternative interpretations" and teaches "the implied reader how to 'read' the text."[16] John *in absentia* effectively utilizes repetition to convey his message to his audience.

Rhetorical Form

Kirby likewise examines the form of these chapters from a rhetorical perspective. While conceding that hellenistic epistles and royal decrees contributed to their final form, Kirby believes the letters are more vivid than an ordinary letter or decree. Because the processes of dictation and public reading are right before us, "the opening of the *Revelation* is, then, a *narration* of an event of primary rhetoric."[17] He identifies four approximate rhetorical correspondences in each letter: προοίμιον ("proem" or introduction)

1. διήγησις ("narration" or statement of facts)
2. πρόθεσις ("proposition" or major point[s])
3. ἐπίλογος (epilogue)

---

14. Cf. Bullinger, *Figures of Speech*, 199–201, 241–42.
15. Diefenbach, "Die 'Offenbarung des Johannes,'" 53.
16. Anderson, "Double and Triple Stories," 84.
17. Kirby, "Rhetorical Situations," 200.

Kirby breaks down each letter into these four sections in a table with the victor and hearing formula found in the epilogue of each letter.[18] Ramsay also recognizes rhetorical form in the seven letters and states that the peroration (epilogue) of each "is modeled in the same way; all contain a claim for attention and promise."[19]

The arrangement of Kirby assumes that the rhetorical species of Revelation is deliberative, "focusing on future action and concerned with expediency."[20] Kennedy, however, notes that the deliberative structure usually has four sections—proem, proposition, proof, and epilogue—adding, "Occasionally a narration is employed; when it does occur, it is often after rather than before the proposition."[21] Kirby's analysis obviously strays from the pattern, omitting the proof section while including a narration section out of the usual order.

The two other species of rhetoric are judicial and epideictic. Kennedy describes these: "The species is judicial when the author is seeking to persuade an audience to make a judgment about events occurring in the past . . . it is epideictic when he seeks to persuade them to hold or reaffirm some point of view in the present, as when he celebrates or denounces some person or some quality. Praise or blame is taken by Aristotle to be the characteristic feature of epideictic."[22] The admonition to remember (μνημόνευε; 2:5; 3:3) is clearly an entreaty regarding the past of the Ephesian and Sardian churches. And the praise and blame sayings, so prominent in the letters, points to an epideictic form. Kennedy summarizes: "In a single discourse there is sometimes utilization of more than one species, and the definition of the species as a whole can become very difficult."[23]

Kirby's identification of a single rhetorical species in the letters—deliberative—conflicts with the evidence. Clearly the species of both judicial and epideictic are also evident. We conclude with Aune[24] that the rhetorical form of the seven letters is a *mixtum compositum*.

---

18. Kirby, "Rhetorical Situations," 200–201.
19. Ramsay, *Letters to the Seven Churches*, 147.
20. Kirby, "Rhetorical Situations," 200.
21. Kennedy, *New Testament Interpretation*, 24.
22. Ibid., 19.
23. Ibid., 23.
24. Aune, "Form and Function," 183n. 5.

Sacramental Liturgy

The influence of Exodus on John is evident in the content of the seals judgment. Prigent believes it is also reflected in the numerous paschal references in Revelation.[25] Thus the literary scheme of the seven letters conforms to the examination of the believers before the eucharist. Its elements are: (1) appreciation directed to the community, and (2) affirmation of the coming of Christ involving (a) warning, threat, and exhortation to repentance, and (b) a gift of the graces conferred by the sacraments. He observes that the leitmotiv, "I am coming" and the eucharistic image, "tree of life," are likewise found in chapter 22, where the liturgical form is most fully developed.[26] The exhortation to repentance received particular attention at the annual Easter occasions, which were the principal celebrations of the early Christian community. "Les chrétiens doivent participer à l'eucharistie en écoutant l'exhortation que la liturgie leur adresse."[27] Prigent concludes that the primary eschatological teaching in the book is sacramental.

Analysis of the text shows that Prigent's observations concerning the presence of paschal imagery in Revelation are valid and important. This is especially proven by the fact that "Lamb" is the most frequent name for Jesus in the book (28x). However, his observations on early liturgical form, drawn from texts such as 1 Corinthians 16:20 and Didache 10:6, are highly speculative. The celebration of Christ's resurrection on Passover rather than Easter Sunday (i. e., quartodecimanism) gives some insight on the paschal practices of the Asian churches. However, too little is known about other early liturgical practices to affirm that the seven letters derive their form from them.

Imperial Edicts

Deissmann in 1901 was one of the first biblical scholars to use an Asian decretal inscription to illuminate a biblical text—2 Peter. While he could not affirm a direct dependence on the decree, he believed "the author of the Epistle, like the author of the Decree before him, simply availed himself of the familiar forms and formulae of religious emotion."[28] Rudberg later saw in a decree of Darius from Magnesia ad Meandrum (5th century BC)

---

25. Prigent, *Apocalypse et liturgie*, 36.

26. Ibid., 42–43.

27. "The Christians must take part in the eucharist by listening to the exhortation that the liturgy addresses to them"; ibid., 45.

28. Deissmann, *Bible Studies*, 367.

a relationship with the seven letters: "Ich glaube, dass wir unter den noch vorhanden kleinasiastischen Inschriften wenigstens *ein* konkretes Vorbild oder eine Parallele besitzen."[29] Rudberg's linkage of the form of the seven letters to a royal decree has recently been revived by Aune. This necessitates extended discussion of the matter.

Definition

The noted classical historian Judge defines an edict as "the proclamation of a magistrate. It is used to regulate the behaviour or thinking of the community under his jurisdiction."[30] The edict differs from a letter in that it is essentially an oral statement and does not make reference to particular individuals. The seven letters are edicts, according to Judge, and open "with the characteristic verb of declaration, λέγει."[31] Benner notes three important features of Roman edicts that bear on Revelation:[32]

1. They were originally read aloud by the magistrate in person or in his presence by a herald;
2. They were directed to everyone; even though their content might not affect everyone, it was supposed that all should know about them;
3. They were always published publicly.

Elements

Stauffer sees similarities between the form of chapters 2–3 and that of imperial edicts: "The preamble of the seven decrees is in unmistakable contrast to the opening words of the edicts of Domitian: 'So speaks he who holds the seven stars in his right hand.'"[33] Stauffer quotes two such edicts: "The Lord our God commands" (Suetonius *Dom.* 13.2) and "Edict of the Lord our God" (Martial *Ep.* 5.8).[34] There are several problems with this comparison. First, the date of Revelation is assumed to be Domitianic,

---

29. "I believe that we possess at least a concrete example or a parallel under the now available inscriptions from Asia Minor"; Rudberg, "Zu den Sendschreiben der Johannes-Apokalypse," 171.

30. Judge, "Regional *kanon* for Requisitioned Transport," 39–40.

31. Ibid., 40.

32. Benner, *The Emperor Says*, 25, 30.

33. Stauffer, *Christ and the Caesars*, 181.

34. Ibid., 158.

which is less preferable.³⁵ Second, Jones calls Suetonius' report, repeated by Dio (67.4.7, 13.4), to be "all but incredible."³⁶ Martial's testimony is that of a flatterer seeking to secure favor from an autocrat. Jones concludes: "He (Domitian) obviously knew that he was not a God, and, whilst he did not ask or demand to be addressed as one, he did not actively discourage the few flatterers who did."³⁷ Like the myth of the Domitianic persecution, the *Dominus et Deus* nomenclature of the imperial degrees is also doubtful.³⁸ Stauffer sees another feature: "The negative continuation with the threat of punishment (2.5, 16) is in the same style as the usual imperial announcements."³⁹ He appeals to the letters of Darius in Herodotus and the royal inscriptions of the Achaemenidae in Behistun as his examples, but how John was to know these documents is left unstated.

Aune updates and broadens the work of Stauffer and Judge, providing an in-depth comparison between imperial edicts and the seven "proclamations." Following Benner, Aune identifies the following elements in a typical edict:⁴⁰

1. *Praescriptio* 2 ("introduction")
2. *Prooemium* (a "preface" to produce benevolence and interest in the addressees)
3. *Promulgatio* (a "proclamation" using a phrase such as "I make known that," etc.)
4. *Narratio* (brief account of the "facts" which caused the enactment)
5. *Dispositio* ("arrangement" expressing the decision, centrally located in the document)
6. *Sanctio* or *corroboratio* ("sanction" or "corroboration"—end clauses used to bring about the observance of the enactment)

---

35. In the article "Early Christians of Ephesus and the Date of Revelation, Again," I presented the arguments for the early and late dating of Revelation, concluding that the internal evidence and historical situation argues better for a date around AD 69, before the fall of Jerusalem; Wilson, "A Pie in a Very Bleak Sky?" 56–76.
36. Jones, *Emperor Domitian*, 108.
37. Ibid., 109.
38. Cf. Thompson, *Book of Revelation*, 105–7.
39. Stauffer, *Christ and the Caesars*, 158.
40. Aune, "Form and Function," 198–201; cf. Benner, *The Emperor Says*, 17.

Examples

While this analysis of imperial edicts is no doubt correct, it again begs the question, what imperial edicts would John be aware of? Aune's examples—Xerxes and Marcus Aurelius—are royal figures removed in time and place from John. The decree of Darius Hystaspes was found in Ephesus' sister city Magnesia, so John might have seen it on public display there.

However, the Roman edicts with which John and his Jewish audience would most likely be aware were those that guaranteed their rights in the empire. Josephus (*Ant.* 14.188, 265–66) mentions that these decrees (δόγματα, not διάταγμα; however, cf. *Ant.* 16.165) were engraved on bronze tablets in the Capitol in Rome[41] as well as displayed in public places in the cities. If Josephus is correct, and the letter of Octavian to the Asian proconsul Norbanus and Norbanus' subsequent letters to the Sardian and Ephesian magistrates were generally known,[42] Aune's claim that "edicts are formal and public, whereas letters are informal and private" is overstated.[43] This is because Aune fails to mention that some official documents are a *mixtum compositum* of letter and edict. Antony's communication on Jewish rights with the Tyrian magistrates, senate, and people opens with a letter directing that his edict be published in Latin and Greek in a very conspicuous place before it gives the text of the edict (*Ant.* 14.319–22). A number of other documents to cities showing this letter/edict form have been found.[44] The apostolic letter/decree issued by the Jerusalem council is an early Christian example (Acts 15:23–29).

An Edict Compared with the Ephesian Letter

One noteworthy edict on Jewish rights was issued by Augustus about 1 BC. The following chart correlates portions of this Augustan edict (Josephus *Ant.* 16.162–65) with the Ephesian letter (Rev 2:1–7). On sound academic grounds we have adopted the nomenclature of decretal analysis utilized by Benner and Aune.[45]

---

41. These archives were destroyed when the Capitol burned in AD 69, but were later replaced by Vespasian (Suetonius, *Vesp.* 8.4).
42. Cf. Johnson, Coleman-Norton, and Bourne, *Ancient Roman Statutes*, §§129, 130, 134.
43. Aune, "Form and Function," 200.
44. Again see Johnson et al, *Ancient Roman Statutes*, §§104, 111, 128.
45. Benner, *The Emperor Says*, 66–67, and Aune, "Form and Function," 201–2.

The Form of the Seven Letters

Sections	Augustus' decree to Ephesus	The Ephesian letter
Praescriptio	Caesar August, Pontifex Maximus with tribunician powers says (λέγει)	Thus says (Τάδε λέγει) him who holds the seven stars in his right hand
Prooemium[a]	Absent	Absent
Promulgatio	Absent	Absent
Narratio[b]	Since the Jewish nation has been found (εὑρέθη) well disposed to the Roman people not only at the present time but also in time past . . .	I know (οἶδα) your works—your toil and your endurance and that you are not able to tolerate evil deeds . . .
Dispositio	it has been decided (ἔδοξε,) by me and my council under oath, with the consent of the Roman people. . . . And if anyone is caught stealing their sacred books or their sacred monies . . . he shall be regarded as sacrilegious and his property shall be confiscated to the public treasury. . . . I order (κελεύω) that it and the present edict be set up in the most conspicuous part of the temple constructed for me by the *koinon* of Asia in Pergamum[c]	Remember from where you have fallen; repent and do your first works. If you do not, I am coming to you and I will move your lampstand from its place, that is, if you do not repent.
Sanctio	If anyone transgresses any of the above ordinances, he shall suffer (δώσει) severe punishment	To the victor I will grant (δώσω) him to eat from the tree of life, which is in the paradise of God.

[a] Aune, "Form and Function," 202, notes, "No counterpart to the *prooemium* is found in any of the seven proclamations." Aune never mentions the *promulgatio*, so he evidently regards it as absent also.

[b] Aune, "Form and Function," 202, believes the *narratio* has "a clear functional counterpart in the οἶδα—clauses in each of the seven proclamations." Although he lists several verbs in the semantic domain of "Learn" (L&N, §27.A), Aune fails to mention the one found in this edict, εὑρίσκω.

[c] Josephus' original reading "Ancyra" is problematic here. First, Censorinus was never a proconsul for Galatia; however, he died as proconsul of Asia in AD 3. Second, the koinon of Asia met in Pergamum, not in Ancyra. Augustus probably sent copies of his edict to be placed in each of his Anatolian temples, with only the names of the governors and destinations changed in the text. Josephus has mistakenly conflated the Galatian and Asian texts. This seems to be born out by Philo (*Legat.* 311) who states that Augustus "sent commandments to all the governors of the different provinces throughout Asia."

The characteristic verb of the *dispositio*—"I command/enjoin" (κελεύω/διακελεύομαι)—found in the edicts of Augustus, Caligula, and Claudius to the Jews (*Ant.* 16.165; 18.304; 19.285; cf. 19.307) is conspicuously absent in the seven letters.[46] Instead they are influenced "by the conditional style of prophetic speech consisting of ethical exhortations, usually matched by conditional threats."[47]

A section similar to the *sanctio*, according to Aune, is "regularly found at the close of each proclamation in the conditional promise of victory."[48] However, a difference of tone distinguishes the decretal sanction from the victor sayings in the seven letters. The typical sanction is negative while the promises are positive. One example of such a sanction is found in the loyalty oath to Augustus (3 BC) taken by the citizens of Gangra in Paphlagonia:[49]

> If I do anything contrary to this oath or not consonant with what I have sworn, I invoke complete and utter destruction upon myself, my body, my soul, my life, my children, and all my family with their possessions in every generation of mine and of my descendants. And may neither land nor sea receive my body, or those of my descendants, nor may they bear fruit for them.

Similar sanctions are found in a decree of Octavian found in Rhosus: "If any city or any magistrate does not do what should be done in accordance with this ordinance . . . they shall be liable to a fine of 100,000 sesterces to be paid to the Roman people," and in an edict to the citizens of Pisidian Antioch: "But if anyone does not obey . . . ."[50] The prophetic curse (Rev 22:18–19) that comes at the end of the book most closely approximates the decretal sanction.

Domitian's Edict

An edict often cited in relation to Revelation is that issued by Domitian in the spring of AD 92. The previous harvest had produced an abundance of wine, but a dearth of wheat. To correct a perceived imbalance in pro-

---

46. Cf. Josephus (*Ant.* 12.120) who paraphrases an earlier edict of Seleucus Nicator (312–281/80 BC) in which he gives an order (ἐκέλευσεν) to the Syrian Jews regarding the purchase of oil.

47. Aune, "Form and Function," 202.

48. Ibid., 203.

49. See Johnson et al, *Ancient Roman Statutes*, §149; cf. the sanction in §183.

50. For Rhosus, see Johnson et al, *Ancient Roman Statutes*, §129.2.7; for Pisidian Antioch see §198.

duction, Domitian ordered that half the vineyards in the provinces be cut down (Suetonius *Dom.* 7.2; 14.2; Philostratus *VitAp.* 6.42; *VitSoph.* 1.21). This order provoked outrage in Asia, and a delegation headed by the Smyrnean orator Scopelianus was sent to Rome to protest the action. Rostovtzeff and others see this edict behind John's reference in 6:6, "Do not harm the olive oil (or "olive orchard" [*BAGD* s. v. ἔλαιον] and the wine."[51] While reference to this edict is one of the few pieces of evidence pointing to a late date for Revelation's composition, it provides no assistance regarding the form of the letters, for the text of the edict is lost.

A Banishment Edict

A final possible parallel not mentioned by Aune is the edict used by the Roman authorities to banish individuals. Certainly John's *relegatio* would have necessitated an official document. The poet Ovid mentions that such an edict relegated him to the port of Tomis on the Black Sea (*Tr.* 2.135–38; 5.2.60–61). The edict was issued neither by the senate nor by a special court but by the *princeps* himself, Augustus. Because the actual form of a banishment edict is unknown, it cannot be determined whether or not John imitated such an edict in composing the seven letters.

Edicts Conclusion

Aune concludes his discussion of edicts: "The seven proclamations of Rev 2–3 are similar in form to ancient royal or imperial *edicts*, in that they exhibit formally and structurally similar *praescriptiones, narrationes, dispositiones* and *sanctiones.*"[52] Aune, however, fails to provide a single edict that parallels the consistent form found in the seven letters. Instead he produces parallels from sections of different decrees. We have attempted to take a decree known to first-century Jews and compare it to one of the letters. While some parallels do exist, there are significant differences as well. Thus Aune's conclusion that the literary genre to which the seven letters belong is that of the imperial edict remains unproven.

---

51. Rostovtzeff, *Social and Economic History of the Roman Empire*, 1:201–2; he also says that the third seal (6:8) "is proved to refer to a widespread famine in Asia Minor by a Latin inscription of AD 93, discovered at Antioch of Pisidia." His confidence regarding the book's date is overstated given the frequency of famine in the East because, as he himself writes, "the Greek cities, even in some parts of Asia Minor, never produced sufficient corn for their population" (1:147). Earlier famines might easily be the referent.

52. Aune, "Form and Function," 204.

If the edict model is accepted, a significant weakness is the psychological effect its use might have on John's Christian audience. The Roman state is depicted as an adversary throughout Revelation, and to adopt such a form might cause confusion since it seemingly suggests complicity rather than hostility. The only valid interpretation for the letters as edicts would suggest that they are parodies of the imperial edict and that John's audience is to appreciate the irony behind the use of this literary form. While possible, this seems unlikely since more probable models exist.

Prophetic Oracles

Old Testament prophetic traditions had a significant influence on John.[53] It should not be surprising then that the form of the seven letters is often seen as based on Old Testament prophetic oracles. Aune in fact earlier classifies the seven letters as "parenetic salvation-judgment oracles."[54] In this section we will look at several texts that have been proposed as models for the seven letters.

The Prophecies of Balaam

The reference to Balaam in the Pergamene letter (Rev 2:14) suggests that John was familiar with his wilderness encounter with Israel. The Christological title, the Morning Star (Rev 2:28; 22:16), is a likely allusion to Numbers 24:17. In Numbers 22–24 seven oracles of Balaam are recorded. The first four oracles are longer, while the last three (Num 24:20–25) against foreign nations are brief.

Two similarities exist between the prophecies in Numbers and in Revelation. First, both prophecies number seven. Wenham writes: "It is difficult to know why they are included, except that they ring up the total of oracles to the mystic number seven."[55] Second, the first three lines of the third and fourth oracles (Num 24:3–4; 15–16) are identical, like the identical openings of the seven letters. Comparing oracles 4–7 to Amos' oracles (see the following section), Smith writes: "The prophecy of victory or defeat, found in the Balaam oracles in Numbers 24:15–24, has the most similarities with Amos. . . . His oracle served as a discouragement to Balak and as a message of assurance to Israel."[56] This emphasis on victory is most

---

53. These traditions were developed in my thesis; see "A Pie in a Very Bleak Sky?" 90–96.

54. Aune, *Prophecy in Early Christianity*, 326.

55. Wenham, *Numbers*, 180.

56. Smith, *Amos*, 30.

pronounced in the fourth oracle: "Edom will be conquered; Seir, his enemy, will be conquered" (Num 24:11 NIV; "be a conquered land" NJB; יְרֵשָׁה). The seven letters likewise close with promises of victory. The oracles of Balaam may be a possible influence on the form of Revelation's seven letters.

The Prophecies of Amos

Rife suggests that the prophecies to the seven nations in Amos 1–2 provide the best literary background for the seven letters.[57] He identifies six formulaic elements found in Amos which simply required John to fill in the blanks:

Amos 1–2	Revelation 2–3
Thus saith the Lord,	To the angel of the church at . . .
for three transgressions . . . ,	write:
yea for four, I will not turn away the punishment thereof; because they (he) . . .	So says the . . . :
But I will send a fire . . . ,	I know . . .
and it shall devour the palaces . . . ,	The one who conquers . . .
Saith the Lord.	Whoever has ears, listen what the Spirit is saying to the churches.

Rife names other areas that Amos and Revelation share—"number, brevity, formulae, prophecy, geographical destination, and use as introduction to a book."[58] Two linguistic similarities are remarkable: the opening formulas are both τάδε λέγει and the closing formula of Amos λέγει κύριος is paralleled by the Apocalypse's τὸ πνεῦμα λέγει. Two items of contrast are that Amos' prophecies are uniformly hostile and that they are shorter in length than the letters, except for the final prophecy against Israel which is longer. In comparing the two, Feuillet states that "we must be careful to distinguish between the similarity of form and the great difference between the intentions of the respective authors: foretelling of divine punishment on the one hand, and, on the other, pastoral exhortations, and consoling promises, both rendered with an inimitable religious fervor."[59]

---

57. Rife, "Literary Background of Revelation II–III," 180.
58. Ibid., 181.
59. Feuillet, *Apocalypse*, 48–49.

Rife's comparison has much to commend it. Yet the most obvious question is whether Amos delivers seven or eight prophecies to Syro-Palestinian nations. Hubbard, like Rife, adopts a sevenfold judgment pattern, while Stuart finds eight, making the prophecy to Israel the climax of the group because Israel was his primary audience.[60] Smith observes regarding this group of eight prophecies: "The uniformity of structure within each oracle is very consistent, thus the final expanded and irregular prophecy against Israel stands out from the rest."[61]

Stuart prefers to call these oracles to foreign nations rather than messenger speeches and lists five aspects to their general format:[62]

1. The messenger introduction (כה אמר יהוה "This is what Yahweh said")
2. Certainty of deserved punishment
3. Evidence (specification of crimes)
4. Announcement of curse (punishment)
5. A concluding formula (אמר יהוה "Yahweh said"; or נאם יהוה "oracle of Yahweh")

Like John's letters, these oracles exhibit minor individual peculiarities. The fifth element is missing with Tyre, Edom, and Judah. This is no problem, according to Stuart, because "variations of style and structure are so common among individual oracles of given prophets . . . ."[63] Barton notes insightfully that "these oracles build up to a climax in the oracle against Israel, and that the prophet's intention is to startle his hearers by suddenly turning on them after lulling them into a false sense of their own security by denouncing their neighbors."[64] In a similar manner John startles the Laodiceans in the final letter by failing to give them praise like the other churches. Amos is not a major source for John, apart from the reference to "his servants the prophets"; however, the form of these prophetic oracles may be a possible influence on the seven letters.

The Prophecies of Ezekiel

John frequently alludes to Ezekiel throughout Revelation. The center section of Ezekiel—the oracles against the nations in chapters 25–32—is

---

60. Hubbard, *Joel and Amos*, 127; Stuart, *Hosea-Jonah*, 308.
61. Smith, *Amos*, 29.
62. Stuart, *Hosea-Jonah*, 308–9.
63. Ibid., 309.
64. Barton, *Amos' Oracles against the Nations*, 36.

perhaps a literary influence on John. Taylor notes two features of these oracles, seven addressees and a geographic design:

> There is probably some significance in the fact that . . . the number of nations dealt with is seven . . . . A further sign of editorial planning is the geographical pattern of the oracles, beginning with Ammon to the north-east of Jerusalem, swinging southwards through Moab to Edom in the south-east, then round to Philistia in the west, and finally going farther afield in a northerly direction to Tyre and Sidon, before ending up with the distant major power, Egypt, in the south.[65]

Stuart finds sixteen nations, not just seven, mentioned in these chapters. However, as he says, many of these are only mentioned in passing as they relate to the nations prominently addressed.[66]

A look at a map of the Near East from Ezekiel's 6th century BC perspective in Babylon shows that geographic design may be a structural factor but not the only one. The first three—Ammon, Moab, and Edom—make geographical sense. Next should come Egypt, but Philistia appears instead. The ordering proceeds up the Mediterranean coast to Tyre and Sidon before moving far south to Egypt. The longest oracle against Egypt—four chapters or one-twelfth of the book—is reserved for the end.

The first four oracles in chapter 25 have a similar form. Stuart identifies four features:[67]

1. "Messenger speech" introduction ("Thus says the Lord God")
2. Crimes of attitude and/or action against the Lord and/or against his people ("because")
3. Announcement of punishment ("therefore")
4. Conclusion ("Then you shall know that I am Lord," or "Then they shall know my vengeance")

These elements likewise appear in the final three oracles, but because the oracles to Tyre and Egypt are so lengthy, they are not as pronounced. John's familiarity with Ezekiel suggests that these oracles to the seven nations might have influenced the form of the seven letters.

---

65. Taylor, *Ezekiel*, 184–85.
66. Stuart, *Hosea-Jonah*, 247, 248.
67. Ibid., 247.

New Testament Prophetic Forms

Hahn suggests that the seven letters altogether are a typical prophetic *gattung*, "wie eine Rede urchristlicher Propheten an eine Gemeinde aussah und welcher Formelemente sie sich bediente."[68] He seeks to find in the letters expressions characteristic of prophetic speech forms. His analysis of the letters, particularly the body, helpfully focuses attention on the formulaic language. Yet to characterize the letters as a whole as typical of early Christian prophecy is problematic.

Aune, in his examination of the prophetic character of the letters, notes the particular relationship of the commissioning formula to prophetic speech.[69] The Christological predication that follows begins with the τάδε λέγει formula, used by both Old and New Testament prophets. Yet the *Weckformel* in the closing is not found anywhere else in early Christian literature. The New Testament tells us little about the form of early Christian prophecy. Paul's directions to the Corinthians (1 Cor 14:29–33) about prophetic revelations in the assembly addresses use rather than content. Thus it is doubtful that the seven letters assist us in determining the larger form of early Christian prophetic speech.

Prophecy Conclusion

While Aune believes that the seven letters derive their form from imperial *edicts*; "[i]n content, however, the narrationes and dispositiones exhibit the complex characteristics of the *paraenetic salvation-judgment* oracles widely used by early Christian prophets."[70] The examples we have examined suggest that Old Testament prophetic oracles influenced the form of the letters more than Aune allows. That John adapts and organizes these oracles to fit his creative purposes is evident, yet the underlying influence of the Old Testament prophets is apparent in the seven letters as in the other parts of the book.

Ancient Letters

The contents of chapters 2–3 are commonly referred to as letters. In this section we will examine Greco-Roman letter forms and attempt to deter-

---

68. "what a speech of early Christian prophets to a church looked like, and which elements of form it used"; Hahn, "Die Sendschreiben der Johannesapokalypse," 391–92.

69. Aune, *Prophecy in Early Christianity*, 275–76, 278.

70. Aune, "Form and Function," 204.

mine their relationship to these two chapters. The influence of other New Testament epistolary traditions upon John will also be discussed.

Individual Letters?

Charles proposes that each of the seven letters was sent at an earlier time to its respective church. John then revised the beginning and ending of each letter to bring the group into conformity with the initial vision of Christ in 1:14–18 and with the theme of conflict between Christ and Caesar. Charles uses the longer Ignatian letters to support his hypothesis.[71]

Surveying the evidence for this theory, Court writes: "When allowance is made for all these features of pattern imposed in the letter collection, what remains of the individual letters, discounting any further patterns in content as well as form, is so small a unit that it is most unlikely to resemble an original letter transmitted independently."[72] For this reason the source analytical approach of earlier commentators has been largely abandoned today. Boring speaks for the modern consensus: "Yet none of the letters in chapters 2–3 are independent letters addressed to a single church. Revelation is one unitary composition addressed, like all the letters, to all the churches."[73] The findings of our research likewise validate the book's unity.

Pauline Letters?

Goodspeed calls the strangest feature of Revelation "that it began with a *corpus* of letters to churches." He suggests that John's model was a Christian collection of letters to churches, which "can only be the newly formed Pauline *corpus*." His main evidence is John's unique use of the typical Pauline greeting "Grace and peace to you." From this he concludes that "the writer of it (Revelation) has before him the collected letters of Paul and is strongly influenced by their form."[74] We noted in chapter 1 that the Muratorian writer reversed the relationship. Paul wrote to seven churches because John had earlier done so. Goodspeed acknowledges the Muratorian Fragment, but answers: "Modern historical study would invert the order, but the coincidence remains striking."[75]

---

71. Charles, *Revelation*, 1:46–47.
72. Court, *Myth and History*, 23–24.
73. Boring, *Revelation*, 85.
74. Goodspeed, *New Solutions of New Testament Problems*, 21, 23, 24, 25.
75. Ibid., 22.

The Muratorian statement is problematic in several ways. First, Paul was dead by the time John wrote Revelation unless a Claudian date is adopted (cf. Epiphanius *Haer.* 51.12, 33), which is most unlikely. Second, to make the number seven fit, the Galatian churches must be considered as one. Third, Crete is not reckoned because the letter to Titus is considered a personal one. Goodspeed's reconstruction is likewise problematic. If an early date is adopted for Revelation, it is improbable that a Pauline collection could be collected and edited by this time. Even a late date is problematic. Although Paul's letters circulated in some form among clusters of churches by the end of the first century (cf. Col 4:16; 2 Pet 3:16; *1 Clem.* 47:1–4), it is unlikely that Paul's letters circulated as a collection until the early second century.[76] Although highly imaginative, Goodspeed's suggestion fails to answer satisfactorily why John wrote in letter form.

One Letter or Seven Letters?

At first glance Revelation displays the tripartite form of Greek documentary letters with an opening, body, and closing.[77] Following the *titulus* in 1:1–2 and the first macarism in 1:3, the opening in 1:4–5 and the closing in 22:21 display familiar biblical epistolary forms.[78] For most of the book John reverts to the mixed genres of prophetic and apocalyptic, and the audience knows this is no ordinary letter. Ramsay's comment that "the form of letters had already established itself as the most characteristic expression of the Christian mind, and as almost obligatory on a Christian writer"[79] is perhaps overstated. Yet by adopting Christian epistolary forms John is clearly identifying his work with other apostolic letters, as discussed in chapter 1.

J. H. Roberts recognizes the Pauline epistolary opening in 1:4 and suggests that the first vision with the seven letters is really the body of a single letter. "A letter ending is missing, but this is not surprising since the letter is followed by other material. In view of this, it would have been inappropriate to include a letter ending."[80] Roberts, however, overlooks the typical ending in 22:21. This indicates that the body extends past chapter 3 to include the entire book. The entire book is thus framed in an epistolary form, albeit an artificial one. Roberts also fails to recognize the individual

---

76. See Bruce, *The Canon of Scripture*, 130.
77. Cf. White, *Light from Ancient Letters*, 198.
78. Cf. Hartman, "Form and Message," 132–35.
79. Ramsay, *Letters to the Seven Churches*, 25.
80. Roberts, "Letter to Seven Churches in the Roman Province of Asia," 21.

character of each of the seven letters. While some situations in the churches are shared, others are unique to the church addressed. To classify the letters as one is thus to ignore their individuality. White observes three characteristics of Christian letters that are apparent in Revelation—friendliness, a discrete body of information, and a longer length.[81]

Letter or Epistle?

Deissman pioneered the study of ancient letters in relationship to the New Testament. He distinguished between "letters" (private personal correspondence) and "epistles" (public literary artifices).[82] Deissman classified the Pauline corpus minus the Pastorals as genuine letters. Regarding Revelation, however, he determined that chapters 2–3

> differ from the rest in the fact that they do not form books by themselves, nor constitute one book together, but only a portion of a book. It is still true, however, that they are not letters. All seven are constructed on a single definite plan,—while, taken separately, they are not intelligible, or, at least, not completely so; their chief interest lies in their mutual correspondence, which only becomes clear by a comprehensive comparison of their separate clauses: the censure of one church is only seen in its full severity when contrasted with the praise of another.[83]

Deissman's observation here that the seven letters are highly stylized is a useful starting point for investigating the form of these letters.

Deismann's two divisions—currently referred to as "real" and "non-real"—remain the most important genre categories used by scholars today. However, Stowers mentions three limitations of Deissman's approach:[84]

1. Papyri from rural Egypt provide only a partial view of ancient epistolography, so letters from urban centers such as Ephesus that are preserved by literary transmission must taken into account.
2. The modern sociological distinction between public and private does not hold for Greco-Roman society in general or for ancient letter writing.

---

81. White, *Light from Ancient Letters*, 19.
82. Deissman, *Bible Studies*, 21ff.
83. Ibid., 54.
84. Stowers, *Letter Writing in Greco-Roman Antiquity*, 18–20.

3. All letters are literature in the broadest sense because they adopt stylized writing conventions; hence the distinction between warm, personal letters and artificial, impersonal epistles is misleading.

Stowers rightly concludes that New Testament letters as a whole "resemble neither the common papyri from the lowest levels of culture and education nor the works of those with the highest levels of rhetorical training. They fall somewhere in between and have the cast of a Jewish subculture."[85]

Epistolary Types

One possible category for chapters 2–3 is that of accusing and apologetic letters which fall under judicial rhetoric. Regarding the presence of this type of letters in the New Testament, Stowers states there are none "unless one considers the letters in Revelation 1–3 [sic] to be accusing letters."[86] Since the Smyrnean and Philadelphian letters contain no words of accusation, such a description could only apply to the other five letters. However, a better alternative exists.

A more probable category is that of epideictic rhetoric—letters of praise and blame. An important social context for ancient letter writing was the client-patron relationship. This hierarchy is reflected in Revelation where God and Jesus are called "Lord" (e.g. 1:8; 22:5) and John and his fellow believers "slaves" (e.g., 1:1). The giving of praise and blame was essential to Greco-Roman institutions. "To praise meant to bestow honor; to blame meant to take away honor and cause shame . . . . Honor provided a person with a status in society."[87] Since epideictic is the rhetoric of praise and blame, most ancient letters are this epistolary type.

In his letters Paul often incorporated words of praise (e.g., Phlp 1:3ff; Col 1:3ff; 1 Th 1:2ff) and words of blame (e.g., 1 Cor 1:10ff; 5:1ff; 6:1ff; Gal 1:6ff). Stowers categorizes John's letters as letters of praise and blame: "Six of the seven letters of Revelation 2 and 3 . . . mix praise with something else such as blaming, threatening, consolation, or promising. In good epistolary form they begin with praise and then turn to blaming or threatening."[88] However, John fails to use such characteristic terms of praising letters as "admire" (θαυμάζω) and "honor" (τιμάω). Based upon

---

85. Ibid., 25.
86. Ibid., 173.
87. Ibid., 27.
88. Ibid., 80–81.

such information, the tendency of some recent commentators to dismiss Revelation 2–3 as letters is not practicable.[89] It is likely that the praise and blame sayings would suggest at least some letter function to the initial Asian audience. Insights from the social scientific approach have thus validated the continued use of the word "letters" to refer to these two chapters.

Papyri Letter Forms

White in *Light From Ancient Letters* draws his letter examples exclusively from Egyptian papyri for the form of Hellenistic royal correspondence.[90] Yet these letters appear to share fewer similarities with John's. While noting Stowers's warning that such papyri may not adequately represent letter writing in a province like Asia, it is nevertheless instructive to note some similarities between Egyptian papyri and the seven letters. For example, the information formulas typically use a form of γράφω and the persuasion statements a form of οἶδα.[91] However, these formulas typically concluded the letter body. A formulaic construction of coercion or persuasion is found in several letters and, according to White, warns the recipient "to attend to some duty or request which was earlier specified in the letter."[92] These expressions urging responsible behavior often include imperatives, and conditional clauses sometimes accompany these. Such warning constructions are found in Revelation 2:5 (εἰ δὲ μή . . . ἐὰν μὴ μετανοήσῃς), 2:16 (μετανόησον οὖν· εἰ δὲ μή . . .), 2:22 (ἐὰν μὴ μετανοήσωσιν . . .), and 3:3 (. . . καὶ μετανόησον. ἐὰν οὖν μὴ γρηγορήσῃς . . .).

White gives two first-century examples to illustrate this formula. PTebt II 408 (AD 3) is from Hippolitos to Akousilaos and in lines 14–15 he wrote: "Therefore, do not act otherwise" (μὴ οὖν ἄλλως ποιήσῃς). The second is PFay 110 (AD 94) from Lucius Bellenus Gemellus, a landowner, to Epagathos, his steward. The letter likewise closes: "Therefore, do not act otherwise" (μὴ οὖν ἄλλως ποιήσῃς). The latter example confirms White's statement that such phrases "tend to occur more often in letters from superiors and in administrative correspondence."[93] This precisely accords with the relationship of Jesus and John to the seven churches. The appearance of the construction here is common: "They do not always

---

89. Cf. Aune, "Form and Function," 204.
90. Cf. Welles, *Royal Correspondence in the Hellenistic Period*, xii–l.
91. White, *Light from Ancient Letters*, 204, 205.
92. Ibid., 206.
93. Ibid.

stand in final position in the body, but they almost always depend upon earlier instructions or requests in the body, and consequently, they gravitate toward the end of the message rather than the beginning."[94]

Letters Conclusion

The seven letters, while employing recognizable epistolary forms, have clearly been adapted by John to fit his purposes for the overall work. Rhetorical style is clearly evident, and perhaps decretal forms are borrowed. The letters likewise clearly draw from prophetic messenger oracles. The resulting work is a *mixtum compositum* in form (to borrow Aune's phrase), yet with a clearly recognizable structure. As Schüssler Fiorenza observes cogently, "In spite of this uniformity in structure the seven prophetic letters are not monotonous."[95] To classify Revelation 2–3 as prophetic letters is perhaps the closest we can come to describing the form and content of these chapters.

The Seven Prophetic Letters[96]

From a literary perspective each letter is one unit, so chapters 2–3 can be divided into seven letters. As we have seen in the proposals reviewed earlier in this chapter, depending on which literary form is adopted, the letters themselves divide into varying numbers of rhetorical sections. The chart below represents the attempt by five leading commentators on the letters to divide them.[97] We will interact with these outlines and then suggest a synthesis drawn from the text of these prophetic letters.

---

94. Ibid.

95. Schüssler Fiorenza, *Book of Revelation*, 165.

96. The outline at the end of this chapter is a useful tool for evaluating the discussion on the seven letters particularly in this section.

97. Aune, "Form and Function," 184; Boring, *Revelation*, 86–91; Hubert, "L'architecture des lettres aux Sept Églises," 349–50; Roberts, "Letter to Seven Churches," 27; and Hahn, "Die Sendschreiben der Johannesapokalypse," 366–90. The translation of Hubert's section headings are: 1) The address; 2) The title of Christ ; 3) The positive assessment; 4) The negative assessment; 5) The exhortations; 6) The threats; and 7) The reward. The translation of Hahn's heading are: 1) The messenger formula; 2) οἶδα—section; 3) The wake-up call; and 4) The victor saying.

The Form of the Seven Letters

	Aune[a]	*Boring*	*Hubert*	*Roberts*	*Hahn*
1	Adscriptio	Address to the angel	L'adresse	Instruction to write	die Botenformel
2	Command to write	The city	La titulature du Christ	Announcement of sender	διδα—Abschnitt
3	τάδε λέγει formula	Prophetic messenger formula	Le bilan positif	Diagnosis of the situation	der Weckruf
4	Christological predications	Christological ascription	Le bilan négatif	Call to conversion (not to Thyatira)	der Überwinderspruch[b]
5	Narratio begun by οἶδα—clause	The divine knowledge	Les exhortations	Threats, rewards, encouagements, counsel[c]	
6	Dispositio	The "body"	Les menaces	Warning to listen	
7	Proclamation formula	The call to attention and obedience	La récompense	Promise to those who triumph	
8	Promise of victory	Eschatological promise to the victors			

[a] Aune's earlier prophetic outline is: 1) commissioning formula with Christological predications; 2) central "I know" section: a) praise, b) censure, c) demand for repentance, d) threat of judgment, e) promise of salvation; 3) call for attention; 4) exhortation to conquer (*Prophecy in Early Christianity*, 275–79).

[b] Pohl, *Die Offenbarung des Johannes*, 1:105, calls the saying "der Siegerspruch."

[c] Threats to Philadelphia, Thyatira, and Laodicea; rewards for obedience to Thyatira, Sardis, Philadelphia, and Laodicea; encouragement to Sardis; and counsel to Laodicea.

The three parts of the hellenistic letter—the greeting, body, and closing—can be observed in the seven letters. However, it is apparent that each of these can again be subdivided. In the greeting is the address and epithet sayings; in the body is the praise, blame, and coming sayings, and in the closing is the hearing and victor sayings. The greeting and closing sections each consist of two sentences, making the address, epithet, hearing, and victor sayings easily recognizable grammatical units. A textual analysis of the seven letters seems to support best the models of Aune and Hubert, although I remain unconvinced that Aune's decretal paradigm is the predominant form of chapters 2–3. In the following discussion we will interact primarily with these two models.

Aune's Model

The analysis of Aune is the most comprehensive, so we will interact the most with his outline. Like Boring, he identifies eight structural features to the letters. Unfortunately, these stereotypical phrases and formulas do not conform to the observable literary units, but rather are elements within them. For example, the *adscriptio* and the command to write comprise the letter address, and the τάδε λέγει formula and the Christological predication comprise the letter sender (Boring makes a similar distinction). In our proposed model we delineate two sections, not four, here—the address and epithet sayings. These follow the natural grammatical units found in each letter.

The final two sections—the proclamation formula and the promise of victory—likewise fall into distinct literary units. These are called the hearing and victor sayings in our model. The promise to the Smyrnean church is an anomaly, however. The verb in every other victor saying is in the future tense except here. The future δώσω is used in four other letters (Ephesus, Pergamum, Thyatira, and Laodicea), yet its use in the letter to Smyrna is outside the victor section in 2:10. Because the promise of the crown of life is clearly eschatological and links the concepts of the first and second death, this appears to be a promise placed outside its defined saying. Aune's model fails to account for this exception, and the entirety of 2:10 is placed in the *dispositio*. This tendency toward structural "bleed" was likewise noted in our discussion of chiastic structure. Outlines proposed for Revelation must, of necessity, be flexible enough to incorporate such structural anomalies.

The center section—the body—is difficult to analyze. The οἶδα-clause and the *dispositio* are distinguished, even though this is difficult because, as Aune notes, the latter "is not formally marked with a stereotypical phrase used consistently in all seven proclamations."[98] While Hahn's outline may be the briefest, he compensates by identifying six major elements in the οἶδα section[99] (abbreviations utilize each church's first letter[s]):

---

98. Aune, "Form and Function," 192.
99. Hahn, "Die Sendschreiben der Johannesapokalypse," 370–77.

1. The church's situation either with approval (E, T, Ph, L) or disapproval (Sa, L)
2. The phrase "but I have against you" (E, P, T)
3. The call to repentance (E, P, Ph, L)
4. The "behold" clause (S, T, Ph, L)
5. The statement "I am coming quickly" with variations (all but S)
6. A statement about what each church has and should keep (all but S)

Although the οἶδα-clause begins the body in all seven letters, the clause functions differently among the letters. In the letters to Ephesus, Smyrna, Pergamum, Thyatira, and Philadelphia (2:1, 9, 13, 19; 3:8) the οἶδα-clause initiates a word of praise; however, in the letters to Sardis and Laodicea (3:1, 15) it initiates a word of blame. Even the five uses of the expanded phrase οἶδα σου τὰ ἔργα (or ἔργα σου) fail to clarify here because Ephesus, Thyatira, and Philadelphia are positive while Sardis and Laodicea are negative. Thus stereotypical language alone cannot determine the form of the letters; the function of such language must also be addressed.

The adversative ἀλλά begins a second distinguishable section of the body. Its fullest form—ἀλλα ἔχω κατὰ σοῦ (ὀλίγα) ὅτι—is found only in the letters to Ephesus, Pergamum, and Thyatira (2:4, 14, 20). In these letters the adversative begins a blame section. However, in the Smyrnean letter (2:9) ἀλλα, is found in the praise saying, while in the Ephesian and Sardian letters (2:6; 3:4) ἀλλα, begins a brief praise before the letter closing. The negative and positive uses of the adversative again highlight the different functions that a stereotypical word might perform. Because there is no blame given to Philadelphia or praise to Laodicea, neither form used either negatively or positively is found in these letters.

The Coming Sayings

Aune perceptively notes that these positive uses of ἀλλά in the Ephesian and Sardian letters form an *inclusio* to frame a third section which he identifies as the *dispositio*.[100] Often this third section, which Aune calls "the central section of the proclamations, the reason for which they were written,"[101] is overlooked because it is so amorphous in the other letters. Since

---

100. Aune, "Form and Function," 191.
101. Ibid.

these two letters are clearly marked, let us examine them for distinguishing words or phrase. Following the brief blame saying (2:4) is a section (v, 5) beginning with the imperatives μνημόνευε[102] and μετανόησον. Following these are two conditional conjunctions εἰ δὲ μή and ἐὰν μή. The verb ἔρχομαι (a present with future implications) and the future κινήσω then follow. The Sardian letter (3:2–3) likewise displays this pattern: a string of five imperatives including the same two followed by the conditional ἐὰν οὖν μὴ and the future ἥξω (2x).

Having identified stereotypical language in the demarcated section of these two letters, let us seek to distinguish this section in the other letters. The imperative μετανόησον followed by a conditional conjunction and a future form of ἔρχομαι occurs also in the letters to Pergamum and Laodicea (2:16; 3:19b–20). The break after the praise section in the Philadelphian letter is difficult to determine. Aune begins the new section in 3:9 with ἰδοὺ διδῶ.[103] My preference is to leave this sentence in the praise section with the initial phrase ἰδοὺ δέδωκα, and begin the coming section with the third phrase ἰδοὺ ποιήσω in the future tense. In the Laodicean letter Aune begins this section in verse 16 largely because of the use of μέλλω σε ἐμέσαι following a causal clause.[104] While a future act is indicated here, the main perspective in 3:16–19a is a present one dealing with correction and instruction (v. 19a). A better start for this section is with the two imperatives, ζήλευε οὖν καὶ μετανόησον (v. 19b). The emphasis on the coming of Jesus is significant in this section. Only in the letter to Smyrna is a form of ἔρχομαι absent. Hemer attributes this absence to the fact "that the Parousia was expected to terminate the church's interim period of suffering. That would be the occasion when Christ would bestow the crown of life. There was no need to stress it as a warning or threat."[105] However, imminent persecution and martyrdom, not the parousia, better account for the preclusion of judgment upon the Smyrneans.

---

102. Aune's comment (ibid., 192) on the use of μνημόνευε is specious: "This emphasis on remembering the past constitutes the idealization of the past implying that all perceived forms of slippage including the appearance of dissident views and behaviours are based on a nostalgic conception of the purity of the pristine era (compatible with the composition of Revelation later than earlier in the first cent. AD)."

103. Ibid.

104. Ibid.

105. Hemer, *Letters to the Seven Churches of Asia*, 74.

Thyatiran Letter Divisions

The letter to Thyatira (2:18–29) is the longest and most complex of the letters "because the author carefully distinguishes *two* groups within that community and delivers a different message to each."[106] Besides speaking to Jezebel and her followers as well as the faithful, he also addresses the other six churches. As a result, several of the sections are repeated. To the first group the use of singular pronouns, as in the other letters, is maintained. The second group (the other churches and the faithful in Thyatira) is easily identified through the use of plural pronouns. The following chart demonstrates this:

Address	Epithet	Praise	Blame	Coming
To the Jezebelites				
Καὶ τῷ ἀγγέλῳ τῆς ἐν Θυατείροις ἐκκλησίας γράψον·	Τάδε λέγει ὁ υἱὸς τοῦ θεοῦ, ὁ ἔχων τοὺς ὀφθαλμοὺς αὐτοῦ ὡς φλόγα πυρός καὶ οἱ πόδες αὐτοῦ ὅμοιοι χαλκολιβάνῳ·	Οἶδά σου τὰ ἔργα καὶ τὴν ἀγάπην καὶ τὴν πίστιν καὶ τὴν διακονίαν καὶ τὴν ὑπομονήν σου, καὶ τὰ ἔργα σου τὰ ἔσχατα πλείονα τῶν πρώτων.	ἀλλὰ ἔχω κατὰ σοῦ ὅτι ἀφεῖς τὴν γυναῖκα Ἰεζάβελ, ἡ λέγουσα ἑαυτὴν προφῆτιν καὶ διδάσκει καὶ πλανᾷ τοὺς ἐμοὺς δούλους πορνεῦσαι καὶ φαγεῖν εἰδωλόθυτα. καὶ ἔδωκα αὐτῇ χρόνον ἵνα μετανοήσῃ, καὶ οὐ θέλει μετανοῆσαι ἐκ τῆς πορνείας αὐτῆς.	ἰδοὺ βάλλω αὐτὴν εἰς κλίνην καὶ τοὺς μοιχεύοντας μετ᾽ αὐτῆς εἰς θλῖψιν μεγάλην, ἐὰν μὴ μετανοήσωσιν ἐκ τῶν ἔργων αὐτῆς, καὶ τὰ τέκνα αὐτῆς ἀποκτενῶ ἐν θανάτῳ.
To the Faithful				
			To the Victor	
καὶ γνώσονται πᾶσαι αἱ ἐκκλησίαι	ὅτι ἐγώ εἰμι ὁ ἐραυνῶν νεφροὺς καὶ καρδίας		καὶ δώσω ὑμῖν ἑκάστῳ κατὰ τὰ ἔργα ὑμῶν	

---

106. Scobie, "Local References in the Letters to the Seven Churches," 613.

Address	Epithet	Praise	Blame	Coming
τοῖς λοιποῖς τοῖς ἐν Θυατείροις,	ὑμῖν δὲ λέγω	ὅσοι οὐκ ἔχουσιν τὴν διδαχὴν ταύτην, οἵτινες οὐκ ἔγνωσαν τὰ βαθέα τοῦ Σατανᾶ ὡς λέγουσιν·	καὶ ὁ νικῶν καὶ ὁ τηρῶν ἄχρι τέλους τὰ ἔργα μου, δώσω αὐτῷ ἐξουσίαν ἐπὶ τῶν ἐθνῶν καὶ ποιμανεῖ αὐτοὺς ἐν ῥάβδῳ σιδηρᾷ ὡς τὰ σκεύη τὰ κεραμικὰ συντρίβεται, ὡς κἀγὼ εἴληφα παρὰ τοῦ πατρός μου, καὶ δώσω αὐτῷ τὸν ἀστέρα τὸν πρωϊνόν.	οὐ βάλλω ἐφ' ὑμᾶς ἄλλο βάρος, πλὴν ὃ ἔχετε κρατήσατε ἄχρι[ς] οὗ ἂν ἥξω.

There is a double address in the letter—first to the angel in Thyatira and then to the rest in Thyatira. The verb λέγω is used twice in the double epithets. This is also the only use of ἐγώ εἰμι in the letters; in its other four occurrences in Revelation it is always used with other Christological epithets (1:8, 17; 21:6; 22:16). Two sets of works are commended. The initial laudatory remarks seem problematic if they are addressed only to the Jezebel party. There is no blame saying for the faithful group, and only to them are promises given. The word βάλλω sets apart the coming section. The Jezebel party is told to repent, while the others are told to hold on until Jesus comes. The complex construction of this letter shows John's ability to adapt his letter structure when needed, and its threefold nature is not mentioned by Aune in his analysis.

Hubert's Analysis

Hubert suggests that the letters be divided into seven columns with seven sectional rows producing forty-nine blocks of text.[107] This I have produced in the letter sayings outline. Such a parallel format allows a ready verbal and subject comparison among the letters.

---

107. Hubert, "L'architecture des letters," 350.

Hubert's analysis is not as in-depth as Aune's and difficult to follow since he fails to give verse references for his discussion. Nevertheless, he makes several important observations. The verb that characteristically begins the exhortation section is μετανοεῖν, which is found in letters 1, 3, 5, 7. It is altogether lacking in letters 2 and 6, yet found three times in letter 4, the central letter. But in the Thyatiran letter only the Jezebel party is directed to repent and not the church itself. This is consistent with our earlier observation that the Thyatiran letter is essentially two letters. Hubert shows the symmetry of this relationship between these two groups of churches like this:[108]

1	2	3	4	5	6	7
	S		T		Ph	
E		P		Sa		L

The bottom row of churches likewise demonstrates an interesting arrangement concerning the praise sayings. Ephesus receives the most—8; Pergamum—2; Sardis—1; and Laodicea—0. The scheme is thus one of diminishing order. This observation is confirmed by noting the word count in the praise sayings of the respective churches.

The victor sayings display a unique relationship between Smyrna and Philadelphia. A crown is mentioned only in these two letters. The Smyrneans are promised a crown, while the Philadelphians already possess it. Both of these churches are likewise being harassed by the Jews who are called the synagogue of Satan.

Hubert's examination of the threats of chastisement is not convincing.[109] Making Ephesus the benchmark, he sees the tone of the threats to churches 2, 4, and 6 becoming less negative while that to churches 3, 5, and 7 more negative. It is difficult to see how the removal of the Ephesian lampstand (if this is the correct understanding) can be better than Jesus spitting the Laodiceans out of his mouth. He rightly notes the entreaty to all the churches in the Thyatiran letter, but according to his diagram the placement of this church is not central. The chiastic structure proposed in chapter 1 better accounts for the position of this entreaty.

---

108. Ibid., 351.
109. Ibid., 352.

The Seven Beatitudes and the Coming/Victor Sayings

Little recognized is the verbal and thematic relationship between the seven beatitudes and the seven letters, particularly the coming and victor sayings.[110] Beatitudes 1–4 and 6 are related to the coming sayings, while beatitudes 5 and 7 are related to the victor sayings. The following chart outlines the thematic relationships:

	Beatitude ("Blessed...")	Church	Coming/Victor Sayings
1	Those who hear the words of the prophecy and keep them (1:3)	Sardis	You have heard, now keep and repent (3:3)
2	The dead who die in the Lord from now on (14:13)	Smyrna	Become faithful until death (2:10)
3	Those watching for his coming as a thief (16:15)	Sardis	Become watchful or Christ will come as a thief (3:2–3)
4	Those invited to the marriage dinner of the Lamb (19:9)	Laodicea	Christ will dine with him (3:20)
5	Those in first resurrection because second death has no authority over them (20:6)	Smyrna	Second death will not harm victors (2:11)
6	Those keeping the words of the prophecy (22:7; cf 22:9)	Philadelphia	You have kept my word (3:10; cf. 3:8)
7	Those washing their robes have the right to the tree of life (22:14)	Ephesus	Victor to eat from the tree of life (2:7)

The following observations are further evidence of such verbal and thematic relationships:

- Example 1 has the only two uses of ἀκούω and τηρέω together.
- Example 2 has a thematic relationship of death.
- Example 3 has the only two uses of κλέπτης and the three uses of γρηγορέω.[111]

---

110. Cf. Mazzaferri, *Genre of the Book of Revelation*, 299.

111. A connection also exists between this beatitude and the blame saying of the Laodicean letter (3:17, 18). Here are found the two references to believers as naked (γυμνός/γυμνότητός) with its resulting shame (αἰσχύνη/ἀσχημοσύνην).

- Example 4 has the only use of δειπνέω and its noun form δεῖπνον (apart from 19:17)
- Example 5 features the use of the distinctive phrase "second death" (also in 20:14; 21:8)
- Example 6, apart from the first beatitude, has the only other conjunction of λόγος and τηρέω.
- Example 7 features the use of the distinctive phrase "tree of life" (also in 22:2, 19).

A relationship connected to the chiastic structure of the book also exists. In terms of the outline presented in chapter 1, sections A and B contain one beatitude and seven victor sayings, while B´ and A´ contain one victor saying and four beatitudes. While the balance is not exact, it strongly suggests that the recipients of the beatitudes and the promises are one and the same—the victors. In the letters the promises are couched in imagery addressed to the victors in each local church; in the beatitudes many of these same images are applied to the blessed victors in all the churches. John uses these exhortations in the form of beatitudes to "bring pressure upon the readers both to perceive the crisis and to act with total resolution."[112]

Trench suggests another internal thematic relationship in the letters: "It is deeply interesting and instructive to observe how in this [Ephesus], and probably in every other case, the character of the promise corresponds to the character of the faithfulness displayed."[113] Charles likewise believes that the form of the letter endings "may in some cases be determined by the diction or thought of the respective letters of which they form the close."[114] Trench delineates such a correspondence in the first six promises, which is outlined next.[115] An asterisk (*) denotes my additions or changes.

Church	Faithful works	Promise
Ephesus	Abstain from works of Nicolaitans, i.e., eating idol meat	Eat from tree of life
Smyrna	Do not fear suffering and death	Not harmed by second death
Pergamum	Abstain from eating idol meat (Hold on to my name*)	Eat hidden manna (New name written on white stone*)

---

112. Minear, *I Saw a New Earth*, 214.
113. Trench, *Commentary on the Epistles*, 97.
114. Charles, *Revelation*, 1.45n. 1.
115. Trench, *Commentary on the Epistles*, 97–98.

Church	Faithful works	Promise
Thyatira	Not vanquished by the world (Ignorant of Satan's deep things*)	Have dominion over the world (Have the morning star*)
Sardis	Keep garments white (Negatively, name alive but dead*)	Clad in white and shining garments (Positively, name not erased from book of life*)
Philadelphia	Overcome Jewish pretensions	Made free of a heavenly Jerusalem
Laodicea	(Focus on temporal wealth and power*)	(Receive eternal throne*)

Trench concludes that "the only Church in which any difficulty occurs in tracing the correlation between the form of the victory and the form of the reward, is the last."[116] Since the Laodiceans are not commended for any faithful works, their preoccupation with temporal status is instead contrasted with eternal rule. The letters therefore demonstrate an inner coherency and show a relationship between the faithful works of the victors in each church and the promises they receive.

Prophetic Letters Conclusion

The analyses of Aune and Hubert have significantly advanced our understanding of the letters. While our division of the letters resembles their outlines, nevertheless we have made significant modifications. Our model has seven sections divided into the following sayings: (1) address, (2) epithet, (3) praise, (4) blame, (5) coming, (6) hearing, and (7) victor. The text of the seven letters divided into these seven sections is found in the Appendix at the end of the book. The word length of each letter and its seven sections is presented for purposes of comparison.

Churches	Total	Address	Epithet	Praise	Blame	Coming	Hearing	Victor
Ephesus	147	7	20	54	11	28	10	17
Smyrna	98	8	12	26	0	25	10	17
Pergamum	147	8	10	38	36	18	10	27
Thyatira	230	13	36	41	38	41	10	51
Sardis	143	8	13	21	12	46	10	33

116. Ibid., 98.

Churches	Total	Address	Epithet	Praise	Blame	Coming	Hearing	Victor
Philadelphia	196	8	22	47	0	57	10	52
Laodicea	188	8	16	0	97	33	10	24

While length must be recognized as only one criterion for evaluation, it is significant that the central letter to Thyatira is the longest. Its victor saying is second in length (by one word) only to that of Philadelphia.

The elements of the praise and blame sayings were mentioned while discussing the rhetorical situation of the seven churches. The coming sayings will be touched on in future discussions. Christ's warnings to come in judgment undoubtedly had a great impact on the Asian miscreants, since his judgment against the Jews was in the process of being fulfilled at Jerusalem. The address, epithet, and hearing sayings will be discussed next before we focus on the victor sayings.

The Address Sayings

Each letter begins with the phrase, "To the angel." This dative singular τῷ ἀγγέλῳ is used again only in 9:14 where the sixth angel is told to release four angels. In the New Testament the only other occurrence is found in Luke 2:13 at the angelic announcement of Jesus' birth. This form is found six times in the Old Testament (Num 22:34; 2 Sam 11:18; 24:16; 1 Chr 21:16; Zech 1:11, 13) and twice in the Apocrypha (Tob 6:6, 14). Only 2 Samuel 11:18 refers to a human messenger. The reference in Numbers is found in the Balaam account. The first reference in Zechariah is in the context of the report of the four colored horses, while the second relates to God's word to the angel who was interpreting the visions to Zechariah. The dative plural is found three times in Revelation—7:2, 15:7, and 16:1. In each of these texts the angels are charged to carry out activities related to divine judgments. The phrase, "To the angel," thus serves a dispatch function in biblical literature, whereby angels are sent as divine messengers.

Angels in Biblical and Apocalyptic Literature

Angelic mediators have a rich background in the Old Testament. The law was given through angels (Deut 33:2 LXX; cf. Acts 7:53; Gal 3:19; Heb 2:2). Angels were sent to interpret the visions of Daniel (Dan 10:4ff.) and of Zechariah (Zech 1:8ff.) among others. The presence of angelic intermediaries is a characteristic of apocalyptic literature. As Collins notes, "In every apocalypse the revelation is mediated by an otherworldly, angelic figure."[117] The multiplicity of angels in Revelation is one of the most prominent features linking it with the apocalyptic genre.

Paul's enigmatic remark in 1 Corinthians 11:10—a woman should wear long hair "because of the angels"—is understood by some commentators to indicate that angels were in attendance at early church meetings. Witherington suggests that in Christian worship "even angels, as guardians of the creation order, are present, observing such worship and perhaps even participating in it."[118] While such an interpretation provides some insight into the functional relationship between the angels and the seven churches, one cannot be dogmatic given the multiplicity of suggested interpretations for this text.

Angels in Asia

Angel (ἄγγελλος) was also an important word for the residents of Asia. Arnold has recently reviewed a number of inscriptions from Asia Minor that speak of angelic mediators. His epigraphic evidence is drawn not only from pagan sources, but also from Jewish and Christian ones. In all three contexts Arnold notes that angels "were perceived as accessible supernatural beings who came to the aid of people in need . . . . In the Jewish and Christian texts, the angels are best interpreted as the supernatural servants and emissaries of Yahweh." He concludes that ἄγγελλος "was an important term in the religious life of the people of Asia Minor."[119]

Although Arnold's research focuses primarily on the angel cults associated with the Colossian church, his study may have implications for our understanding of angels in Revelation. Clearly John's congregations were not venerating angels as had Laodicea's sister church in the Lycus valley (Col 2:18). Yet the prominent mention of angels at the beginning of each letter suggests that the Asian audience was familiar with their mediatorial role in the churches. Such cognizance is consistent with the Anatolian inscriptional evidence described by Arnold and others.[120]

Angels in Revelation

"Angel" is a common noun in Revelation used sixty-seven times. An angel is identified in 1:1 as the mediator for John's vision. The "son of man" figure

---

117. Collins, "Jewish Apocalypses," 21.

118. Witherington, *Conflict and Community in Corinth*, 236.; cf. Fee, *First Epistle to the Corinthians*, 521–22, for other interpretations

119. Arnold, "Mediator Figures in Asia Minor," 26, 27.

120. Cf. Mitchell, *Anatolia*, 2:46.

that John sees in his opening vision is holding seven stars (1:16).[121] The use of metaphorical language here is evident because, when the speaker places his same right hand on the prostrate John, he never drops the stars (1:17). Instead he comforts the seer and interprets the stars to be the angels of the seven churches (1:20). Thus each church has its complementary angel. Wojciechowski's attempt to identify the seven stars with the sun, moon, and five planets lacks any textual basis and thereby seems improbable.[122]

Seven angels are connected later with the seven trumpets (8:2, 6) and the seven bowls (15:1, 6, 7; 16:1). It is unlikely that these are the same angels as those assigned to the churches. For these angels are said to be standing before God (8:2) and coming out of the heavenly temple (15:6). A review of every other occurrence in Revelation indicates that ἄγγελλος is a celestial being rather than an earthly one, hence "angel" is the proper translation.

The identification of the ἄγγελος as the human leader (e.g., the bishop) in each church is clearly inadequate.[123] Widely accepted today is the view "that the angels are personifications of the prevailing spirit of the churches, the spiritual counterpart of the earthly reality."[124] This position is alien to the reality of angels as spiritual beings as seen in Revelation and in the rest of the Bible. Throughout Revelation angels are the exclusive agents in executing the divine commands. Stuckenbruck plausibly suggests that the angel in each congregation, to whom John is instructed to write, serves as a mediator—patron or guardian—who ensures that Christ's message is safely and accurately delivered.[125] Just as John is sent an angel to mediate God's word to him (1:1), so the churches are similarly sent an angel to mediate Jesus' word to each. Finally, Park argues convincingly that the use of angel reflects John's tendency to emphasize "that there is a heavenly representative reality (seemingly better) for an earthly transient entity."[126]

---

121. Beasley-Murray, *Revelation*, 70, asserts that seven stars were "a symbol of the political power exercised by the Roman Caesars over the world, and in this sense the seven stars often occur on imperial coins." He draws his information from Stauffer, *Christ and the Caesars*, 150–53, who refers specifically to a coin type of Domitian honoring his dead son (illustrated in Ehrman, *New Testament*, 405 fig. 27.2). However, Burnett, Amandry, and Ripollès in *Roman Provincial Coinage* give no examples of Flavian *provincial* coinage inscribed with seven stars.

122. Wojciechowski, "Seven Churches and Seven Celestial Bodies," 48.

123. Cf. Trench, *Commentary on the Epistles*, 58–61.

124. Watson, "Angels of the Seven Churches," 2:1.255.

125. Stuckenbruck, *Angel Veneration and Christology*, 234–38.

126. Park, "More than a Regained Eden," 285n. 67.

The command to write (γράψον) to the angel of each church reiterates an earlier command given to John who is in the Spirit on the island of Patmos. He hears a loud voice behind him: "Write (γράψον) what you see in a book and send it to the seven churches" (1:11). What follows is the initial listing of the seven churches in the same order as they are addressed in chapters 2–3. Here John is commanded to write directly to the churches without mention of angelic mediators. The command is renewed in 1:19 when the First and the Last again commands: "Write (γράψον) therefore the things you saw." This literary device of addressing each church through an ἄγγελος using second person singular verbs and singular pronouns breaks down within the letters. A plural pronoun is first used in 2:10 when the Smyrneans are warned that the devil is going to throw some of you (pl.; ἐξ ὑμῶν) into prison. These will be tested and experience tribulation for ten days. Thereupon "the author seems to forget his angelic addressee and refers to the entire community using second-person plural forms."[127]

The command to write occurs on three other occasions in the book.[128] In 14:13 John is commanded by a heavenly voice to record the contents of the second beatitude. In 19:9 an angel commands him to write the fourth beatitude. And in 21:5 John receives the final command: "Write, 'These words are faithful and true.'" This oath precedes the final saying to the victor given by the one sitting on the throne, who identifies himself as the Alpha and Omega, the Beginning and the End, and is a chiastic complement to the opening command.

The Epithet Sayings

Following the τάδε λέγει saying most letters include a present participle in the presentation—ὁ κρατῶν ... ὁ περιπατῶν (2:1), and ὁ ἔχων (2:12, 18; 3:1, 7). These participles have a structural symmetry with the present participle ὁ ἔχων that begins the call the hear. Aune assigns the use of ὁ ἔχων in 2:12 and 3:7 to the semantic subdomain of Grasp, Hold, like that of ὁ κρατῶν.[129] This is questionable since ὁ ἔχων in both cases better fits the semantic subdomain of "Have, Possess," as in 2:18 and 3:1.[130] In 2:12 Jesus does not hold the sword, for it proceeds out of his mouth (cf. 1:16; 2:16). In 3:7 Jesus does not literally hold the

---

127. Aune, "Form and Function," 186n. 16.

128. A similar command to write is found in Hermas (*Vis.* 8.3): "Therefore you will write (γράψεις) two books, and you will send one to Clement and one to Grapte."

129. Aune, "Form and Function," 189; cf. L&N, §18A.

130. L&N, §57A.

key; he holds the seven stars. Rather the key of David is a metaphor of the authority he possesses (cf. 1:18).

The Epithets in Revelation

The presentation of Christ in each letter is drawn from the opening vision in chapter 1. Many of the names and images are likewise depicted in the closing visions of the book. The following chart shows the intratextuality related to the epithets in Revelation.

Church	Epithets	Opening Epithets	Other Epithets
Ephesus	Holds 7 stars in right hand; walks among 7 golden lampstands (2:1)	Has 7 stars in right hand (1:16); among 7 golden lampstands (1:13)	Has the 7 stars (3:1)
Smyrna	First and Last; dead and lived again (2:8)	First and Last (1:17); dead and now lives again forever (1:18)	First and Last (22:13)
Pergamum	Has sharp double-edged sword (2:12)	Sharp double-edged sword out of mouth (1:16)	Sword of his mouth (2:16); sharp sword out of mouth (19:15)
Thyatira	Son of God; eyes like blazing fire; feet like bronze (2:18)	Son of man (1:13); eyes like blazing fire (1:14); feet like bronze in a blazing furnace (1:15)	Eyes like a blazing fire (19:12)
Sardis	Has 7 spirits of God and 7 stars (3:1)	7 spirits (1:4); has 7 stars in right hand (1:16)	7 spirits (4:5; 5:6); holds 7 stars in right hand (2:1)
Philadelphia	The Holy, the True; has key of David; opens and closes (3:7)	Has keys of death and Hades (1:18)	Holy and True (6:10)
Laodicea	Amen; faithful and true witness; beginning of God's creation (3:14)	Faithful witness (1:5)	Faithful and True (19:11; cf 21:5); Beginning and End (21:6; 22:13)

In the opening vision Christ is depicted as the eschatological judge. Features of this vision are seen in each of the seven letters, where both temporal and eschatological judgment are in view. The appearance of these epithets in chapters 19–22, where the eschaton itself is depicted, is equally significant. Mazzaferri overstates when he writes that the primary purpose of the eschaton is "divine judgment upon the wicked, especially as they persecute believers."[131] While such judgment is an aspect, more importantly it is a time of reward for the believers who have maintained their witness.

The Epithets in the Old and New Testaments

Revelation's intertextual use of the Old and New Testaments can again be observed in the epithet sayings. In the chart below such allusions are noted.

Church	Epithets	Epithet Backgrounds
Ephesus	7 stars in right hand; 7 golden lampstands	12 stars = 12 tribes? (Gn 37:9); golden lampstand with 7 bowls (Zech 4:2)
Smyrna	First and Last; dead and lived again	First and Last (Isa 44:6; 48:12); cf died and lived again (Rom 14:9)
Pergamum	Sharp double-edged sword	Mouth like sharp sword (Isa 49:2; cf Ps 149:6); cf rod of mouth (Isa 11:4)
Thyatira	Son of God; eyes like blazing fire; feet like bronze	My son (Ps 2:7); eyes as lamps of fire and feet as bronze (Dan 10:6)
Sardis	7 spirits of God	7 spirits of God? (Is 11:2–3 LXX; cf Zech 4:2, 10)
Philadelphia	The Holy, the True; has key of David (3:7); opens and closes	Holy (Isa 40:25; Hab 3:3); True (Exod 34:6; Ps 86:15; Isa 65:16); key of the house of David that opens and closes (Isa 22:22)
Laodicea	Amen; faithful and true witness; beginning of God's creation (3:14)	God of Amen? (Isa 65:16 Sym); faithful witness in heaven? (Ps 88:38 LXX); firstborn of all creation . . . the beginning (Col 1:15, 18)

---

131. Mazzaferri, *Genre of the Book of Revelation*, 243.

Although it is difficult to identify the precise background of all of the epithets, it appears that John again relies on the Old Testament for many of these names and images.

The reference in the Laodicean letter to Jesus as the "beginning of God's creation" has a striking parallel in the use of κτίσις and ἀρχή in Colossians 1:15, 18. Regarding John's possible acquaintance with Paul's letter to Colossae, Charles believes it highly probable, while Mounce thinks it all but certain.[132] Based on geography and verbal parallelism, it is an attractive hypothesis that the source of the Laodicean epithet is the Colossian letter.

The Hearing Sayings

The use of the plural "churches" in the hearing sayings—"the one who has an ear, let him hear what the Spirit is saying to the churches"—contrasts with its singular form in the address. Does this mean that each letter is directed not only to the addressed church, but also to all the churches? The unique situation of each church makes this unlikely. The only other use of "churches" in the seven letters is found in the Thyatiran letter (2:23) when Jesus wishes all the churches to understand the error of Jezebel and her followers. Does the plural form perhaps point to the universal nature of the promises then? Is it these that are available to every Asian believer who overcomes? This perspective seems more viable. That the victor sayings follow the hearing sayings in the first three letters points to such a logical progression.

Another hearing saying is found in 13:9 following John's vision of the first beast. Its length is abridged—"If anyone has an ear, let him hear"—with the refrain mentioning the Spirit omitted. Enroth accounts for its distinctiveness, saying, "In chapter 13 the prophet himself is speaking in his own person and not through a supernatural authority as in the letters."[133] The participial form found in the letters has been changed to a conditional sentence beginning with εἴ τις (cf. Mk 4:23), which introduces the two succeeding sentences adapted probably from Jeremiah 15:2 and 43:11.

Here it precedes the first of four *Hode* (Ὧδέ) sayings: "Here is the obedience and faith of the saints" (13:10). A similar saying without the hearing saying is found in 14:12: "Here is the obedience of the saints, those who keep the commandments of God and the faith in Jesus." The

---

132. Charles, *Revelation*, 1:94; Mounce, *Book of Revelation*, 124.
133. Enroth, "Hearing Formula in the Book of Revelation," 605.

plural "saints" functions as the equivalent of "churches" in these hortative texts. And, to make a wordplay in English, the "here" functions as an attention device just like the earlier "hear."

The two other *Hode* sayings are likewise instructive. The first in 13:18 follows John's vision of the second beast: "Here is wisdom. The one who has a mind, let him calculate the number of the beast." The pattern of the present participle of "have" (ἔχων) plus a cognitive body part, here "mind" (νοῦν) instead of "ears" plus an aorist imperative singular, here "let him calculate (ψηφισάτω)," clearly suggests a modified hearing saying. The final saying in 17:9 incorporates the first seven words of 13:18: "Here is the mind which has wisdom" (Ὧδε ὁ νοῦς ὁ ἔχων σοφίαν). Bauckham observes, "The resemblance between the two passages is clearly deliberate, and the variation between them typical of John's stylistic habit of varying the precise form of expressions he repeats."[134] Enroth, however, sees a subtle change of purpose between these two latter sayings and 13:9: "When the author wants to indicate a deeper meaning to his hearers and readers, he directs his call to "understanding" (νοῦς) not to the "ear" (οὖς)."[135] Whether to the ears or to the mind, the hearing sayings and their variations were designed to gain the attention of the same intended audience.

A final, but condensed, hearing saying—"the one who hears, let him say, 'Come'"; ὁ ἀκούων εἰπάτω," Ἐρχου—is found in 22:17. Ἀκούων is a substantival participle, not an imperative; the command is to "speak," not to "hear." The Spirit is again speaking to the Asian churches, with the bride, saying "Come." The faithful hearers are likewise invited to say, "Come." Two other substantival participles with imperative verbs follow: "And the one who thirsts let him come (ὁ διψῶν ἐρχέσθω) and the one who wishes, let him take (ὁ θέλων λαβέτω) from the gift of the water of life." This couplet contains imagery related to the final victor saying in 21:6–7. The hearing sayings placed throughout Revelation underscore that the believers in the seven churches remain the intended audience.

The Role of the Spirit

The Spirit is initially presented in 1:4 as the seven spirits (cf. 4:5; 5:6), a symbol probably drawn from Zechariah 4:1–10.[136] However, in the seven letters the Spirit is presented in the singular, τὸ πνεῦμα. The plurals of

---

134. Bauckham, *Climax of Prophecy*, 394.
135. Enroth, "Hearing Formula," 607.
136. Cf. Bruce, "Spirit in the Apocalypse," 336.

chapter 1—seven Spirits, seven churches, seven angels, indicating totality and completion—become singular in chapter 2. While Jesus speaks (λέγει) to each individual church, it is the Spirit's role to speak (λέγει) also, applying the message to the other churches.

The relationship of Jesus to the Spirit in the letters has occasioned much discussion. "When John writes what Christ dictates to each church, it is equally the Spirit who speaks. So there is no need for a distinct position in the hierarchy."[137] This interrelationship is also depicted in 5:6 where the slain Lamb has eyes which are the seven Spirits of God. These eyes sent throughout the earth symbolize divine omniscience. A related Christological epithet—eyes of blazing fire (2:18)—combines the aspect of omniscience with that of purification, since fire is often a symbol of the Holy Spirit in the New Testament (e.g., Matt 3:11; Acts 2:3).

Kirby sees in the hearing saying an early formulation of trinitarian doctrine. The warning/refrain "is also important for Jesus' *ethos* because it represents the collocation of two elements: [1] the phrase familiarly associated with him in the Gospels: 'He who has ears to hear,' and [2] the identification of the speaker here in *Revelation* as *the Spirit*."[138] The presence of other trinitarian collocations (cf. Rev 1:4–5 and 5:6) make this observation highly likely.

In neither the eighth hearing saying nor the *Hode* sayings is the Holy Spirit identified as the speaker. In fact, no one is explicitly mentioned so the Spirit could well be the speaker. Following the declaration of the second beatitude (14:13), the Spirit responds by saying, "Yes."

Biblical Co-texts

This aphorism occurs seven times in the Synoptics (Matt 11:15; 13:9, 43; Mark 4:9, 23; Luke 8:8; 14:35) and occurs as a variant reading six times (Matt 25:29; Mark 7:16; Luke 12:21; 13:9; 21:4). Hadorn declares, "Die Mahnung zu hören, schliesst an ein bekanntes jesuswort an."[139] This relationship with the Synoptic sayings has likewise been noted by Vos: "With respect to the speaker of this characteristic exhortation, it is significant that in the synoptic Gospels it is found only in contexts which are ascribed to our Lord," observing also that this "exhortation is not used by the apostles in their speeches, as they are recorded."[140] The similarity

---

137. Mazzaferri, *Genre of the Book of Revelation*, 300.
138. Kirby, "Rhetorical Situations," 206n. 29.
139. Hadorn, *Die Offenbarung des Johannes*, 40.
140. Vos, *Synoptic Traditions in the Apocalypse*, 74.

between Matthew 11:15, which speaks of John the Baptist as the expected Elijah, and the "endings of the prophecies to the seven churches" provides evidence to Ford that the Baptist was the author of Revelation.[141] Such a conclusion seems unwarranted given the phrase's usage in the parable tradition, particularly in the parable of the sower, which has no relationship to the Baptist. Enroth rightly infers from the Synoptic background that John took the hearing formula from tradition "but he edits it and uses it in a new context."[142]

Mazzaferri believes the "call to hear" (*Weckruf* or *Weckformel*) has much in common with the Old Testament "attention formula": "The AF builds on the imperatival שמע and the object דבר. It occurs at least 40 times with seven variants. Most common is שמעו דבר יהוה . . . . The AF appears in the major prophets some 31 times in all."[143] Aune disagrees, however: "The formula has no close verbal parallel in ancient literature with the exception of the parable tradition in the Synoptic Gospels."[144] Aune, however, overlooks the strong verbal tie to this Old Testament form. The most familiar verse in the Torah—the Shema ("Ἄκουε' Ἰσραὴλ . . . ; Deut 6:4 LXX)—was a hearing saying that could be heard in the synagogues of the Diaspora every sabbath.

The 3 + 4 Pattern

An interesting change in pattern occurs between the final two sayings of the letters. In the first three the call to hear precedes the victor saying; in the last four letters the promises to the victors come first. "This grouping of the sections into 3 + 4 (letters) or 4 + 3 (seals and trumpets) is found in three series; it is entirely absent from three other sections (vials, voices and vision)."[145] Whether there is any significance to this switch in the letters has been debated. Bauckham concludes that "it is difficult to discern any reason within the letters for this distinction between the first three and the last four churches."[146] Giblin, however, suggests the change "helps show that the promise is tied to the Lord"s communication as a whole, not just

---

141. Ford, *Revelation*, 29.
142. Enroth, "Hearing Formula," 601.
143. Mazzaferri, *Genre of the Book of Revelation*, 121.
144. Aune, "Form and Function," 193.
145. Loernetz, *Apocalypse of Saint John*, xviii.
146. Bauckham, *Climax of Prophecy*, 10.

to the last thing he said, and indeed, that the promise is paired with the hearing-formula."[147]

Farrer, commenting on John's use of the half-week pattern, notes that within the four sequences of seven, each is divided into a greater and lesser half-week (4 + 3 = 7). About the letter sequence, "the letters fall into two cycles, the last three going back over the ground traversed by the first four."[148] This analysis is problematic both structurally and thematically. The half-week is broken differently in the letters than in the seal, trumpet, and bowl judgments. The division here is 3 + 4 = 7. And the Nicolaitan/Balaam/Jezebel problem found in three of the first four letters is unmentioned in the last three.

Given John's conscious manipulation of structure, some purpose probably lies behind this setting apart of the first three city churches. Benedict suggests that "in the first three letters an understanding of the truth leads to an appropriation of the promise and so to victory . . . in the last four letters obedience leads to victory and is the key to the understanding of the truth."[149] While understanding and obedience are doubtless the keys to victory, their use here appears undesigned. Even Benedict admits that Philadelphia is an exception in the final group. With Ramsay, I believe John is reflecting the historical reality that Ephesus, Smyrna, and Pergamum were the "First of Asia," a title featured on coinage of the province. In the first century all were conventus cities as well as neocorates for cult temples, whether for Artemis or the emperor.[150]

Another deviation is the twofold use of the dative τῷ νικῶντι only in the victor sayings of the letters to Ephesus and Pergamum. Again, is there a reason for this stylistic variation or is it simply an example of a figure of speech called polyptoton—the repetition of the same noun in several cases?[151] Perhaps Ephesus and Pergamum are further distinguished from Smyrna because they were the political centers in Asia both for the Romans and for the *koinon* of Asia.

---

147. Giblin, *Book of Revelation*, 51n. 44.
148. Farrer, *Revelation of St. John*, 11.
149. Benedict, "Use of NIKAΩ in the Letters to the Seven Churches," 6, 23.
150. Ramsay, *Letters to the Seven Churches*, 148, 125. According to Bach, "La structure au service de la predication," 295, these cities "étaient trois métropoles, des centres important du point de vue politique, culturel et religieux" (". . . were three metropolises, which were important centers from a political, cultural, and religious point of view").
151. See Bullinger, *Figures of Speech*, 267.

Chapter Summary

The literary influences upon the letters to the seven churches have been found to be diverse. John has not slavishly adopted a specific form, preferring instead to be eclectic with his sources. However, we have determined that Old Testament prophetic oracles and Greco-Roman letters, with particular indebtedness to the Pauline correspondence, were the predominant forms behind the letters. We have accepted Schüssler Fiorenza's term "prophetic letters" as the best description for the contents of chapters 2–3. At first glance the seven letters appear to follow a stereotypical form with familiar phrases and catchwords. However, the letters are in fact amazingly complex with varying patterns adapted to the individual churches. The letters are interconnected with the rest of the book through the Christological epithets and the coming, hearing, and victor sayings. Such intratextuality proves that the letters never existed apart from the book. In the next chapter we will begin our investigation of the victor sayings by looking at the identity of the victors and the background of victory in the ancient world.

3

The Victors and the Victor Sayings

Introduction

SINCE THE promises in the seven letters are commonly called victor sayings (*Siegersprüche*), it is necessary to examine the meaning of victor in its biblical and cultural context. We begin by examining two Greek verbs prominent in the sayings, δίδωμι and νικάω, focusing especially on νικάω. Because of the centrality of νικάω to our topic, we will look at its usage first in Revelation and other Johannine literature as well as in the New Testament, Extrabiblical, and Old Testament writings.

The second section of the chapter deals with the victor motif in three contexts—Christian, Greco-Roman, and Jewish. Important here is the value placed on victory in the ancient world. First the subject of the victors in the church is discussed. Whether the reference to Laodicean nakedness has any relevance to Greek athletics is questioned. An important issue concerning the identity of the victors in Revelation is reviewed. The internal evidence relating the victor to other names of Christians is first detailed. Then the two predominant views—victors as only martyrs and victors as all Christians—are evaluated. This chapter provides an important link between our discussion in the previous chapters and the victor sayings themselves.

The background of athletic games in Greece is presented. The honor attached to victory within Greek culture is noted. As in Greece, agonistic games were popular in Asia, and their role in the Asian cities is discussed. We conclude with the Jewish perspective on victory. The Jews initially had strong feelings against athletic games in Judea, and the games served as a flashpoint when the Greeks attempted to hellenize the Jews. The reaction of the Jews in the Diaspora was less polemical, and their situation will be examined.

The Verb Δίδωμι

The verb δίδωμι ("I give") occurs frequently in Revelation (57x). Its passive form ἐδόθη, used twenty times beginning in 6:2, has much theological significance. The opening of the seven seals and the blowing of the seven trumpets are totally under the control of the risen Lamb. The resultant judgments that fall upon the earthdwellers are therefore divine in origin. Likewise, whatever authority accrues to the beast and false prophet is derived from the dragon (cf. 13:2, 4–5), who himself is portrayed under divine authority bound with a chain (20:1–3). Finally, the privilege of the saints to wear white garments (6:11; cf. 19:8) and to judge from thrones (20:4) is given by God. This use of the passive form appears to indicate "that which has already been fixed in the will of God."[1]

The future δώσω is found in every victor saying except those to Sardis and Philadelphia where other future verbs are used. Its eight occurrences include once in the promises to Ephesus (2:7), Smyrna (2:10), and Laodicea (3:21), and twice in the double promises to Pergamum (2:17) and Thyatira (2:26, 28) with an additional use in the promise to all the churches (2:23). Its use in the Smyrnean letter outside the victor saying helps to identify the phrase as part of the saying.

Black calls the verb's occurrences in 2:7 and 3:21, where δίδωμι = נתן, the "best-known and best-attested Hebraism in the New Testament."[2] Δίδωμι when followed by an infinitive, according to Charles, means "to permit" and "is the normal construction in this sense in our book."[3] This sense is in fact conveyed in two contemporary translations—"give permission" (2:7 NRSV) and "give the right" (2:7; 3:21 NIV). Δώσω is used in two other places in Revelation—11:3 and 21:6. The former is not a promise per se, but a familiar Hebraism which means, "I will commission my two witnesses to prophesy"[4]; the latter is part of the final victor saying.

The first promise to Thyatira (2:26) alludes seemingly to a promise found in Psalm 2:8–9 (LXX): δώσω σοι ἔθνη τὴν κληρονομίαν σου. The text of this promise will be developed later; here we wish simply to show the verbal relationship with δώσω. The epithet in the Philadelphian letter seems to be an allusion to Isaiah 22:22. This Isaianic reference is preceded by a number of promises including: τὸν στέφανόν σου δώσω αὐτῷ καὶ τὸ κράτος καὶ τὴν οἰκονομίαν σου δώσω εἰς τὰς χεῖρας αὐτοῦ...

---

1. Beckwith, *Apocalypse of John*, 599.
2. Black, "Some Greek Words," 146.
3. Charles, *Revelation*, 1:280.
4. Ibid.

καὶ δώσω τὴν δόξαν Δαυιδ αὐτῷ . . . (vv. 21–22 LXX). A related promise by Jesus, likewise alluding to Isaiah 22, is found in Matthew 16:19: δώσω σοι τὰς κλεῖδας τῆς βασιλείας τῶν οὐρανῶν. The promises of Jesus using δώσω found in Revelation 2–3 and Matthew 16 show a probable verbal dependence on Psalm 2 and Isaiah 22.

The high usage of δίδωμι marks it as a verb of special importance in Revelation, particularly in the victor sayings where it is the predominant verb (8 out of 19). A final note concerns the secular usage: Roman magistrates used δίδωμι in their letters "to grant or confirm privileges of various kinds upon cities, organizations, and individuals."[5] God likewise is seen in Revelation as the Giver of both punishment and reward. To the disobedient the lake of fire awaits, while to the victors he promises to give privileges in the heavenly kingdom.

The Verb Νικάω

Νικάω, according to Sweet, is "a keyword in Revelation (and) practically confined to the Johannine writings."[6] The νικ-word group is in fact used forty-four times in the New Testament.[7] Of these occurrences ten are the roots in five proper names—Nicanor, Nicodemus, Nicolaitans, Nicolaus, and Nicopolis. These proper names are mentioned simply because the possibility of a wordplay involving Nicolaus ("victor over the people") and the Nicolaitans is often mentioned by commentators.[8] The thirty-four other uses reflect two verbs, νικάω (28x) and ὑπερνικάω (1x), and two nouns, νίκη (1x) and νῖκος (4x). Four of these are citations from the Old Testament (Matt 12:20; Rom 3:4; 1 Cor 15:54, 55). The remaining twenty-nine are distributed thus in the canonical New Testament: Synoptics (1x); Pauline (4x); and Johannine (25x). The predominant Johannine usage is broken down as follows: Gospel (1x); 1 John (7x); and Revelation (17x).

The formulaic use of τῷ νικῶντι and ὁ νικῶν is found at the beginning of each of the seven victor sayings. John does not use τῷ νικήσαντι or τῷ νενικηκότι, for "the pres. part. here is timeless."[9] Charles, however, sees John being influenced by the use of a Hebrew

---

5. Sherk, *Roman Documents*, 193.

6. Sweet, *Revelation*, 80.

7. According to Bauernfeind, *TDNT*, "νικάω ktl.," the use of the νικάω word group in the Old Testament Greek translations yields "no very striking data."

8. Cf. Charles, *Revelation*, 1:52–53; Kraft, *Offenbarung*, 72–74.

9. Swete, *Apocalypse of St. John*, 29.

participle here, which can have either a perfect or imperfect sense: "in our author ὁ νικῶν = ὁ νενικηκώς."[10] The participle does not suggest completed action; in fact, the example Charles rightly cites from 4 Ezra 7:127 suggests that the struggle for victory is ongoing. The observation of Mulholland is well taken: "The verb tense in Greek stresses the continuous nature of the conquering. *Jesus is not giving promises to the ones who have conquered, but to the ones who are in the process of conquering*" (my emphasis—MW).[11] This discussion of tenses may, however, be irrelevant to John's meaning. For in Revelation 12:11 the martyrs in heaven are said to have triumphed (ἐνίκησαν; aorist) over Satan the accuser through the blood of the Lamb and their testimony. This same group is portrayed in 15:2 as victors (νικῶντας; present) over the beast, his image, and the number of his name. With these martyrs "it is the abiding character of 'conqueror' on which emphasis is laid, and not the fact of conquest."[12]

In the final victor saying in the seven letters (3:21) Jesus ties his promise to the Laodiceans to his own victory—ὡς κἀγὼ ἐνίκησα. Caird states that here John explicitly defines what he means by the mysterious title, the conqueror or victor: "The Conqueror is one who follows Christ along the road which leads to that victory; or rather, because Christ comes in all his victorious power to those who open the door to him, the Conqueror is one in whom Christ wins afresh his own victory, which is also God's victory."[13] This victory is first announced in chapter 1 where Jesus is called the faithful witness, the firstborn from the dead, and the ruler of the kings of the earth (v. 5; cf. v. 18). The use of the aorist in 3:21 verbally ties the seven letters to the vision that follows in chapters 4–5. This triumph is reiterated in 5:5 when John is told that the Lion of the tribe of Judah is able to open the sealed scroll because he was victorious (ἐνίκησεν). Yet when he looks to behold this Lion, John instead sees a Lamb looking as if it had been slain. Jesus' sacrificial death on the cross is the reason for his triumph. "Lamb" now becomes Jesus' title of victory throughout the rest of the book—his most frequently ascribed divine title (28x).

The seven seals open with the rider on the first white horse goes out conquering so that he might conquer (6:2). Interestingly this false Christ is given the crown of victory before he departs. His victory is only illusory and transitory. Although the beast seemingly triumphs over the

---

10. Charles, *Revelation*, 1:54.
11. Mulholland, *Revelation*, 96n. 9.
12. Swete, *Apocalypse of St. John*, 194.
13. Caird, *Revelation of St. John*, 58.

two witnesses at the end of 1260 days by killing them (11:7), the witnesses are resurrected after three days and taken up into heaven (vv. 11–12). In 12:11 the means by which the martyrs were victorious is told: through the blood of the Lamb and the word of their testimony. The first beast is given authority to make war against the saints and to conquer them (13:7). "The word 'conquer,' it should be observed is ironical: the true conqueror is the martyr."[14] In 15:2ff John sees a vision of those who were victorious over the beast and his image standing on the heavenly sea of glass singing with harps. In 17:14 the Lamb is said to conquer the beast and his allied kings because he is the Lord of lords and King of kings. Leivestad argues persuasively that the understood verb in 14b should be νικήσουσιν, not εἰσιν: "and the elect, chosen, and faithful with him (will conquer them)."[15] The final use in 21:7 is a present participial promise like those in the seven letters.

To conclude, in Revelation νικάω is used in three different senses— *first*, of a moral, spiritual victory by Christ and the saints; *second*, a physical, military victory by the beast; and *third*, a moral **and** military victory by Christ and the saints.[16]

Usage in the Fourth Gospel and 1 John

The single use in the Gospel is found in John 16:33. After first warning the disciples that they will encounter tribulation in the world, Jesus exhorts them to be courageous (cf. Acts 23:11) because he has conquered the world. Westcott poignantly observes, "Thus in His last recorded words of teaching before the Passion, the Lord claims the glory of a conqueror."[17] In 1 John the verb is used five times (2:13, 14; 4:4; 5:4, 5) and the noun νίκη once (5:4). In each case the subject is the believers, not Jesus. They have triumphed over the evil one (2:13, 14), the false prophets/spirits (4:4), and the world (5:4). Their victory over the world has occurred because they have conquered with their faith (5:4) whose object is Christ, the victor for all time. 1 John 5:5 displays the same participial form used in Revelation: τίς [δέ] ἐστιν ὁ νικῶν τὸν κόσμον εἰ μὴ ὁ πιστεύων

---

14. Kiddle, *Revelation of St. John*, 250.

15. Leivestad, *Christ the Conqueror*, 231.

16. Cf. Leivestad, ibid., 212, who sees only the first two. Koester, *Revelation and the End of All Things*, 57, on the other hand, sees the term conqueror only as a "military metaphor."

17. Westcott, *Gospel According to St. John*, 234.

ὅτι Ἰησοῦς ἐστιν ὁ υἱὸς τοῦ θεοῦ. The use of this word group is one of the striking similarities among the Johannine writings.

Usage in the New Testament

Four uses of νικάω are found in Romans. In 3:4 Paul cites the Septuagint reading of Psalm 51:4 (v. 6 MT), "So that you may be justified in your words and victorious when you judge." Here νικήσεις translates the Hebrew זכה. This verb, in parallelism with צדק, means "be justified=be regarded as just, righteous" *(BDB)*. The root in Aramaic and Syriac supplies the verb for "to conquer," and, according to Black, the Septuagint "has given this Aramaic meaning to the verb, no doubt because νικᾶν is a much stronger expression."[18] Black sees in this Pauline usage a possible implication for interpreting νικᾶν in Revelation. He asks if its meaning in the promises, where the context is forensic and related to the final Assize and its aftermath, is a nuance which is "the author's equivalent of the Pauline δικαιοῦσθαι (δικαιοσύνη), the divine acquittal, the 'winning of the verdict.'"[19] While such a nuance is possible, we believe an interpretation emphasizing judicial rhetoric or juridical function is unlikely. In 8:37 is found the single use of ὑπερνικάω, where Paul declares that believers are "super-victorious" in the face of constant martyrdom. Finally, in 12:21 he gives an ethical exhortation to the Romans not to be conquered by evil but instead to conquer evil with good.

Νῖκος is used three times in Paul's teaching on the resurrection of the dead in 1 Corinthians 15. In verse 54, which quotes Isaiah 25:8a, when the believers are clothed with imperishability and immortality, "death has been swallowed up in victory." This Isaianic text is the probable source for Revelation 21:4 (Isaiah 25:8b is likewise alluded to in Revelation 7:17[20]). Hosea 13:14 is freely rendered in 1 Corinthians 15:55, "Where, O death, is your victory?" Paul translates the Hebrew קטבך ("your destruction") as τὸ νῖκος, forgoing the Septuagint's δίκη ("penalty, judgment"). This taunt looks ahead to the ultimate victory of the believers at their resurrection. In verse 57 Paul affirms that God gives victory over death through the resurrection of the Lord Jesus Christ. The use by John and Paul of the same Old Testament texts emphasizing victory over death suggests a common eschatological *testimonia*. Victory over death is a noteworthy theme in Revelation, particularly in the Smyrnean promise (2:10–11).

---

18. Black, "Some Greek Words," 139.
19. Ibid., 140.
20. Cf. Fekkes, *Isaiah and Prophetic Traditions*, 170–72; 253–55.

There is only one example of νικάω in the Synoptics—in the parable of the strong man (Lk 11:22). The context is the exorcism of a mute man by Jesus (v. 14). Some in the crowd accuse Jesus of casting out demons by the power of Beelzebub (v. 15). Jesus responds with a saying about a kingdom divided against itself (vv. 17–18). The parable of the strong man follows, with Satan representing the strong man and Jesus the stronger one. The imagery clearly depicts a spiritual warfare occurring in the heavenly realms that Jesus has already won. The parallel passages in Matthew 12:29 and Mark 3:27 use δέω synonymously with νικάω. In Revelation 20:1–2 an angel seizes Satan and binds (ἔδησεν) him for a thousand years. John's use of the same verbs for conquering and binding Satan, which are found in the Synoptics, again suggests the prophet's likely familiarity with the Synoptic tradition, particularly Luke.

Usage in Extrabibiblical Literature

The word group is found in each of the four books of Maccabees—1 (1x), 2 (8x), 3 (2x), and 4 (17x)—books that recount the Jewish struggle against Seleucid hellenization. Probably contemporaneous with Revelation and also originating in the coastlands of Asia Minor, 4 Maccabees deals with the subject of martyrdom—that of Eleazar, the mother, and her seven sons (4 Macc 1:8). The struggle of these martyrs against the Antiochus Epiphanes is portrayed as an athletic contest. In 1:11 they conquered (νικήσαντες) the tyrant by their endurance (ὑπομονῆς). The elderly priest Eleazar is severely tortured by Antiochus, yet like a noble athlete he is victorious over his tormentors (6:10). Likewise, the brothers, in spite of torment and pain, are not conquered (11:20). Through their endurance victory (νῖκος) is accomplished resulting in immortal life (ζωῇ; 17:12, cf. v. 15). The concept of the martyrs as victors permeates this document. Although these remarkable parallels in terminology do not imply John's dependence on 4 Maccabees,[21] such Jewish martyrological literature provides one of the "nearest material analogies."[22] It likewise demonstrates an existing mind-set of resistance and martyrdom among the Hellenistic Jewish communities of Anatolia. According to Pfitzner, here are the begin-

---

21. Such dependence, however, may be found in the second-century *Martyrdom of Polycarp*, and patristic authors such as Augustine and Jerome "treat the Maccabean heroes as Christian protomartyrs" (Stowers, "4 Maccabees," 925).

22. Leivestad, *Christ the Conqueror*, 216.

nings of the standard vocabulary of Christian martyrdom and the first coupling of this tradition with the athletic metaphor.[23]

Two other texts celebrate the victory of the righteous. 1 Enoch 50:2 declares that "the righteous ones shall be victorious in the name of the Lord of the Spirits." 4 Ezra 7:127 also states, "This is the meaning of the contest which every man who is born on earth shall wage, that if he is defeated he shall suffer what you have said, but if he is victorious he shall receive what I have said." In the latter one the author again sees life within an agonistic context.

The Nicolaitans

The Nicolaitans (literally, "victors over the people") are mentioned by name in the Ephesian and Pergamene letters and by practice in the Thyatiran letter. Bauckham argues convincingly that Nicolaitan alludes to Revelation's keyword νικάω and suggests that "Their teaching made it possible for Christians to be successful in pagan society, but this was the beast's success, a real conquest of the saints, winning them to his side, rather than the only apparent conquest he achieved by putting them to death."[24] The particular mention of Nicolaitans in 2:6 is a dualistic construct providing a parallel to the theme of the victors in the promises. The Asian audience would appreciate the irony of these would-be victors over the people contrasted with the true spiritual victors over the beast and false prophet.

The Nicolaitans, according to Boring, "may like 'Balaam' and 'Jezebel,' be John's own symbolic name for his opponents, since 'conquer' is a key word in John's theology and since 'Nicolas' is the rough equivalent of 'Balaam' in Hebrew ('ruler of the people')."[25] Kirby approaches from a different tact, "The paronomasia of Νικολαϊτῶν/νικῶντι in this context would have not a whimsical but an oracular tone for the ancient ear. That word-play is audial; Νικόλαος / בלעם is conceptual."[26] The insights of both Boring and Kirby are valid; for the word play is audial *and* conceptual. Nicolaus need not simply be a symbolic name, however, but was probably an actual person who promulgated such teaching in the churches. "Indeed, supposing his existence, we may see a play on an actual man's name as a suitable basis for a slogan of current controversy."[27] By mentioning the

---

23. Pfitzner, *Paul and the Agon Motif,* 64.
24. Bauckham, *Theology of Revelation,* 124.
25. Boring, *Revelation,* 93.
26. Kirby, "Rhetorical Situations," 207n. 41.
27. Hemer, *Letters to the Seven Churches of Asia,* 89.

Nicolatians, John establishes a contrast between two groups (at least) in the Asian churches—those victorious over the people and those victorious unto God. The Nicolaitans' solution to conflict is compromise. Their victory is only apparent though; the true victors will be manifested at the Lord's coming.

Translations of ὁ νικῶν and τῷ νικῶντι

The substantival participial phrases ὁ νικῶν and τῷ νικῶντι have been translated variously in different language versions.

- "He who overcomes" (AV, NASB, NIV), "wer überwindet" (Lutherbibel 1984; 1994 Elberfelder), "hom wat oorwin" (1933 Afrikaans translation)
- "One who conquers" (NRSV)
- "Victor" (NAMB), "Victorious" (PHILLIPS), "those who are victorious" (REB; TNIV), "those who prove victorious" (NJB), "Qui vaincra" (Segond), "wer siegt" (Einheitsübersetzung), "die wat die oorwinning behaal" (NAB)

The versions adopt one of three basic translation options—overcomer, conqueror, or victor. "Overcomer" is the most general of the three and conveys little of the connotation of ancient usage. However, in modern therapy parlance it suggests someone who has overcome some addiction such as drugs, alcohol, or gambling. "Conqueror" brings a militaristic connotation favored by Giblin: "The promise is couched, of course, in militant terms, as befits an apocalyptic document."[28] It suggests the spiritual nature of the believer's warfare; however, military imagery is a secondary aspect of the victor imagery. "Victor" has an agonistic connotation and best fits with the related imagery of the ancient games—wreaths, palm branches, and white robes. It is a comprehensive term that incorporates the strengths of all the options while avoiding their weaknesses. It is therefore the translation preferred in this study.

Victors in the First-Century Church

The Asian Christians, particularly the Gentiles, would be well-acquainted with Greek athletic games because "spectacles were public institutions, organized (and sometime financed) by government authorities."[29] Like

---

28. Giblin, *Book of Revelation*, 52.
29. Veyne, "Roman Empire," 201.

Plato (*Phaed.* 256A) and Philo (*Praem.* 13 passim), the early church came to see the human struggle between virtue and vice in terms of the Greek games. Paul writes to the Corinthians from Ephesus: "Don't you know that although all run the race in the stadium, only one receives a prize? Run therefore to win the prize. Everyone who competes in the games goes into strict training. They run to win a perishable crown; but we run to win a perishable crown" (1 Cor 9:24–25). He follows with an analogy of himself as a boxer who buffets his body, so "I myself will not be disqualified for the prize" (v. 27).[30]

Likewise, the victor sayings (and Revelation in general) prominently utilize athletic motifs to portray the Christian life. If it was a great distinction then to compete in the Greek athletic competitions, how much more so to compete in the spiritual race for an immortal, heavenly reward! And if death was an honored outcome of the games, how much more was martyrdom to be honored by the community of saints! Thus arose the predilection in the postapostolic church to compete until death, if that was called for. The attitude of Ignatius toward martyrdom has been characterized by Holmes as "vivid, almost macabre eagerness."[31] That this ideal was practiced is evident in the second century when bishops had to forbid saints from willingly offering themselves up to martyrdom, even though it was unnecessary (*Mart. Pol.* 4).

In his prophetic word to the Laodiceans, Jesus criticizes the church members for their nakedness and exhorts them to buy white garments (Rev 3:17). In the related third beatitude the believers are likewise exhorted to keep their garments, lest they walk naked and reveal their shame (Rev 16:15). The final horror for the prostitute is that she is left naked (Rev 17:16). For both Jesus and John, shame and disgrace is associated with nakedness.

Athletic exercises were conducted in the gymnasium, derived etymologically from the Greek word γυμνός, "naked." The athletes in the gymnasium and in the games always participated in the nude. Chambers asserts that the impulse to nudity was primarily philosophical: "Nudity allowed the athlete to demonstrate how near he came to the ideal of man as the gods had made him."[32] One of the Maccabean objections to Jason's

---

30. Paul was ministering in Corinth in AD 51 when the Isthmian Games were held. Thus he probably had firsthand experience with the athletic images he later uses here writing from Ephesus; cf. Chambers, "Greek Athletics," 63. Paul might have also witnessed games in Ephesus during his stay there.

31. Lightfoot, Harmer, and Holmes, *Apostolic Fathers*, 131.

32. Chambers, "Greek Athletics," 33.

hellenizing efforts was that he made his fellow Jews conform to Greek customs (2 Macc 4:10ff). Jewish athletes now began to compete in the nude, greatly offending traditional sensibilities. "The fact that Jewish ephebes attempted to undo the effects of circumcision by epispasm shows how far the tendency to assimilation went."[33] The author of Jubilees was later to write that "all who will know the judgment of the Law that they should cover their shame and they should not be uncovered as the gentiles are uncovered" (*Jub* 3:31). The Jews of the Dispersion were probably more accommodating to the practice of nudity. Chambers effectively underscores this point: "If Greek gymnasium life could induce Romans to abandon the mores of their ancestors to the extent that they were not ashamed to exhibit themselves nude before women (Plut. *Cat. Mai.* 3), it is unreasonable to assume that among the Jews there would not be many who could be lured away from the traditions of their fathers."[34] Although Pfitzner rejects the thesis that Paul had firsthand experience with Greek athletics,[35] a more likely perspective is that Paul viewed them as *adiaphora*, amoral conduct that was permissible for the strong in faith while perhaps problematic for the weak (cf. 1 Cor 8:1–13; 10:23—11:1).

Returning to the Laodicean letter: perhaps one reason for the church's apathy was an over-enthusiasm for athletics. Maybe its members were encouraged to compete because victory in the games would bring honor to the fledgling Christian community and approbation from the Roman authorities. Thus Jesus, through the ironic contrast of nakedness/clothing, is calling the believers to reorder their priorities and gain the true honor given to the spiritual victors. Even though "naked" has verbal links with the imagery of the games in the Laodicean letter, its use as a compound predicate adjective with "poor" and "blind" suggests that an interpretation connecting it with the consequence of poverty is still preferred. Its use in the third beatitude (Rev 16:15), however, points to a generalization of the problem among all the Asian believers.[36]

---

33. Hengel, *Judaism and Hellenism*, 1:74.

34. Chambers, "Greek Athletics," 55–56. One paradox of Greco-Roman culture was that while men could be seen naked, even husbands could never see their wives totally nude. Only true libertines "made love to a woman from whom he had removed every stitch of clothing" (Veyne, "Roman Empire," 203).

35. Pfitzner, *Paul and the Agon Motif*, 188.

36. Charles, *Revelation*, 1:188 believes, however, that the reference to nakedness in these two passages is "the same thing as in 2 Cor. v.1–5, and denotes the loss of the spiritual body." The objection to this interpretation, of which Charles is aware, is that the context in Revelation is the present, not the future.

The Old Testament background of this image should also be noted. In Isaiah 47:1–3 nakedness and shame are mentioned as the result of the judgment on Virgin Babylon, images also prominent in Revelation. Ezekiel assails unfaithful Jerusalem, threatening that her nakedness will be exposed if she does not repent of her idolatrous practices (Ezek 16:37; 23:29; cf. Mic 1:11). And Nahum warns the harlot Ninevah that, unless she repents of her witchcraft, her nakedness and shame will be shown (Nah 3:4–5). Therefore to "walk naked" suggests moral and spiritual turpitude. John's frequent use of imagery from the prophetic books makes this is the likely background for the allusion to nakedness in Revelation. However, given John's propensity to use multivalent imagery, an allusion to Greek athletics might also be found in this language.

The Identity of the Victors: Their Nature and Role in Revelation

The identity of the victors in Revelation has been much debated. The designation "victor" is but one of many descriptions given to believers in Revelation. The following chart presents the range of names with their location, either on earth or in heaven.

Name	On Earth	In Heaven
Servants	1:1; 2.20, 7.3, 10.7, 11:18; 15:3; 19:2; 22:6	19:5; 22:3
Fellow servants	6:11; 19:10; 22:9	6:11
Hearers (of the words)	1:3; 22:8, 17, 18	
Keepers of the words/ works/commandments	1:3; 2:26; 12:17; 14:12; 16:15; 22:7, 9	
Church(es)	1:4, 11, 20; 2:1, 7, 8, 11, 12, 17, 18, 23, 29; 3:1, 6, 7, 13, 14, 22; 22:16	
Kingdom	1:6; 5:10	
Priests	1:6; 5:10	20:6
Brothers	1:9; 6:11; 12:10; 19:10; 22:9	6:11
Partner in tribulation	1:9	
Apostles	2:2	18:20; 21:14
Those who have an ear	2:7, 11, 17, 29; 3:6, 13, 22; 13:9	
Victors	2:7, 11, 17, 26; 3:5, 12, 21; 21:7	15:2
Faithful witness	2:13	
Witness(es)	11:3; 22:20	

Name	On Earth	In Heaven
One who is watchful	16:15; cf. 3:2	
Saints	5:8; 8:3, 4; 11:18; 13:7, 10; 14:12; 16:6; 17:6; 18:24; 19:8; 20:9; 22:11	18:20
Souls who were slaughtered/beheaded	18:24	6:9; 20:4
Those who were sealed	7:4, 5, 8	Cf. 14:1
144,000	7:4	14:1, 3
Tribe(s) of Israel	7:4, 5, 6, 7, 8	21:12
Great multitude		7:9; 19:1, 6
Prophets	10:7; 11:10, 18; 16:6; 18:24; 22:6, 9	18:20
Those who fear him or his name	11:18	19:5
Offspring of the woman	12:17	
Virgins		14:4
Those who follow the Lamb		14:4
Firstfruits		14:4
My people	18:4	
Wife		19:7; 21:9
Holy City		21:2, 10
New Jerusalem		21:2, 10
Bride		21:2, 9; 22:17
My son	21:7	
Righteous one	22:11	

Several observations can be drawn from this chart. Like victors, descriptions such as servants, priests, and saints are used whether on earth or in heaven. "Saints" is the most common name and is used fourteen times. The reference to the first beast conquering the saints in 13:7 is particularly illuminating. Looking backward, the verse's language is nearly identical to that in 11:7, which speaks of the beast conquering the two witnesses. The beast makes war and conquers both groups, indicating the witnesses/saints have a singular identity. Looking forward to 13:9, before the second beast is seen, a hearing saying similar to that found in the seven letters is interjected. This is followed by a *Hode* saying to the saints. The saints and the victors are one and the same. Likewise, in 17:6 saints and witnesses are linked, and in 20:6 priests and saints associated.

"Servants" is the second most common designation and the one used in 1:1. It is used in 2:20 to describe the Thyatirans whom Jezebel was attempting to deceive, thus the same audience to whom the promise of victory was given. It is difficult to conclude, as Swete does, that two groups are depicted in 20:4. He believes οἵτινες . . . distinguishes a group who, while persecuted and despoiled, were not martyred.[37] A group, with similar characteristics, is depicted as martyrs earlier in 12:11. Apart from Jesus (cf. 4:11; 5:2, 9, 12), no one is found worthy (ἄξιος; 5:4) except the faithful in Sardis (3:4) and the martyred saints and prophets.

The Victors as Only Martyrs

Tertullian advances the view of the victors as only martyrs in his treatise on martyrdom, *Scorpiace*. After recalling the promises to the victors, the church father asks, "Who, pray, are these so blessed conquerors, but martyrs in the strict sense of the word? For indeed theirs are the victories whose also are the fights; theirs, however, are the fights whose is also the blood" (*Scor.* 12).

Rosscup likewise asks the question, "Who is the overcomer who receives the reward?" The three options he proposes are admittedly from a pastoral perspective: (1) a saved person who retains salvation, which some forfeit; (2) a saved person who conquers, distinguished from a defeated Christian; and (3) every saved person.[38] His theological presuppositions, however, lead him to adopt the third view before even reviewing the evidence in Revelation.

Johnson shares this view but seeks to answer the question from a biblical perspective: "Certainly they are Christ's true disciples, those who are fully loyal to Him, and who are identified with Him in His suffering and death (1 John 5:4–5). Compare those who do not overcome in the letters (e.g., the 'cowardly,' 2:10, 13; the 'sexually immoral,' 2:14, 20; the 'idolaters,' 2:14, 20; and the 'liars,' 2:2, 9, 20; 3:9) with those in 21:8."[39]

This latter comparison of the victors in 21:7 with those specified sinners in 21:8 indicates that the former have a specific moral quality to their witness that is absent from their counterparts. This moral erosion prompted by false teaching is what is threatening the churches. The victors are to withstand such error in their congregations. Conquering, as

---

37. Swete, *Apocalypse of St. John*, 262.
38. J. E. Rosscup, "Overcomer of the Apocalypse," 261–63.
39. Johnson, *Revelation*, 40.

defined by Mulholland, is "the experience of living fully as citizens of New Jerusalem unencumbered by the bondages of Fallen Babylon though not removed from their sphere of activity."[40] Kiddle concurs with this definition: "The conqueror must vanquish the temptations of this life, and demonstrate in action his possession of the Christian virtues. This idea is implicit in all the promises to the conqueror. It is a necessary qualification of the second meaning of "conqueror"—that is, he who wins a victory over persecution and death, the martyr."[41] Kiddle believes that in the promises to Laodicea and Thyatira, the conqueror can only be the martyr: "if in two, then in all."[42]

The Victors as All Christians

Beasley-Murray gives an extended discussion concerning the identity of the martyrs and reaches the conclusion that the victors are all Christians. After rejecting Kiddle's assertion that the victors are only martyrs, he observes that "the promises to the conquerors are fundamentally assurances to the faithful of the benefits of Christ's redemption, expressed in the language of apocalyptic."[43] The letters never suggest that all Asian believers will die or that participation in Christ's redemption is restricted to a select group. Rather "the essential characteristic of the conqueror, therefore, is that he participates in Christ's conquest by faith, and through persistence in faith he continues to share in Christ's victory to the end—whether the end be death or the parousia of Christ."[44] Laws apprehends correctly the dilemma for modern readers: "[Martyrs] dominate his vision, at times it seems to the exclusion of all else. We cannot look to the author of the Apocalypse for an exposition of Christian living as the imitation of Christ by those who live everyday lives and may expect to die peacefully in their beds."[45] A comparison of the descriptive names for Christians in the chart above reveals that the victors are all the Asian believers who by faith enter into Christ's victory. The conclusion from John's perspective is that "every disciple of Jesus must be in principle a martyr and be ready to lay down his life for his faith."[46]

---

40. Mulholland, *Revelation*, 96.
41. Kiddle, *Revelation of St. John*, 61–62.
42. Ibid., 63.
43. Beasley-Murray, *Revelation*, 78.
44. Ibid., 79.
45. Laws, *In the Light of the Lamb*, 67.
46. Ladd, *Revelation of John*, 41.

Symbols of Victory Used in Revelation

White was a color of victory in the ancient world. When the Lamb opens the first seal, a rider on a white horse goes out as a victor bent on conquest (6:1–2). He is given a crown, or wreath, another prominent symbol of victory to be discussed later. This rider is most likely the Antichrist going forth in apparent victory, not the Parthians. In 19:11 the Word of God is seen riding a white horse. Swete rightly suggests that "In both passages the 'white horse' is the emblem of victory."[47] Likewise the armies of heaven that follow are riding white horses (19:14). Since angels are never seen in Revelation riding horses, this group should best be identified as the victors. Revelation 17:14 confirms this, stating that the elect and called and faithful followers of the Lamb will make war with him against the beast and the ten kings.

Vergil (*Aen*. 3.537) mentions how the appearance of four snow-white horses was viewed as an omen of victory. Plutarch (*Cam*. 7.1) describes how Camillus celebrated a triumph by hitching four white horses to a chariot and driving through Rome, although he states that no commander either before or after did such a thing. Yet Cassius Dio (43.14.3) writes that the senate granted Julius Caesar permission to drive a chariot drawn by white horses through Rome to celebrate his victory in North Africa. During such triumphs Rome became a *candida urbs*, "city in white," which Juvenal (*Sat*. 10.45) describes as "the imposing procession of white-robed citizens marching." Ramsay summarizes: "Thus though the triumph itself could never have been seen by the readers of this letter, they knew it as the most typical celebration of complete and final victory, partly from report and literature, partly from frequently seeing ceremonies in the great imperial festivals which were modeled after the triumph."[48]

I. R. Arnold, however, cites inscriptional evidence that suggests that the Asians might have had firsthand knowledge of such triumphs. Ephesus and Laodicea were centers of the ἐπινίκια festivals, which "were no doubt instituted on the occasion of some military victory of the Romans."[49] Although these inscriptions date later than the first century AD, Arnold believes the ἐπινίκια festivals had their forerunner in Boeotian contests celebrating a Roman victory in the Mithridatic War (first century BC). Thus, such triumphs with their attendant appearance of white horses and clothing might have been observed by John's audience.

---

47. Swete, *Apocalypse of St. John*, 250.
48. Ramsay, *Letters to the Seven Churches*, 283.
49. Arnold, "Festivals of Ephesus," 21.

Military iconography was well known in Asia. The emperor was often depicted in a curiass (military breastplate) to depict his image as a triumphant ruler. Coins circulating in the province likewise showed the emperor as victor. An Asian tetrdrachma from the Claudian period depicts the cuirassed emperor inside the imperial cult temple with a spear in his right hand, and the goddess Rome is crowning the victorious emperor.[50]

A large multitude out of the great tribulation is seen in 7:9 standing before the throne in white robes with palm branches in their hands. The palm tree is indigenous to the tropical Mediterranean climate, and its range extends as far as Smyrna. To the ancient Greeks and Romans the palm tree was a symbol of victory, and palm leaves were given to the victors in athletic games. Pausanius (8.48.2–3) provides the background: "But at most games they use a wreath of palm, and everywhere the winner has a palm branch put in his right hand. The reason for the tradition is this: they say when Theseus came home from Crete he held games at Delos for Apollo, and crowned the winners with palm. They say it started from there, and even Homer mentioned the palm tree at Delos in Odysseus's prayer to Alkinoos's daughter."

At the beginning of the third century BC in the Roman games "for the first time palm branches were presented to the winners, a custom taken over from the Greeks" (Livy 10.47.3). One of the supernatural events that foreshadowed Julius Caesar's defeat of Pompey at Pharsalus (48 BC) was the spontaneous growth of a palm tree out of the pavement inside the temple of Victory at the Asian city of Tralles (Caesar *Bell. civ.* 3.106; Plutarch *Caes.* 47; Dio 41.61.4).

Palm branches are often found on the obverse and reverse of provincial coin types. A particular favorite with issues from nearly forty cities, including Smyrna, Sardis, and Laodicea, was a standing Nike, both left and right, with a wreath and palm.[51]

The palm branch likewise became a symbol of victory for the Jews. After Simon captured Gaza in 141 BC, he and his men entered the city rejoicing and carrying palm branches "because a great enemy was crushed and removed from Israel" (1 Macc 13:51; cf. 2 Macc 10:7). When Jesus made his triumphal entry into Jerusalem shortly before his passion, the crowds heralded his arrival by waving palm branches (John 12:13). It is this victorious Jesus (Rev 5:5) who is the focus of the heavenly choir in

---

50. See Friesen, *Imperial Cults*, 30, where also an illustration of the coin is provided.

51. Burnett et al, *Roman Provincial Coinage*, 1992. Examples from Asia are Smyrna (l. 2465/1; r. 2473), Sardis (l. 3010), Laodicea (l. 4403A–14), and Colossae (r. 2891). In fact, Burnett et al list thirty-seven coin issues of Nike that include a palm branch.

chapter 7. Coupling this Jewish background with the aforementioned Greco-Roman background, the palm branches in the hands of the martyrs are a powerful statement of their victory over the forces of evil. Likewise, they depict "a victory celebration, in which Jesus and the Father are being welcomed."[52]

Ulfgard, however, questions whether an anti-pagan document like Revelation would use such non-biblical symbolism to describe the people of God before the throne. While not excluding the symbolic meaning of victory, he prefers to associate the palm branches with *lulavs* used by the Jews in their celebration of the Feast of Tabernacles.[53] This association of palm branches with the Feast of Tabernacles in chapter 7 is usually given little credence by interpreters.

Victors in the Greco-Roman World

Nike was the Greek goddess of victory and often identified with Athena. Statues represent her as a winged maiden, usually as alighting from flight, holding in each hand her most frequent attributes—a palm branch and a wreath, or crown.[54] In Ephesus the Hercules Gate carried an arch with a flying Nike holding a laurel wreath in her left hand and a palm branch in her right. Although the Nike relief dates from the fourth century AD, its iconography is typical.[55] Hesiod (*Theog.* 383ff.) says Nike was the daughter of Pallas and Styx; her siblings were Rivalry, Strength, and Force. She and her family were honored by Zeus for fighting with the gods against the Titans. "She is here an abstraction or symbol of decisive victory for the gods."[56]

Her role in the athletic games is strikingly portrayed by the poets. Standing next to Zeus on Olympus, she judges the award for excellence both to gods and people (Bacchylides 11.1). Pindar (*Nem.* 5.42) describes the victorious athlete Euthymenes falling twice from Aigina into the arms of Nike. "Here Nike is already victor of an athletic, not only of a military, contest. She rules over all contests."[57] Cults of Nike flourished at Olympia and Athens (Pausanius 5.14.8) as well as in the Asian city of Tralles, be-

---

52. Mealy, *After the Thousand Years*, 217.
53. Ulfgard, *Feast and Future*, 90.
54. See Avery, "Nike," s.v.
55. Scherrer, *Ephesus*, 98.
56. S.v. "Nike," *OCD*, 2nd ed.
57. Ibid.

tween Ephesus and Laodicea.⁵⁸ Athena Nikephoros was the chief goddess of Pergamum and her temple, patterned after the Parthenon, is the oldest known temple in the city. Following Eumenes II's military success against the Seleucids, he constructed new stoas at the Athena temple (ca. 160 BC). A restored inscription from its architrave reads, "King Eumenes to the victory-bringing Athena."⁵⁹

What was the value of victory in the ancient Mediterranean world, and how was the victor thought of by his fellow men and women? This is an important question about a culture regarded as *agonistic*. Pilch has recently examined the phenomenon of lying and deceit in the seven letters and notes that honor-status was important to the residents of Asia, and that "everyone seeks to augment honor."⁶⁰ One way to achieve honor was victory in the public games (ἀγῶνες στεφανῖται). "[F]ame and victory itself are the true goals, because they grant the victor that which is in essence the goal of every Greek, that he might become the object of awe and admiration, and that his name might be remembered even in death."⁶¹ Inscriptions found in mainland Greece show residents of Asia traveling as far as Thessaly, Boeotia, Aegina, and Arcadia to participate in the agonistic festivals there.⁶²

Regarding the role of the games in public life, Young writes, "Perhaps nothing else is more distinctive of ancient Greece than athletics."⁶³ Competition in the Greco-Roman world was followed with passionate interest. Veyne describes how "Greeks flocked not only to great games (*isolympicoi, periodicoi*) and lesser games (*stephanitai*), which were associated with fairs, but also to minor games (*themides*)."⁶⁴ The most prestigious athletic event at the Big Four Crown games—Olympian, Isthmian, Nemean, and Pythian—was a sprint of 192 meters called the *stade*. The victor of this event was listed first on the Olympic summaries, and a nearly complete list of these victors remains for the millennium that the games were held (776 BC–AD 217).

---

58. For visitors to Ephesus today, one of the most familiar images is the 4th century AD marble of the flying Nike holding a wreath, which was part of the Heracles Gate located at the beginning of Curetes Street; cf. Erdemgil, *Ephesus*, 55.

59. Akurgal, *Ancient Civilizations*, 77.

60. Pilch, "Lying and Deceit," 128.

61. Pfitzner, *Paul and the Agon Motif*, 17.

62. Ringwood, *Agonistic Features*, 16, 45, 62, 96.

63. Young, "Athletics," 2:1131.

64. Veyne, "Roman Empire," 200.

The great lyrical poet Pindar (ca. 518–438 BC) wrote odes to celebrate the victors in each of the crown games. These odes follow a literary form known as the Epinician Ode: "a reference to the victor is required and to the place and nature of his victory; allusions to other victories won on earlier occasions may be added, as may compliments to his trainer."[65] A standard Epinician motif is the *Siegewunsch*, which makes "specific and unambiguous reference to hoped-for future victories."[66]

The victors at the Big Four games, also called ἱεροί, received no rewards except a symbolic crown (στέφανος) made of olive, pine, wild celery, or bay leaves respectively. In his conversation with Solon, Anacharsis mocks the insignificance of such a prize (Lucian *Anach.* 10). Although Lucian writes in the middle of the second century AD, Solon's reply epitomizes the Greek attitude to victory from the seventh century BC onwards:

> They are merely tokens of the victory (νίκης) and marks to identify the winners. But the reputation that goes with them is worth everything to the victors (νενικηκόσιν), and to attain it, even to be kicked is nothing to men who seek to capture fame through hardships. Without hardships it cannot be acquired; the man who covets it must put up with many unpleasantnesses in the beginning before at last he can expect the profitable and delightful outcome of his exertions.

However, at other games called θεματικικοί, lucrative prizes were awarded. A well-known inscription IG II².2311 (400–350 BC) lists the amphorae to be given to the victors at the Panathenaic games.[67] Noteworthy about this inscription is the repetition of ΝΙΚΩΝΤΙ in the list of awards.[68] In another type of contest called eiselastic, the victor was accorded a triumphal entry into his native city as well as other civic privileges. In Sibylline Oracle 2:39 entry into the heavenly city is likened to that of the victor in the eiselastic games.[69] Vitruvius (*Arch.* 9.1) observed about these victors "that they not only receive praise publicly at the games, as they stand with palm and crown, but also when they go back victorious to their own people they ride triumphant with their four-horse chariots into

---

65. Grant, *Greek and Latin Authors*, 332.
66. Miller, "Apolline Ethics," 462 n. 3.
67. Van Nijf, *Civic World*, 225.
68. Cf. Johnston, "*IG* II2 2311," 126–27.
69. An inscription found in Pergamum contains a decree of the Senate and an edict and letter of Trajan (AD 112/117) giving instructions concerning the Pergamene eiselastic games (Johnson, *Ancient Roman Statutes*, §221; cf. Pliny *Ep.* 10.118–19).

their native cities, and enjoy a pension for life from the State." The theater, dating from the Augustan period, in the Pisidian city of Termessus had a row of seats dedicated to the victors (ἱερονίκαι) in the sacred games.

The cities of Asia had enthusiastically embraced the Greek athletic tradition, especially after Greece's conquest by Rome. "The celebrations appear to have followed the traditional mainland program; there is little indication that any strictly local customs . . . were introduced."[70] This Hellenistic conservatism in maintaining traditional celebrations likewise characterized the Asian attitude toward victory in athletic competitions.

The principal festivals in Ephesus were the Ephesia, dating to the early fourth century BC, and the Artemesia. These festivals included all types of contests. In the latter half of the first century AD the Balbillea festival gained prominence. The emperor Vespasian gave a citizen and benefactor of the city named Balbillus permission to begin these games. (Balbillus was an astrologer of Nero, procurator under Claudius, and prefect of Egypt.) Inscriptional evidence shows that gymnastic contests comprised most of the events.[71]

The κοινά festivals were initiated in 29 BC by the *koinon* of Asia. The chief priest of the emperor cult and leader of the *koinon* often served as the *agonothetes* of the festival. The principal festivals were celebrated every five years (penteteric) in Ephesus, Smyrna, and Pergamum, with each city having its own cycle. The Ionian games in Smyrna are given particular mention by Pausanius (6.14.3). Lesser koina. Festivals were also held in Philadelphia, Laodicea, and Sardis. Thus each of the seven cities except Thyatira is known to have sponsored such games. Gladiatorial combats and fights were also held at Ephesus, Pergamum, and Laodicea, with Ephesus being the first site in Asia where this brutal sport was introduced (71/70 BC).

A letter of Antony to the *koinon* of Asia (ca. 42/42 or 33/32 BC) highlights the extraordinary status of athletes in the Greco-Roman world:[72]

> On a former occasion also I was petitioned in Ephesus by Marcus Antonius Artemidorus, my friend and gymnastic trainer, along with the eponymous priest of the synod of sacred victors and crown-winners (ἱερονικῶν καὶ στεφανειτῶν) from the inhabited world, Charopinus of Ephesus, to ensure that the existing [privileges] of the synod should remain untouched, and to request, concerning the other honors and privileges which they asked from me, exemp-

70. Arnold, "Festivals of Ephesus," 17.
71. Ibid., 19–20.
72. Cf. Millar, *Emperor in the Roman World*, 454; Sherk, *Roman Documents*, 291.

tion from military service, from all liturgies, and from providing lodgings, as well as the rights of truce, asylum and the wearing of the purple in relation to the festival, that I should agree to write at once to you.

The participants in the games were all volunteers. Thus it was not considered cruel for gladiators to die in the arenas; they had volunteered to commit murder and suicide. "In Greek regions the death of a boxer during a match was not a 'sports accident.' It was a glory for the athlete to die in the arena, just as if he had died on the field of battle. The public praised his courage, his steadfastness, his will to win."[73] Plutarch (*Mor.* 239D; cf. Lucian *Anach.* 38) describes an annual Spartan competition called "The flagellation" or "Contest of endurance," where boys were lashed all day at the altar of Artemis Orthia, with some even dying. Plutarch states the consequence: "And the one who was victorious was held in especial repute." Christian martyrdom thus had an athletic antecedent.

Victors in the Jewish World

What would be the reaction of the believing Jews in the seven churches to the exhortation to be victors? Although we have demonstrated a more general background to such imagery from Old Testament and Extrabiblical literature, relating particularly to spiritual endurance and persecution, connotations regarding Greek athletics nevertheless prevail.

Most of the games were held in connection with the worship of a local deity. Before the deity's image the contestants brought offerings and prayers for victory and, if successful, their statuettes and crowns. If possible, games were held near the sanctuary, and "it became a firm practice to cut the victor's crown, wreath or palm branch from a tree in the sacred grove."[74] For example, in Pergamum the middle city, which contained the three gymnasia and the fields where the athletic games took place, was dominated by the temple of Hera.[75] Such idolatrous veneration was guaranteed to provoke Jewish sensibilities. Josephus (*Ag. Ap.* 2.217–18) expressed the alternative Jewish hope:

> For those, on the other hand, who live in accordance with our laws the prize is not silver or gold, no crown (στέφανος) of wild olive

---

73. Veyne, "Roman Empire," 202.
74. Pfitzner, *Paul and the Agon Motif*, 20.
75. Akurgal, *Ancient Civilizations*, 90–101; cf. Chambers, "Greek Athletics and the Jews," 18–21.

or of parsley with any such public mark of distinction. No; each individual, relying on the witness of his own conscience and the lawgiver's prophecy, confirmed by the sure testimony of God, is firmly persuaded that to those who observe the laws and, if they must needs die for them, willingly meet death, God has granted a renewed existence and in the revolution of the ages the gift of a better life.

Although Pfitzner insists that the religious significance of the games persisted into the Christian era, Ringwood avows that by this time "the great majority of contests are of purely secular significance."[76] In his study Chambers adopts the latter perspective—the essential genius of the Greek games was humanistic. However, "it is important to know that enthusiasm for either the gymnasium or the public games would involve some degree of compromise on the part of a Jew if he identified himself with the religious tradition of his people."[77] Yet it is noteworthy that the synagogue in Sardis is located in the monumental bath and gymnasium complex (dating, however, third century AD).[78] The proximity of the synagogue and the gymnasium in Sardis suggests little tension between the two in the early Christian era.

During the Intertestamental period the attempt by the Seleucids to hellenize Judea brought them into sharp conflict with the Jews. As we have seen, athletics epitomized the Greek spirit so the vanguard of hellenization became the establishment of a gymnasium in Jerusalem at the foot of the citadel (2 Macc 4:9–12). The best of the Jewish young men participated, and even the priests forsook their temple duties to seek Greek prizes instead of traditional honors (vv. 12–15). The provocation given by Greek athletics was to be one of the causes of the subsequent Maccabean rebellion (166–160 BC).

Greek athletics were absent from Judea until 25 BC when Herod the Great reintroduced quinquennial games in honor of Caesar (Josephus *Ant.* 15.268). Athletes were attracted from throughout the Greco-Roman world, lured by the glory of victory (τῆς νίκης εὐδοξίᾳ; 15.269). Although upset by the games in toto, the Jews were most offended by the trophies, which they considered idols (15.276). Herod diffused their anger by showing the complainants the true nature of the trophies (15.277–80) and thwarted an assassination attempt by a core of traditionalists who refused to concede (15.281–91). Greek athletics were in Judea to stay.

76. Pfitzner, *Paul and the Agon Motif*, 20; Ringwood, *Agonistic Features*, 12.
77. Chambers, "Greek Athletics and the Jews," 30.
78. Cf. Seager and Kraabel, "Synagogue and the Jewish Community," 168ff.

Harris writes, "The intermingling of Jewish and Greek culture may not have gone so far in Palestine as in the Dispersion, but it had gone far enough to permit the Jews there a considerable experience of Greek athletics."[79] Thus Paul, a Pharisee trained in the school of Gamaliel in Jerusalem, could feel no qualms about using athletic imagery. And John, especially if he is the apostle whose origins are in Judea, likewise uses athletic imagery without hesitation.[80]

The Diaspora, which sent Jews into Asia and throughout the Mediterranean, gave them an even greater exposure to athletics. The writings of the Alexandrian Jew Philo are a case in point. He refers numerous times to the games and uses such imagery to commend virtue.[81] In the contest of evil he states ironically that the real victor is the one who loses to the evildoer: "Do not allow either the herald to announce or the judge to crown the enemy as victor, but come forward yourself and present the prizes and the palm, and crown" (*Agr.* 112). Old Testament figures such as Noah, Abraham, Isaac, Jacob, Moses, and Joseph are commended as moral victors in the holy contests, where victory is of the soul rather than the body. For their triumph these victors along with other Old Testament role players receive prizes that include a crown. "But the decisive point is that the prize or crown is *not claimed* by the athlete, *but granted* by God, for it is God who rewards and crowns all toil."[82] Philo is significant because, though he still thought of himself as a Jew, he could appreciate Hellenism and use its images as examples in his teaching. As Chambers observes, "He was not attacking or abusing the religion of Israel but uncovering and revealing its true meaning and significance."[83]

Chapter Summary

The numerous references to victory in Revelation shows that νικάω was an important catchword for John. The Nicolaitans were a heretical group condemned for seeking temporal victory through accommodation rather than spiritual victory through resistance. In 1 Corinthians Paul uses victory

---

79. Harris, *Greek Athletics and the Jews*, 95.

80. Harris, ibid., makes a fanciful suggestion that "when St John outran Peter in their rush to the empty tomb on the first Easter morning, he was using a skill which he had acquired in the days when as a boy he imitated the runners he had watched in the stadium of Tiberias."

81. A full discussion of these texts can be found in Pfitzner, *Paul and the Agon Motif*, 38–57, and Harris, *Greek Athletics and the Jews*, 51–95.

82. Pfitzner, *Paul and the Agon Motif*, 48.

83. Chambers, "Greek Athletics and the Jews," 143.

in an eschatological sense regarding the resurrection of the dead, while the sole use of the motif in the Synoptics centers around victory over Satan. 4 Maccabees uses the victor motif extensively in its portrayal of Jewish martyrs resisting hellenization. The promises of Jesus found in Revelation 2–3 bear a striking resemblance to promises found in Psalm 2 and Isaiah 22, particularly the language of giving some reward to the victors.

An examination of the descriptions for believers in Revelation shows that "victors," "saints," and "servants" are used synonymously. Thus the identification of the victors as only the martyrs is problematic, for John presents the victors as being all Christians. This has important implications for the promises, because they are addressed to all believers in the seven churches who persist in doing good deeds and in remaining faithful. The reference to nakedness in the Laodicean letter seems to be primarily a metaphor related to spiritual poverty, although an allusion to Greek athletics is still possible.

Athletics were the quintessence of the Greek experience of victory and pride, and victors in the games were highly honored within the culture. Athletic contests were held throughout Asia, with the most prominent being the *koinon* games in Ephesus, Smyrna, and Pergamum. Although the Jews under the Maccabeans initially rebuffed the establishment of athletic traditions in Judea, later under Herod such games were finally accepted. Jews in the Diaspora became very familiar with the Greek games. Thus the victor motif is found in the two most prominent Jewish writers of the first century—Philo and Paul. In the next chapter we will look at the focus of our thesis—the victor sayings and their background in biblical literature.

4

The Text of the Victor Sayings

Introduction

IN THIS chapter we will examine the text of the victor sayings in chapters 2–3, particularly the key images. The preceding chapters have laid the necessary foundation for such a discussion. Upon the initial reading of the letters, what might be the reaction of the Asian audience to these promises? Such a response would be based on a number of literary, cultural, and historical factors. In this chapter we will seek to gain an understanding of the promises from these backgrounds as well as from intratextual usage within Revelation's first three chapters. In chapter 5 we will examine other references to the promises throughout the rest of Revelation to clarify further our understanding of these images. Our overview in these chapters cannot be comprehensive in the sense of including every comment or opinion on these texts. So much has been written that such a treatment would be impossible. Therefore the most viable perspectives compatible with sound hermeneutics have been selected. Several of the images are difficult to interpret, and new lines of interpretation are presented.

Before beginning the discussion of the victor sayings, we first examine the important question of local references and whether they play a legitimate role in interpreting the letters. The victor sayings in the letters are investigated in turn. General matters including textual issues are examined first. Relevant local references related to the situation of each church are discussed next. Then the co-texts of each image in New Testament, Extrabiblical, and Old Testament literature are presented. These co-texts are often presented with minimal comment. Although these presentations may not necessarily present fresh evidence, such a compilation is useful to show the development of these images in the Jewish and Christian communities. The heading "Extrabiblical" is used as a catch-all for works in the Apocrypha and Pseudipigrapha as well as nonbiblical historical and literary writings from the Greco-Roman world. Occasional reference from the Apostolic Fathers are also brought in. We conclude each section by suggesting how the promises may have been understood by the audience in the Asian churches.

While the influence of Old Testament prophetic literature on John was overarching,[1] it would be imprudent to ignore totally the numerous verbal parallels with the promises found in Extrabiblical literature. It is clear that John dips into a common well of language and imagery. Charles argues persuasively that "without a knowledge of the Pseudipigrapha it would be impossible to understand our author."[2] Therefore, how the Jewish apocalyptists used various symbols *may* guide us in understanding John's symbolism. Yet John's Revelation stands apart from these works both from a literary and a spiritual perspective. As Caird has observed about certain of these apocalypses, "The *Book of Enoch* has been justly called one of the world's six worst books. The *Ezra Apocalypse*, which somehow found its way into the Vulgate, and so into the Apocrypha under the title of 2 Esdras, is responsible for many of the most deplorable features of mediaeval theology. It is therefore quite unjust to John to insist that he must be judged by such company as this."[3] Circumspection is therefore called for in drawing any parallels between this literature and Revelation.

The Question of Local References

W. M. Ramsay is well known for his advocacy of local references: "The letters were written by one who was familiar with the situation, the character, the past history, the possibilities of future development, of those seven cities. The church of Sardis, for example, is addressed as the church of that actual, single city: the facts and characteristics mentioned are proper to it alone, and not common to the other churches of the Hermus valley."[4] Rudwick and Green, Wood, and Porter are scholars who have built upon Ramsay's labors by attempting to refine the understanding of the local references in Laodicea, Pergamum, and Sardis.

The outworking of Ramsay's view was a sort of environmental determinism to which Court objected:[5]

---

1. See the section on "Old Testament prophetic situations," in "A Pie in a Very Bleak Sky?" 90–95.
2. Charles, *Revelation*, 1:lxv.
3. Caird, *Revelation of St. John the Divine*, 10.
4. Ramsay, *Letters to the Seven Churches*, 28.
5. Court, *Myth and History in the Book of Revelation*, 27.

Expressed in its most extreme form, this belief in the determining influence of the environment would leave little opportunity or justification for a pastor's praise or blame. In a situation where, granted the weakness of human nature, conformity was almost inevitable, the function of a writer in letters such as these would amount to stating the reality of the situation for those who had failed to recognize it. The characteristic expression of the promise to the one who overcomes cannot have been made with much hopefulness or conviction.

Barr has likewise sought to discredit the theory: "These places and their associated ideas are not merely historical correlations, as Ramsay saw, but they are an oratorical device which would enable easy memorization of the order and scope of these letters."[6]

Hemer recognized the weaknesses in Ramsay's approach and updated and expanded his focus. The result was to make the recognition of local references historically and hermeneutically more credible. He has refined this approach to audience criticism by reconstructing a viable social history of the seven churches, asserting that "the symbolism of the letters was forcibly applicable to the original readers."[7]

Scobie has recently answered the objections of Prigent concerning local references by contending, "If only two or three local references can be convincingly demonstrated this would be sufficient to uphold the theory of local references; these would then greatly increase the possibility that at least some further such references exist."[8] Although he discusses only a few of the fifty or so suggested local references (many of which are "farfetched" in his opinion), the recognition of such references "does shed light on the nature of the letters as Christian prophetic oracles and on John's relation to the local situations addressed."[9] Rowland explains rightly how the inclusion of local color highlights the close link between religion and culture: "It is expected that the Christians in Laodicea will have imbibed the dominant ethos of the place in which they live, and so their outlook will be more governed by that than by Christ."[10] Thus the risen Christ must directly and forcefully challenge those situations and experiences that have impeded the spiritual development of each church.

---

6. Barr, "Apocalypse of John as Oral Enactment," 245–46n. 9.
7. Hemer, *Letters to the Seven Churches*, 210.
8. Scobie, "Local References," 616–17.
9. Ibid., 624.
10. Rowland, *Revelation*, 63.

The matter of local references in the seven letters is analogous to the question of historical references in Revelation. The fact that John had firsthand knowledge of events happening in the Roman Empire, especially in Asia, is an important consideration in interpreting the so-called local references.[11] We accept the likelihood of local references as the direct context for the victor sayings and therefore in our discussions will present suggested references in the seven cities.

Are the promises individualized to each church? Ramsay believes so: "The promise contained in the perorations of the seven letters is different in every case, and is evidently adapted in each instance to suit the general tone of the letter and the character and needs of the city."[12] Hemer agrees that in the letters "we find a pointed appropriateness in the promises to the conquerors" because "John is deeply concerned with the specific needs of his readers."[13] The suggestions of these and other scholars will be scrutinized regarding each promise. Two questions we will attempt to answer are: What might this promise have communicated to the initial Asian audience, and what might their response have been?

The Ephesian Victor Saying

The victor saying in this letter is found in 2:7. Jesus promises to grant (δώσω) the victor permission to eat from the tree of life in the paradise of God. Some texts include μέσῳ in the final clause: ἐν μέσῳ τῷ παραδείσῳ and ἐν μέσῳ τοῦ παραδείσου. These variants[14] undoubtedly arose from an attempt to harmonize the text with the Septuagint readings of Genesis 2:9 and 3:3 (cf. Gen 3:8).

This is the first of six uses of αὐτῷ in the promises (cf. Rev 2:17 [2x], 26, 28; 3:21). Speaking of its use here and in 2:17; 2:26; and 3:21 (cf. 21:7), Benedict suggests this explanation: "Without the use of the pronoun, the meaning would have been clear, but its usage is an emphatic, specific and restrictive way of showing that the promised reward applies only to the conqueror."[15] Zerwich provides a more likely explanation.

---

11. For example, the fire in Rome, the Roman civil war, and the Nero *redivivus* myth. This historical background is developed at length in chapter 2 of my thesis in the section, "The Historical Situation of the Roman Empire." A map illustrating the Nero redivivus myth can be found in Wilson, *Charts on the Book of Revelation*, 116.

12. Ramsay, *Letters to the Seven Churches*, 179.

13. Hemer, *Letters to the Seven Churches of Asia*, 42.

14. The manuscripts supporting the variants here and in subsequent references can be found in NA27.

15. Benedict, "The Use of ΝΙΚΑΩ," 42. As we have discussed in chapter 3, the

Here and in 2:17 use of τῷ νικῶντι δώσω with the pleonastic addition of αὐτῷ "shows that the participle, although put in the dative, is in the author's mind pendent, in accordance with the Semitic idiom of nominal sentences."[16] The pendent logical subject is normally followed by a sentence that takes it up by using a pronoun.

The Tree of Life

The possibility of a local reference has been challenged by Beckwith: "This promise, like the epithet of Christ in v. 1, does not have specific reference to the circumstances of the Ephesians, it is applicable to all alike; and it is placed appropriately in this introductory epistle as fundamental to the promises in all the others."[17] Lilje likewise notes its importance: "The greatest promise, which will be the last to be fulfilled (Rev 22:14) stands first in the letters; for the tree of life is the sign of the restoration of Paradise."[18] Although the primary reference is to the creation account in Genesis, a local reference need not be precluded. In this section we will explore several possibilities.

A group called the Nicolaitans is first mentioned in this letter. Eating in the pagan temples was a major concern for John. An implicit contrast is drawn between those who compromise by eating idol meat, thereby forgoing their heavenly reward, and those who abstain, thus gaining the right to eat from the tree of life for eternity. Thompson identifies such a reversal of truth as irony: "The irony of Christian proclamation and imitation occurs in a more subtle form in the message to the Ephesians where those conquering are promised to eat from the 'tree of life'...."[19] However, the Nicolatians were also a problem in Pergamum as well as in Thyatira (i.e., the Jezebelites). The believers in these churches would therefore understand the irony of this promise to the Ephesians. Hence, while there is a local reference, its scope encompasses more than just one church. We find this true in the promises in the other letters as well.

The tree of life imagery may also have some parallels in the local Artemis context. Outside of Ephesus was the grove Ortygia, the traditional birthplace of Artemis. The site of this sacred grove, called a *paradeisos*, was

---

promises are not just restricted to the victors.

16. Zerwick, *Biblical Greek*, §26.

17. Beckwith, *Apocalypse of John*, 451.

18. Lilje, *Last Book of the Bible*, 72.

19. Thompson, *Book of Revelation*, 48, cites other examples of irony in the letters to Smyrna, Philadelphia, and Laodicea.

still known in the first century (Strabo *Geogr.* 14.1.5, 20). The background of the Artemesium as a tree shrine is mentioned both by Callimachus (*Hymn. Dian.* 237–39) and Dionysius Periegetes (826–29).

Ford postulates that the symbol of the tree of life was perhaps suggested "because the sacred tree associated with the worship of the nature goddess appears on Ephesian coins."[20] Hemer likewise cites the abundant evidence for use of the tree on coinage, but his evidence is all pre-Roman dating from 400–350 BC.[21] An examination of Roman coins mainly from the Ephesian mint, shown in Trell and Burnett and depicting the Artemesium, produced no evidence suggesting that the tree of life was a motif connected to Artemis.[22] It is doubtful whether John's audience would be familiar with the symbolism of pre-Roman coinage because such coinage was no longer in circulation. The purpose of the large-scale production of imperial coinage in first-century Asia was to establish a uniform coinage in the province.[23]

Biblical and Extrabiblical Co-texts

The phrase "tree of life" is used nowhere outside of Revelation. Ξύλον is used five times in reference to the crucifixion of Jesus, both in a Petrine (Acts 5:30; 10:39; 1 Pet 2:24) and a Pauline (Acts 13:29; Gal 3:13) context. Its use by Paul in Galatians follows the Septuagint reading of Deuteronomy 21:23, a text clearly alluded to in the other four uses as well.

Some expositors have suggested a relationship between the tree of life and the cross. Roberts asks, "May it not be that the word was used in this special sense by the early Christians, and that John is also thinking of the Cross when he speaks of the 'tree of life'?"[24] Although John never uses the word σταυρός, the redemptive sacrifice of the Lamb is clearly presented in his second vision (Rev 5:6–12). Giblin likewise writes, "Ultimately, the tree of life is the cross as bearing the fruit of salvation, namely, the resurrection. Its placement in God's garden, paradise, symbolically includes both the abode of the just in the heavenly kingdom (cf. Luke 23:42–43) and the new creation at the final resurrection (cf. Rev 22:2)."[25] The source of this

---

20. Ford, *Revelation*, 388.

21. Hemer, *Letters to the Seven Churches in Asia*, 45–46.

22. Hemer, ibid., 46, however, cites an issue from Elagabalus showing the huntress Artemis standing beneath the palm. His other example better shows the relationship of the palm tree to Nike.

23. See Burnett et al, *Roman Provincial Coinage*, 23.

24. Roberts, "Tree of Life," 332.

25. Giblin, *Book of Revelation*, 54.

The Text of the Victor Sayings

association is found in early Christian art—a common motif shows the living trunk of the cross bearing twigs and leaves.[26] Schneider relates, "In the tomb paintings of the 2nd century it is thus depicted for the first time as the symbol of victory over death."[27] This devotional association, though theologically intriguing, is anachronistic and belies a background different from John's use in Revelation. It therefore must be rejected.

The ministry of the new priest mentioned in the Testament of Levi 18:11 is that he will open the gates of paradise and δώσει τοῖς ἁγίοις φαγεῖν ἐκ τοῦ ξύλου τοῦ ζωῆς. The similarity of the language in this text to Revelation is remarkable. In 4 Ezra 2:12 (cf. 8:52) the tree of life providing fragrant perfume is but one benefit Ezra promises to the people in the restored Jerusalem. What distinguishes these texts from Revelation is that the tree of life is transferred to the temple in the earthly Jerusalem rather than to the heavenly Jerusalem.

Enoch in his vision saw seven mountains resembling a throne, and on the highest was a special tree that looked and smelled like no other (*1 En.* 24:3–5). The angel Michael tells Enoch that following the great judgment the righteous will be presented with the tree's fruit for life (*1 En.* 25:4–5). In 2 Enoch 8:3 the tree of life, found in paradise, "is indescribable for pleasantness of fragrance."

This promise has its initial background in the creation account which tells how God planted a garden (παράδεισον) for Adam in Eden and therein grew τὸ ξύλον τῆς ζωῆς ἐν μέσῳ τῷ παραδείσῳ beside the tree of the knowledge of good and evil (Gen 2:8–9 LXX). Although forbidden to eat from the latter tree, Adam and Eve, goaded by the serpent, ate its fruit and the fall of humanity resulted. Because of their transgression, God declared the tree of life out of bounds for Adam and Eve lest they eat of it and live forever (Gen 3:22). The two are then banished from paradise, and cherubs and a flaming sword are placed before the tree of life to guard it (Gen 3:24–25).

Another reference to the tree of life is found in the Septuagint reading of Isaiah 65:22, where the translators have given an eschatological reading to the Masoretic text העץ "the tree." In the new heaven and new earth, referred to as Jerusalem (Isa 65:17–18), κατὰ γὰρ τὰς ἡμέρας τοῦ ξύλου τῆς ζωῆς ἔσονται αἱ ἡμέραι τοῦ λαοῦ μου. The people

---

26. Such a tree/cross, dating from the early fifth century AD, is depicted on a large flask found in the residence of a Byzantine dye merchant in Sardis; see Crawford, "Multiculturalism at Sardis," 41, 44.

27. Schneider, "ξύλον," *TDNT* 5:40–41.

will grow old laboring at their works (ἔργα), suggesting that immortality is conferred by the tree.

The Paradise of God

Paradise (παράδεισος) is an Old Persian loan word (*pairi-daeza*) meaning "enclosure," then "park" or "garden."[28] At the nearby temple of Apollo at Didyma (cf. Iamblichus *Myst.* 3.11), "while the questioners waited and sacrificed, they could lodge in the housing which we know to have spread on the second-century [BC] precinct, or *paradeisos*, as it was still touchingly described, in a word of Greco-Persian origin."[29] The designer of this sanctuary was Paionius, who was also one of the architects of the Artemis temple in Ephesus. The temples in Ephesus and Didyma were the first and third largest temples in the ancient world respectively, and the remains of the Didyma temple "convey a striking impression of what the Artemesion itself may have looked like"[30] It is probable that the Artemesium likewise contained a *paradeisos* precinct for lodgers to dwell in.

Biblical and Extrabiblical Co-texts

The shift from a secular to a religious meaning is seen in the Septuagint rendering of the creation account where paradise is seen as God's garden. This religious meaning, according to Charlesworth, "entered Jewish thought and vocabulary after the Babylonian Exile" and "combined with the hope of a blessed eschaton."[31]

Paradise is mentioned in only two other New Testament passages. On the cross Jesus tells the repentant thief that "today you will be with me in paradise" (Luke 23:43). Paradise is thus portrayed as the place of the righteous dead (Hades the place of the unrighteous; cf. Luke 16: 23). And Paul, describing a visionary experience, states that he was caught up to paradise (2 Cor 12:4). In these texts paradise is a heavenly rather than an earthly reality, and in Paul's case spiritually present now rather than only a future expectation.

Paradise imagery is found throughout Extrabiblical literature. The Testament of Levi 18:11 predicts the raising up of a priestly Messiah who will open the gates of paradise by removing the sword that has threatened

---

28. The etymology and background of the word is surveyed thoroughly by Jeremias, "παράδεισος," *TDNT* 5:765ff.
29. Fox, *Pagans and Christians*, 182.
30. Yamauchi, *New Testament Cities*, 130.
31. Charlesworth, "Paradise," *ABD* 5:154.

since Adam. Andersen gives this extended summation of the paradise traditions in 1 Enoch:[32]

> It has the "garden of life" (60:23; 61:12), "the garden where the elect and just live" (60:8), "the garden of justice" (77:3). It is across the ocean (77:3) "at the extremities of the earth" (106:7–8). This sounds more like the place where Gilgamesh goes to consult Utnapishtim. This is where Enoch himself eventually goes (1En 60:8), and presumably the paradise to which Michael took Melkizedek in 2En 72:9. This is where Methuselah and Noah go to consult Enoch (1En 65:2). Paradise is differently located in other parts of 1En. In chs. 37–71 he goes to the west (52:1), "to the extremity of the skies" (39:3). But in 70:1–4 he goes northwest. In the mythological journey of Enoch in 1En 17f., 23–25, Paradise is a marvelous garden to the northwest, near the divine mountain. It has the tree of life, and rivers come from it.

In 2 Enoch 8:1–8 (cf. 42:3) paradise is located in the third heaven, with four rivers flowing with honey, milk, oil, and wine; in 65:10 the righteous will be collected to live for eternity in a great and incorruptible paradise.

4 Ezra has several passages that mention paradise. In 4 Ezra 6:3 God contrasts the beginning of the earth when the foundations of paradise were laid with the coming end of the age. In chapter 7 the furnace of hell and its opposite, the paradise of delight, are disclosed on the day of judgment (v. 36), and Ezra laments that because of Adam's sin many will not enter paradise, with its unspoiled fruit, abundance, and healing (v. 123). Upon the opening of paradise the tree of life is planted (8:52).

In Ode of Solomon 20:7 the reader is exhorted to put on the Lord's grace and "come into his Paradise, and make for yourself a crown from his tree." 2 Baruch, though later than Revelation (2nd cent AD), likewise has several references to paradise. God created paradise but denied it to Adam after he sinned (2 Bar. 4:3). God subsequently showed it to Abraham and Moses (vv. 4–5). Paradise, like the new Jerusalem, is preserved for the future (v. 6).

Paradise is the setting for the tree of life. The phrase ὁ παράδεισος τοῦ θεοῦ is found only in the Septuagint reading of Genesis 13:10 and Ezekiel 28:13; 31:8 (2x; cf. Isa 51:3, ὡς παράδεισον κυρίου). In Genesis 2:15 and 3:24 it is also called the paradise of delight, translating τρυφῆς for עדן ("Eden"; cf. Ezek 31:9). The restoration of Eden is a theme found in the Prophets. In Isaiah 51:3 the deserts and wastelands of Zion are to become a paradise of God; in Ezekiel 36:35 "Eden follows desolation in

---

32. Andersen, "2 Enoch," 1:115n. 8b.

a promise oracle."³³ The curse upon the earth resulting from the Fall is finally counteracted in eschatological redemption.

This distinctive Old Testament background has prompted Hemer to link its usage in this letter with the long-established Jewish community in Ephesus.³⁴ The numerous other Old Testament allusions throughout the book make it unlikely that John has especially singled out the Jewish believers in Ephesus for this promise.

Ephesian Saying Conclusion

What might the Ephesians have made of this promise when they heard it? The imagery of the tree of life and paradise was no doubt familiar through Old Testament and Extrabiblical literature. A complete reversal of the Fall, which had occurred in Eden, would probably be suggested. Swete allows further that "Man's exclusion from the Tree of Life . . . is repealed by Christ on condition of a personal victory over evil. To eat of the Tree is to enjoy all that the life of the world to come has in store for redeemed humanity."³⁵ By giving this promise to the victors, Jesus shows he is the expected messiah-priest prophesied in the Testament of Levi.

Lilje points rightly to the eschatological nature of the motifs: "Thus all the promises about 'victory' point beyond this world to another, and this first one most decidedly of all."³⁶ Although we have yet to examine the other promises, Lilje's claim about this one is overstated because several others also have a clear eschatological focus. Rather, as Mealy has pointed out, "this is a promise of everlasting life in God's presence. Everything else from now on will be seen to build on this basic promise."³⁷ Interpreting this promise from an anthropological perspective, Pilch writes, "The reward of eating . . . suggests that truly honorable people will not allow themselves to be taken advantage of, but will have food in abundance."³⁸ This observation seems banal in light of the theological and eschatological implications of the motifs.

---

33. Stuart, *Ezekiel*, 251.
34. Hemer, *Letters to the Seven Churches of Asia*, 1986:37ff.
35. Swete, *Apocalypse of St. John*, 30.
36. Lilje, *Last Book of the Bible*, 72.
37. Mealy, *After the Thousand Years*, 82.
38. Pilch, "Lying and Deceit," 130.

The Text of the Victor Sayings

The Smyrnean Victor Saying

The first part of this promise lies in 2:10 between the coming and hearing sections with the victor saying in 2:11. The promise thus consists of a positive and a negative element. According to Rissi, "The message to the church in Smyrna is dominated by the life-death motif."[39] This tone is set in the epithet saying where Jesus declares he was dead and now lives again (2:8). Hemer says it even more emphatically, "The themes of suffering, death and resurrection pervade every verse of our letter."[40]

What type of genitive is τῆς ζωῆς? It could be one of quality—the crown is enduring and living in contrast to one that fades or tarnishes. However, Zerwick thinks that in the New Testament it is more probably epexegetical—the crown consists of life itself or the life of the age to come.[41] Swete sees the phrase as practically equivalent in meaning to "tree of life" (2:7).[42] The similar construction of "book of life" (3:5 et al) is also comparable. The epexegetical construction in these texts suggests the likelihood of a similar meaning for the images.

The phrase οὐ μή with the aorist subjunctive or future indicative, according to Blass, Debrunner and Funk, "is the most definite form of negation regarding the future." In some examples the future and aorist subjunctive forms are so similar they are difficult to differentiate; here "the subjunctive is absolutely certain due to its distinctive form."[43] This construction is used eighteen times in Revelation; twice in the promises to Sardis (3:5) and Philadelphia (3:12). The reference in 3:5 is a clear example of a future following the negation.

There are ten occurrences of ἀδικέω in Revelation. Charles says that it is always used in the sense of "to hurt," except in 22:11 where it means "to act unjustly," "to sin."[44] Black doubts rightly whether "hurt" or "harm" does full justice to John's usage of this verb. He points to the stronger Hebrew sense "to smite" that is reflected in the hiphil verb הפה in Isaiah 10:20, translated by ἀδικέω in the Septuagint (cf. *T Sim.* 5:4). Because this sense is required in 7:2, 3, and 9:4, 10, Black suggests that a similar nuance is required in 2:11—"he who is victorious will not be stricken down by the second death." His alternate suggestion, "destroy in

---

39. Rissi, *Future of the World*, 108n. 209.
40. Hemer, *Letters to the Seven Churches of Asia*, 59.
41. Zerwick, *Biblical Greek*, §45; cf. Laws, *In the Light of the Lamb*, 68.
42. Swete, *Apocalypse of St. John*, 33.
43. BDF, §365.
44. Charles, *Revelation*, 1:59; 2:222.

judgment," seems preferable given the use of κρίνω with "second death" in 20:13–14.[45]

The Crown of Life

The condition of faithfulness is linked to the promise of the crown of life. The faithfulness of Smyrna is linked to her faithfulness to Rome. Jesus is perhaps calling the Smyrneans to a new allegiance related to their heavenly responsibilities rather than to their civic ones. Because of the familiarity of the crown image in antiquity, Beckwith thinks it is not necessary to look for a local origin of the metaphor, for example, in the games for which Smyrna was famous.[46] Numerous suggestions have been advanced, however. Hemer mentions seven possibilities, and of these only three appear plausible—the crown as a symbol of victory, as a symbol of honor, or as a topological reference.[47] Our discussion will center around these.

As we have seen in chapter 3, the crown was a familiar image of victory in antiquity. "A victor's crown in the games was regarded as supreme earthly fortune."[48] The most famous of the athletic contests held throughout the Greco-Roman world was the Olympics. Pausanius (5.15.3) mentions a wild olive tree, "called the crown olive, from which tradition dictates that the Olympic winners should be given their wreaths." In Revelation the figure seems to be borrowed from the wreath awarded to the victor in the games. These games were held in nearly all of the seven cities. Because of such associations, the wreath was also a popular image on the reverse of provincial coins. The standing Nike with wreath and palm was a popular issue. Burnett lists twenty-three coin types of Nike holding a wreath and a palm branch.[49]

The crown was also a symbol of honor. When Antony visited Ephesus in 41 BC, the Judean Jews sent an embassy to petition Antony regarding an injustice to the Jews. This delegation brought him a golden crown (Josephus *Ant.* 14.304). In his reply to Hyrcanus the high priest and the Jewish nation Antony acknowledged that "the crown (στέφανον) which you have sent, I have accepted it" (*Ant.* 14.313). "A gift of this kind was a common practice, for the historian records this gesture of nearly every

---

45. Black, "Some Greek Words," 143–44.
46. Beckwith, *Apocalypse of John*, 455.
47. Hemer, *Letters to the Seven Churches of Asia*, 72–73.
48. Grundmann, "στέφανος, στεφανόω," *TDNT* 7:620.
49. See Burnett et al, *Roman Provincial Coinage*, passim.

Jewish embassy."[50] The Smyrneans gave a golden crown to distinguished individuals to bestow civic honor. Cicero (*Flac.* 75) refers sarcastically to this practice in the context of a state funeral for a businessman named Castricius upon whose corpse was placed the city's crown. Hemer comments, "The promise of a 'crown of life' might readily be contrasted with this institution of a city whose highest honour was awarded posthumously."[51]

Numerous inscriptions from Smyrna and other cities of Asia document an office of "Crown-Wearer" (ὁ στεφανηφόρος). Although the office was largely honorary, it cost its holder a great amount of money. The holder, sometimes a woman, could serve in the office multiple times as well as hold it concurrently with other civic offices.[52] Another group entitled to wear crowns were the Asiarchs (cf. Acts 19:31). These were the leading Roman citizens of Asia who served as high priests of the *koinon*[53] and presided over the imperial cult. Candidates for this prestigious office were elected to represent the cities of the province. Dio Chrysostom (35.10) describes this honored group: "I refer to the 'blessed ones,'[54] who exercise authority over all your priests, whose title represented one of the two continents in its entirety. For these men too owe their 'blessedness' to crowns (στέφανος) and purple and a throng of long-haired lads bearing frankincense." According to Yamauchi, "These priests wore unusually ornate crowns adorned with miniature busts of the imperial family, and were given the title *stephanophorus*."[55]

Benefaction was a dominant aspect of Greco-Roman society. "Stephanoi had been a quintessentially civic form of honouring major benefactors in classical Athens."[56] During the Hellenistic and imperial periods crowns were likewise awarded to the benefactors of private cult associations, foreign trade associations, and occasionally occupational associations. Kearsley writes, "The ultimate response of a grateful

---

50. Johnson et al, *Ancient Roman Statutes*, §126n. 8.
51. Hemer, *Letters to the Seven Churches of Asia*, 74.
52. Cadoux, *Ancient Smyrna*, 195–96.
53. Kearsley, "Civic Benefactor," 7:240.

54. It is interesting that Dio calls these representatives of the imperial cult "blessed ones" (μακαρίους). Perhaps God's "blessed ones," to whom John directs the seven beatitudes, are contrasted with the Asiarchs.

55. Yamauchi, *New Testament Cities*, 110. A statue of such an imperial priest with a crown on his head, dating from the second century AD, was found by archaeologists in the East Gymnasium at Ephesus. It is now displayed in the Izmir Museum. For a picture of the priest, see Scherrer, *Ephesus*, 71.

56. Van Nijf, *Civic World of Professional Associations*, 63.

beneficiary . . . was the awarding of some tangible item or exceptional privilege." Benefactors commonly chose crowns made of gold for that item. Dio Chrysostom (*Or.* 2.29–30) criticizes the politicians of Tarsus for their preoccupation with crowns, purple, and front-row seats, all images found in Revelation. All three were highly coveted by citizens of the Greek cities. Arrian (*Epict. diss.* 1.19.29) suggested that being able to wear the gold crown was the chief incentive for individuals to become a priest of the emperor.

The crown as a topological reference is described by Apollonius (Philostratus *Vit. Apoll.* 4.7). He encouraged the Smyrneans to take pride in themselves rather than in the beauty of their city: "It was more pleasing for the city to be crowned with men than with porticos and pictures." Concerning "the crown of Smyrna," Ramsay writes that "there can be no doubt that the phrase arose from the appearance of the hill Pagus, with the stately public buildings on its rounded top and the city spreading out down its rounded sloping sides."[57] Aristides gives varied descriptions of the city in his *Orations* (15.20–22). "Several of his highly ornate sentences become clearer when we notice that he is expressing in a series of variations the idea of a crown resting on the summit of a hill."[58] A similar topographical reference is sometimes observed in the letter to Pergamum. Wood asks, "The expression 'Satan's throne' may well bear reference to the strength and multiplicity of pagan cults, but could it not also bear reference to the actual shape of the city-hill towering, as it still does, like a giant throne above the plain?"[59] The reference here is best understood as the emperor cult and its temple in the city. And as Hemer observes rightly, "A topographical understanding of the 'crown' at Smyrna is better founded, the use of the metaphor being authenticated by ancient evidence."[60]

Biblical and Extrabiblical Co-texts

Four references to "crown" are found in an eschatological context in the New Testament. Paul calls the Thessalonians his crown of boasting at the parousia (1 Thess 2:19). All those who long for the appearing of the Lord as righteous judge will receive a crown of righteousness (2 Tim 4:8).

---

57. Ramsay, *Letters to the Seven Churches*, 186.

58. Ibid., 186–87. Similarly, E. J. Young, *Book of Isaiah*, 2:264, suggests that the reference in Isaiah 28:1–4 to Samaria as a crown is "a topological reference, for Samaria was situated on a hill, which is thought to have suggested a crown."

59. P. Wood, "Local Knowledge in the Letters of the Apocalypse," 264.

60. Hemer, *Letters to the Seven Churches of Asia*, 238n. 39; cf. Ramsay, "Smyrna," 4:555.

The Text of the Victor Sayings

Deissman notes that the official visit of a ruler was called a parousia and upon his arrival he was given a golden crown. He finds such a background for these Pauline verses: "While the sovereigns of this world expect at their parousia [sic] a costly crown for themselves, 'at the parousia of our Lord Jesus' the apostle will wear a crown. . . ."[61]

Peter tells his Anatolian audience that at the appearing of the Chief Shepherd, they will receive an unfading crown of glory (1 Pet 5:4). And James 1:12 contains a beatitude using language and imagery similar to that in Revelation: "Blessed is the person who endures temptation because after being tested, he will receive the crown of life (τὸν στέφανον τῆς ζωῆς) which God promised to those who love him." Martin observes regarding this promise: "'life' belongs to the world of victory enjoyed by those who win through in their battle with temptation (πειρασμός) to emerge as victors."[62]

Vos believes the references in Revelation, 2 Timothy, and James recall a promise given by Jesus during his earthly ministry. He finds three analogous features between the three texts: "1) a promise is made to those who endure temptations, sufferings, or persecution; 2) a crown of life/righteousness is the reward, 3) the Lord is both the one who apparently makes the promise and the bestower of the crown."[63] The text in 1 Peter also shares these features. It is probable that these four texts are based on a common saying of Jesus.[64]

Beasley-Murray suggests that the symbol may be "the representations applied in the ancient world, alike to divine beings and to blessed mortals, of a crown of light surrounding the head, to indicate the glory of the one on whom it rests."[65] The meaning would be: "I will crown you with glory in the life of the age to come." This meaning is tenuous since the eschatological sense is already present as written, and the phrase "crown of light" has no background in the Old and New Testaments.

The immortal righteous in Wisdom of Solomon 5:15–16 receive their rewards of a glorious kingdom and a beautiful crown. In 4 Ezra 2:42–47 the Son of God places a crown on the head of each person in the heavenly multitude. The reference to the goal of a crown of glory in Testament of Benjamin 4:1, according to Charles, indicates "the idea of

---

61. Deissman, *Light from the Ancient East*, 369.

62. Martin, *James*, 33.

63. Vos, *Synoptic Traditions in the Apocalypse*, 192, 193.

64. Another reference is found in the Shepherd of Hermas 68.1, where the angel of the Lord crowns the faithful with crowns made of palm leaves.

65. Beasley-Murray, *Revelation*, 83.

crowns as the reward of righteousness is pre-Christian."⁶⁶ Ascension of Isaiah 9:24–26 refers to three elements found in the promises—crowns, robes, and thrones. Many in the world will receive these rewards through believing. And the odist in Odes of Solomon 9:11 exhorts, "Put on the crown in the true covenant of the Lord, and all those who have conquered will be inscribed in his book." The Odes emphasize a present experience of immortality, unlike Revelation where the presentation is largely future.⁶⁷

Kraft writes, "Einen „Lebenskranz" oder eine „Lebenskrone" kennt das Alte Testament nicht."⁶⁸ However, there is much crown imagery in the Old Testament related especially to the monarchy. For example, God gives a crown of precious stone to the righteous king (Ps 20:4 LXX). Metaphorically it also symbolizes blessing and honor (cf. Prov 1:9; 4:9; 12:4; 16:31; 17:6). Other possible backgrounds for the crown imagery are found in Isaiah 22:21, Ezekiel 28:12, and Zechariah 6:10–11, all sources for other imagery in the letters. In Isaiah Eliakim is promised: "And I will give him your crown."⁶⁹ The passage in Ezekiel speaks of the ruler of Tyre possessing a crown: "And you had a beautiful crown in the luxury of the paradise of God." In both texts the current holder of the crown is losing possession of it for disobedience. In Zechariah the prophet is commanded to garnish silver and gold from several newly arrived exiles and to make it into a crown. He is then to set the crown on the head of the high priest Joshua. Another possible source is Isaiah 62:3: "And you will be a beautiful crown in the hand of the Lord and a royal diadem in the hand of your God." Here crown and diadem are used in parallelism. In the Septuagint the two words are often used interchangeably, unlike the New Testament where a distinction in meaning is usually preserved.⁷⁰

---

66. Charles, *Revelation*, 1:129.

67. Cf. Aune, "Odes of Solomon," 455.

68. "A 'wreath of life' or a 'crown of life' are not known in the Old Testament"; Kraft, *Offenbarung*, 61.

69. However, the Hebrew text ואבנטך אחזקנו reads "sash" instead of "crown." The promise immediately preceding this, "And I will clothe him with your robe (στολήν)," is a possible source for the imagery of the white robes (στολή) found in 6:11; 7:9, 13, 14; and 22:14.

70. The translators failed to distinguish between στέφανος and διάδημα when translating עטרה (cf. Pfitzner, *Paul and the Agon Motif*, 51). For the distinction in meaning, see Purves, "Crown," *HBD* 1:530.

The Second Death

A connection between death and Smyrna existed in antiquity. This resulted from its etymological link to the Greek word for myrrh σμύρνα. Myrrh was commonly used for embalming, and was one of sweet-smelling spices in which the body of Jesus was wrapped (John 19:39). After summarizing several such proposed links, Hemer suggests "that the name of Smyrna was fitting and expressive to the ancient mind for a city which seemed to exemplify characteristics which myrrh symbolized."[71] A number of mourning myths became associated with the city. Perhaps the best known was the story of Niobe, whose children were killed by Leto and Artemis. Following their funeral Niobe wandered to Mount Sipylus, northeast of Smyrna, where Zeus changed her into a marble statue whose face was continually wet with tears. Such myths "suggested and perpetuated the picture of a city of suffering, a concept symbolized by its very name."[72]

Biblical and Extrabiblical Co-texts

There is no mention of "second death" outside of Revelation. In 1 Corinthians 15:21 Paul recalls the account in Genesis where physical death—the first death—entered the human race through Adam.

The phrase occurs in Plutarch's *Moralia* (Fac. 9434F), where he says that after death the good lead a most easy life, but are not blessed or divine "until the second death." From Plutarch's Platonist perspective the righteous, not the unrighteous, experience the second death. At the first death all humans, who are tripartitely constituted, lose their body; at the second death the righteous have their minds separated from their souls, which have been living on the moon (Fac. 943C). Certain of this group are called victors (νικηφόροι) for their steadfastness and are crowned with wreaths (στεφάνοις).

Philo likewise mentions two deaths in his treatise on rewards and punishments. In his discussion of the punishment of Cain, he writes: θανάτου γὰρ διττὸν εἶδος, τὸ μὲν κατὰ τὸ τεθνάναι . . . τὸ δὲ μετὰ τὸ ἀποθνῄσκειν, ὃ δὴ κακὸν πάντως (*Praem.* 70).[73] While the first death is either good or indifferent, the second death is entirely bad because it is painful and perpetual punishment given in Cain's case for fratricide (*Praem.* 71). In an earlier section on rewards (*Praem.* 52) Philo

---

71. Hemer, *Letters to the Seven Churches of Asia*, 58.
72. Ibid., 59.
73. "For there are two kinds of death; the one that of being dead . . . the other that of dying, which is in every respect an evil" (Yonge trans.).

declares that the virtuous man in the sacred contests was proclaimed the winner of the crown. The use of the images, crown and two deaths, together in both Plutarch and Philo suggests that John is using associations familiar to his audience.

Several targumic parallels are cited by Charles: "let Reuben live in this age and not die the second death" (TgJ on Deut 33:6); "let them die the second death and not live in the next world" (TgNeb on Jer 51:39, 57), and "this sin shall not be forgiven you till you die the second death" (TgNeb on Isa 65:6, 15).[74] The frequency of "second death" in the Targums indicates it was "a common Jewish phrase denoting a second and retributive death in the future state."[75] Calling the targum on Deuteronomy 33:6 the Old Testament *locus theologicus* in rabbinic Judaism that proves the resurrection of the dead, Johnson states rightly, "Not to die the second death, then, means to rise again to eternal life."[76]

There is also no mention of the phrase "second death" in the Old Testament. Death first came to the human race following the sin of Adam and Eve (Gen 2:17). In the letter to Smyrna, imagery of the Fall follows the promise of Edenic restoration given to the Ephesians. Because of the link with fire and brimstone in Revelation 20:14, Peake sees the second death as a reminder of the destruction of Sodom and Gomorrah.[77] Hort, following Temple, sees the allusion as also referring to the flood, with fire and flood commonly linked in Jewish eschatology (cf. 2 Pet 2:5–7; Jude 7).[78] Such typological interpretations, however, are inadequate for understanding the present literary context of this promise.

Smyrnean Saying Conclusion

The familiarity of the images in this victor saying assured their comprehension by the Smyrneans. Beckwith observes rightly that this promise "is determined directly by the peril of the readers."[79] Although the church in Smyrna faces a period of testing, "to die under the wrath of man is small compared with the prospect of suffering the judgment of God."[80] Charles, following Bousset, understands correctly the crown as one which belongs to

---

74. Charles, *Revelation*, 1:59.
75. Hort, "Apocalypse of St John I–III," 26.
76. Johnson, "Revelation," 12:585.
77. Peake, *Revelation of John*, 240.
78. Hort, "Apocalypse of St John I–III," 27.
79. Beckwith, *Apocalypse of John*, 455.
80. Beasley-Murray, *Revelation*, 83.

eternal life: "As the tree of life . . . is a symbol of the blessed immortality in Christ, so the crown of life appears to symbolize its full consummation."[81]

The reverse of the promise of a crown of life is the promise of escape from the second death. Impending physical (first) death for some is contrasted with the promise that none will be harmed by a future (spiritual) second death. "To participate in the first death is also to escape the second death and to enter into the promised reign of God's grace and peace."[82] A fuller explication of the "second death" is reserved for chapters 20–21, where John himself defines "second death" (21:8). If the audience perceived chiastic structure in the document, it would then anticipate that such a definition would be forthcoming.

The mention of "your crown" in 3:11 is significant because it is found in the complementary letter to Philadelphia and "states negatively the possibility which the promise to Smyrna puts positively."[83] It is not found in the victor section there and presupposes knowledge of its mention in the Smyrnean letter. This is another indicator of the interrelationship among the letters, that their message is not totally individualized to each church but applicable to the others. Kiddle believes that the Philadelphians already possess their crown, while the Smyrneans have yet to earn theirs.[84] John, however, asserts that both ideas are true. Like those whose names are written in the book of life (Rev 3:5), believers are already marked for membership in the messianic community. Kiddle continues, "But the name could be erased. The crown could be lost, through unworthy conduct."[85] Yet, because neither Smyrna nor Philadelphia receives any censure, their promised reward is guaranteed if they persevere in the trial with their opponents in the local synagogues.

The Pergamene Victor Saying

The promise to the church of Pergamum, found in 2:17, is one of the most obscure sayings. It and the victor saying to Thyatira are the only examples of double promises introduced by δώσω. Hemer observes rightly, "The corresponding promises in the other letters, even when complex, as at

---

81. Charles, *Revelation*, 1:59.
82. Wall, *Revelation*, 74.
83. Beasley-Murray, *Revelation*, 101.
84. Kiddle, *Revelation of St. John*, 53.
85. Ibid.

Philadelphia, are developments of a single concept."[86] The two concepts in this double promise, with the second complex promise divided also, are:

1. Jesus will give the victor (to eat) the hidden manna.
2. (a) He will give the victor a white stone, and
   (b) upon the stone he will write a new name known only to its receiver.

Several variants are found in the text. The first is αὐτῷ φαγεῖν. This is a probable scribal attempt to bring agreement with the language in the Ephesian promise (2:7). The second is ἀπό τοῦ μάννα. According to Blass et al, the partitive genitive with verbs meaning "to eat of" has been replaced in the New Testament with prepositional phrases using ἀπό or ἐκ; therefore Blass argues that the adopted reading "is not credible."[87] Charles, however, contends that τοῦ μάννα is the only example of a simple partitive genitive after δίδωμι in the New Testament.[88] Stuart confirms John's proper use of the genitive case here to speak partitively, claiming "This belongs to Attic writers of the nicest idiom."[89] Hemer cites an additional example in 3:9 of a partitive genitive, ἐκ τῆς συναγωγῆς.[90] However, the latter is not an example of a partitive genitive; instead the construction "is being driven out by the use of the preposition ἐκ."[91]

The Hidden Manna

Court, citing Pliny the Elder and Galen of Pergamum, mentions that manna in pagan Greek and Latin literature indicated a crumb of frankincense or pinch of incense used to prove loyalty to the emperor.[92] Pliny (*Nat.* 12.32) does identify manna as a fragment obtained by shaking the frankincense tree, but he never states in what context the incense was used. The reference in Galen was never found.

Biblical and Extrabiblical Co-texts

In John 6:31 Jesus speaks of the manna given in the wilderness and quotes Exodus 16:15. He tells his audience that Moses did not give the true bread

---

86. Hemer, *Letters to the Seven Churches of Asia*, 252n. 67.
87. Blass et al, 1961:§169, §169.2.
88. Charles, *Revelation*, 1:65.
89. Stuart, "White Stone of the Apocalypse," 464–65.
90. Hemer, *Letters to the Seven Churches of Asia*, 241n. 78.
91. Blass et al, 1961:§164.
92. Court, *Myth and History in the Book of Revelation*, 33.

of heaven; the Father has now given it through his Son who is the bread coming down from heaven (vv. 33, 41, 58). He is the bread of life (ἄρτος τῆς ζωῆς; vv. 35, 48). Those who come to him and believe will never hunger or thirst again (v. 35; cf. 7:37–38 where Jesus is likewise the source of living water). Israel ate the manna in the desert and died; those who partake of his flesh which is the living bread will not die but live forever (vv. 50–51, 57–58). Jesus here corrects erroneous thinking about manna and its source—that he himself is the true bread of God who gives life in the age to come. Beasley-Murray gives the reason, "It is hidden from the Jews, and can be received only through the confession of Jesus as Lord."[93] The promise of the bread of heaven/life is a realized one in the Fourth Gospel, while the promise of hidden manna in Revelation is future, though the second is obviously predicated on the first.

In the context of teaching on idolatry and the Lord's Supper, Paul makes a historical reference to Israel's wilderness wanderings and calls manna "spiritual food" (1 Cor 10:3). The writer of Hebrews mentions the gold jar of manna that rested in the ark (Heb 9:4).

The adjective "hidden" suggests the veiled nature of Jesus' teaching. The meaning of the parables was mostly hidden to his audience (Matt 13:34–35). His teaching about his coming death was also hidden from his disciples (Luke 18:34). The verb κρύπτω is used in an eschatological context in Colossians 3:3. Since the Colossians have died through identification with Christ's death in water baptism, their lives are hidden in Christ who is seated at the right hand of God (vv. 1–3). At Christ's appearing, they will also appear in glory (v. 4). In conclusion I resonate with the comment of Dunn regarding the Colossians, which also has relevance to John's audience: "Despite the present hiddenness of their 'life,' which might make their attitudes and actions in their present living somewhat bewildering to onlookers, they could nevertheless be confident that Christ, the focus of their life, would demonstrate to all the rightness of the choice they had made in baptism."[94]

After the destruction of Jerusalem and the temple in 586 BC, a tradition states that Jeremiah rescued the ark and other sacred objects such as the pot of manna and hid them in a cave on Mount Nebo until God should re-gather his people (see 2 Macc 2:4–8). Another tradition declares that an angel hid these sacred temple objects in the earth and was to guard them "until the last times" (*2 Bar.* 6:8). 1 Maccabees 1:23 speaks of the hidden treasures from the temple that Antiochus took to Syria. Although

93. Beasley-Murray, *Revelation*, 88.
94. Dunn, *Colossians and to Philemon*, 208.

these accounts use the "hidden" imagery related to the temple objects, none mentions manna specifically. We conclude that these descriptions are too generalized to provide a background for the promise of hidden manna.

2 Baruch speaks of a twelve-fold period of tribulation (26:1—27:15) after which the Messiah will be revealed (29:3). During a period of earthly restoration "the treasury of manna will come down again from on high, and they will eat of it in those years because these are they who will have arrived at the consummation of time" (29:8). Therefore Wall concludes that the hidden manna imagery "probably draws upon rabbinic commentaries on Exodus 16:31–35 by which Jews expected to be nourished by this same manna in the age to come."[95] Beckwith thinks the reference to "a delightful drink of sweet honey from heaven" in Sibylline Oracle 3.746 may refer to manna.[96] While these suggestions demonstrate the vitality of the manna image in Jewish communities, they fail to provide a convincing connection to our text.

During their forty years of wilderness wanderings God gave Israel manna to eat every day except the Sabbath (Exod 16:31; Num 11:6–9; Deut 8:3, 16; Jos 5:12; Neh 9:20; Ps 78:24). It is called "bread from heaven" (Exod 16:4; Neh 9:15; Ps 78:24 LXX) and "bread of angels" (Ps 78:25). The tradition preserved in Psalm 78 and Nehemiah 9 links the provision of water from the rock with that of the manna. A golden pot of manna was to be set aside by Aaron as a testimony to future generations (Exod 16:32–34). Charles suggests rightly that our text refers to the heavenly manna of the wilderness, not to this later pot of manna which was in the ark.[97]

The White Stone

The identification of the white stone is very difficult, and many interpretations have been proposed. Because of this, our format will be modified in this section. Tenney justifiably calls the white stone and the pillar (3:12) the two unexplained symbols in the seven letters.[98]

The main difficulty relates to the meaning of ψῆφος. Although its primary sense is a "stone" or "pebble," the ψῆφος was used in counting, in games, and in voting for acquittal or condemnation (cf. Acts 26:10) and thus acquired those meanings. Pythagorean mathematics represented num-

---

95. Wall, *Revelation*, 76.
96. Beckwith, *Apocalypse of John*, 461.
97. Charles, *Revelation*, 1:65.
98. Tenney, *Interpreting Revelation*, 189.

bers using figures made with pebbles.⁹⁹ Hence the verbal form ψηφίζω is used in 13:18 to mean "count up, to calculate" (cf. Luke 14:28) the number of the beast.

Ψῆφος likewise stood for a resolve or decree.¹⁰⁰ A further use was as an amulet (*BAGD* s.v.). This variety of meanings is reflected in the various interpretations for this promise. Hemer has compiled the seven most credible suggestions:¹⁰¹

1. A jewel in Old Testament or rabbinic tradition (Exod 28:17-21; Yoma 75a).
2. The judicial *calculus Minervae*, the casting vote of acquittal (Ovid *Metam.* 15:41–42; Theophrastus *Char.* 17.8; Heliodorus *Aeth.* 3.3ff; Aeschylus *Eum.* 744).
3. A token (*tessera*) of admission, membership, or recognition (*CIG* 3173=*IGRR* IV.1393; *IGRR* IV. 353d14; *CIG* 3278).¹⁰²
4. An amulet with a divine name (Artemidorus *Onir.* 5.26).
5. A token (*tessera*) of gladiatorial discharge (Horace *Ep.* 1.1.1-3).
6. Allusion to a process of initiation into the service of Asclepius (Aristides *Hym. Asklep.* 6.69).
7. Simply as a writing material whose form or color was significant.

Hemer provides a comprehensive review of these suggestions. After evaluating each, he discounts views 1 and 5; allows as possible views 2,

---

99. Bauckham, *Climax of Prophecy*, 391.

100. *Liddell and Scott* s.v. See also Mason, *Greek Terms for Roman Institutions*, 130, 131; cf. McLean, *Introduction to Greek Epigraphy*, 216 n. 6.

101. Hemer, *Letters to the Seven Churches of Asia*, 96.

102. In this category Ramsay (*Letters to the Seven Churches*, 222) also speaks of "an entrance ticket to distributions," that is, the *tesserae frumentariae*. Such tokens were tendered for a single corn ration and began to be used by Augustus in 22 BC in the midst of a famine in Rome. The use of *tesserae* led to greater efficiency in grain distribution in the capital (see Rickman, *Corn Supply of Ancient Rome*, 62). Although Augustus attempted to give out tesserae for four month' supply three times a year, at the request of the plebs he returned to the previous custom of distributing the share monthly (Suetonius, *Augustus* 40). Only the citizen body of Rome comprised the *plebs frumentaria*, ranging in size from 150,000–200,000 persons, received the ration during the food crisis of AD 6 (Rickman, Ibid., 184–85). At the Great Festival Nero had all kinds of presents thrown each day to the people including *tesserae frumentariae* (Suetonius *Nero*, 11).

3, 4, and 7; and thinks view 6 most likely.[103] Given the background of the athletic games, a version of view 3 is attractive. Swete, citing Arethas, regards the white stone as a symbol of victory.[104] Apparently victors at the games were given tokens entitling them to rewards courtesy of the cities. However, no other authority mentioning such a use of *tessarae* can be found, so this view founders on lack of evidence.[105] View 4, which proposes that the white stone is a Christian magical amulet, has been adopted by both Beckwith and Charles.[106] This interpretation seems unlikely given John's frequent denunciation of sorcery in Revelation. View 7 relates to the subject of decrees, to be addressed next.

Inscriptional Co-texts

McLean notes that inscriptions from the Propontis, just north of Pergamum, "frequently bear the formula ἀναγράψαι εἰς τελαμῶνα λευκοῦ λίθου (engrave on a white stone stele)."[107] About 9 BC a decree (*OGIS* 458[108]) was issued by the *koinon* of Asia confirming an epistolary request of the proconsul Paullus Fabius Maximus. It stated that Augustus' birthday be made an official holiday in the province as well as the beginning of the municipal new year. [109] This letter/decree has several verbal parallels with Revelation. In his letter Fabius calls the birth of Caesar Augustus "the beginning of breath and life" (ἀρχὴν τοῦ βίου καὶ τῆς ζωῆς, l. 10; cf. Rev 3:14). The honor of Augustus should "remain forever" (εἰς τὴν τειμήν ... αἰώνιον, l. 28; cf. Rev 4:9; 5:13; 7:12). In the decree the birthday of the god Augustus is declared the beginning of "good news" (εὐαγγελί[ων]; Rev 14:6) for the world (ll. 41–42). At the end of this decree is a state-

---

103. Ibid., 96–102.
104. Swete, *Apocalypse of St. John*, 40.
105. Cf. Hemer, *Letters to the Seven Churches of Asia*, 243n. 96.
106. Beckwith, *Apocalypse of John*, 461; Charles, *Revelation*, 1:66–67.
107. McLean, *Introduction to Greek Epigraphy*, 36.

108. The decree was apparently distributed throughout the province because copies have been found in five Asian cities. A copy was found in 1826 at Apamea, a conventus city, with damaged copies also being found at Priene, Dorylaeum, Eumenea, and Maionia; see Hemer, *Letters to the Seven Churches of Asia*, 87; cf. Boring et al., *Hellenistic Commentary*, §225. We wish to thank the staff at the Manisa Museum for permission to examine the Maionian fragment of the marble *tabula* in its collection; cf. Malay, *Greek and Latin Inscriptions*, §5.

109. Although the Asian calendar was formally changed to synchronize with the Roman Julian calendar, tradition won out, however, and such important Asian cities as Ephesus, Smyrna, Miletus, and Cyzicus did not change their old calendars to the Julian one; see Magie, *Roman Rule in Asia Minor*, 1:481.

ment related to this promise: "The tablet-writing of the proconsul and the decree (ψήφισμα) of Asia are to be inscribed (ἀναγραφῆναι) on a white-stoned stele (στήλῃ λευκολίθωι), which is to be set up in the temenos of Rome and the emperor" (ll. 63–64; cf. 65–67).

A cognate of ψῆφος, ψήφισμα, is used in this inscription (cf. Est 3:7; 9:24; 2 Mac 6:8; 12:4; Josephus *Ant.* 16.165). This decree was to be placed in the temple of Rome and Augustus in Pergamum, which "served as a repository for decrees of the Koinon, letters from Rome and decrees honoring provincial priests or other officials of the Koinon, with stelai set up in the temenos or even in the temple itself."[110] The Pergamenes, as well as the other Asian Christians, probably had knowledge of this inscribed stele displayed in the central Augustan temple in Pergamum. The promise of a new name written on a white stone thus stands in contrast with the "gospel" of the emperor Augustus written on a white stone. Although this inscriptional link to the promise cannot be proven conclusively, its interpretive connection must be considered. Whose new name is written on the white stone—that of Christ or the believer—will be addressed later.

Biblical Co-texts

Fekkes declares that "There is no OT or early Christian parallel to the motif of the white stone . . . ."[111] However, two motifs of the rock/stone as a Christological image are prominent in Scripture. Since the manna imagery comes from the wilderness context (Exod 16:1–36), might not the imagery of the white stone come from that context also? Immediately following the manna story is the account of Moses bringing forth water from a rock after the Israelites complain about the lack of water (Exod 17:1–7). This miraculous provision of drink is repeated in Numbers 20:1–13, wherein Moses is disciplined for striking the rock rather than speaking to it. In Deuteronomy 8:15–16 the miracles of rock and manna are again recounted regarding Israel's experience in the wilderness. This miracle is also recalled in Psalms 78:15–25 and 105:40–41.

Israel's wilderness experience is treated as typological for the church by Paul in 1 Corinthians 10. They all ate the same spiritual food—manna—and drank the same spiritual drink—water from the rock (vv. 3–4). Then Paul provides a Christological interpretation of this spiritual rock: it was Christ in a pre-incarnate manifestation (v. 4). This perspective grows directly out of Jesus' teaching about himself in John 6, reviewed earlier. He is the bread of heaven, but in John 7:37–39 Jesus also presents

---

110. Mellor, *ΘΕΑ ΡΩΜΗ: Worship of the Goddess Roma*, 141.
111. Fekkes, *Isaiah and Prophetic Traditions*, 128.

himself as the source of living water. The linkage of manna and water in all these texts is noteworthy.

Jesus is described figuratively as the chief cornerstone in Ephesians 2:20. A spiritual temple is being built on the foundation of the apostles and prophets. The believers are the building materials—the stones—being used to construct the dwelling place of God (v. 22).

A catena of Old Testament scriptures is used in 1 Peter 2:6–8, which presents Jesus in imagery like that of Ephesians. Isaiah 28:16 is quoted first: God will lay a stone in Zion, a chosen and precious cornerstone. This stone is then personalized: whoever trusts in him will never be shamed. Psalm 118:22 is quoted next: the stone rejected by the builders has become the capstone. Isaiah 8:14, quoted last, speaks of a stone that causes people to stumble and a rock that makes them fall. Peter uses these texts to support his identification of Jesus as the Living Stone (v. 4). By extension then his Asian audience is to be living stones built into a spiritual house as a holy priesthood (v. 5). Three Greek words referring to the rock/stone as a building material—ἀκρογωνιαῖος, λίθος, and πέτρα—are used in these texts.

God as the Rock—a source of protection and strength—is also a prominent Old Testament motif.[112] However, according to Mundle, "the LXX avoids the word *petra* in translating these passages, and makes use of circumlocutions."[113] Two references to God as the Stone (אבן) are found in Genesis 49:24 (untranslated in the Septuagint) and in Zechariah 3:9 (λίθος LXX). In the Genesis text God is also called Shepherd, the identification in the next Thyatiran promise.

The passage in Zechariah 3 begins with the *Weckformel*, "Listen" (ἄκουε LXX). Then an oracle with messianic implications promises unconditionally that God will send "my servant the Branch" (v. 8). A promise to set a stone before Joshua comes next. The stone has seven eyes (cf. Zech 4:10), even as the slain Lamb seen by John in Revelation 5:6 has seven eyes (the sevenfold Spirit).[114] Then God promises to engrave an inscription on the stone (Zech 3:9). (The Septuagint omits this reference to an inscrip-

---

112. סלע Ps 18:2; 31:3; 42:9; 71:3; צור, 2 Sam 22:3; Ps 18:31, 46; 28:1; 31:2; 61:2; 62:2, 6, 7; 71:3 78:35; 89:26; 92:15: 94:22.

113. Mundle, "Rock," *NIDNTT* 3:381.

114. Baldwin discusses another possible translation of עינים as "springs." This association with water unifies the message of verses 8–10; the living water of the fountains causes the Branch to shoot up. "The stone, according to this translation, is no longer an engraved jewel but rather takes its meaning from the rock struck by Moses in the desert . . . . It is not impossible that Zechariah was incorporating both meanings, in a play on the word" (*Haggai, Zechariah, Malachi*, 117, 118).

tion, translating instead "Behold, I am digging a pit.") After reviewing a few of the interpretations for this inscribed stone, Petersen concludes that the inscription relates to the stone in the high priest's headdress inscribed with the name "Holy to Yahweh" (Exod 28:36–38).[115] This explanation seems likely since this stone is linked with the bearing and removal of Israel's guilt. "What the Israelites and the high priest were to do from the perspective of Ex 28 is, from the perspective of this writer, to be undertaken by Yahweh. . . . Yahweh will do that which no human could accomplish, even if he were the high priest."[116] This expiatory role has strong links with John's portrayal of Jesus as the slain Lamb.

A relationship between the Pergamene promise and these Rock/Stone traditions seems attractive except for one thing—ψῆφος is used instead of πέτρα or λίθος. The mention of white is easily explained because of its symbolic use throughout Revelation. However, πέτρα is used only in 6:15–16 to speak of a place of hiding from the wrath of the Lamb. Λίθος is used eight times to speak of precious stones, with the most significant usage to be discussed in chapter 7. The verbal cognate of ψῆφος is used in 13:18, where the saints are encouraged to calculate (ψηφίζω) the number of the beast's name—666. The verbal relationship in 13:18 with the promise of a new name written on a white ψῆφος must have been apparent to the Asian audience. Genesis 49:24 and Zechariah 3:9 provide the most probable biblical background for the image of an inscribed stone. Because the Septuagint failed to translate "Stone" in Genesis 49:24 and deleted the inscription imagery in Zechariah 3:9, perhaps John chose to translate אבן as ψῆφος. The divine Jesus could be the messianic white Stone promised to the victors in Pergamum.

The New Name

Ὄνομα is used eleven times in the seven letters and found in two other promises. The Sardians are promised that their names will never be blotted out of the book of life and that their names will be acknowledged before God and his angels (3:5). The phrase "new name" is also used in the Philadelphian promise where the reference is to Jesus (3:12). Both of these texts will be discussed later in turn.

---

115. Petersen, *Haggai and Zechariah 1–8*, 212. He also attempts to link the seven eyes with the name " 'Holy to Yahweh' [which] can be construed as having seven consonants.' The explanation is unconvincing because the inscription actually has eight (קדש ליהוה).

116. Ibid.

"New" (καινός) is used nine times in Revelation to speak of the coming age when all things become new (21:5)—new name (2:17; 3:12), new Jerusalem (3:12; 21:2); new song (5:9; 14:3); new heaven and new earth (21:1). Mulholland (1990) points out that two words exist in Greek for "new"—νέος indicates something brand new that has never existed before, while καινός indicates something new in quality or nature. Revelation always uses the latter because "the 'new name' is something that is new in quality or nature."[117] Louw and Nida, however, avoid such a contrast: "Though this distinction may be applicable to certain contexts and is more in accordance with classical usage, it is not possible to find in all occurrences of καινός and νέος this type of distinction."[118] While exegetical judgments should be avoided based on such tenuous distinctions, it is nevertheless true, as Behm states, "'new' is a leading teleological term in apocalyptic promise [e.g., in Revelation]."[119]

The magical papyri demonstrate a belief in the ancient world that names have power. To know someone's name gives power over that person. Acts 19:13–20 describes how Jewish exorcists in Ephesus attempted to use the name of Jesus to cast out evil spirits. A demon responded that he knew the names of Jesus and Paul, but not their names. When the demonized man beat up the exorcists, the name of the Lord Jesus became honored in the city. An account immediately follows of the Ephesians burning their magical scrolls. They exchanged their magical names for the most powerful name of the Lord Jesus.

The Ephesian *grammata* with their occultic powers were closely linked with Ephesus. These "letters" consisted of six magical names—ἄσκιον, κατάσκιον, λιξ, τετράξ, δαμναμενεύς, and αἴσια.[120] Two of the letters "Lix Tetrax" are coupled in Testament of Solomon 7:5 to name the demon of the wind. Beckwith sees a background of magic behind this promise—the white stone is "a secret charm which will give him power against every assailant and avert every evil."[121] Yet in paradise what need is there for protection against the fornicators and idolaters outside the walls of the messianic kingdom?

---

117. Mulholland, *Revelation*, 110.
118. L&N, 1:594n. 9.
119. Behm, "καινός," *TDNT* 3:449.
120. Cf. Arnold, *Ephesians: Power and Magic*, 15.
121. Beckwith, *Apocalypse of John*, 461.

Court notes that Aristides received a vision of Asclepius during incubatio at Pergamum.[122] To commemorate this occasion he was given a token associated with his new name Theodorus (*Hym. Asklep.* 518). Ramsay discusses at length the transformation of Aristides' life as a consequence of this experience.[123] Hemer concludes that this example "probably offers the most complete analogue for our passage and sets it in sharp contrast with a practice likely to have been current in Pergamum."[124] He concedes, however, that "the evidence for the postulated custom remains circumstantial and inferential."[125] Without further information it is not possible to choose this interpretation conclusively.

Biblical and Extrabiblical Co-texts

In the kenosis passage in Philippians 2:5–11 Paul describes how, after Jesus Christ died on a cross, God exalted him to the highest place, giving him a name above every name—Lord—the equivalent of Yahweh (v. 11).[126]

Levi is told that his posterity will be divided into three offices (*T. Levi.* 8:11). The third will be given a new name, "because from Judah a king will arrive and shall found a new priesthood in accord with the gentile model and for all nations" (v. 14). Kee explains, "That new role, which is said to follow the model of the gentiles, may allude to the Maccabean priest-kings, with their increasingly secular discharge of the dual role."[127]

In the Old Testament and in other ancient literature "the name of a person sometimes revealed his character, his personality, even his destiny. In fact, a person's name was often considered to be but an expression, indeed a revelation, of his true nature."[128] When God gave the covenant promises to the patriarchs, he gave them new names—Abram became Abraham (Gen 17:5) and Jacob became Israel (Gen 32:28). Jacob's new name is given after he wrestles all night with an angel (vv. 24–26).[129] In

---

122. Court, *Myth and History*, 33.

123. Ramsay, *Letters to the Seven Churches*, 227–30.

124. Hemer, *Letters to the Seven Churches of Asia*, 100.

125. Ibid., 101.

126. Fee, *Philippians*, 222–23, discusses whether "Jesus" or "Lord" is the name and opts for "Lord," the name often given to Caesar. He concludes, "Paul well knows to whom he is writing these words, especially since he is now one of the emperor's prisoners and the Philippians are suffering at the hands of Roman citizens as well."

127. Kee, "Testaments of the Twelve Patriarchs," 791n. d.

128. Hawthorne, "Name," *ISBE* 3:481.

129. Neall, *Concept of Character in the Apocalypse*, 133, makes this interesting analogy with Revelation, "As Jacob in his time of trouble (Jer 30:7), under threat of death (Gen

Isaiah two promises are given to God's people concerning a name. God promises the eunuchs who keep his sabbaths: "I will give them an eternal name" (56:5 LXX). And before the creation of the new heavens and new earth, "my servants will be called a new name (ὄνομα καινὸν; 65:15 LXX).

Pergamene Saying Conclusion

The reference to "hidden manna" in the promise is obscure. A spiritual victual now concealed will be restored for the victors to partake of. Boring proposes that this image reflects "the Jewish despair over the destruction of the temple by the Babylonians in 586."[130] Such a historical allusion seems too obscure to be viable. The image of manna naturally follows the reference to Balaam, both being notable aspects of Israel's wilderness wanderings. The Asian churches in a sense are in a wilderness period with obstacles and enemies seeking to turn them aside. The goal of the victors will not be the Promised Land, but the soon-to-be-mentioned New Jerusalem. Charles suggests that part of the victory of the Pergamenes consists in their abstinence from forbidden meats eaten by the unfaithful; the faithful will eat of the heavenly manna.[131] This meaning is sustained by Fekkes and best fits the context: the hidden manna "is an appropriate spiritual compensation for those who have refused the earthly sustenance of food sacrificed to idols . . . ."[132] This is also the second promise with a food motif.

The image of the white stone remains obscure. The white stele in the temple of Augustus is a promising local reference for this image. Because of the Pauline and Petrine letters to the Asian churches, John's audience would be familiar with the traditions of the rock as the source for water and the stone as a building material. The use of ψῆφος does not seem to fit these traditions, however. To alleviate this impasse, we proposed that John himself translated into Greek the familiar reference to God as a Stone that was untranslated in the Septuagint. A fuller identification, perhaps related to John's prophetic ministry in the church, may be lost, making a conclusive determination for this image impossible to resolve.

32:6–7), obtained victory by weeping, seeking a blessing, and prevailing with the angel (Hos. 12:4), so the saints in their great tribulation obtain victory through the persistent struggle with God which issues in divine blessing."

130. Boring, *Revelation*, 90.

131. Charles, *Revelation*, 1:66.

132. Fekkes, *Isaiah and Prophetic Traditions*, 128.

Is the new name on the white stone to be that of the believer or of Jesus? Trench answers that the understood object of λαμβάνων which ends the promise should be "white stone" and not "new name." The new name is therefore not the victor's but something better: "It is the new name of God or of Christ, *'my new name'* (cf. iii.12); some revelation of the glory of God, only in that higher state capable of being communicated by Him to his people, and which they only can understand who have actually received."[133] Fekkes, however, responds, "Despite the similar terminology, it seems best to see 2.17 and 3.12 as separate promises, each with a different focus and aim."[134] In the Gospel of John Jesus presents himself as the manna and the living water; in Ephesians and 1 Peter he is the living Stone and the Rock. The listeners at this point would probably be thinking of these Jesus traditions as well as the various names under which Jesus is presenting himself in the epithets, rather than their own new names. Since a reference to the new name arises again in the Philadelphia letter, we will defer further discussion until then.

The Thyatiran Victor Saying

The victor saying in the letter to Thyatira is found in 2:26–28. Hemer (1986:124) justifiably calls this promise "probably the most difficult of the seven." Zerwick cites the opening of the main promise as an example of pendent nominative. It is a form of anacoluthon consisting "in the enunciation of the local (not grammatical) subject at the beginning of the sentence, followed by a sentence in which that subject is taken up by a pronoun in the case required by the syntax."[135] This is seen in ὁ νικῶν καὶ ὁ τηρῶν ... τὰ ἔργα μου ... δώσω αὐτῷ ἐξουσίαν....

This is the only promise where the present participle τηρῶν is added. The verb τηρέω is a key word in Johannine literature—Gospel (18x), 1 John (7x), and Revelation (11x). Noteworthy is its usage in four beatitudes—1:3; 14:12; 16:15; and 22:7. These are likewise closely linked to the promises (cf. chapter 2), because the blessings of the beatitudes are going to the victors.

Ἔργον is likewise a prominent word in Johannine literature—Gospel (27x), Epistles (5x), and Revelation (20x), with 12 occurrences in the seven letters. Earlier in the Thyatiran letter (2:23) Jesus declares to all the churches that he searches the hearts and minds. He promises them that

---

133. Trench, *Commentary on the Epistles*, 141.
134. Fekkes, *Isaiah and Prophetic Traditions*, 128–29.
135. Zerwick, *Biblical Greek*, §25.

rewards will be issued based on each person's works (cf. Isa 40:10; Rev 22:12). The reference in 2:23 suggests a likely reason that works are also mentioned at the beginning of this victor saying. Jesus emphasizes that the victor must keep his works until the end (cf. Matt 24:13). This "must mean that he does the same works as Jesus did or acts according to his will."[136] Beasley-Murray cogently states that "this is the nearest we have in the seven letters to a definition of the conqueror."[137]

Under the Attalids Thyatira associated itself with Pergamum and was regarded as the most southerly city in the district of Mysia, although later it was considered a city of Lydia. This relationship between the two cities is seen by Ramsay as also evident in Revelation: "There may be traced a common type both in the preliminary addresses and in the promises at the end of those two letters. The spirit . . . is throughout of dazzlingly impressive might, the irresistible strength of a great monarch and a vast well-ordered army."[138] The promise sets the victorious Christian in the place of the Roman emperor, who was the ruler of the nations and destroyed his enemies with his legions. Ramsay sees irony here because Thyatira (perhaps also Philadelphia) was the smallest, weakest, and least distinguished of the seven cities. Thyatira "seemed in every way the least fitted by nature and by history to rule over the nations."[139] Such an explanation, while possible, remains indeterminate.

The image of the shepherd's rod must have been a familiar one to the Thyatirans. As a city noted for its trade guilds and home of Lydia the purple seller (Acts 16:14–15), the preparation of garments made from wool supplied by local shepherds was a thriving industry. Wool was the material most used by the Greeks for warm clothing.[140] Sardis was likewise noted for its garment industry, and Laodicea, as we will see, was famous for the wool of its black sheep. That the rod of authority used by such local shepherds symbolized the future rule of the victors must have been astounding to the Thyatiran believers.

Shepherd the Nations with a Rod of Iron

The initial clause promises authority over the nations, while the second clause describes how the victor will exercise that authority. Charles makes

---

136. Leivestad, *Christ the Conqueror*, 214.
137. Beasley-Murray, *Revelation*, 93.
138. Ramsay, *Letters to the Seven Churches*, 241–42.
139. Ibid., 244.
140. See Bonfante and Jaunzems, "Clothing and Ornament," 3:1376.

a point regarding the use of "authority" in Revelation: "when a limited authority is implied, ἐξουσία stands without the article . . . , with the article full authority in the circumstances defined in the context is implied."[141] However, his examples in 9:3 (without) and 9:19 (with) contravene his point: the locusts of the fifth trumpet and the horses of the sixth trumpet receive similar authority to work their judgments. Again, the authority mentioned in 17:12 (without) and 17:13 (with) is identical, so any variation is related to style rather than to meaning.

The substitution of ἐξουσία for κληρονομία lies in the Septuagintal background of Psalm 2:8. The idea there is one of lasting possession obtained through conquest, expulsion, and extermination, particularly in relation to the conquest of Canaan (cf. Num 34:2). Foerster also cites Ezekiel 25:4 as a background, where inheritance "can be used of the possession of alien peoples."[142] The inheritance of the victors is in fact rule over the nations. The conjecture of Hemer—that the substitution might be noteworthy because "the Christian in Thyatira might have seemed in a condition of powerlessness"[143]—seems to miss the point.

Biblical and Extrabiblical Co-texts

This promise shows the clearest relationship to an Old Testament text—Psalm 2:8–9. Whether it is a quotation or an allusion is debatable. Many commentators echo the familiar truism that no quotations from the Old Testament are found in Revelation.[144] Fekkes, however, argues convincingly otherwise: "Thus the contextual visibility of this messianic promise based on a messianically understood OT text is undoubtedly intentional and goes beyond the bounds of an allusion."[145] Archer and Chirichigno assign an A/A- rating to the two parts of the quotation, which indicates a reasonably or completely accurate rendering from the Masoretic text and the Septuagint.[146] The textual basis of this promise—whether the Masoretic text or the Septuagint—is a matter of intense debate.

---

141. Charles, *Revelation*, 1:75.
142. Foerster, "κλῆρος κτλ," *TDNT* 3:778.
143. Hemer, *Letters to the Seven Churches of Asia*, 124.
144. E.g., see Caird, *Revelation of St. John the Divine*, 45.
145. Fekkes, *Isaiah and Prophetic Traditions*, 68.
146. Archer and Chirichigno, *Old Testament Quotations*, 57.

Psalm 2:8–9 MT	Revelation 2:26–27	Psalm 2:8–9 LXX
תְּרֹעֵם בְּשֵׁבֶט בַּרְזֶל וְאֶתְּנָה גוֹיִם נַחֲלָתֶךָ כִּכְלִי יוֹצֵר תְּנַפְּצֵם	δώσω αὐτῷ ἐξουσίαν ἐπὶ τῶν ἐθνῶν καὶ ποιμανεῖ αὐτοὺς ἐν ῥάβδῳ σιδηρᾷ ὡς τὰ σκεύη τὰ κεραμικὰ συντρίβεται	δώσω σοὶ ἔθνη τὴν κληρονομίαν σου... ποιμανεῖς αὐτοὺς ἐν ῥάβδῳ σιδηρᾷ ὡς σκεῦος κεραμέως συντρίψεις αὐτούς

The Septuagint translators derived תרעם from רָעָה and vocalized it תִּרְעֵם, hence ποιμανεῖς, while the Masoretic text derived it from רעע and vocalized it תְּרֹעֵם, hence Symmachus' translation συντρίψεις.[147] Black states: "There seems little doubt that ποιμαίνειν at Revelation 2:27=LXX Psalm 2:9 is a *mistranslation* of the Hebrew word (*ra'ah* or *ra'a*), taken over by the writer of the Apocalypse."[148] However, Archer and Chirichigno maintain that תְּרֹעֵם is from רָעָה, not רָעַע (=רָצַץ).[149] Craigie summarizes persuasively, "Although either reading is possible . . . the context as a whole suggests the more powerful 'break them.'"[150]

Caird presents a novel alternative: "The preferable theory is that John, independently of the Septuagint, made the same mistake which the Septuagint translator made before him—a perfectly understandable mistake for one to whom Greek was a foreign language—of supposing that, because the Hebrew *r'h* can mean both to pasture and to destroy, its Greek equivalent must be capable of bearing both meanings also."[151] Caird presents a good argument on the level of practical likelihood; however, it seems unrealistic to suppose John had no knowledge of the Septuagint reading, which he appears to have followed here. Trudinger, however, argues that the quotation as a whole is closer to the Hebrew original than to the Septuagint.[152]

What then did John mean by ποιμαίνω? Johnson calls a paradox the combination of this mild word with those of "iron rod" and "shatter."[153] The word is used positively in 7:17 where, speaking of the white-robed survivors of the great tribulation (7:17), the Lamb will shepherd them and lead (ὁδηγήσει) them. Mealy calls this "a veiled promise that Jesus

---

147. Cf. Swete, *Apocalypse of St. John*, 46; Charles, *Revelation*, 1:75–76.
148. Black, "Some Greek Words," 137.
149. Archer and Chirichigno, *Old Testament Quotations*, 57.
150. Craigie, *Psalms 1–50*, 64.
151. Caird, *Revelation of St. John*, 45.
152. Trudinger, "Some Observations," 84–85.
153. Johnson, "Revelation," 12:446.

will lead the overcomers to himself and to God the Father (as similarly in 2:17, etc.)."[154] Both of these verbs are found in the shepherd Psalm 23 (22 LXX), where the rod (ῥάβδος; Heb שבט) is likewise mentioned. While rod originally described a shepherd's club tipped with iron nails (cf. Mic 7:14), the term came to be associated with authority (Ps 45:6; 44:7 LXX), hence the translation "scepter," and punishment (2 Sam 7:14). The rod (שבט) in Genesis 49:10 was already understood messianically when it was translated as "ruler" (ἄρχων). It seems clear that John gives two meanings to ποιμαίνω—the first pastoral towards his people and the other authoritarian toward the nations.

Instead of translating "rule" for the latter, Charles argues that the secondary Hebrew meaning of רעה "to devastate" (usually "to shepherd") should be understood in 2:27, 12:5, and 19:15.[155] The parallel verbs συντρίβω and πατάσσω, he believes, point to such a translation. To translate as "destroy" in 19:15 is particularly attractive since the scene is one of total annihilation. Yet Black questions whether John understood the word in this sense or intended to convey this meaning to his readers.[156] Since John has already rejected the stronger Hebrew connotation by following the reading of the Septuagint in 2:27, Charles's suggestion must be qualified.

The latter half of the quotation might have been omitted; in fact, it is not repeated in 12:5 and 19:15. It is a metaphor of the Messiah's rule over the nations. Again the translation is problematic. In the Septuagint the verb συντρίψεις is future and a coordinate of "will rule"; in Revelation it is a present passive. Charles recommends that συντρίβεται be taken as a Hebraism and therefore regarded as a future συντριβήσεται, a reading favored by a number of later manuscripts. He rejects a translation like "as pottery is broken," preferring one like "he will break them as pottery."[157] In Jeremiah 19:11 both verbal forms are used: συντρίψω τὸν λαὸν τοῦτον καὶ τὴν πόλιν ταύτην καθὼς συντρίβεται ἄγγος ὀστράκινον. Here the judgment upon Judah and Jerusalem is also likened to broken pottery (cf. Isa 30:14; Jer 18:1–11). Determining which translation to adopt in the promise is difficult because both are defensible. It seems best, however, to read it as a present passive—"is broken"—even though it produces an awkward translation.

---

154. Mealy, *After the Thousand Years*, 175n. 2.
155. Charles, *Revelation*, 1:170; cf. Beasley-Murray, *Revelation*, 93.
156. Black, "Some Greek Words," 137.
157. Charles, *Revelation*, 1:177.

Psalm 2, because of its messianic nature, played a visible role in early Christian *testimonia*. Verses 1–2 are quoted in Acts 4:25–26 and verse 7 in Acts 13:33 and Hebrews 1:5; 5:5. These New Testament texts emphasize the relationship between the Father and the Son regarding Jesus' resurrection, superiority over angels, and eternal priesthood. This emphasis is likewise seen in Revelation 2:28, which states that the victor will receive even as Jesus did from the Father. Such a qualifying statement in the promise is similar to that in 3:21. Because of ellipsis, the object of his reception must be supplied. Authority, or a rod of iron, are the most obvious choices from the preceding verse, but as we have seen, the figure represents the same reality.

Jesus' reception of authority from the Father is a theme in the Gospels. The so-named Great Commission in Matthew 28:18 begins, "All authority has been given to me." And in his high priestly prayer following the Last Supper Jesus emphasizes that his authority over all people has been given him by the Father (John 17:2; cf. 3:35; 13:3).

In Psalm of Solomon 17:22–24 the messianic king is "to destroy the unrighteous rulers, to purge Jerusalem from gentiles . . . to smash the arrogance of sinners like a potter's jar; To shatter all their substance with an iron rod; to destroy the unlawful nations with the word of his mouth." Testament of Judah 24:6, after referring to a Star from Jacob, reads, "and from your root will arise the Shoot, and through it will arise the rod of righteousness for the nations, to judge and to save all that call on the Lord."[158]

A final text that speaks of authority over the nations is Daniel 7:14. The nations serve the Son of Man because his authority is everlasting. In 7:27 he hands over this authority to the saints.

The Morning Star

Ramsay links this part of the victor saying with the military imagery found in the city's history and in the earlier promise to rule: "The brightness, gleam, and glitter, as of 'an army with banners' which rules through the opening address and the concluding promise, is expressed in a milder spirit without the terrible character, though the brilliance remains or is even increased in the images of 'the morning star.'"[159] Such an interpretation is surely a bit fantastic!

---

158. Collins, *Scepter and the Star*, 63, 91–92, believes that, although there are Christian elements in this text, this verse is part of its Jewish core which preserves Jewish traditions.

159. Ramsay, *Letters to the Seven Churches*, 245.

Lohmeyer links the morning star to the planet Venus, which from Babylonian times was a symbol of rule: "In römischer Zeit ist deshalb Venus die Verleiherin von Sieg und Herrschaft."[160] The victorious generals Sulla and Pompey erected temples to Venus, and Julius Caesar erected a temple in her honor before the battle of Pharsalus (Appian *Bell. civ.* 2.68–69). The Roman legions carried her zodiac sign, the bull, on their standards. The morning star was thus a familiar image of victory and rule throughout the Greco-Roman world. The contrast between the sovereignty of Christ and the prevailing Roman powers "would help to explain how the language of Num 24.17 had been brought into the arena of the church's current conflict."[161]

Biblical and Extrabiblical Co-texts

The morning star is generally understood to be an allusion to Balaam's third oracle: "a star will rise out of Jacob" (Num 24:17).[162] The certainty of this observation is reinforced when the next line is noted, "and a rod (בֵט) will rise out of Israel." The image of the rod figured prominently in the first promise drawn from Psalm 2:9. Reference to the morning star seems less obscure and out of place when this dynamic relationship is understood. As already noted, the rod was interpreted messianically in Genesis 49:10 (LXX) which reads, "a ruler ($ἄρχων$) will not fail from Judah." Here the rod is likened to a man destined to rule. Philo (*Praem.* 95) says that this man will come forth "leading a host and warring furiously, who will subdue great and populous nations." John's use of the prophetic form and the prophetic curse in the Balaam chronicle plus his mention of Balaam by name in the Pergamene letter (2:14) make this allusion certain.

Daniel 12:3 speaks of the wise who will shine as stars forever. The immediate background is 11:33–45, which describes the end time when these same wise saints will fall by sword, fire, and captivity at the hands of the wicked king of the north.[163] Young summarizes, "Those who during the period of persecution have dealt prudently and wisely . . . shall receive the glorious reward of their labors in that they shall shine eternally as the brightness of the firmament and as the stars."[164]

---

160. "In Roman times Venus is therefore the bestower of victory and rule"; Lohmeyer, *Offenbarung*, 30.

161. Hemer, *Letters to the Seven Churches of Asia*, 126.

162. Cf. Bauckham, *Climax of Prophecy*, 323ff.

163. The reference in 11:30 to the ships of Kittim (Cyprus) is based upon Balaam's prophecy in Numbers 24:24.

164. Young, *Prophecy of Daniel*, 256.

Luke 1:78 refers to Christ's birth as the "dayspring" or "dawn" (ἀνατολὴ). This Christian messianic interpretation of ἀνατολὴ is based on the Septuagint translation of "shoot" (צמח) as "a rising" (ἀνατολὴ) in Numbers 24:17, Jeremiah 23:5, and Zechariah 3:8; 6:12. Schlier, after reviewing the interpretation of ἀνατολὴ among various church fathers, opts for the translation, "star shining from heaven."[165] The verb form is found 2 Peter 1:19: "and the morning star will rise (καὶ φωσφόρος ἀνατείλῃ) in your hearts." This is again a probable allusion to Numbers 24:17, whose messianic interpretation seems to have become a fixed Christian exegetical tradition.[166]

4 Ezra 7:97 speaks of the seven orders of the sleep of the righteous dead, the sixth being they are "made like the light of the stars." 1 Enoch 104:2 states that the suffering righteous will "shine like lights in heaven." These two texts have an obvious dependence upon Daniel 12:3. For his service in the temple, Simon the high priest is likened to the morning star (ἀστὴρ ἑωθινὸς; Sir 50:6). Testament of Levi 18:3 states of the coming priest: "His star shall rise in heaven like a king," while Testament of Judah 24:1 reads: "And after this there shall arise for you a star from Jacob in peace" (cf. 1QM 11:6–7; 4QTestim 9–13). The Damascus Document calls the star the interpreter of the law (CD 7:18–19). After reviewing these texts, Collins persuasively concludes that "Balaam's oracle was widely understood in a messianic sense."[167]

Thyatiran Saying Conclusion

The double promise to Thyatira is the only saying with proximate co-texts in the Old Testament. The Asian audience must have recognized the ambivalence in the main verb—"rule" or "destroy." Trench proposes: "Instead of the mere unmingled judgment which lay in the passage as it originally stood in that Psalm, He expresses by it now judgment mingled with mercy, judgment behind which purposes of grace are concealed, and only waiting their due time to appear."[168] The transfer of rule from the Son of Man to the saints in Daniel is likewise seen in Revelation. Johnson notes that "John seems to alternate between the rule of Christ (1:5; 11:15) and the rule of the saints (1:6; 2:26–27)."[169] This promise in Revelation,

---

165. Schlier, "ἀνατολὴ," *TDNT* 1:353.
166. Cf. Bauckham, *Jude, 2 Peter*, 226.
167. Collins, *Scepter and the Star*, 64.
168. Trench, *Epistles to the Seven Churches*, 157.
169. Johnson, "Revelation," 12:514.

according to Craigie, "contains an anticipation of the ultimate rule and triumph of the man born to be King in the language and imagery of Ps 2...."[170] Those who are victorious are promised a share of that rule and triumph at his coming.

Ancient expositors presented a range of interpretations for the image of the morning star. Victorinus thought it was the first resurrection, Andreas suggested the saints putting the fallen Lucifer under their feet, and Beatus and Bede thought it Christ himself.[171] The star motif in the scriptural background cited indicates rule and sovereignty. Wall suggests that the morning star "again symbolizes the eschatological situation of the community of overcomers by pointing to its future participation in the triumph of God's rule over all those secular and materialistic pretenders to the Lord's throne."[172] Yet above all, the Septuagint reading of Numbers 24:17 suggests that the star is a person. An important part of the reward given at the parousia is the presence of Jesus himself. Mealy thinks "it is more than conceivable that along with the promise of the morning star, two other cryptic promises refer to Jesus as well, namely the promise of a white stone, and the promise of hidden manna (Rev 2.17)."[173] We have made a similar suggestion in our discussion of the white stone and hidden manna. However, any definitive conclusion regarding the morning star will be deferred until the next chapter.

The Sardian Victor Saying

The text of the Sardian promise is found in 3:5. A variant of οὕτως, perhaps early, is οὗτος. Hemer suggests it "could easily have arisen from dictation, being easier and a phonetic equivalent."[174] Beckwith questions whether οὕτως should be translated "likewise"; to do so (1) "would imply a certain distinction between the ὁ νικῶν and the unsullied, whereas the latter must be included in the former," and (2) "blending of the class introduced by the formula ὁ νικῶν with the preceding sentence is at variance with the usage of all the other epistles."[175] He proposes that οὕτως be understood to repeat the participle νικῶν, "thus," for example, being a conqueror. In the two other occurrences of οὕτως in the letters—2:15

---

170. Craigie, *Psalms 1–50*, 69.
171. See Swete, *Apocalypse of St. John*, 47.
172. Wall, *Revelation*, 79.
173. Mealy, *After the Thousand Years*, 215.
174. Hemer, *Letters to the Seven Churches of Asia*, 147–48.
175. Beckwith, *Apocalypse of John*, 476.

and 3:16—both link what precedes. If the usage is debatable here, it would be best to follow these other examples. The "unsullied" in Sardis will be among the victors, if they continue to walk worthy. There is no distinction of persons, only of time—present and future.

Beckwith's second objection is invalid, because "promise bleed" was shown to occur in both the Smyrnean (2:10) and Thyatiran (2:23) letters. In fact, John specifically moves the praise saying to precede the victor saying in this letter because of the connection in imagery. Beckwith invalidates his point by acknowledging that an eschatological promise is introduced before the victor formula in 2:10 as well as in 3:4 and 3:20. Οὕτως should therefore be translated "likewise" or "in this manner."[176]

The fourfold use of ὄνομα is noteworthy. The Sardians have a name (i.e., a reputation) that they are alive, but in fact are dead (v. 1). A few names (i.e., individuals) in the city have not compromised but remain worthy (v. 4). The other two uses are in the victor saying. The promise never to erase the victor's name from the book of life alludes to Deuteronomy 9:14 (LXX), where ὄνομα is likewise used. Swete comments pointedly, "The 'few names' in Sardis which are distinguished by resisting the prevailing torpor of spiritual death find their reward in finally retaining their place among the living in the City of God."[177]

White Garments

The ἱματίοιν was the most common outer garment for men and women in the Greco-Roman world. This rectangular garment came in various sizes and was draped around the body. The quality of the fabric distinguished the social status or wealth of the wearer. Related terms are ἔνδυμα, ἐσθής, and χιτών—all used almost synonymously in the biblical literature.[178] Besides ἱματίοιν (3:4, 5, 18; 4:4), στολή (6:11; 7:9, 13) and βύσσινος (19:14; cf. 19:8) are two other words used for clothing in Revelation. The adjective λευκός is used in each of these texts, suggesting that their meaning is synonymous. The semantic relationship between these terms will be developed further in chapter 5.

White is used five times in chapters 1–3 (out of fifteen times in the book). In 1:14 the Ancient of Days is pictured with hair white as snow and wool. White is here portrayed as a color both heavenly and divine. The Pergamenes are promised a white stone (2:17). In the Sardian praise

---

176. Ibid., 475.
177. Swete, *Apocalypse of St. John*, 52.
178. Cf. L&N §6.162.

The Text of the Victor Sayings

saying (3:4), the image of white garments is first used. A few have not soiled (ἐμόλυναν) their garments and thus walk with Christ in white. Those in white are called "worthy," in contrast to those called to repentance who are living in sin. Garber comments, "The white clothing marks their identification with the cause of God and his kingdom. It is a gift and cannot be earned, although the character of the heavenly robe or body is conditioned by the character and actions of the earthly body (cf. I Cor. 6:18)."[179] Garber's linkage of the soiled garments to unfaithfulness regarding baptismal vows draws too heavily on Pauline imagery (e.g., Gal 3:27; Rom 13:14) and fails to grasp John's perspective.

This promise is reiterated in the final letter where the Laodiceans are told to buy white garments to hide the shame of their spiritual nakedness (3:18). This may be an allusion to the Fall account in which God clothes Adam and Eve after they discover they are naked (Gen 3:10–11, 21; cf. chapter 3 regarding nakedness in athletics). While the Laodiceans are exhorted to purchase their white garments, the Sardians will be given theirs. In both cases white garments are related to moral worthiness. These statements regarding white garments are two sides of the same spiritual coin. As Ulfgard fittingly states, white garments are "both an earthly possession which qualifies for heavenly existence and a feature of heavenly existence."[180]

In the last chapter we discussed the relationship of the color white to victory; here we will examine its significance in antiquity as the color of purity and innocence. Ramsay asserts that wearing white garments "was appropriate for those who were engaged in the worship of the gods, for purity was prescribed as a condition of engaging in divine service, though usually the purity was understood in a merely ceremonial sense."[181]

Deissman explains the scene of the white-robed multitude in Revelation 7 as a heavenly panegyric modeled after religious ceremonies seen throughout Asia Minor. He quotes a decree from the Asian city of Stratonicea prescribing that hymns be sung daily in the bouleuterion to honor the city's patron deities by thirty boys, "clothed in white and crowned with a twig, holding a twig in their hands." He suggests that John modeled his heavenly choir after similar choirs of sacred singers.[182] What his audience "beheld in heaven was something that had, by associa-

---

179. Garber, "Symbolism of Heavenly Robes," 257.
180. Ulfgard, *Feast and Future*, 81.
181. Ramsay, *Letters to the Seven Churches*, 282.
182. Deissman, *Bible Studies*, 368–70.

tion with their native soil, become familiar and dear to them—a choir of pious singers in festive attire; and if they had an ear to hear what the Spirit said to the churches, they could also, of course, surmise that in this instance what came from holy lips was a new song."[183] Charles rightly calls this suggestion "a complete misconception of our text."[184] Moffat suggests another ceremonial function, that "the language reflects that of the votive inscriptions in Asia Minor, where soiled clothes disqualified the worshipper and dishonoured the god."[185] Philostratus describes a visit by Apollonius to a cave at Lebadea. Those who visited the oracle were dressed in white raiment (*Vit. Apoll.* 8.19).

The allusion to the wool industry at Sardis, according to Johnson, "intensifies the image of soiled and defiled garments."[186] Sardis and Laodicea were noted for their wool, and the image of white garments appears in both letters. Commentators as early as Trench saw a reference in 3:18 to the black sheep for which Laodicea was famous.[187] Their wool was used to make expensive black glossy garments. After surveying the ancient literary sources, Hemer accepts the premise of a contrast between the white garments and the black wool.[188] Beckwith, however, challenges such an application because "in that case we should expect in the following purpose clause reference to such garments rather than to nakedness."[189] What is more probable here is the use of irony—the Laodiceans, who come from a place noted for its clothing, are found naked by Jesus. The mention of white garments in this victor saying diminishes the likelihood of an individualized local reference in the Laodicean letter. Yet it is significant that the reference to white garments is found in the letters to Sardis and Laodicea, both of which were textile centers.

Biblical and Extrabiblical Co-texts

White is an eschatological or heavenly color in every New Testament text except Matthew 5:36 and John 4:35.[190] In the parable of the weeds Jesus tells how after the harvest at the end of the age, the righteous will shine

---

183. Ibid., 370.
184. Charles, *Revelation*, 1:211.
185. Moffat, "Revelation of St. John," 5:364.
186. Johnson, "Revelation," 12:449.
187. Cf. Trench, *Epistles to the Seven Churches*, 212.
188. Hemer, *Letters to the Seven Churches*, 199–201.
189. Beckwith, *Apocalypse of John*, 490.
190. Cf. Michaelis, "λευκός," *TDNT* 4:246–47.

like the sun in the heavenly kingdom (Matt 13:43). At his transfiguration Jesus' garments appeared dazzlingly white as light (Matt 17:2; Mark 9:3; Luke 9:29). The reference to the glistening character of Jesus' clothing reflects the Old Testament concept that "the glory of God is always conceived as shining brilliance or bright light."[191] The angel standing outside the empty tomb was wearing a white garment (Mark 16:5; cf. Luke 24:4; John 20:12). The two angels who spoke to the disciples at Jesus' ascension were also dressed in white clothing (Acts 1:10). These white garments worn by the angels "are not so much descriptive as an expression of the transcendent character of their δόξα."[192]

In the parable of the wedding banquet every guest except one is wearing a wedding garment; that one is thrown into the outer darkness (Matt 22:1–13). Hill points to the likely interpretation: "The wedding garment probably symbolizes righteousness (*dikaiosune*), that faithfulness and obedience which can be expected of those who are members of the Kingdom, or Church."[193] In Hermas' vision (68.3) the faithful are rewarded with white garments.

In 2 Maccabees 11:8 God sends a good angel dressed in white to lead the Jews to victory. Ezra sees those at the messianic feast clothed in white (*4 Ezra* 2:38–40), in garments called "immortal clothing" (v. 45). Enoch sees the Great Glory sitting on his throne wearing a gown that was shining more brightly than the sun and whiter than snow (*1 En* 14:20; cf. 71:1 for a similar description of angels). In 1 Enoch 62:15–16 the righteous are said to wear garments of glory, which will become garments of life that will never wear out. The Lord tells Michael to remove the earthly clothing from Enoch and put him into clothes of glory (*2 En* 22:8), no doubt a heavenly, or spiritual, body. Regarding the Ascension of Isaiah, "the heavenly robes which the saints put on after death are a symbol of their transformed state; they are mentioned frequently in the Christian portions of AscenIs; cf. 3:25; 4:16f.; 7:22; 8:14, 26; 9:2, 9–11, 17f., 24–26; 11:40."[194] 1QS 4:7–8 speaks of a "crown of glory with majestic raiment in eternal light." Philo (*Contempl.* 66) describes a monastic group called the Therapeutae who dressed in white garments for their greatest feast on the fiftieth day. Rabbinic sources reflect a great fondness for white clothes, which "are worn on joyous occasions or feast days, but they are also

---

191. Lane, *Gospel of Mark*, 318.
192. Kittel, "ἄγγελος," *TDNT* 1:84n. 67.
193. Hill, *New Testament Prophecy*, 302–3.
194. Knibb, "Martyrdom and Ascension of Isaiah," 2:157n. p.

regarded as a mark of distinction."[195] In first-century Judaism the dead were buried in white clothing.

Job is asked by the Lord if he is able to adorn himself with glory and splendor (Job 40:10). And the psalmist declares that God is "clothed with splendor and majesty; He wraps himself in light as a garment" (Ps 104:2). Garber writes, "Job agrees with Psalms in linking God's sovereignty with imagery of glorious clothing."[196] The preacher enjoins his audience that their garments should always be white (Eccl 9:8). Isaiah 61:10 combines wedding imagery with that of clothing: "for he has clothed me with a garment of salvation (ἱμάτιον σωτηρίου) and a tunic of joy." The Ancient of Days sat on a throne wearing white garments, with hair white as wool (Dan 7:9). The angelic messenger whom Daniel sees is clothed in (white) linen (βύσσινα; Dan 10:5). Zechariah sees a vision of Satan accusing the high priest Joshua (Zech 3:1–2). The high priest's sin is represented as dirty garments (ἱμάτια ῥυπαρὰ; v. 3). After God takes away Joshua's sin, he commands that the high priest be clothed with a new robe.

The Book of Life

The Sardians have a name (i.e., reputation) for being alive but are in fact dead (Rev 3:1). Those who are worthy are promised that their name will be maintained in the real book of life. Ramsay finds the contrast between life and death in the Sardian letter significant: the history of Sardis was in the past; she was a city whose better days were over.[197]

The Jews around AD 85–90 adopted Eighteen Benedictions, the twelfth enjoining that "the Nazarenes and the *minim* . . . be blotted out from the book of life."[198] This "Heretic Benediction" was "probably intended as a means of marking out Jewish Christians and excluding them from the synagogue community."[199] If Revelation is dated late to around AD 95 and the synagogues in Smyrna, Sardis, and Philadelphia were using this injunction for exclusionary purposes, this promise by Jesus counters the Jewish attempt to keep Asian believers from their heavenly reward.[200] Though this interpretation is attractive, it is precluded because an earlier date for Revelation's writing (ca. AD 69) is more consistent with the evi-

---

195. Michaelis, "λευκός," *TDNT* 4:244.
196. Garber, "Symbolism of Heavenly Robes," 23.
197. Ramsay, *Letters to the Seven Churches*, 274–75.
198. Barrett, *New Testament Background*, §200.
199. Barrett, *Gospel According to St. John*, 362.
200. Cf. Hemer, *Letters to the Seven Churches of Asia*, 9.

dence.²⁰¹ Because this image is so pervasive in biblical literature, its background is probably not found in the twelfth benediction.

Greek cities maintained a list of its citizens in a public register. When someone committed a criminal action and was condemned, he lost his citizenship and his name was subsequently erased from the register. Moffatt cites several inscriptions that mention this action, which use the same Greek verb ἐξαλείφω to describe the act of removal.²⁰²

Biblical and Extrabiblical Co-texts

Following the return of the seven-two, Jesus tells them to rejoice because their names are written in heaven (Luke 10:20). Concerning this verse, Schrenk writes that "we have a particularly solemn image which carries with it the thought of the ancient custom of inscribing in a list of citizens, but which is also linked with the idea of the book of life."²⁰³ Paul similarly tells the Philippians to rejoice always because his fellow workers, like themselves, have τὰ ὀνόματα ἐν βίβλῳ ζωῆς (Phil 4:3). Hawthorne sees the background of Philippi being a Roman colony as important here: "Just as Philippi, and other cities like it, must have had a civic register that included all the names of its citizens, so the heavenly commonwealth (cf. 3:20) has its own roll where God inscribes the names of those to whom he promises life."²⁰⁴

The writer of Hebrews tells his audience that they have come to Mount Zion, the heavenly Jerusalem, as members of the church of the firstborn whose names are written in heaven (Heb 12:23). The perfect προσεληλύθατε used in verse 22 suggests the writer's eschatological perspective differs from John's—that the believers are already enjoying the benefits of heavenly citizenship. The writer of Hebrews, like John, understands that it is through faith these blessings are enjoyed (cf. 11:1ff) and that the full manifestation of the heavenly city is yet to come (13:14). Smith rightly summarizes, "There is a general consensus that all of the NT references to the book of life, including Luke 10:20 and Heb 12:23 which do not use the exact phrase, designate the same book."²⁰⁵

---

201. In "The Early Christians in Ephesus and the Date of Revelation, Again," I present a lengthy discussion of the arguments for the early and late dates, concluding that the internal evidence of Revelation coupled with the historical situation of the Roman Empire argue for a date of writing before the fall of Jerusalem in AD 70.

202. Moffatt, "Revelation of St. John the Divine," 5:365.

203. Schrenk, "γράφω κτλ," *TDNT* 1:770.

204. Hawthorne, *Philippians*, 181.

205. Smith, "Book of Life," 221–22.

1 Enoch makes a number of references to the heavenly book. In 47:3 Enoch sees the Ancient of Days sitting on the throne with the books of the living ones open before him. Again Enoch is shown the heavenly tablets and told to read them: "I read that book and all the deeds of humanity . . ." (81:2; cf. 90:20; 93:1–3; 103:2). In 108:3 Enoch is told that "the names of (the sinners) shall be blotted out from the Book of Life and the books of the Holy One." Jubilees 5:13 states that judgment upon people is based on their works written in the heavenly tablets (cf. 16:9; 23:32). 1QM 12.2–3 refers to a book with the names of the heavenly armies who, after receiving their rewards, will rule for eternity.

After Israel had sinned at Mount Sinai by making the golden calf, Moses interceded with God for the nation. If God would not forgive the people's sin, Moses asked that his name be erased from God's book (Exod 32:32). The Lord replied, "If anyone has sinned before me, I will erase (αλείψω) him from my book" (v. 33; cf. Deut 9:143). Jesus' promise here in Revelation is the denial (οὐ μή) of these statements in the Pentateuch. Isaiah declares that on the day when the Branch appears, holy are "all those who are recorded for life in Jerusalem" (Isa 4:3; cf. 48:19). Lightfoot summarizes, "The 'book of life' in the figurative language of the Old Testament is the register of the covenant people. . . . Hence 'to be blotted out of the book of the living' mean 'to forfeit the privileges of the theocracy,' 'to be shut out from God's favour.'"[206]

Daniel sees books opened in the heavenly court (7:10); Michael tells him what is written in the book of truth (10:21). Following the great distress everyone whose name is written in the book will be delivered (12:1). Goldingay makes an unwarranted distinction between this latter book and the first two by stating that the book in 12:1 is "not the 'reliable book' of 10:21, which included the future acts of the wicked as well as those of the people of God, nor one of the 'books' mentioned in 7:10, which recorded the past basis for God's judgment, but a list of those who belong to God's people, the citizen list of the true Jerusalem."[207] Beale correctly observes "That the book of Daniel 12 should be thought of in relation to that of Daniel 7 is natural since both appear in contexts of eschatological persecution."[208]

---

206. Lightfoot, *Philippians*, 159.
207. Goldingay, *Daniel*, 306.
208. Beale, *Use of Daniel in Jewish Apocalyptic Literature*, 239.

The Confession of a Name

Jesus next promises to confess (ὁμολογήσω) the victor's name before his Father and his Father's angels. *BAGD*, s.v., suggests the sense of "acknowledge," which is the translation found in the NIV and NJB. This is the second of three occurrences in the victor sayings where Jesus speaks of "my Father" (cf. 2:28; 3:21). It is the only place in Revelation where the angels are called "his" (αὐτοῦ) in relationship to the Father.

Biblical and Extrabiblical Co-texts

Jesus' statement to the Twelve in Matthew 10:32 is a closely related text, "Therefore everyone who confesses me before others, I will also confess (ὁμολογέσω) him before my Father in heaven." Whoever denies Christ will likewise be denied by him before the heavenly Father (v. 33). This eschatological promise then has both a positive and a negative side. The parallel in Luke 12:8 reads "before the angels of God" rather than "my Father in heaven." The preposition ἐνώπιον is used synonymously with ἔμροσθεν in the denial clause (v. 9). The use of ἔμπροσθεν, according to Marshall, "stresses that a public acknowledgement is meant, and it may refer specifically to standing before a judge; the fact that the second part of the saying alludes to the heavenly court does not demand that a forensic situation be seen on the earthly level also, but it is not impossible that Jesus may have had this in mind."[209] In these sayings "importance is attached to the correspondence between human conduct here on earth and the eschatological word of the Judge or Witness."[210] The promise in Revelation conflates a word of Jesus found in these two Synoptic sources, without mentioning the aspect of denial. Also, by adapting the Jesus saying into a victor saying, John "has destroyed the verbal correspondence of protasis and apodosis that characterized the Synoptic *logion*, though it is possible that he intended his readers to recall the original protasis."[211]

A negative form of this saying is found in Mark 8:38 and Luke 9:26: "For whoever is ashamed of me . . . ." These words are mercifully withheld in Revelation, Swete observes, where "the last note is one of unmixed encouragement and hope."[212]

The use of ἐνώπιον in the Sardian promise similarly puts the setting in a heavenly courtroom with Jesus before the Father and his angels.

---

209. Marshall, *Luke*, 515.
210. Michel, "ὁμολογέω," *TDNT* 5:208.
211. Bauckham, *Climax of Prophecy*, 95–96
212. Swete, *Apocalypse of St. John*, 52.

Giblin, who interprets the seven spirits in the epithet as the angels of the presence, says, "The promise to the victor repeats the motif of the seven spirits by assuring the faithful of public proclamation of the victor 'before my God and before his angels.'"[213] The link between the Sardian epithet and the promise here is probable, although his denial of the pneumatological reference is unnecessary. Angels are already in the epithet because the seven stars were previously identified as angels (1:20). It is doubtful that there are two angelic references here. Jesus who hold the angels will also confess the victor before them.

2 Clement 3:2 quotes the saying of Jesus in Matthew 10:32 and then interprets what the believer's confession should be: "By doing what he says and not disobeying his commandments."

Sardian Saying Conclusion

The metaphor of garments is closely related to that of light. Clothing in a literal sense is unnecessary in heaven, for believers there are clothed with the imperishable (cf. 1 Cor 15:53–54). The glory of Jesus at his transfiguration and of his angels at the resurrection and ascension hints at the meaning of white garments. They speak of transformation into a heavenly sphere. Charles rightly links white garments with "the spiritual bodies in which the faithful are to be clothed in the resurrection life."[214] Ladd also sees this as "a promise of victory and purity in the messianic Kingdom. . . ."[215] The future verb περιπατήσουσιν should therefore be understood eschatologically. Swete finds here an express description of the end of the victors: "The 'few names' in Sardis which are distinguished by resisting the prevailing torpor of spiritual death find their reward in finally retaining their place among the living in the City of God."[216]

Smith contends that the grammar and context of the verse, particularly the emphatic double negative οὐ μὴ (cf. 2:11; 3:12), deny any possibility of blotting from the book of life. "It is not a threat; rather it is an emphatic promise that the names of overcomers (i.e., Christians) will *never*, under any circumstances, be blotted from the book."[217] However, the promise is not unconditional to all Sardian believers, since it is directed only to those who are victorious.

213. Giblin, *Book of Revelation*, 61.
214. Charles, *Revelation*, 1:82.
215. Ladd, *Revelation of John*, 57.
216. Swete, *Apocalypse of St. John*, 52.
217. Smith, "Book of Life," 229.

The phrase "before my Father" finds its antecedent in 3:2 where Jesus finds the works of the Sardians fulfilled "before my God." The confession of the victor's name is thus linked to the successful completion of his or her works. Michel appropriately includes this promise under the classification "judicially 'to make a statement,' in the legal sense 'to bear witness.'"[218] Jesus as the eschatological Witness or Judge will proclaim the righteousness of each victor before the heavenly throne.

The Philadelphian Victor Saying

The victor saying is found in 3:12. Gundry make this grammatical comment regarding the verse: "Christ promises to make overcomers pillars 'in the temple of my God,' which in view of 21:22 we should read as 'the temple that is my God' (genitive of apposition)."[219] To translate this as an objective genitive rather than a subjective genitive based a future text is exegetically flawed. The phrase τοῦ θεοῦ μου is used as a subjective genitive three other times in this verse, and this is the likely reading in Gundry's example too.

Some manuscripts show the variant ποιήσω αὐτῷ for ποιήσω αὐτόν. This appears to be a scribal attempt to put the pronoun in the victor sayings in the same case following the future verb, as in δώσω αὐτῷ (2:7, 17 [2x], 26; 3:21). Since John had already correctly put the pronoun in the accusative case in 3:9 (ποιήσω αὐτούς), it is clear that αὐτόν is the correct reading.

The lack of grammatical concord in appositives, especially with participles, occurs frequently in Revelation (cf. 9:14; 11:15; 14:6; 19:20).[220] An example is found in this victor saying: τῆς καινῆς Ἰερουσαλήμ ἡ καταβαίνουσα.... Instead of agreeing with the genitive case of its antecedent, a nominative participle is used. The scribal attempt to bring agreement has produced the textual variant τῆς καταβαινούσης here. Such confusion is understandable given the agreement found in two parallel verses— τὴν πόλιν τὴν ἁγίαν' Ἰερουσαλὴμ [καινὴν] καταβαίνουσαν ... (21:10; cf. 21:2).

A final variant ἀπο, for ἐκ before τοῦ οὐρανοῦ found in several manuscripts is unlikely given the reading καταβαίνουσαν ἐκ τοῦ οὐρανοῦ, which is found in the two parallel texts just mentioned (21:2, 10).

---

218. Michel, "ὁμολογέω," *TDNT* 5:207-8.
219. Gundry, "New Jerusalem," 262.
220. Zerwick, *Biblical Greek*, §13.

The first half of the victor saying combines two aspects:
1. The victor will be made a pillar in the temple of the Lord,
2. The victor will never go out of the temple anymore.

Since pillar is apparently used metaphorically, temple is likewise presumed to be used metaphorically. In the second half ἐπ' αὐτον could refer either to στῦλον or to ὁ νικῶν. The distinction is really immaterial because the two merge in the first half of the saying—the victor *is* a pillar metaphorically.

In the second part of the saying Jesus promises to write upon the pillar/victor three things:
1. The name of his God,
2. The name of his heavenly city,
3. His own new name.

Points 1 and 3 will be considered first, then point 2 will be considered. Ramsay asserts that one, not three, names, are implied—a name that has all three characters and is simultaneously the name of all three.[221] This assertion will be investigated. Four times in the promise Jesus refers to God as "my God" (cf. Mark 15:34; John 20:17). This suggests that the intimacy Jesus has with God will become the privilege of the priestly "pillars" who serve in the heavenly city.

Though not part of the victor saying, Johnson believes the pledge to keep the believers from the coming hour of trial (3:10) "may be taken as a promise to all the churches."[222] The Philadelphians have met the condition—to heed Christ's command to endure patiently. The hour of trial to come upon the earth unfolds through the seal, trumpet, and bowl judgments. The distinctive substantival participle κατοικοῦντες is found here and in ten other texts (6:10; 8:13; 11:10 [2x]; 13:8, 12, 14 [2x]; 17:2, 8). Exemption from the hour of trial is not deliverance from persecution, because the slain souls given white robes were martyred at the hands of the earthdwellers (6:9–11). We agree with Johnson that the hour of trial is "a specific type of trial (God's wrath) that is aimed at the rebellious on the earth."[223] Schüssler Fiorenza rightly notes, "In the 'hour of trial' which is coming on the whole world (3:10) only the Christian community will

---

221. Ramsay, *Letters to the Seven Churches*, 302.
222. Johnson, "Revelation," 12:453.
223. Ibid., 12:455.

be saved (7:1–8; 11:1–2)."²²⁴ Because this promise is not eschatological, it will not be discussed further.

The Pillar in the Temple

Tenney points out that the temple symbolism is taken directly from contemporary architecture: "Every city in the Roman world had temples adorned with colonnades which supported the roof of the shrine or which made the porches where the public assembled."²²⁵ Coin types from the Asian cities often featured their temples. The Temple of Artemis appears on many coins of Ephesus. Some coins show the correct number of eight pillars fronting the temple, while other types are miniaturized, showing only four. According to Pliny the Elder (*Nat.* 36.96), the Artemesium contained 127 support pillars, which were 60 feet high, slender and beautifully fluted. Trell describes their uniqueness: "Their elaborate bases consisted of mouldings like rings of marble supporting sculptured reliefs that 'ran around' the bottom drums, an architectural delight almost but not entirely without precedent in the ancient world. Exquisite Ionic capitals with their expertly and gracefully carved circular sides (volutes) protected the columns and supported the marble horizontal beam above (entablature)." ²²⁶ Upon entering the temple the visitor would literally be surrounded by a forest of pillars. Today only a lone pillar stands at the site of the Artemesium.²²⁷

To experience the visual impact of such pillars today, one must visit the Temple of Apollo at Didyma, connected in antiquity to Miletus by an eleven-mile sacred road. It designer was Paionios, one of the architects of the Artemesium. The Didymaion was the third largest structure of the Greek world. The temple was designed for 124 pillars, although some outer ones were never completed. Smaller temples pillars likewise contained pillars. These pillars could be comprised either of drums connected by a lead rod or chiseled from a single piece of marble.

Inscribed pillars, both fluted and smooth, are found throughout western Turkey. This author has observed such pillars *in situ* at Ephesus, Claros, Euromos, Hierapolis, and Pergamum, and in the archaeological museums at Izmir and Manisa. In the upper agora at Ephesus two smooth inscribed Doric pillars are found in the Prytaneion. Some of the inscriptions found

---

224. Schüssler Fiorenza, *Revelation*, 48.
225. Tenney, *Interpreting Revelation*, 190.
226. Cf. Trell, "Temple of Artemis at Ephesos," 80–81.
227. For a brief discussion of this temple of Artemis, see Scherrer, *Ephesus*, 44–57.

on these pillars list the names of the members of the League of Curetes, a class of priests affiliated with the Artemisium. "The main function of the league was to celebrate the birth of Ephesian Artemis in Ortygia, near Ephesus, each year."[228] A dramatic example of fluted inscribed pillars is found at the temple of Zeus in Euromos (second century BC). Ten of the eleven outer standing pillars on the north and west sides have a placard-type inscription at the same height facing outward on the pillars. A similar fluted inscribed pillar is found at the oracle site of Claros, near Ephesus. It is apparent that the imagery of inscribed pillars was familiar to the Asian believers. Temples were a prominent part of public life in the seven cities, although our knowledge about temples in Philadelphia is limited.

The asseveration that believers will never have to leave the temple is likened by Moffatt to local practice in the imperial cult: "The provincial priest of the Imperial cultus erected his statue in the temple at the close of his year's official reign, inscribing on it his own name and his father's, his place of birth and year of office."[229] He applies this imagery to Christians as priests in the next world. Although not explicit in this promise, priestly imagery does pervade the letters. However, the criticism of Beckwith is apropos: "The circumstances of the victor entering triumphantly into the eternal kingdom are too unlike those of the priest passing out of all relation to the temple, to justify a comparison."[230] An imperial temple never existed in Philadelphia in the first century, and the imperial shrine that Ramsay so confidently mentions is only a conjecture.[231]

Barclay recounts a supposed custom regarding Philadelphia's temples. "When a man had served the state well, when he had left behind him a noble record as a magistrate or as a public benefactor, or as a priest, the memorial which the city gave to him was to erect a pillar in one of the temples with his name inscribed upon it."[232] He suggests that this honorific custom formed the background for Christ's promise. Since Barclay gives no source for his reference, it cannot be validated.

Wilkinson has recently offered another possible interpretation—the pillar analogy is rooted in established coronation rituals practiced in ancient Israel and throughout the ancient Near East. At his coronation Josiah stood by a pillar as was the custom (2 Kgs 11:14). The proximity of

---

228. Erdemgil, *Ephesus*, 52; see page 50 for a photograph of the inscriptions.

229. Moffatt, "Revelation of St. John," 5:369.

230. Beckwith, *Apocalypse of John*, 485. Hemer, *Letters to the Seven Churches of Asia*, 166, has found no evidence for the existence of this oft-cited custom.

231. Cf. Price, *Rituals and Power*, 259; Ramsay, *Letters to the Seven Churches*, 301.

232. Barclay, *Letters to the Seven Churches*, 98.

the king to the pillar perhaps signified the monarch's relationship to the cult or maybe suggested the stability and duration of his rule. The kingship/coronation theme found throughout Revelation and particularly in the seven letters reflects this ancient perspective. Wilkinson believes such coronational connections would be apparent to anyone versed in the Hebrew scriptures, as John was. "Whether the allusion of the pillar would in fact be clearly understood by the readers of Revelation seems beside the point, in regard to such an opaque work."[233] For the readers to respond positively to the promise, the allusion must not be oblique, but understandable. Actual pillars inscribed with names provide a more likely reference than Wilkinson's.

The word that the victor will no longer go out is seen by Ramsay as a promise of stability in the presence of regular earthquakes attributable to Philadelphia's location in the Catacecaumene.[234] The people would naturally be fearful to stay in their city following such seismic shocks (cf. Strabo *Geogr.* 12.8.18; 13.4.10). Both Ramsay and Hemer share firsthand accounts of the trauma following a modern earthquake in the city.[235] The traditional Greek method of building temples was designed to withstand earthquakes. The temple foundations were designed to "float" on the soil like a raft. Each block was joined to another by metal cramps, so that the platform was a unity. For example, the sub-foundation of the Artemesium was built of charcoal covered with fleeces to protect it, not only from earthquakes, but also from sinking into the marshy shoreline (cf. Pliny *Nat.* 36.95).[236] Thus the temple was undoubtedly one of the most secure structures in the city.

Biblical and Extrabiblical Co-texts

Paul in Galatians 2:9 calls James, Cephas, and John the reputed pillars of the Jerusalem church. Wilckens comments, "Presupposed here is the idea of a heavenly building—the Church as God's temple (cf. 1 Cor 3:10 ff., 16 ff.; Eph 2:21; Rev 3:12)—which the three who are mentioned bear up as basic pillars."[237] In 1 Timothy 3:15 the image is less defined; the house of God as the church of the living God is called the pillar and ground of the

---

233. Wilkinson, "ΣΤΥΛΟΣ of Revelation 3:12," 500, cf. 499.
234. Ramsay, *Letters to the Seven Churches*, 298–99.
235. Ibid., 291; Hemer, *Letters to the Seven Churches*, 264n. 14.
236. Cf. Ashmole, *Architect and Sculptor*, 7.
237. Wilckens, "στῦλος, *TDNT* 7:734–35.

truth. Clement describes Peter and Paul as the greatest and most righteous pillars who were persecuted and struggled until death (*1 Clem.* 5:2).

Godly people characterized as pillars are similarly portrayed in several texts. The mother of 4 Maccabees 17:3 was able to withstand her persecution because she was built on the pillar of her seven children. Le Déaut helpfully points out that "in the targum passage for Numbers 20.29 Aaron is called the 'pillar of the prayer of the children of Israel.'"[238] And in the messianic kingdom Enoch sees the ancient house transformed with new pillars set up in the new structure (*1 En* 90:29).

The literal use of στῦλος predominates in the Old Testament. Two well-known pillars named Jakin and Boaz stood on the porch to the north and south outside the Solomonic temple (1 Kgs 7:21; 2 Chr 3:15–17). Upon the temple's destruction these pillars were broken up and their bronze removed to Babylon (Jer 52:17). This reference is an improbable source for the promise. The metaphorical use is suggested when David (Ps 144:12) speaks of a day of victory when the daughters of Israel will be like pillars carved to adorn a palace (ναός; 143:12 LXX). In Proverbs 9:1 Wisdom stands on seven pillars. God makes Jeremiah an iron pillar in his prophetic role against Judah (Jer 1:18).

Accepting a suggestion by Kraft who sees an allusion here to Isaiah 22:23, "I will fasten him (as) a peg in . . . his father's house," Fekkes writes, "The common image of a peg as a symbol of stability, the promise-form, and the fact that John has already used the previous verse of Isaiah (22.22) in the same letter, all support the conclusion that Isaiah's peg metaphor is unlikely to be an accidental parallel to John's pillar metaphor."[239] However, the peg in Isaiah's prophecy will be sheared off and fall (v. 25), unlike the pillar which will never (οὐ μὴ) lose its position in the temple. Because of the inadequacy of the peg imagery in Isaiah 22, the allusion in Revelation moves from the key of David to the pillar in the temple.[240]

Divine Names Written

In the first century Philadelphia on two occasions adopted a new name. An earthquake in AD 17 destroyed the city, and in gratitude for Tiberius' generosity Philadelphia added "Neocaesarea" to its name (Strabo *Geogr.*

---

238. Le Déaut, *Message of the New Testament*, 32.

239. Fekkes, *Isaiah and Prophetic Traditions*, 133; for Kraft see 1974:82.

240. Wilkinson, "ΣΤΥΛΟΣ of Revelation 3:12," 500n. 14, notes, 'It is possible, however, that the Greek text of Isaiah available to the author of Revelation actually read στηλω at this point—as does Codex Vaticanus."

12.8.18; 13.4.10). Under Vespasian "Flavia," the emperor's family name, was also adopted, undoubtedly because of his largesse following a similar natural disaster (Suetonius *Vesp.* 17). Philadelphia was the only one of the seven cities to take a new name, although Sardis took the temporary epithet "Caesarea." The validity of such a reference is weakened when we recall that the new name imagery was first used in the letter to Pergamum (2:17), a city that had no name changes.

The fourfold use of the possessive pronoun "my" parallels the paternalistic relationship the emperor had with his imperial cities. Inscribed on the Archive Wall at Aphrodisias, just south of Philadelphia, are Augustus' words that Aphrodisias is "the one city from all of Asia that I have selected to be my own."[241]

Extrabiblical and Biblical Co-texts

When the people of Israel wanted to honor Simon and his sons, they inscribed a record of his deeds on bronze tablets and put it on "pillars" on Mount Zion (1 Macc 14:27 NRSV, NAB, NJB). However, the text has στήλαις (v. 26 LXX), not στύλοις. The additional instructions in verse 48 suggest that "steles" is the preferred translation. Josephus (*Ant.* 16.165) likewise mentions a decree of Augustus installed in his temple at Pergamum that concludes, "This was inscribed upon a pillar in the temple of Caesar" (LCL). Again the better translation is probably "inscribed upon a stele (ἐστηλογραφήθη)."

A possible reference has been found in Ignatius (*Phld.* 6.1). The bishop looks upon those who are silent about Christ as tombstones and graves of the dead, "upon which is written only the names (ὀνόματα) of people." While this link is attractive, Charles rightly finds no common idea between the two: "Ignatius is comparing false teachers to sepulchres, whereas our text declares that the victors shall be upholders of the spiritual temple of God, with the name of their God blazoned on their brows."[242]

As part of his high priestly garb Aaron wore a gold mitre with the words "Holy to the Lord" engraved over his forehead (Exod 28:36–38). The purpose of the priestly blessing to be offered by Aaron and his sons was to put the name of the Lord upon the children of Israel (Num 6:27). And before Ezekiel sees the wicked destroyed in Jerusalem, God commands an angel to place a mark on the forehead of the righteous, sparing them from the coming slaughter (Ezek 9:4).

---

241. Erim, *Aphrodisias*, 30.
242. Charles, *Revelation*, 1:92.

The New Jerusalem Coming Down from Heaven

In the New Testament Jerusalem is found in two different forms Ἱεροσόλυμα (63x) and Ἰερουσαλήμ (76x). The former was the preferred Hellenistic form (although the LXX did not use it), while the latter was the more Judaistic.[243] John consistently uses the Hebraic form in Revelation[244] and in this case τῆς καινῆς Ἰερουσαλήμ. Jeremias accounts for such usage here and in Hebrews as follows: "Beide Autoren hatten überhaupt keine Wahl, weil sie von der himmlischen (Hebr) bzw. eschatolgischen (Apk) Gottesstadt reden, für die nure die sakrale hebräische Namesform in Frage kam."[245]

Paul contrasts the earthly Jerusalem in slavery with the free Jerusalem that is above (Gal. 4:26). Bruce comments, "In our present text, just as ἡ νῦν Ἰερουσαλήμ is not primarily the geographical site, so ἡ ἄνω Ἰερουσαλήμ is not spatially elevated but is the community of the new covenant."[246] To bear the name of a city is to declare oneself as one of its citizens. Such a heavenly citizenship for believers is assumed by Paul (Phil 3:20).

The writer of Hebrews tells his readers that they have come to Mount Zion, the heavenly Jerusalem, the city of the living God (Heb 12:22; cf. 11:10; 13:14). As in the Old Testament, Zion and Jerusalem are linked and the terms probably synonymous.[247] In contrast to the promise in Revelation, here "[t]his is not our author's perspective: the new Jerusalem has not yet come down to men, but in the spiritual realm they already have access to it."[248] Such participation is now possible for those who believe in Jesus because he is the bread who has come down from heaven (καταβαίνων ἐκ τοῦ οὐρανοῦ; John 6:33, 41, 58). Unlike the nonbiblical writings, "these two passages show no concern for the earthly Jerusalem as a city to be rebuilt, but are solely concerned with the heavenly Jerusalem."[249]

---

243. Cf. De Young, *Jerusalem in the New Testament*, 12.

244. The Gospel of John, however, uses Ἱεροσόλυμα twelve times exclusively. De Young, ibid., 13, assuming the traditional Johannine authorship, accounts for this distinction because "this writer intentionally chose the first form for the earthly, and the other for the heavenly and eschatological city."

245. "Both authors had no choice at all, because they talked about the heavenly (Hebr) and/or eschatological (Rev) city of God; only the sacral Hebraic name form could be used" (Jeremias, "ΙΕΡΟΥΣΑΛΗΜ/ΙΕΡΟΣΟΛΥΜΑ," 275).

246. Bruce, *Galatians*, 221.

247. Cf. Ellingworth, *Hebrews*, 677.

248. Bruce, *Hebrews*, 375.

249. Park, "More than a Regained Eden," 136.

Extrabiblical and Biblical Co-texts

Tobit 14:5 speaks of a restoration to the land of Israel, after which Jerusalem will be rebuilt in splendor and the temple in it. In an allegory of Israel's history found in 1 Enoch 89–90 Jerusalem is repeatedly referred to as a "house." In the messianic kingdom that ancient house will be transformed into "a new house, greater and loftier than the first one" (90:29; cf. *T. Levi* 10:5). Park writes that "it is obvious that the 'ancient house' and the 'new house' are symbols of the old and the new Jerusalem which teaching is in line with that of the OT."[250] 1 Enoch 91:16 predicts, "The first heaven shall depart and pass away; a new heaven shall appear." Testament of Daniel 5:12 makes an explicit reference: "And the saints shall refresh themselves in Eden; the righteous shall rejoice in the New Jerusalem." The Lord, the Holy One of Israel, will live and rule in their midst (v. 13). Here the New Jerusalem is equated with an Edenic paradise.

4 Ezra 8:52 speaks of an age to come when a city is built (i.e., a new Jerusalem; cf. 10:27), following the opening of paradise and the planting of the tree of life. This newly established city is Zion (10:44). In 2 Baruch 4 the Lord tells Baruch that the earthly Jerusalem will be delivered up temporarily (v. 1) to be replaced by another city prepared from eternity at the time he decided to create paradise (vv. 2–3a; cf. 6:9; 32:2–5). This new Jerusalem was revealed to Adam before he sinned, as well as to Abraham and to Moses (4:3b–5). Park aptly summarizes: "In many cases, due to the ambiguity of the extant expressions, we cannot ascertain whether Jerusalem/Zion is presented as descending from heaven as in Revelation or as a reconstruction of the earthly city, although in some cases the city has a copy in heaven, i.e., is pre-existent."[251]

Jerusalem is found 660 times in the Old Testament; its synonym Zion 154 times.[252] David captured the city from the Jebusites and reigned there as king of the united monarchy of Israel and Judah for thirty-three years (2 Sam 5:5ff). He made the city his capital and called it the city of David. Jerusalem was not only the political center of the Jewish people but also its religious center. The ark of the covenant rested on Mount Zion (2 Sam 6:17–19) before Solomon built a temple to contain it (1 Kgs 6:19). Jerusalem is identified numerous times as the place where God's name dwells (cf. Deut 12:11; 1 Kgs 9:3; Ps 74:7; Jer 3:17; 7:12). The complete history of the city can be found in any Bible dictionary or encyclopedia.

---

250. Ibid., 93.
251. Ibid., 112.
252. Cf. Fohrer, "Σιών κτλ," *TDNT* 7:319.

Of particular importance for our discussion is the place of a "new" Jerusalem/Zion in the prophetic books. For example, Dumbrell observes that "Isaiah is dominated by Jerusalem imagery. The book's structure is . . . informed by Jerusalem orientated theology."[253] Chapters 1–39 describe the rejection of Jerusalem, chapters 40–66 its restoration. For her future reward Zion/Jerusalem is promised that "he will call you a new name (τὸ ὄνομα τὸ καινὸν) which the Lord will name" (62:2). Park suggests three points regarding the restoration motif in Isaiah:[254]

1. A new and glorified Jerusalem is presented as the world's center attracting all nations in the last days (2:1–5; 18:7; 59:20; 60:1–62:12).
2. The continuity of the new Jerusalem with the earthly, national capital is unclear; however, it seems to transcend the bounds of the earthly realm (51:3; 53:1, 7; 55:1–3). The life promised in the new heavens and new earth (65:17–25) is described with paradise motifs.
3. No distinction exists between Zion/Jerusalem as a city (i.e., a sacred space; 46:12–13; 52:1) and the saved community (i.e., a sanctified people; 51:16; 59:10). The two concepts are used interchangeably and simultaneously.

Park summarizes his finds: "Although there is the impression of an unquestioned elevation of the historical Jerusalem as the place of God's special favor, it is superficial since *the idea of God's presence with his people is more important* although it is depicted in Jerusalem language."[255] Park correctly elucidates an Isaianic emphasis likewise found in Revelation.

Historically the book of Ezekiel was written during the period of the destruction of Jerusalem and the temple (586 BC). Chapters 1–32 deal largely with the themes of judgment and destruction. Only in the final sixteen chapters does the hope of restoration appear. This hope centers on the rebuilding of a new temple described in chapters 40–48. The book closes with a revelation of the new name of the city where the temple resides, "The Lord is there" (יהוה שׁמה; 48:35). Zechariah 14:5–21 also gives a picture of a restored Jerusalem, which follows the defeat of the nations when the Lord himself comes.

---

253. Dumbrell, *End of the Beginning*, 5.
254. Park, "More than a Regained Eden," 72–77.
255. Ibid., 77.

Philadelphian Saying Conclusion

To the Philadelphians a pillar would be a familiar metaphor for worthy persons. Being likened to the pillar of a temple would assure the victors of stability and permanence as they endure the coming hour of trial. As pillars, each believer is "built permanently into its structure and bearing its proportion of responsibility for the maintenance of God's worship."[256] Their present worship was disrupted through strife with the Jewish community. "To compensate for exclusion from the place of honour in the synagogue Christ promises them a place (as pillars) in God's temple."[257] Finally, as Swete astutely quips, "a λυχνία may be removed (ii.6), but not a στῦλος."[258]

The Pergamenes had been promised a new name written on a white stone (2:17); the Philadelphians are now promised names to be written on pillars, including the new name of Jesus. In the ancient world "[t]o know the name of a deity was to share his power—to be enabled to invoke him successfully, to enjoy a consequent security and protection."[259] The victor is assured that he belongs to God, the heavenly city, and to Christ, and "that he will everlastingly share in all the blessings and privileges of all three."[260] We have earlier seen that a name symbolizes the essential nature of a person. Wall summarizes well: "in this case, it indicates the identity of the community of current overcomers as the eschatological community that will experience transformed human existence at Christ's return."[261]

R. H. Gundry asserts about this promise: "At 3:12 he presented Christ's promise to write on the overcomer—i.e., on the professing believer who proves to be genuine—the name of the New Jerusalem as well as the name of God and his own (i.e., Christ's) new name." In other words, "Christ identifies the New Jerusalem with the person who overcomes much as he identifies his own person and that of God his Father with the overcomer."[262] Turner answers, stating that "John does not mean to assert that the overcomer is the new Jerusalem but rather that the overcomer is associated with his or her ultimate destiny, the new Jerusalem, as well as with Christ

---

256. Tenney, *Interpreting Revelation*, 190.
257. Farrer, *Revelation of St. John*, 80.
258. Swete, *Apocalypse of St. John*, 57.
259. Kiddle, *Revelation of St. John*, 54.
260. Hendrickson, *More than Conquerors*, 75.
261. Wall, *Revelation*, 85.
262. Gundry, "New Jerusalem," 256.

and God."²⁶³ This question of identification will be addressed further when the fulfillment of this saying is discussed in the next chapter.

The Laodicean Victor Saying

The final victor saying to the Seven Churches is found in 3:21. As in 2:7, δώσω here means to "permit," "grant." In 3:20 Jesus promises the repentant Laodiceans that he will come in and eat with them. Gager, quoting Schweitzer, believes this verse refers to a primitive form of an eschatological sacrament, which "anticipated the return of Jesus and the messianic feast with him in the immediate future."²⁶⁴ Wall denies the eucharistic imagery; "rather it celebrates the restoration of fellowship."²⁶⁵ However, both perspectives are possible because in the early church the most intimate picture of fellowship surrounded the Lord's Supper (cf. Acts 2:42ff.).

What is the relationship between the promise to eat in verse 20 and the victor saying in verse 21? Beckwith states that here are brought together the two promises of eating with the Messiah and sharing his rule, as Luke 22:29–30 does also.²⁶⁶ He believes Revelation 3:20, along with 2:10 and 3:4, are examples of an eschatological promise being introduced "before that connected with the formula ὁ νικῶν."²⁶⁷ Charles, however, suggests that verse 20 refers to repentance in the present; it is not eschatological and thus does not refer to the messianic banquet in chapter 19.²⁶⁸ Charles's perspective best accords with the purpose of the other coming sayings, whose function in the letters was discussed in chapter 2. Jesus is presently at the door of the church, knocking and asking it to repent. If the Laodiceans heed his reproof and correction, Jesus promises to renew his spiritual presence with them at the Lord's table. Because verse 20 is not being considered eschatological, it is not included in the Laodicean victor saying.

The Divine Throne

Most commentators see little evidence of a local reference in this promise. Brewer describes how in the ancient theaters the seats in the front row

---

263. Turner, "New Jerusalem in Revelation 21:1—22:5," 287.
264. Gager, *Kingdom and Community*, 56.
265. Wall, *Revelation*, 87.
266. Beckwith, *Apocalypse of John*, 492.
267. Ibid., 475.
268. Charles, *Revelation*, 1:100.

were often shaped like thrones. These would be occupied by city officials, leading officials, or priests. For example, the Ephesus theater had twelve thrones for accommodating dignitaries. The victors on their heavenly thrones would thus receive the honor and status accorded to those who occupied them in the Asian civic theaters.[269] Such an association appears to have little warrant, although I agree with Brewer that many of the believers would be acquainted with Greek drama in the Asian theaters.

Hemer recalls the elevation of a citizen Zeno to the kingship of Cilicia in 39 BC and of Pontus in 36 as a reward for barring Laodicea's gates to the invading Labienus Parthicus in 40 (Strabo *Geogr.* 14.2.24). Although the Zenoid family continued to play some role in the rule of Anatolia over the next century, its history is incomplete. The branch of the family that remained in Laodicea figures prominently on its coinage. Because the city produced a dynasty of kings who greatly influenced its character, Hemer sees the appropriateness of the promise of thrones to the Laodicean believers. Yet he rightly concedes that the application of this background is still questionable.[270]

Another approach may be considered. θρόνος was used in 2:13 to describe Pergamum as the throne of Satan. The latter was interpreted in chapter 1 as related to the city's centrality in the emperor cult, the imperial government, and the commune of Asia. As a conventus city Laodicea was a secondary "throne" in the province. The Romans had established textile factories there to manufacture the sleeved tunic (*dalmatica*) and the hooded cloak (*birrus*), making the city an economic center as well.[271] For the Laodicean church to be prospering to the degree it was, its members must have been well connected politically and economically. This preoccupation with influence and money was wreaking spiritual consequences.[272]

The promise of authority in the messianic kingdom might well be a counterbalance to the temporal power upon which the church was now focused. Boring seems to have overestimated the Laodicean's spirituality. He thinks that their riches "were probably not only or even primarily material riches but the spiritual riches enjoyed by Christians who supposed they were already living in the fulfilled time of prophetic phenomena and

---

269. Brewer, "Influence of Greek Drama on the Apocalypse of John," 80.

270. Hemer, *Letters to the Seven Churches of Asia*, 205–6.

271. Cf. Bonfante and Jaunzems, "Clothing and Ornament," 3:1402.

272. Despite the shortfalls of the historical-prophetical interpretation, it is nevertheless apparent why people continue to be attracted to its perspective. The European/North American church, with its materialistic orientation and concern with temporal power, rings true as a type of the lukewarm Laodicean church.

spiritual bliss."[273] Such a realized eschatology does not appear to be the problem of the Laodiceans.

Biblical and Extrabiblical Co-texts

Jesus is presently exalted on his heavenly throne at the right hand of the Father (Acts 5:31; Rom 8:34; Heb 4:16; 8:1; 12:2). At the renewal of all things Jesus will sit on his glorious throne. He promised the apostles that they too would sit on twelve thrones, judging the twelve tribes of Israel (Matt 19:28; cf. 1 Cor 6:2–3). From his throne in glory the Son of Man will judge the nations, as a shepherd separates the sheep from the goats. The criterion for his judgment is whether righteous works such as feeding the hungry or visiting the prisoner were done. The wicked are sent to eternal punishment while the righteous receive eternal life (Matt 25:31–46). The faithful saying written to Timothy in Ephesus has a remarkable thematic parallel: "If we died with him, we will also live with him; if we endure, we will also reign with him" (2 Tim 2:11–12).

Wisdom is said to be a co-adjudicator (πάρεδρον) on the throne (Wis 9:4). The Maccabean martyrs, who triumphed in the contest (ἀγῶν) through endurance, now stand around the divine throne living a blessed life (4 Macc 17:18). Hellenistic writers, such as Josephus and Philo, did not speak of the throne of God, believing the concept to be too anthropomorphic.[274]

Among the writings of Palestinian Judaism, "ein Sitzen des Messias auf dem Thron der göttl. Herrlichkeit kennen nur die der vorchristl. Zeit angehörenden Bilderreden des Buches Henoch."[275] In 1 Enoch the Son of Man is seated on his glorious throne executing eschatological judgment on the unrighteous (45:3), the righteous (51:3), the fallen angels (55:4; 69:29), the holy angels (61:8), and the rulers and landlords (62:2–5). 1 Enoch closes with this promise: "I shall bring them out into the bright light, those who have loved my holy name, and seat them each one by one upon the throne of his honor" (108:12). 4Q521 2.ii.7 promises that the Lord "will honour the devout upon the throne of eternal royalty."

The throne was the most visible symbol of the power and authority of the earthly king. The two are closely linked in the Old Testament: "as soon as he (Zimri) began to reign and was seated on the throne . . ."

273. Boring, *Revelation*, 94.
274. Cf. Schmitz, "θρόνος," *TDNT* 3:163.
275. "A sitting of the Messiah on the divine throne of Glory is only known in the picture speeches of the book of Enoch, which belongs to the pre-Christian time"; Strack and Billerbeck, *Kommentar zum Neuen Testament*, 1:978.

(1 Kgs 16:11; cf. 2 Sam 14:9). The king could share his throne with his son (Exod 11:5; 2 Kgs 21:1) or his mother (1 Kgs 2:19), and co-regencies were a common feature of the southern kingdom (e.g., Asa/Jehoshaphat, Jehoshaphat/Jehoram, etc). By metonymy, the throne of David stands for the eternal dynasty promised by God to David (1 Chr 17:12–14; Pss 89:4, 29, 36; 132:11–12). The Messiah accedes to the throne of David when he comes (Isa 9:7).

The Old Testament conception of the throne of God derives it imagery from the earthly throne, as seen in the juxtaposition of the two in 1 Kings 22:10 and 19. God declares that "heaven is my throne, and the earth is my footstool" (Isa 66:1). When Isaiah saw the Lord, he was seated on a throne in the heavenly temple (6:1). And when Ezekiel saw the glorious likeness of the Lord, he appeared to be seated on a throne of sapphire (1:26; 10:1).

The core of the issue is: the throne of God thus functions as an important symbol of the eschatological kingdom and judgment. At Israel's restoration Jerusalem will again become the throne of the Lord, where all nations will gather to worship him (Jer 3:17). In Ezekiel's vision of the restored temple God shows the prophet where his throne will sit forever in the midst of his holy people Israel (Ezek 43:7). In his night vision Daniel sees multiple thrones set up, with the Ancient of Days seating himself on a throne as the heavenly court opens the books (Dan 7:9–10). The vision's interpretation emphasizes that the saints are to receive a kingdom that they will possess forever (v. 18). The court strips the fourth beast and its ten kings of their authority to blaspheme the Most High and to oppress the saints, who are at last given total sovereignty and power to rule in the everlasting kingdom (vv. 23–27).

The clearest announcement of the messianic co-regency is found in Psalm 110:1: "The LORD says to my Lord: 'Sit at my right hand until I make your enemies a footstool for your feet.'" Kidner explains, "King David speaks in the psalm as the prophet who declaims the enthronement oracle to the Messianic King."[276] This psalm, quoted by Jesus (Matt 22:44; Mark 12:36; Luke 20:42–43) and the basis of apostolic teaching on his exaltation and session (Acts 2:34–35; Eph 1:20; Heb 1:13), is one of the most quoted passages in the New Testament.

---

276. Kidner, *Psalms 73–150*, 392.

Laodicean Saying Conclusion

The concept of messianic reign is articulated earlier in Revelation where the believers are declared to be "a kingdom, priests to his God and Father" (1:6). Beckwith makes a likely proposal that "The past tense in ἐποίησεν denotes what has been ideally or potentially accomplished in the act or purpose of God, while the actual realization is in the future."[277] The promise to the Thyatiran church likewise concerns sharing Christ's future reign in the eschatological kingdom. Thus victory in the Laodicean promise, according to Roberts, "consists of partaking in the rule of the Lord who Himself has triumphed."[278]

The promise in Revelation is an extension of the one given to the apostles in Matthew 19:28. This scriptural background would no doubt be familiar to the Laodiceans. In Extrabiblical literature the function of the throne is summed up in Wisdom 3:8: the righteous "will judge the nations and have power over the peoples, and their Lord will reign forever." In the Old Testament the image of the throne as the seat of judgment is found throughout, with Psalm 110:1 being a primary text.

Vanni reiterates an important point made in chapter 3: "tra la vittoria e l'intronizzazione di Cristo e del cristiano c'è un nesso di dipendenza. La vittoria del cristiano è determinata dalla vittoria di Cristo, che sola la rende possibile."[279] The reward for Jesus' victory over death and the grave was to sit with his Father on the heavenly throne. A difference in rewards is articulated here: the victor is not told that he will share the throne with the Father.

Black believes the context here is forensic: "the victory is that of one who shares Christ's 'session' with God in heaven after the Judgement."[280] Collins qualifies this observation: "The function of judgment is often associated with enthronement but is not necessarily implied."[281] Concerning this closing promise, Lohmeyer states: "Dieser Spruch verheißt die letzte und höchste Würde; er schließt so wirkungsvoll den Kranz der 7 Ueberwindersprüche wie der 7 Sendschreiben."[282] Whether or not the

---

277. Beckwith, *Apocalypse of John*, 429.

278. Roberts, "Letter to Seven Churches," 31.

279. ". . . between the victory and the enthronement of Christ, for the Christian there is a nexus of dependency. The victory of the Christian is determined from the victory of Christ, which alone makes it possible"; Vanni, *L'Apocalisse*, 162.

280. Black, "Some Greek Words," 140.

281. Collins, *Scepter and the Star*, 144.

282. "This saying promises the final and highest grandeur; it closes effectively as the wreath of the 7 overcomer sayings of the 7 letters"; Lohmeyer, *Offenbarung*, 40.

Asian churches would have seen this promise as an especially appropriate conclusion is unknown.

An Epilogue to the Seven Letters?

Ramsay sees the final promise as part of an epilogue to the seven letters that begins in verse 19 because it "has no apparent relation to their situation and character."[283] His conception of the letters as a literary composition demands that an epilogue complete them. Even Ramsay admits it is difficult to separate the Laodicean letter from the epilogue but uses the criterion of local reference to make that distinction. He argues that surely after such a sharp condemnation, "it seems hardly consistent to give it the honor which is awarded to the true and courageous church of Philadelphia alone among the seven, and to rank it among those whom the author loves."[284] Such specious reasoning precludes God's divine grace; it also fails to see chiastic emphasis on the subject of love in the first (2:4), fourth (2:19) and seventh (3:19) letters. We disagree with Ramsay that the promise in 3:21 is part of an epilogue but find it an integral part of the Laodicean letter.

Commentators have also debated the transitional character of the victor saying. Charles characterizes the transition to chapter 4 as "an entire change of scene and subject. The dramatic contrast could not be greater."[285] On the other hand, Bauckham proposes: "Whereas the others are framed in terms appropriate to the church addressed, this last promise seems to be placed last, not because of any special appropriateness to the church at Laodicea, but rather because it anticipates chapter 5. Christ's own 'conquest' and his consequent enthronement with his Father in heaven is what John sees announced and celebrated in chapter 5."[286]

While we are unwilling to concede that the promise has no individual characteristics, it seems incontrovertible (contra Charles) that the promise functions as a transition to the rest of the book. Such a transition was built into the proposed chiastic outline in chapter 1; section B ended with 4:2 whereas section C began in 3:21. Hence commentators who artificially divide the book at this point create a problem. Williamson astutely observes that the promise "provides a compact summary of some of the heart of

---

283. Ramsay, *Letters to the Seven Churches*, 318.
284. Ibid., 318–19.
285. Charles, *Revelation*, 1:102.
286. Bauckham, *Theology of the Book of Revelation*, 6.

Revelation's theology."[287] The thrust of the whole argument in the visionary John's mind is: the way to victory so as to join Jesus on the throne is to follow him. By willingly laying down his life Jesus became victorious and was then himself enthroned with the Father in heaven.

Chapter Summary

The key images of each victor saying have been presented. Crucial textual and grammatical matters were discussed. The relevant literary co-texts for each image have been presented. All the images except the second death and the white stone had recognizable associations in biblical literature. For the white stone, traditions related to Jesus as the Stone/Rock were presented and a new interpretive solution proposed. Although the promise of the confession of a name has no Old Testament background, it clearly refers to a Jesus saying in Matthew 19:28. Most of these images were found in Extrabiblical literature, usually within eschatological texts.

Clusters of images were found in certain texts in Extrabiblical and Old Testament literature. Texts with three or more image clusters are presented next. There are three texts from Extrabiblical literature that feature promise clusters—1 Enoch 90, 4 Ezra 8, and Ascension of Isaiah 9.

1 Enoch 90	*4 Ezra 8*	*Ascension of Isaiah 9*
Shepherd with a rod (v. 18)	Paradise opened (v. 52)	Robes (vv. 9–11, 17–18, 24–26)
Throne (v. 20)	Tree of life planted (v. 52)	Crowns (vv. 12, 18, 24–25)
Books opened (v. 20)	City built (i.e., New Jerusalem, v. 52)	Thrones (vv. 10–12, 18, 24–25)
Abyss of fire (v. 24)	Death of unrighteous (v. 58)	Books (v. 22)
New house (i.e., Jerusalem, v. 29)		
New pillar (v. 29)		
Snow-white (clothes, v. 31)		

There are four Old Testament passages that feature promise clusters—Isaiah 60–62, Ezekiel 28 LXX, Daniel 7, and Zechariah 3–6.

287. Williamson, "Thrones in the Book of Revelation," 135.

Isaiah 60–62	Ezekiel 28 LXX	Daniel 7	Zechariah 3–6
Morning star (60:3)	Crown (v. 12)	Thrones (v. 9)	Rich garments (3:4)
Garments (61:3, 10)	Paradise (v. 13)	White garments (v. 9)	Inscribed stone (3:9)
New name (62:2)	Stone (v. 13)	Books opened (v. 10; cf. 12:1)	Crown (6:11)
Crown (61:3; 62:3)	Holy mountain (i.e., Zion, v. 14)	Authority over nations (v. 14)	
Jerusalem established (62:7)			

Additional promise imagery can be found in these documents because of their prophetic and apocalyptic nature. However, these charts focus on the texts that have the largest promise clusters.

Promise images recur within the seven letters and are presented on the next chart.

Image	Eph	Smyr	Perg	Thy	Sard	Phila	Laod
Life	2:7—tree	2:10—crown			3:5—book		
Crown		2:10				3:11	
Garments					3:4, 5		3:18
Death		2:10, 11		2:23			
Name	2:3		2:13, 17		3:1, 4, 5	3:8, 12	
Star	2:1			2:28	3:1		
Throne			2:13				3:21

The significance of this observation relates to the question of local references. Because images like "crown," "new name," and "white garments" are used in more than one letter, this diminishes the likelihood of a local reference in these cases. It does not exclude one either; for example, both Sardis and Laodicea were textile centers and familiar with garment production. The images related to local references were either generic or familiar enough to the other churches that the entire Asian audience could understand the references in the letters. Thus U. Müller can write regarding each promise, "Es geht nicht mehr um die Glieder dieser oder jener Gemeinde, sondern um die Überwinder in der kirche überhaupt."[288]

Minear observes that each reward involving a share in Jesus' power (e.g., rod, throne) "links its recipient to God so that an unbroken communion is established from the lowest participant to the highest. This communion clearly provides the essentials of life: food, clothing, home, name, security, power."[289] Such essentials, more or less, are presently being denied the believers in every church except Laodicea. Minear's list of essentials suggests the possibility of classifying the promise images in three areas—provision, place, and person. These are outlined in the following chart.

Provision	*Place*	*Person*
Tree of life	Paradise of God	Hidden manna
Crown of life (no second death)	Pillar in the temple	White stone?
White stone?	New Jerusalem	New name
Shepherd the nations		Morning star
White garments		Divine names
Book of life		
Confession of name		
Divine throne		

Concerning the provision images, we can relate only those of "shepherd the nations" and "divine throne" directly to ruling.

The phenomenon of restating the same promise using different images is particularly seen regarding immortality. The characterization by Mealy that these are all promises of eternal life is too broad.[290] However, the images of tree of life, crown of life, second death, book of life, and confession of name all assure the victor of the same reality—eternal life in the new Jerusalem. Roloff suggests that "in the final analysis in these promises the important matter is not receiving certain gifts from God but rather the relationship to God himself, the giver of all gifts."[291] While relationship

---

288. "It does not concern any longer the members of this or that congregation, but instead it is about the overcomer in the church generally"; Müller, *Offenbarung*, 94.

289. Minear, *I Saw a New Earth*, 60.

290. Mealy, *After the Thousand Years*, 170.

291. Roloff, *Revelation*, 237.

may be the ultimate outcome, the images themselves relate predominantly to the victor's spiritual provisions in the heavenly kingdom. This emphasis is even greater if the images of the pillar in the temple as well as the new Jerusalem and divine names, both to be written on the victor, are shifted to the first column (they could be placed in either).

A crucial and fundamental question should be asked next: When the letters were heard originally, would the promises be understood by the Asian audiences? Charles thinks not, "The endings would in many respects be incomprehensible but for the later chapters, to which in thought and diction they are most intimately related, and apart from which they would be all but inscrutable enigmas."[292] This assessment is certainly true regarding several of the images. But, as we have demonstrated, most of the images were familiar enough to the believers that they could be largely comprehended. Regarding the audience's recognition of such imagery, Mealy well states, "This is not to claim that they would necessarily be unfamiliar with the term or its significance, but only that they would be forced to wait to see exactly how it would be developed *in Revelation*"[293] (my emphasis—MW). This development of the fulfillment of the promises in Revelation is the subject of chapter 5.

---

292. Charles, *Revelation*, 1:44-45.
293. Mealy, *After the Thousand Years*, 82n. 2.

5

The Fulfillment of the Victor Sayings

Introduction

IN CHAPTER 4 the victor sayings were examined within the context of the seven letters. This chapter surveys the development of the theme of victory in the rest of Revelation, culminating with their fulfillment in chapters 19–22. Modern readers, like the original audience, encounter a plethora of promise imagery after that in the seven letters in chapters 2–3. Such imagery is there for a reason, according to Fekkes: "The expectation of this future consummation and renewal is kept alive in earlier parts of the book by John's strategic placement of eschatological 'reminders.'"[1] We will demonstrate that these fulfillments relate fundamentally to the integrity and trustworthiness of Jesus' promises to the Asian believers, especially those encountering severe tribulation.

John's frequent use of *intra*textuality reminds us that the primary grid for interpreting Revelation is the book itself. Because of this, reference to outside literary sources will be minimal in this chapter. The organization of the promises and their fulfillments in chapters 4 and 5 is in a specific sequence stemming from the hermeneutical concept of *cotextuality*. This should minimize the need to provide continual cross references between the chapters. Fekkes aptly summarizes, "Thus, the manifestation of divine renewal and reward outlined in Rev 21.1—22.5 was already presupposed in the promises of chs. 2–3 . . . . These promises serve as a preview to the main presentation and development of salvation oracles in Revelation 21–22."[2] While disagreeing with Fekkes's demarcations in the final chapters, we concur that a unique relationship exists between the two sections. Before examining these fulfillments, we must first look at a final promise given in Revelation's closing chapters.

---

1. Fekkes, *Isaiah and Prophetic Traditions*, 92.
2. Ibid.

A Final Victor Saying

A final victor saying resembling the victor sayings in Revelation 2–3 is found in section B′. Swete calls this "an eighth promise that completes and in effect embraces the rest."[3] This final victor saying is found in 21:6–7: "To the one who thirsts I will give free drink from the spring of the water of life. The victor will inherit these things, and I will be God to him and he will be a son to me." Apart from the absence of a hearing formula, it is similar to the promises in chapters 2–3. The characteristic δώσω and ὁ νικῶν are found. In the Ephesian and Pergamene letters the dative participle τῷ νικῶντι was used to begin the promises; here τῷ διψῶντι is used. The seven letters do not contain an explicit promise of living water, which is here given to the victor who thirsts for God. This promise is repeated under the image of inheritance as God's son in verse 7. Thus "the thirst for God will be satisfied in the relation of perfect sonship with God."[4] Mealy identifies the thirst here as "not so much a symbol of their *desire* for God as it is emblematic of their *weary condition* which is the result of earthly faithfulness."[5] Yet it is surely the victor's desire for God that sustains him or her through persecution (cf. Matt 5:6).

This final saying is introduced by the epithets, "I am the Alpha and the Omega, the Beginning and the End." In 1:8 "Alpha and Omega" is also used as an epithet for the Lord God Almighty. Fekkes comments, "The promise follows the same structural pattern as the eschatological rewards of the letters (Rev. 2–3), except that here God is the speaker."[6] But can Jesus be ruled out definitively as the speaker? "Beginning" (ἀρχή) is likewise an epithet for Christ in the Laodicean letter (3:14). Both God and the Lamb occupy the same heavenly throne in 22:3. And the similar declaration containing the epithets "Alpha and Omega, Beginning and End" is repeated in 22:13, but here Jesus is clearly the speaker. Beasley-Murray rightly observes, "Accordingly as judge of the world the Christ claims the divine title affirmed by the Lord God Almighty in 1:8."[7] Jesus can do this because he shares God's nature. The change of language from

---

3. Swete, *Apocalypse of St. John*, 281; Beasley-Murray, *Revelation*, 313, likewise states that "The promises to the conquerors, declared in the seven letters in chapters 2–3, therefore find their summary expression at this point."

4. Beckwith, *Apocalypse of John*, 752.

5. Mealy, *After the Thousand Years*, 263.

6. Fekkes, *Isaiah and Prophetic Traditions*, 262.

7. Beasley-Murray, *Revelation*, 338–39.

"father" to "God" suggests that ambiguity concerning the speaker's identity is deliberately introduced.

The new Jerusalem in the new heaven and new earth and the victors' place there are briefly introduced in the opening verses of chapter 21. But before the heavenly city can be described more fully, the Asian audience is once again confronted with a choice. With which city will they align themselves—Babylon/Rome or the new Jerusalem? "Each has its inhabitants and its destiny. Those who drink from salvation's springs supplied by God himself are true followers of Christ."[8] The fate of the sinners is spelled out in verse 8; their promise is the water of the second death—the lake of fire.

The Spring of the Water of Life

In 7:16–17 the multitude out of the great tribulation is told that they will never again thirst. For the Lamb shepherding them "will guide them to the springs of waters of life" (v. 17).[9] During the judgments of the trumpets (8:10–11), the two witnesses (11:6), and the bowls (16:4–5), the earthdwellers are deprived of their water supply. They instead become intoxicated on the wine of the prostitute (17:2). Ladd offers, "Perhaps a contrast is intended with those who drink from the golden cup full of the wine of impure passion (17:4; 18:3) offered men by the great harlot."[10]

The promise in 21:6 is repeated in contracted form in 22:17: "And let the one who thirsts come; let the one who desires partake freely of the living water." The threefold invitation to "Come" begins with that of the Spirit and the bride. The Spirit is always mentioned in connection with the hearing sayings in Revelation 2–3. Here it is the same, and what follows is a modified hearing saying, "And let the one who hears say, 'Come.'"

Charles believes these ἔρχου sayings are directed "to the world of men that were still thirsting for life and truth or were willing to accept them."[11] This identification seems improbable because of the interplay between Jesus' threefold announcement, "I am coming soon" (22:7, 12, 20) and the threefold invitation to "Come" (vv. 17, 20). The object of the invitation is specifically identified in verse 20, "Come, *Lord Jesus*."

---

8. Johnson, "Revelation," 12:594.

9. Friesen, *Imperial Cults*, 200, writes: "Rather than simply quoting Isaiah 49, however, John used the verb ὁδηγήσει ("he will lead") from Psalm 23 (Ps 22:3 LXX) and thereby injected the image of the Lord as shepherd."

10. Ladd, *Revelation of John*, 279.

11. Charles, *Revelation*, 2:180.

The image of water is considered to be particularly significant in the Laodicean letter. Because they are neither hot nor cold but lukewarm, Jesus is going to spit them out of his mouth (3:15–16). The travertine hot springs at Hierapolis, visible from Laodicea six miles north, are mentioned both by Strabo (*Geogr.* 13.4.4) and Vitruvius (8.3.10). Colossae, about ten miles east of Laodicea, was known for its cold pure waters. Laodicea, on the other hand, received its water supply through an aqueduct, whose source lies in springs two miles south near the modern city of Denizli. This water would be lukewarm when it arrived in the city, and its high mineral content made it petrifying (cf. Strabo *Geogr.* 13.4.14).[12] Rudwick and Green convincingly suggest that lukewarmness is not a reference to believers who lack zeal or are halfhearted, but rather to those whose works are barren and ineffective.[13] For the Laodiceans who were spiritually parched but did not know it, this final promise to quench their thirst would have been especially significant.

Biblical and Extrabiblical Co-texts

The saying in Revelation 21:6 and its couplet in 22:17 echo a familiar word of Jesus in John 7:37–38 (cf. 6:35). Mealy notes that determining a specific Old Testament antecedent for these two "thirst" passages in Revelation "is somewhat complicated by the possibility that John is adopting the conventional vocabulary of a living water tradition which was already current in Johannine circles."[14]

Because Jesus' invitation to drink in John 7:37–38 is directed to thirsty unbelievers, Beasley-Murray believes the invitation to drink in Revelation likewise "is extended to any who have not yet responded to the appeal of Christ in the gospel."[15] Such an identification is problematic, however. The synonyms—bride, hearer,[16] and thirsty—are all names used earlier in Revelation for the faithful victors and not for unbelievers.[17] Wall rightly identifies one audience as immature believers who have compro-

---

12. Hemer, *Letters to the Seven Churches of Asia*, 186–91, gives a notable summary of the water situation in Laodicea.

13. Rudwick and Green, "Laodicean Lukewarmness," 178.

14. Mealy, *After the Thousand Years*, 260.

15. Beasley-Murray, *Revelation*, 346.

16. The reference to the hearers in 22:17–18 again forms a chiastic frame with the initial mention in 1:3. This reiterates that the same Asian audience is in view throughout the prophecy.

17. Didache 10:6 likewise exhorts, "If anyone is holy, let him come (ἐρχέσθω); if anyone is not, let him repent."

The Fulfillment of the Victor Sayings

mised their faith. He points to a similar interplay in James between an invitation for Christ to return and for backslidden believers to return to God: "The imminence of the Lord's parousia (James 5:7–9) provides incentive to bring back those believers who 'wander from the truth' (James 5:19), since they will be saved from the eschatological consequences of 'a multitude of sins' (James 5:20)."[18]

The reference to water here makes explicit a possible inference of the meaning of "white stone" discussed in chapter 4. There the tradition of the rock as a source of living water, which Jesus develops in John 6–7, was examined. Schüssler Fiorenza notes that "Whereas the author of Revelation understands it ['living water' or 'water of life'] as an image for eschatological salvation . . . the Fourth Gospel clearly understands the metaphor in a christological sense . . . ."[19] Such a marked dichotomy cannot be sustained. For in John's Gospel living water is likewise a soteriological image (cf. 4:10–15), whereas in Revelation rock as a source of water may be a Christological image.

Enoch sees a fountain of righteousness that never becomes depleted and is surrounded by many other fountains of wisdom. "All the thirsty ones drink (of the water) and become filled with wisdom" (*1 En.* 48:1). Ode of Solomon 30:1–2 invites, "Fill for yourselves water from the living spring of the Lord, because it has been opened for you. And come all you thirsty and take a drink, and rest beside the spring of the Lord" (cf. 6:8–18).

Water and thirst are familiar Old Testament metaphors for spiritual life. The psalmist declares that all the righteous will drink from God's river, because with him is the fountain of life (Ps 36:8–9; πηγὴ ζωῆς, 35:10 LXX). Barrett (1978:327) sees a probable indirect allusion here and in 22:17 to Isaiah 55:1. Although Mealy believes that use of the verb διψάω in these passages is not distinctive enough to confirm an allusion to Isaiah 55:1, he contends, however, that the use of δωρεάν = ἄνευ ἀγυρίου (בלוא כסף) "is most significant and changes the character of the allusion from possible to probable."[20] John uses Isaiah's water metaphor to symbolize the restored covenant between the victors, the new remnant Israel, and God. Joel 3:18 declares that on the day of the Lord a spring (πηγή; 4:18 LXX) will flow out of the house of the Lord. Both Ezekiel (47:1ff.) and Zechariah (14:8) see waters of life flowing out of the eschatological Jerusalem. These depictions of life-giving waters are hyperboles,

---

18. Wall, *Revelation*, 268.
19. Schüssler Fiorenza, *Book of Revelation*, 100.
20. Mealy, *After the Thousand Years*, 261.

according to Stuart, used "as a symbolic depiction of the coming age of abundance."[21]

Inherit All Things as God's Son

Biblical and Extrabiblical Co-texts

The words in Revelation closely parallel those spoken to David through the prophet Nathan: "I will be a father to him, and he will be a son to me" (2 Sam 7:14). Here David is told that God will establish the throne of his kingdom forever (v. 14). Further, "because of its typological use in 2 Corinthians 6:18 and Hebrew 1:5, v. 14a has long been considered messianic in a Christological sense."[22] Anderson suggests that the father-son terminology may be an adoption formula based on a legal covenant.[23] Such covenant language is found in similar divine promises to Abraham (Gen 17:7–8) and to Solomon (2 Chr 7:14).

The term "father" in 2 Samuel is replaced by "God" in Revelation. This change of idiom for God is required "when John transfers the messianic formula from Christ to Christ's bride."[24] To John, Jesus alone has the right to regard God as Father (cf. Ps 2:7; Heb 1:5). Beasley-Murray aptly summarizes, "Believers are God's sons, but derivatively through their relation to the Christ, who is the unique Son of the Father."[25]

Paul also speaks of the relationship between the heavenly Father and his adopted sons and daughters (2 Cor 6:18). Furnish comments, "Here and in Rev 21:7 it is cited as a promise that those who are faithful to God's will shall know him as their father."[26] Paul likewise speaks of their inheritance: "Since you are a son, then also an heir through God" (Gal 4:7). He shares a similar sentiment in Romans 8:17, "If we are sons, then also heirs—heirs of God and fellow heirs with Christ." The single usage of κληρονομέω in Revelation where the word has the same reference as these texts "is one indication among many of the radical agreement between St John and St Paul."[27]

---

21. Stuart, *Ezekiel*, 412.
22. Youngblood, "2 Samuel," 3:891.
23. Anderson, *2 Samuel*, 122.
24. Wall, *Revelation*, 248.
25. Beasley-Murray, *Revelation*, 313–14.
26. Furnish, *II Corinthians*, 374.
27. Swete, *Apocalypse of St. John*, 281.

Final Victor Saying Conclusion

The promise of the water of life complements the earlier "life" promises—tree of life (2:7), crown of life (2:10), and book of life (3:5). These "life" metaphors emphasize that quality of life will be a hallmark of the new Jerusalem. The divine promise to quench the thirst of the saints (7:16; 21:6) is here realized. Does this promise apply only to the right to drink from the spring of the water of life? The promise to inherit all things (ταῦτα) seems to be broader. Johnson believes the victor "will inherit all the new things of the city of God,"[28] that is, everything described in 21:1–4. Mounce suggests that "all this" refers to the promises in chapters 2–3; they are "the inheritance of those who remain constant in their faith during the period of final testing."[29] As we have discovered, each of these fulfillments points to a similar spiritual reality. These rewards to the victors follow the reward of the unrighteous—second death in the lake of fire—described immediately before (20:11–15). The victors are promised an inheritance because they are sons of God. Given the repeated emphasis on deeds in the seven letters, it is noteworthy that here only the deeds of the unrighteous are mentioned (21:8); between God and his children relationship is emphasized.

The Ephesian Fulfillment

The Tree of Life

Three references to the tree of life are found in chapter 22—verses 2, 14, and 19. These verses will be discussed in turn around the specific themes which they address. Nicol recalls that the tree of life in Genesis 3, guarded by the cherubim and the flaming sword, symbolizes a threat: "In Rev 22, however, the image is of free access to the tree of life . . . . [and] symbolizes a promise."[30]

The initial reference in verse 2 mentions the location and purpose of the tree of life in the new Jerusalem. In verse 1 John is shown a river of the water of life proceeding from the throne of God and the Lamb. Charles observes that "it is noteworthy that no spiritual significance is attached to this river here, whereas the tree of life (xxii.2) is full of significance in this respect."[31] Yet in another place Charles makes a careful distinction between

---

28. Johnson, "Revelation," 12:594.
29. Mounce, *Book of Revelation*, 374.
30. Nicol, "The Threat and the Promise," 136.
31. Charles, *Revelation*, 2:175.

the tree of life and the water of life: "The latter is a free gift (xxii. 17, xxi. 6), given without money and without price to every one that thirsteth for it. It symbolizes the divine graces of forgiveness and truth and light, etc. (cf. vii. 17). If a man is faithful to the obligations entailed by these graces he becomes a victor (νικῶν) in the battle of life, and thus wins the right to eat of the tree of life."[32] This is true and therefore the river seen by John *is* spiritually significant: it contains the water of life promised in 21:6.

Whether the words ἐν μέσῳ τῆς πλατείας αὐτῆς καὶ τοῦ ποταμοῦ ἐντεῦθεν καὶ ἐκεῖθεν should be construed with verse 1 or 2 is debated. If with verse 1, the phrase ἐντεῦθεν καὶ ἐκεῖθεν has a prepositional force (cf. Dan 12:5 Theod); if with verse 2, the words function as adverbs (Exod 26:13; Ezek 47:7). Beckwith prefers to link with verse 1, referring to the waters "proceeding out . . . in the midst of the street thereof."[33] The rivers thus run down the street, lined on both sides with trees of life. Swete, however, prefers to align with verse 2, translating "between the street of the city and the river, on this side and on that."[34] The river flows across the broad street intersecting the city, each bank lined with a row of trees. Beasley-Murray suggests a third option, "In the midst of the city's street stands a single tree, the tree of life, *situated between either side of the river*, which at this point has diverged into two branches."[35] Since the city's street is earlier described as made of pure gold, like transparent glass (21:21), the view that places the river in the street seems most problematic.

The image appears to be drawn from Ezekiel 47:12, where Ezekiel sees the waters flowing first from the temple (v. 1), then into its courts and the city (v. 2) before moving beyond the eastern gate (v. 3). There is no mention of a street, and multiple fruit trees are growing on both banks of the river. Through Ezekiel's influence, Charles suggests that "our author departs here from the conception of a single tree of life as in Gen ii.9, iii.22; I Enoch xxiv.4, xxv.4–6."[36] Tree of life is thus used collectively. Hendrickson takes this collective sense a step further—"the city is full of rivers of life. It is also full of parks containing trees of life."[37] In 4 Ezra 2:18 the single tree of life likewise becomes twelve trees, each loaded with

32. Charles, *Revelation*, 1:155.
33. Beckwith, *Apocalypse of John*, 765.
34. Swete, *Apocalypse of St. John*, 299.
35. Beasley-Murray, *Revelation*, 331.
36. Charles, *Revelation*, 2:176.
37. Hendrickson, *More than Conquerors*, 206.

various fruits. But given its function in Revelation as the antitype of the tree in Eden and the two subsequent references that suggest a singular use as in the Ephesian promise, the tree of life should be regarded as one, not many (cf. *1 En.* 24:4).[38]

Because the difficulty of the grammar precludes a definitive translation, perhaps a commonsensical reading should be adopted which preserves the image of a single tree: "in between the street and the river, along the side of each, stood the tree of life." A reading similar to this has been proposed by Delebecque who argues that the best translation for ἐν μέσω A καὶ B, where A and B are genitives, is "between A and B."[39] Comparing the adverbial expression ἐντεῦθεν καὶ ἐκεῖθεν to a similar one in John 19:18, he suggests the location of the tree should be in relation to the river and the street. His proposed translation reads: "Au milieu, entre son esplanade et le fleuve, en venant d'ici et en venant de là, un Bois de vie."[40]

In 22:2 the purpose of the tree of life is given—to bear twelve crops of fruit, one each month. The clause κατὰ μῆνα ἕκαστον ἀποδιδοῦν τὸν καρπὸν αὐτοῦ renders freely the Hebrew text of Ezekiel 47:12 לחדשיו יבכר, where the Septuagint has τῆς καινότητος αὐτοῦ πρωτοβολήσει. Charles sees this as further evidence of John's independent usage of the Hebrew text.[41] The number twelve is used repeatedly in chapter 21 to speak of gates (vv. 12, 21), angels and tribes (v. 12), foundations and apostles (v. 14), and pearls (v. 21). The city is a cube measuring 12,000 stadia. The reference to twelve fruit in 22:2 is the final use of twelve and "seems to indicate that the provisions of the city for the nurture of its people are adequate. Just as its people are twelve, so is its capacity to sustain the life of those people."[42] The tree of life with its continuous fruit-bearing epitomizes the transformation in the new order by forgoing the seasonal cycles of seedtime and harvest (Eccl 3:2).[43]

---

38. The thought of the prophecy from *Barnabas* 6:13 is appropriate here: "He made a second creation in the last days. And the Lord says: 'Behold, I make the last things as the first.'"

39. Delebecque, "Où situer l'arbre de vie," 128; cf. Xenophon *Anab.* 2.2.3.

40. "In the middle, between its street and the river coming from here and from there, is a Tree of life"; Delebecque, "Où situer l'arbre de vie," 129. My translation was composed before I discovered Delebecque's article, which thus corroborated my own conclusion.

41. Charles, *Revelation*, 2:177.

42. Turner, "New Jerusalem in Revelation 21:1—22:5," 289.

43. Lucian (*Ver. hist. 13*) provides an interesting parallel when he describes horticulture on the Island of the Blessed: "The grape-vines yield twelve vintages a year, bearing every month; the pomegrantes, apples and other fruit-trees were said to bear thirteen times a year, for in one month, the Minoan, they bear twice."

The leaves of the tree of life are for the healing of the nations, an image probably drawn from Ezekiel 47:12 (cf. *4 Ezra* 7:123; *Apoc. Mos.* 6:2). The Hebrew ועלהו לתרופה is again followed rather than the Septuagint ἀνάβασις αὐτῶν εἰς ὑγίειαν. When John speaks of healing here, Ladd is surely correct in his observation that "we are not to think of nations of men living on the new earth in the age to come who will need healing from pain, sickness, and dying. The contrast is between this age, inhabited by suffering and dying peoples, and the age to come."[44] Freedom from sickness and pain has already been promised (21:4). Thus the imagery of abundant fruit and medicinal leaves symbolizes the far-reaching effects of Christ's death among the redeemed.

The nations, according to Mulholland, are "a consistent image for the realm in opposition to New Jerusalem."[45] These nations were destroyed by the smiting of Jesus (19:15) at the battle of Gog and Magog (20:8; cf. 16:14). Now in the new Jerusalem the nations have been transformed—populated by victors who walk by the light of the glory of God (21:24; cf. Tob 14:6–7). The victors were seen proleptically as those redeemed from every nation (5:10; 7:9). The kings of the earth bring the splendor of their nations into it (21:24). Du Rand reflects that "It is odd for kings to bring glory when the kings of the earth were relegated to the lake of fire (cf 19:11–26; 20:1–15)."[46] Rather, these kings are again the victors whose previously announced kingdom is finally realized and who will reign forever and ever (1:6; 5:10; 22:5). This understanding goes against du Rand's view that "the kings who were once enemies in chapter 16 and 19 become worshippers in chapter 21."[47]

This perspective that the healing of the nations means their conversion is likewise held by Bauckham, who believes the universalistic hope of the Old Testament prophets, yet unrealized, is taken up by John. "It will not be Israel alone that will be God's people with whom he dwells. It will not even be the eschatological Israel, redeemed from every nation. Rather, as a result of the witness of the church called from every nation, all nations will be God's people."[48] Bauckham cites the account of the two witnesses (typifying the church) as an example *par excellence* of such a conversion. Following the miraculous resurrection and ascension of the

---

44. Ladd, *Revelation of John*, 288.
45. Mulholland, *Revelation*, 331.
46. Du Rand, "Imagery of the Heavenly Jerusalem," 81.
47. Du Rand, "Imagery of the Heavenly Jerusalem," 82.
48. Bauckham, *Climax of Prophecy*, 311; cf. pp. 238–336.

witnesses (11:11–12) and a destructive earthquake (v. 13), the nations became fearful and gave glory to the God of heaven. "In 11:13 we see that what judgments alone failed to effect (9:20–21), the witness of the two witnesses does effect."[49] However, Kiddle issues a strong rebuttal:[50]

> But this is not what it seems; John does not share the optimism of Isaiah and the psalmists. In fact, he knows that the great mass of mankind will have committed the unpardonable crime of deifying evil. They will have pledged themselves to the cause of Satan, and damned themselves eternally (xiii. 8, 14, xiv. 9–11). In these circumstances, there is no question of any general 'conversion' of mankind in the last days. Men give *glory to the God of heaven* when it is too late for their own salvation—when they are compelled by overriding terror to recognize that the true Lord is Christ and not Antichrist. Remorse and not repentance is their condition. The scene should be compared with that in vi. 15–17, where the terror of men is equally an acknowledgment that at last they have understood God's omnipotence and the approach of inexorable judgment.

Jesus, at the conclusion of the Olivet discourse, likewise speaks of a judgment of the nations at the parousia (Matt 25:31–46). As the nations are gathered before his throne, Jesus separates the righteous from the unrighteous, as a shepherd separates the sheep from the goats. Although the people are first gathered collectively in nations, they are judged individually on the basis of their works. The wicked receive eternal punishment, while the righteous go to eternal life (v. 46). Blomberg comments, "The upshot here, then, as with the culmination of all Scripture in Rev 20–22, is to assert that ultimately there will only be two kinds of people in the world. These will be distinguished on the basis of their response to the gospel and its emissaries, and their eternal destinies will be as distinct as is conceivable."[51] Revelation 21:27 substantiates this: no abominator or liar among the nations shall enter the city—only those whose names are written in the Lamb's book of life. Giblin astutely observes that John never attempts to resolve the interplay between human free will and God's grace. "Nevertheless, the promises to the 'victor' enunciated in the seven proclamations to the Churches and the 'inheritance' (a gracious gift)

---

49. Ibid., 279.
50. Kiddle, *Revelation of St. John*, 206.
51. Blomberg, *Matthew*, 379.

promised to the 'victor' in 20:7 suppose that the apparent duality does not entail a dichotomy."[52]

The second reference (22:14) is found in the midst of the seventh and final beatitude: Blessed are those who wash their robes ἵνα ἔσται ἡ ἐξουσία αὐτῶν ἐπὶ τὸ ξύλον τῆς ζωῆς. The mixture of constructions—the future after ἵνα—is frequent in Revelation (3:9; 6:4, 11; 9:5, 20; 13:12, 14:13). Swete comments, "And if it is to be distinguished in meaning from the conjunctive, it may point to the certainty, the actuality, of the result, while the conjunctive suggests that there are conditions which must be fulfilled first."[53]

The close relationship between the promises and the beatitudes was noted in chapter 4. Their purpose in Revelation is very similar. Here in the midst of the description of the new Jerusalem is a hortative reminder to the Asian believers to purify themselves lest they be unable to enter the city and partake of the tree of life. Hatfield fittingly mentions, "Access to the tree of life in the holy city is a measure of divine forgiveness that expresses the full delight of paradise."[54] The authority to partake of the tree, denied after the Fall, is now restored by Jesus to those who live in faith and righteousness.

The final mention of the tree of life (22:19) is found in the prophetic curse that closes the book. The reading of the King James version here, "book of life," has no manuscript support. It follows the Textus Receptus based on Erasmus's reconstruction of the Greek text which follows the Vulgate.[55] Those who take away from, that is, distort or minimize, the words of John's prophecy, God will take away his share (τὸ μέρος) in the tree of life and in the holy city. This is the third and final use of μέρος as part of fulfillment imagery. The beatitude in 20:6 declares that the blessed are those who have a share in the first resurrection. Benedict makes this association: "μέρος is the same word used by the Lord in John 13:8 in reference to *fellowship*. The thought is similar in Revelation 22:19."[56]

At the Fall humanity lost access to the tree of life and received the curse of death (Gen 3:22), perhaps alluded to by the difficult term κατάθεμα (22:3). The share of the tree—the right to live forever—that was promised to the believers contrasts with that share of the lake of fire

---

52. Giblin, *Book of Revelation*, 193.
53. Swete, *Apocalypse of St. John*, 307–8.
54. Hatfield, "Function of the Seven Beatitudes," 166.
55. Cf. Johnson, "Revelation," 12:603n.
56. Benedict, "Use of ΝΙΚΑΩ in the Letters," 9.

The Fulfillment of the Victor Sayings

and brimstone—the second death—consigned to the unbelievers (21:8; cf. Mt 24:51; Lk 12:46). This warning is addressed to John's opponents in the Asian churches, such as the Nicolaitans and the followers of Jezebel. Whatever opposition they might muster is tempered with a fear that resistance to John's prophetic authority may well result in eternal exclusion from the new Jerusalem.

The Paradise of God

The phrase "paradise of God" is never found again in Revelation. Even though the word "paradise" is not used in these latter chapters, Jeremias believes "the garden of God is in Rev. the epitome of the glory of the consummation. The Jerusalem of the last time is depicted as Paradise when ref. is made to the trees of life by the water of life (22:1f., cf. 14, 19), to the destruction of the old serpent (20:2, cf. 10), and to freedom from suffering, affliction and death (21:4)."[57] He lists a number of paradise motifs found in the Old Testament.[58] These are now correlated with other similar motifs found in Revelation 20–22.

Motif	Revelation	Prophets
Peace among animals	5:13	Isa 11:6–7; 65:25
Peace between humans and animals		Isa 11:8; Hos 2:18
Longevity	20:6; 22:5	Isa 65:20, 22; Zech 8:4
New heaven and new earth	21:1	Isa 65:17; 66:22
Fellowship with God	21:3, 7; 22:3	Jer 31:33; Ezek 43:7, 48:35; Hos 2:19–20; Zeph 3:15–17
No death	21:4	Isa 25:8; 26:19
No mourning or crying	21:4	Isa 25:8; 65:19; Jer 31:13
No disease	21:4; 22:2	Isa 65:20; Ezek. 47:12; Mal 4:2
Abundant water	21:6; 22:1, 17	Isa. 35:6–7; 41:18–19; 43:19; 55:1; Ezek 47:1–12; Joel 3:18; Zech 14:8
Glory of God present	21:23	Isa 66:18–19; Ezek 43:2–5; 44:4
Salvation of the nations	21:24	Isa 66:20–21

57. Jeremias, "παράδεισος," *TDNT* 5:770.
58. Ibid., 5:767n. 15.

Motif	Revelation	Prophets
Peace among the nations	21:25	Isa 2:4; 9:6–7; Hos 2:18; Mic 4:3–4; Zech 9:10
Worship by all nations	21:26	Isa 2:2–3; 19:21; 66:23
Place of moral purity	21:27; 22:15	Ezek 36:25; 43:7; Zech 13:1–2; Mal 3:2–5
Great fruitfulness	22:2	Isa 35:1–2; Jer 31:12; Ezek 47:12; Hos 2:22; Joel 3:18; Amos 9:13–14
Curse lifted	22:3	Isa 65:22–23

All the paradise motifs identified by Jeremias are found in chapters 20–22 except those involving animals. This omission is inexplicable except that perhaps John failed to see animals as part of the new earth and he therefore reinterprets the Isaianic prophecies. Regarding this issue, Young suggests that animals in the new order "no longer are at enmity one with another, because evil has departed from men."[59] Dispensationalists see this transformation of the animal kingdom occurring during the millennium, but this is unlikely because their scenario still envisions sin upon the earth during the thousand years.[60] For it is only after the thousand years and the arrival of the new Jerusalem that paradise will be established. It is the aggregate of motifs that describe the heavenly city, not the specific phrase, that fulfills the promise of paradise, for it heralds the advent of the age of paradise.

Ephesian Fulfillment Conclusion

To interpret the fulfillment of each promise in the letters, we must recognize the multivalence of the imagery. The predominance of the chiliastic method of interpretation in the early church shows that these images were taken literally. "They believed that, when Christ returned to earth, Christians who had died would rise from the grave and inherit an earthly paradise together with believers who were alive."[61] From the perspective of the first hearers then, it is likely the promises would not just be interpreted metaphorically or spiritually.

---

59. Young, *Book of Isaiah*, 1.391.
60. Cf. Martin and Martin, *Isaiah*, 65.
61. Wainwright, *Mysterious Apocalypse*, 23.

For example, Ladd suggests that the tree of life "is a biblical way of expressing the promise of eternal life in the consummated Kingdom of God," while paradise describes "the dwelling place of God" and is "equivalent to the heavenly Jerusalem."[62] Yet the antitype of the tree of life in the paradise of God in Genesis suggests that the Ephesian audience would anticipate some tangible expression of a similar reality in the eschaton. Renewed spiritual life through the Holy Spirit had been experienced by the congregation. Yet the complete expression of that renewal lay ahead. The fruit produced each month by the tree is to be consumed by the nations for their healing. Since Jesus ate food while in his resurrection body (Luke 24:42–43; John 21:13–15), it was perhaps reasonable for the audience to expect some sort of heavenly repast like this and manna to feast on at the heavenly banquet.

While paradise is not specifically mentioned in the new Jerusalem, the concept is conveyed effectively through the numerous motifs from the Old Testament that suggest the heavenly city is a paradise. The original garden of Eden, lost in the Fall, is regained in a garden city given as the new and eternal home of the victors. Gundry fittingly summarizes, "As often in apocalyptic, *Endzeit* recaptures *Urzeit*."[63]

The Smyrnean Fulfillment

The Crown of Life

The crown or wreath (στέφανος) is mentioned seven other times in Revelation. The Philadelphians are told to hold on so they might receive their crown (3:11). The twenty-four elders seated on thrones wear golden crowns (4:4) and later lay them around the heavenly throne as they worship its occupant (4:10). The rider on the first horse (6:2) likewise wears a crown in his conquering role as a false Christ, and the locusts of the fifth trumpet have something resembling golden crowns upon their heads (9:7). The celestial woman of 12:1 wears a crown of twelve stars. Finally, the Son of Man seated on the white cloud is wearing a golden crown (14:14).

Another headdress called a diadem is found in the New Testament only in Revelation. Some English translations (e.g., NIV) fail to distinguish between the two and translate διάδημα as "crown" also. In 12:3 the dragon wears seven diadems, in 13:1 the beast wears ten diadems on his horns, and in 19:12 Jesus mounted on his white horse has many

---

62. Ladd, *Revelation of John*, 41.
63. Gundry, "New Jerusalem," 264.

diadems on his head. The diadem was always the sign of ancient royalty, and in Revelation "it symbolizes respectively the empire of the dragon, the beast, and of the royal Christ."[64] Trench questions whether crown in the Smyrnean promise is the diadem of royalty or the garland of victory. He chooses the former while acknowledging that στέφανος is seldom used in this sense.[65] John's clear distinction between the two in Revelation requires garland of victory as the choice.

The phrase "crown of life" is not used outside the Smyrnean promise. Yet the picture of the martyrs wearing white robes and holding palm branches (7:9) is closely related. As mentioned in chapter 3, the images of the wreath and the palm appear together frequently in literary and numismatic sources. This proleptic glimpse of the future inheritance of the victors shows the victorious church, which has survived the great tribulation, now alive and standing before the heavenly throne. This same group is seen again in 20:4–6. The occasion when they "came to life," or "lived again" (ἔζησαν; v. 4), is called the first resurrection. The rest of the dead did not "live again" until after the thousand years (v. 5), thus implying a second physical resurrection. According to Ladd, "The New Testament does not elsewhere clearly teach a twofold resurrection, although it is implied in such passages as John 5:29 and I Cor 15:24–25."[66]

This latter text is part of Paul's teaching on the resurrection in 1 Corinthians 15:12ff., the most extensive passage on the resurrection in the New Testament. It concludes with quotations in verses 54–55 from Isaiah 25:8a and Hosea 13:14 which declare victory over death. Isaiah 25:8b provides the allusion that John uses in Revelation 7:17 and 21:4a regarding the victors: God will wipe away every tear from their eyes. In Revelation 21:4b, ὁ θάνατος οὐκ ἔσται ἔτι is a probable paraphrase of Isaiah 25:8a. It is likely that John was familiar with Paul's use of this text, since both use "death" as the subject.[67] The intertextuality exemplified in these passages establishes that the crown of life is received at the first resurrection.

Whether the first resurrection includes only the martyrs or all believers is debated. Does the "rest of the dead" (20:5) include believers or only the unrighteous? Charles sees this resurrection as a special one for the martyrs which precedes the general resurrection of the dead: "Therefore

---

64. Purves, "Diadem," *HDB* 1:604.
65. Trench, *Epistles to the Seven Churches*, 115.
66. Ladd, *Revelation of John*, 268.
67. Cf. Fekkes, *Isaiah and Prophetic Traditions*, 254.

The Fulfillment of the Victor Sayings

not even the righteous, who had died a peaceful death, have part in this first resurrection."[68] Wall counters: "This resurrected body is not the martyr church as some argue . . . ; rather, this is the whole community of 'overcomers.' The eschatological community is composed of two groups of believers, the martyred and unmartyred faithful."[69] Wall's identification is correct because the victors have already been identified as all the saints, not just the martyrs. Also, given the use of the same Old Testament texts by Paul and John emphasizing victory over death at the resurrection, it is difficult to imagine John presenting two separate resurrections of believers in this passage. That all faithful believers are included in the first resurrection best agrees with the scriptural evidence.

The Second Death

The expression "second death" is used three times in chapters 20–21. In 20:6 it is found in the fifth beatitude. Whatever juridical authority sin had to produce death is now broken for the saints who participate in the first resurrection. Here the second death is contrasted with the first resurrection. A first death is presumed for all; for the believers that death is imminent (2:10) or has already happened (2:13; 20:4). While the first resurrection is selective and the second universal, the first death is universal (except for those raptured at the parousia; cf. 1 Thess 4:17) and the second is selective.[70] The time of the first resurrection is neither the intermediate state after death nor the believer's spiritual resurrection following his or her baptism; rather it occurs at the parousia.

Rissi presents a curious twist to the concept of the second resurrection. He says both resurrections can only designate the bestowal of eternal life. "Since the first resurrection brings redemption from the first death situation, it is proper to understand the second resurrection as redemption from the second death situation."[71] According to Rissi, the purpose of the second resurrection is to redeem those suffering under God's judgment and to bring reconciliation to all humanity, even the universe. Beasley-Murray provides an appropriate response: "Candour compels us to state

---

68. Charles, *Revelation*, 2:184; cf. Mounce, *Book of Revelation*, 360.

69. Wall, *Revelation*, 238; Beale, *John's Use of the Old Testament*, 162, likewise well states: "It is not just the way people die which proves them to be overcomers, but the whole of their Christian lives are to be characterized by 'overcoming,' which is a process completed upon death."

70. Cf. Farrer, *Revelation of St. John*, 206.

71. Rissi, *Time and History*, 124.

that John has given no clear indication of any such teaching."[72] Rissi fails to preserve the antimony present in Revelation between the Lamb who loved and shed his blood for the forgiveness of sins (1:5) and the Lamb whose wrath is so great that no one can stand against it (6:16).

In 20:11–15 the last judgment following the thousand years is depicted. This is the punishment Jesus warned about: "Fear the One who can to destroy the soul and body in Gehenna" (Mt 10:28). All the dead, excluded from the first resurrection, are given up by the sea and the grave to appear before the heavenly throne for resurrection bringing eternal death. Daniel 12:2 speaks of multitudes sleeping in death who will awake to shame and eternal contempt. Upon hearing the voice of the Son of Man, those practicing evil will come out their graves to be condemned to the resurrection of judgment (John 5:28–29). The dead are judged according to their works (Rev 20:12–13). These ἔργα, according to Rissi, "are, therefore, in all likelihood to be understood only in the negative sense as *sinful 'works'* and the 'books' as *registers of sins*."[73] Those whose names are missing from the book of life are condemned to the lake of fire (20:15). Lastly, death and hades are cast into the lake of fire, specifically called the second death (v. 14).[74] He who holds the keys of death and Hades (1:18) has finally locked the door.

The lake of fire is first mentioned in 19:20. Following the defeat of the beast and the false prophet by the rider on the white horse, the two are cast alive into the lake of fire, described as burning sulfur or brimstone (θεῖον). Jesus makes a curious statement about the last judgment: the King will ask the cursed to depart from him into the eternal fire prepared for the devil and his angels (Mt 25:41). Speaking of these texts, Swete observes, "It is remarkable that here as in Mt. *l.c.* the qualification for the Second Death is a negative one (οὐχ εὑρέθη, οὐκ ἐποιήσατε). The negation of eternal life is eternal death."[75] Whereas God was forced in the beginning to provide a place of punishment for Satan and his rebellious angels, that abode was never intended for humanity, which was created for fellowship

---

72. Beasley-Murray, *Revelation*, 304.

73. Rissi, *Future of the World*, 36.

74. The order of resurrection and judgment in chapter 20 parallels that given by Paul in 1 Corinthians 15:23–26 (contra Swete, *Apocalypse of St. John*, 263): first, Christ; at the parousia those who belong to him (the saints in the thousand years); then the end when all dominion, authority, and power are destroyed (Armageddon, Gog and Magog); finally, death, the last enemy, is destroyed (the lake of fire).

75. Swete, *Apocalypse of St. John*, 274.

The Fulfillment of the Victor Sayings

in the eternal kingdom. But following the Fall, those who freely chose to rebel found themselves likewise destined for the eternal fire.

Following the battle of Gog and Magog, the devil is cast into the lake of fire and brimstone where he joins the beast and the false prophet (20:10). The three will be tormented (βασανισθήσονται) day and night forever. Caird writes, "In justice to John let it be noted that the lake of fire is not for men, as it is for the demonic enemies of God, a place of torment."[76] Caird, however, overlooks 14:10 where an angel announces that anyone who worshiped the beast and received his mark would be tormented with fire and brimstone before the holy angels and the Lamb. To suggest that the second death is annihilation is to import a theological concept absent in the text. Rissi responds to the annihilationist perspective: "The wording of 20:10 forbids thinking of a dissolution into nothingness."[77] Swete adopts a mollifying tone on this issue, "Whether the function of the fire is to destroy or to punish or to purify is not within the scope of the revelation entrusted to the Seer."[78] Yet Swete's statement regarding the function of the lake of fire is unsatisfying. Whatever its ultimate outworking in the divine plan, the lake of fire for John's audience was meant to be a hard saying to cause false teachers to repent and to strike fear into potential apostates.

The initial vision of the new Jerusalem brings an announcement that there will be no more death for God's people (21:4). The victors addressed in the final promise saying (vv. 6–7) are contrasted with the sinners whose lot is the lake of fire (v. 8). This antithetical formula "shows clearly the character of those slaves who do not become victors."[79] Here is the final mention of the second death—it is the lake of burning fire and brimstone.

In 21:8 is the first of three vice lists that conclude the book (cf. the first one in 9:20–21). Park makes an interesting observation that the unique vices—cowardice and faithlessness, uncleanness and baseness—stand at the head of each list and "are closely related to the context in which the list is given."[80] Certainly cowardice and faithlessness would be temptations to the Asian believers facing the pressures of the imperial cult; uncleanness and baseness are perhaps synonymous with the fornication and idolatry of Jezebel and the Nicolaitans. Gundry concludes, "To save their necks, they [the professing Christians] participated in the vile practices of non-

---

76. Caird, *Revelation of St. John*, 260.
77. Rissi, *Time and History*, 124.
78. Swete, *Apocalypse of St. John*, 283.
79. Minear, *I Saw a New Earth*, 61.
80. Park, "More than a Regained Eden," 183.

Christians and murderously betrayed their fellow Christians to the persecuting authorities and practiced the sexual immorality and magic that went along with idolatry."[81]

The three lists are compared for similarity, not for order, in the following chart. Texts in the seven letters that mention these vices are also included in the left column.

21:8	21:27	22:15
	Common (e.g., unclean)	Dogs (e.g., base)
Cowards (cf. 2:13)		
Faithless (cf. 2:10)		
Abominators (cf. 3:4, 18)	Abominators	
Murderers		Murderers
Fornicators (cf. 2:14, 20)		Fornicators
Sorcerers		Sorcerers
Idolaters (cf. 2:14, 20)		Idolaters
Liars (cf. 2:2, 9, 20; 3:9)	Liars	Liars

Regarding the first list in 21:8, "[m]ost of the terms are traditional in the descriptions of paganism (cf. Rom 1.28 ff.), but the first two in particular make it clear that the loser means primarily the faithless, he who has failed to keep the words and works of Christ to the end, who has denied his name and become 'conformed to this world.'"[82] The cowards and unfaithful are undoubtedly those who have apostatized in the face of the beast's threats.[83]

The source of the lake of fire imagery is obscure. Gehenna, the usual biblical expression for hell (cf. Matt 5:29–30; Mark 9:43–49), is missing in Revelation. The linkage with brimstone/sulfur suggests the destruction of Sodom and Gomorrah upon which God rained fire and brimstone (Gen 19:24; cf. Deut 29:23; 3 Macc 2:5; Luke 17:29; *1 Clem.* 11:1). The psalmist (11:6; cf. 1QpHab 10:5) states that the Lord will rain fire and brimstone upon sinners. The final verse of Isaiah 1 (v. 31) and the book's final verse (66:24) both state that the fate of the wicked is to burn and no

81. Gundry, "New Jerusalem," 258.
82. Leivestad, *Christ the Conqueror*, 214.
83. False teachers may also be in view. Ignatius (*Eph.* 7.1), speaking of false teachers, says, "For they are mad dogs that bite by stealth; you must be on your guard against them, for their bite is hard to heal."

one can quench the fire (cf. Mark 9:48). Isaiah (34:9; cf. 30:33) prophesies the destruction of Edom with sulfur and burning pitch that will never be quenched. And Ezekiel (38:22) prophesies to Gog that God will rain fire and brimstone upon him and his allied nations. A similar judgment is declared by the angel of the sixth trumpet—plagues of fire, smoke, and sulfur kill one-third of humanity (Rev 9:17–18). The combined allusions in chapter 20 to Gog and to fire and brimstone suggest John's dependence in part on Ezekiel.

1 Enoch contains several examples of this theme. In 10:12–13 the unrighteous burn and die for eternity as their punishment on the day of judgment; 48:9 paints a macabre portrait of the unrighteous burning in the presence of the righteous. In 90:25–26 the guilty shepherds and their blind sheep are cast into the fiery abyss to burn in the sight of Enoch. The great judgment into which the souls of the sinners are cast is characterized as darkness, nets, and burning flame (103:8).

Tenney suggests this possible local background: "Perhaps the imagery was affected by the widespread knowledge of the eruption of Vesuvius in AD 79, when the city of Herculaneum perished in a flow of molten lava."[84] If the early dating of the book is held, such a connection would not be relevant.

The background of "lake" is even more difficult. In 1 Enoch 67:13 Michael says that the punishment of the angels will be an example to the kings and rulers: "For these waters of judgment are poison to the bodies of the angels as well as sensational to their flesh; (hence) they will neither see nor believe that these waters become transformed and become a fire that burns forever." Like Revelation, 1 Enoch identifies water as a medium for judgment.

Smyrnean Fulfillment Conclusion

The first resurrection is contrasted with the second death in 20:6. The juxtaposition of first resurrection/second death parallels that of crown of life/second death in the Smyrnean promise. Participation in the first resurrection is thus the fulfillment of the promised crown of life. Perhaps at that first resurrection the Smyrneans hoped for a crown to be placed on their heads, like that like placed on the victors at their own Smyrnean games. Such would be the public acknowledgment for their willingness to suffer.

The second death is the final penalty of the ungodly, an eternal death in the lake of fire. According to Wall, it is a euphemism "for the fate of

---

84. Tenney, *Interpreting Revelation*, 192.

those who do not share in the eschatological blessing of eternal life."[85] The juxtaposition seen most basically in the life/death motif is likewise developed in the holy city/unholy lake of fire imagery. A thick and high wall surrounds this city (21:12) to keep out the unholy (22:15). "Thus, for the seer, the wall of jasper does not serve as a menacing defence against enemies, but rather as an announcement to the world of condemnation outside the city of the radiant glory of God's community in the new Jerusalem."[86] An eternal demarcation exists then between those experiencing the first resurrection and the second death. Whereas the crown is the prize for the victor, the lake of fire is the awful "reward" for the sinner.

The Pergamene Fulfillment

The Hidden Manna

There are no other references to manna in Revelation. For a fulfillment Meyer suggests, "As in contemporary Jewish literature, the manna of Rev. 2:17 has a counterpart in water."[87] The failure to mention water in the victor sayings in chapters 2–3 need not preclude its connection in the minds of John and his audience. Whereas the image of manna disappears, the image of water appears in later chapters. In 7:16–17 the martyrs out of the great tribulation are promised that never again will they hunger or thirst because the Lamb would lead to springs of living water (cf. John 6:35). The final promise in 21:6 reiterates the sense of this promise. It is further realized in chapter 22 with the appearance of the river of living water (v. 1) which is freely given to those who are thirst (v. 17).

A number of commentators see the fulfillment of this promise in the messianic banquet. Giblin believes that "since all the other promises to the victor have a fully eschatological sense, referring to one's final status in heaven and/or the new Jerusalem the 'hidden manna' probably refers directly to the wedding-feast of the Lamb, and would only *connote* the Eucharist as an anticipation of that event."[88] Caird suggests that the main course at the messianic banquet will consist of heavenly manna.[89] Without knowing how delectable such an entrée might be, we should hope it is more appetizing than the manna the Israelites received. Johnson spiritual-

---

85. Wall, *Revelation*, 239.
86. Rissi, *Future of the World*, 71.
87. Meyer, "Μάννα," *TDNT* 4:466.
88. Giblin, *Book of Revelation*, 227 n. 185.
89. Caird, *Revelation of St. John*, 42.

The Fulfillment of the Victor Sayings

izes the purpose of this metaphor, "To those at Pergamum who refused the banquets of the pagan gods, Christ will give the manna of his great banquet of eternal life in the kingdom (John 6:47–58)."[90] Because John fails to make an overt connection between manna and the wedding supper, such a linkage remains inconclusive.

The White Stone

In the last chapter we examined the scriptural prominence of the theme of stone as a building material. It should not be surprising then that such imagery is also prominent in John's vision of the new Jerusalem. In chapter 21 an amazing list of twelve stones is found. These form the twelve foundations of the heavenly city. The following chart compares this list with that of the twelve stones found on the high priest's vestment in Exodus and the identical list that adorned the king of Tyre in Ezekiel (cf. also Is 54:11–12). The names of the stones are presented in Greek because their varied English translations obscure the relationship between the lists.

Rev 21:19–20	Exod 28:17–20; 39:10–13 LXX	Ezek 28:13 LXX
ἴασπις (6)	1. σάρδιον	σάρδιον
σάπφιρος (5)	2. τοπάζιον	τοπάζιον
χαλκηδών	3. σμάραγδος	σμάραγδον
σμάραγδος (3)	4. ἄνθραξ	ἄνθρακα
σαρδόνυξ	5. σάοφειρπς	σάπφειρον
σάρδιον (1)	6. ἴασπις	ἴασπιν (+ἀργύριον, χρυσίον)
χρυσόλιθος (10)	7. λιγύριον	λιγύριον
βήρυλλος (11)	8. ἀχάτης	ἀχάτην
τοπάζιον (2)	9. ἀμέθυστος	ἀμέθυστον
χρυσόπρασος	10. χρυσόλιθος	χρυσόλιθον
ὑάκινθος	11. βηρύλλιον	βηρύλλιον
ἀμέθυστος (9)	12. ὀνύχιον	ὀνύχιον

Charles draws a correspondence between the jewels in Revelation and the signs of the zodiac, stating that the former list is exactly the reverse of the usual zodiacal order. John "regards *the Holy City which he describes*

---

90. Johnson, "Revelation," 12:442.

as having nothing to do with the ethnic speculations of his own and past ages regarding the city of the gods."[91] Jart counters this assertion by pointing to zodiacs arranged both clockwise and counterclockwise that decorated synagogues between the third and sixth centuries AD: "Thus, Charles' theory according to which an ulterior motive might be involved in the 'counterclockwise' arrangement is hardly tenable."[92] Why John reordered the stones remains open, although various other explanations have been proposed.[93]

The ascription of the title "priests" to the saints in Revelation (1:6; 5:10; 20:6) suggests a possible relationship to the high priestly vestment. However, John's rearrangement and omission of the stones suggests that he had other purposes in mind. John rearranged the traditional order of the tribes in 7:5–8 to emphasize Judah, the tribe from which the Messiah Jesus came. Here his rearrangement emphasizes the jasper stone. When John has his initial vision of the One seated on the throne (4:3), the first image given of his likeness is that of jasper (ἴασπις) and carnelian (σάρδιον), the two stones that head the lists in Revelation and in the Old Testament. When this throne is seen again in 20:11, it is described as great and *white*.[94] In 21:11 the new Jerusalem descends shining with the glory of God, brilliant like jasper said to be clear as crystal. Thus the colors suggested in 4:3 are probably transparent white and red. "Der Jaspis ist in der Apokalypse nicht der unansehnliche Stein, den wir so nennen, sondern einer der edelsten Steine, der nach Ansehen und Aussehen auf den Diamanten hinausläuft."[95] The objections of Jart to this identification as a diamond are unconvincing, so Kraft's conjecture remains just that.[96]

The walls of the new Jerusalem are composed of jasper (21:18), and jasper is then mentioned as the first precious stone to decorate the foundations of the wall (v. 19). The walls contain twelve gates inscribed (ἐπιγεγραμμένα) with the names of Israel's twelve tribes; the foundations are inscribed with the names of the twelve apostles (vv. 12–13). Apart from the Pergamene promise in 2:17, this is the only text in Revelation

---

91. Charles, *Revelation*, 2:168; for the zodiac see page 167.

92. Jart, "Precious Stones in the Revelation," 164.

93. Cf. Swete, *Apocalypse of St. John*, 291; Farrer, *Revelation of St. John*, 219.

94. The throne of God seen in 1 Enoch 18:8 is made of alabaster. Alabaster was used in antiquity for making ointment jars and various ornaments. "When pure it is white or translucent" (Bowes, "Alabaster," 1:95).

95. "In the Apokalypse jasper is not the unattractive stone, which we so named, but is one of the most precious stones, suggesting the reputation and appearance of diamonds"; Kraft, *Offenbarung des Johannes*, 268.

96. Jart, "Precious Stones in the Revelation," 171–72.

that speaks of a stone being inscribed. Finally, the city has no sun or moon for light because the glory of God, permeating its walls of jasper, lights it (21:23). John's description of the new Jerusalem suggests that the city's beauty comes from the dwelling of God from which the light of his glory emanates throughout the city.

The New Name

Although ὄνομα is used twenty-six times outside the seven letters, there appear to be no other occurrences directly related to this image. The reference in 19:12 to a name not known to anyone but himself pertains to Christ only and not to the victor. For the names written in the book of life are presumably each believer's given personal name (20:15; 21:26). And the names of the twelve tribes written on the gates and the names of the twelve apostles written on the foundations of the new city are well known (21:12, 14). Our discussion of 2:17 in chapter 4 left unresolved whether the new name applied to the individual believer or to Christ. The lack of any individual fulfillment or a fulfillment related to Christ's new name leads to the conclusion that the promise of such a new name is not individualized.

Pergamene Fulfillment Conclusion

Because manna is never mentioned again in Revelation, proposed links with the messianic banquet are only speculative. Hidden manna, like the fruit of the tree of life, is the spiritual sustenance of the heavenly city. It suggests fellowship with Jesus himself, the bread of life. The identification of the white stone remains problematic. The list of twelve inscribed stones that form the foundation of the new Jerusalem presents intriguing parallels. Perhaps the white stone inscribed with a new name is related to the victor's place in the holy city, where he or she becomes a part of the foundation of the city with the twelve apostles. White jasper is associated in several texts with the throne of God. Perhaps the promise to sit on a throne is to join Jesus in ruling from a white throne, following the great white throne judgment. The new name is probably not a personal one given to believers, but related to Christ's new name.

The Thyatiran Fulfillment

Shepherd the Nations with a Rod of Iron

Craigie observes "that one of the NT books which contains many references to Ps 2 is the Revelation of St. John."[97] Besides the Thyatiran promise, he references among others 12:5 and 19:15, both verses to be examined in this section. The placement of these references (2:27; 12:5; 19:15) in the key places of chiastic structuration (B, F, B′) suggests their significance in the book. Although this theme of the judgment over the nations is an important eschatological role for the victors, Mealy believes "the eschatological role which *is* most emphasized is that which the overcomers are to enter in relationship to God and Christ."[98] We agree with Mealy that the interpretation of 2:26 suggesting that the nations survive to be ruled by the saints "is not at all a likely reading of the promise, since in this context it would connote despotism, which is highly out of character for Revelation."[99]

In 12:5 the woman gives birth to a male child, "who is to rule all the nations with a rod of iron." The child is then snatched up to God and his throne (θρόνον). The purpose for the birth of the Messiah is singular—to rule the nations. Mounce fittingly comments, "As a shepherd defends his flock against the wild beasts of prey, so will Christ at his return strike the nations which oppress and persecute his church . . . (in 2:27 the overcomers at Thyatira are promised a part in this rule)."[100] Nothing is mentioned of a sacrificial death for redemption of the nations (the song of the martyrs does so in verse 11, however). The immediate reference to throne indicates that "rule" is the verb's meaning here.

This promise shares an affinity with the Laodicean promise which also speaks of thrones. The fulfillment of that promise is found in chapter 20, whose language closely parallels this text. A precondition for ruling the nations with a rod of iron is the defeat of Satan on earth, a theme found in both chapters. Botha rightly observes, "The names given to Satan in 12:9 are here repeated—thus identifying him as one and the same adversary."[101] The verbal relationship between chapters 12 and 20 is outlined below:

---

97. Craigie, *Psalms 1–50*, 69.
98. Mealy, *After the Thousand Years*, 80.
99. Ibid., 121n. 1.
100. Mounce, *Book of Revelation*, 238.
101. Botha, "Authorship; Final Judgment," 138.

The Fulfillment of the Victor Sayings

Satan	Chapter 12	Chapter 20
Names	καὶ ἐβλήθη ὁ δράκων ὁ μέγας, ὁ ὄφις ὁ ἀρχαῖος, ὁ καλούμενος Διάβολος καὶ ὁ Σατανᾶς (v. 9)	καὶ ἐκράτησεν τὸν δράκοντα, ὁ ὄφις ὁ ἀρχαῖος, ὅς ἐστιν Διάβολος καὶ ὁ Σατανᾶς, καὶ ἔδησεν αὐτὸν χίλια ἔτη (v. 2)
Activity	ὁ πλανῶν τὴν οἰκουμένην ὅλην (v. 9); εἰδὼς ὅτι ὀλίγον καιρὸν ἔχει (v. 12)	ἵνα μὴ πλανήσῃ ἔτι τὰ ἔθνη ἄχρι τελεσθῇ τὰ χίλια ἔτη. μετὰ ταῦτα δεῖ λυθῆναι αὐτὸν μικρὸν χρόνον (v. 3)
Heavenly action	ἐβλήθη εἰς τὴν γῆν, καὶ οἱ ἄγγελοι αὐτοῦ μετ᾽ αὐτοῦ ἐβλήθησαν (v. 9)	καὶ ἔβαλεν αὐτὸν εἰς τὴν ἄβυσσον καὶ ἔκλεισεν καὶ ἐσφράγισεν ἐπάνω αὐτοῦ (v. 3)

Whereas the fall of Satan in chapter 12 is to the earth because of his defeat in heaven, the fall in chapter 20 appears to be from the earth to the Abyss. The similarity of language and subject indicates that the two accounts are closely related.

In 2:12 and 16 Jesus vows to use the sharp sword proceeding out of his mouth to rebuke the unrepentant in the Pergamene congregation. In 19:15 the purpose of the similar sharp sword is that he might smite (πατάξῃ) the nations and rule (ποιμανεῖ) them with an iron rod, again following 2:27. The actual destruction of the heathen is likened to a trampling in the winepress of God's wrath (cf. 14:19–20). The holy war motif is prominently seen here, according to Giblin. Like the classic example in the Exodus, "God's people do not engage in belligerent action here. Their role is to follow God's directives, and their physical activity amounts to little more than local motion from one dwelling to another."[102]

Caird asks when the victor will smash the nations with an iron rod, and concludes it cannot be either in the heavenly city or in the millennial kingdom. "We are compelled therefore to look for the fulfilment of this promise *within the present order*; and since the Christian becomes a Conqueror in this world only in the moment of his leaving it, the fulfilment must be the actual death of the martyrs."[103] He overlooks the preceding verse 19:14 where the armies of heaven, riding white horses and wearing white garments, both symbols of victory, are following the messianic rider on the white horse. This is the one who smites the nations (v. 15). I agree

---

102. Giblin, *Book of Revelation*, 250.
103. Caird, *Revelation of St. John*, 46.

with Mealy that the Thyatiran promise is "exhausted in the picture of their participation with Christ in the 'battle of the witnesses' in ch. 19."[104] Likewise, nothing in Revelation 20:1–6 suggests that the nations of the world are spared judgment at the parousia.[105] The nations mentioned later in chapters 21–22 are comprised of the redeemed, not unbelievers.

The Morning Star

The fulfillment of this promise is found in 22:16 where Jesus says, "I am . . . the bright morning star." The adjective λαμπρός is added to Christ's self-identification here. Earlier it is used positively to speak of shining garments (15:6; 19:8) and shining crystal (22:1) or negatively of the splendors of Babylon (18:14). The noun form is used in Isaiah 60:3 which says that "kings will come to your light and nations to your brightness" (λαμπρότητι, LXX; cf. *1 Bar.* 5:3). Bauckham writes, "It is worth noticing that the last two words of Isaiah 60:3, which are paraphrased by this designation of Jesus, are precisely those which were omitted from John's adaptation of Isaiah 60:3 in Revelation 21:24. He has saved them for this designation of Jesus as the one who draws the nations into the New Jerusalem."[106]

Bauckham notes an interesting pattern in Revelation of combined allusions to pairs of prophecies of the Davidic Messiah:[107]

Rev 2:26–28	Ps 2:9	+	Num 24:17
Rev 5:5	Gen 49:9	+	Isa 11:10
Rev 19:15	Ps 2:9	+	Isa 11:4
Rev 22:16	Isa 11:10	+	Num 24:17

These four Old Testament passages share in common the catchword שׁבט (rod or scepter). Because these passages refer to a destructive judgment on the nations, allusions are made to them in the first three texts to advance the theme of messianic victory over the nations. However, in 22:16 the image is positive. Jesus' coming precipitates the arrival of the multinational church (7:9) into the heavenly city. Speaking of this image in Jude, Bauckham comments: "Thus the rising of the morning star is a symbol

---

104. Mealy, *After the Thousand Years*, 238.

105. The usual New Testament word for the Lord's coming παρουσία is never used in Revelation. "One thousand years," used six times in chapter 20, seems to be John's metaphor for the same reality.

106. Bauckham, *Climax of Prophecy*, 325.

107. Ibid., 323.

for the Parousia of Christ which inaugurates the eschatological age."[108] The reference in 21:24 validates this: "The nations will walk by its light." The future of περιπατέω is found only in the Sardian letter, where those who have not soiled their garments "will walk with me in white" (3:4). The victors are those who will walk in the glorious light of Jesus, the bright morning star.

Finally, a ligature, or abbreviation, consisting of the initial Greek letters—iota (I) and chi (C)—of the name Jesus and his title Christ is known from Christian antiquity. Finnegan describes it as "essentially the combination of a cross mark and a vertical stroke and, in its simplest form, would look like a six-pointed star."[109] The star thus symbolized Jesus Christ.

Thyatiran Fulfillment Conclusion

The promise that the oppressive world system would soon come under the lordship of Christ would be eagerly anticipated by the Thyatirans. At his appearing they would constitute the heavenly army that would shatter the strength of the ungodly nations and establish a godly rule. It must have been reassuring that with all the military imagery, an actual battle is never depicted. The nations led by the dragon, the beast, and the false prophet simply dissolve at the word issuing from Christ's mouth.

In chapter 4 we concluded that the promise of the morning star certainly pointed to a person, an opinion validated here. Trench sustains this opinion that Christ himself will be given to the victor. However, Beckwith demurs, "The meaning cannot be, as some take it, that he will give himself to the victor, a conception not possible in our Apocalyptist's idea of the eschatological kingdom."[110] However, Lenski rightly affirms that "The Victor King Jesus is the brilliant Morning Star in royal splendor; and he gives to every faithful believer the gift to be like him in royal splendor. He and all these other victors shall shine together, all being as morning stars in brilliance, our brilliance being derived from him."[111] This seems the most satisfactory explanation of the image.

---

108. Bauckham, *Jude, 2 Peter*, 226.
109. Finnegan, *Archaeology of the New Testament*, 353.
110. Trench, *Epistles to the Seven Churches*, 160; Beckwith, *Apocalypse of John*, 471.
111. Lenski, *Interpretation of St. John's Revelation*, 124–25.

The Sardian Fulfillment

White Garments

Besides ἱματίοιν (3:4, 5, 18; 4:4; 16:15; 19:13, 16), three other words are used in Revelation for clothing—στολή (6:11; 7:9, 13, 14; 22:14), βύσσινος (18:12, 16; 19:8 [2x], 14), and λίνον (15:6). Charles (1920: 1.186–87) regards the first three as synonymous, while Louw and Nida also regard βύσσινος and λίνον as synonymous.[112] This example again demonstrates John's propensity to use synonyms throughout the book (cf. "dragon," etc; Rev 12:3ff, 20:2). The rider on the white horse is dressed in a ἱματίοιν at his return (19:13) and inscribed on the garment over his thigh is the name "King of kings and Lord of lords" (v. 16). Angels are robed in white linen in 15:6. The references in 15:6 and 19:14 contain the characteristic verb of clothing or dressing ἐνδύω.

The twenty-four elders (4:4), ministering around the heavenly throne with the four living creatures, are wearing white garments. Because of this, Michaelis believes they are probably angels because "the white clothes show that the elders belong to the heavenly world."[113] However, the elders are wearing crowns and sitting on thrones—rewards likewise promised to the victors. And the elders are clearly distinguished from the angels who appear in 5:2 and 11,[114] so to identify them as angels seems improbable. If human, who are they? And what does their number represent, since twenty-four is never used as a symbolic number except in Revelation?

Ford writes, "Just as the creatures represent the universe, so do the elders represent Israel."[115] Such an exclusive identification is unprecedented in Revelation. Swete concludes that this vision is proleptic and represents the whole church, Jew and Gentile, "seen as already white, crowned, and enthroned in the Divine Presence—a state yet future (ἃ δεῖ γενέσθαι), but already potentially realized in the Resurrection and Ascension of the Head."[116] When the martyrs first appear in 6:9–11, they are under the altar, not seated on thrones. When they appear again in chapter 8, the

---

112. Charles, *Revelation*, 1:186–87; L& N 1:73n. 16.

113. Michaelis, "λευκός," *TDNT* 4:249n. 56; cf. Charles, *Revelation*, 1:130.

114. Johnson, "Revelation," 12:470n., rightly notes that the proper reading of 5:10 is crucial to the identification of the elders. "If *hemas* is original, it would be difficult to argue that the elders are angelic beings." He adopts the shorter reading (like NA26), yet still views the elders as angels. He likewise concedes that white garments and crowns of gold generally belong to the saints in Revelation, yet begs an exception in the case of the elders.

115. Ford, *Revelation*, 80.

116. Swete, *Apocalypse of St. John*, 69.

The Fulfillment of the Victor Sayings

elders are clearly distinguished from this group (v. 13). Some connection may exist between these twenty-four elders and the twenty-four courses of priests which ministered in the temple (1 Chr 24:1ff.). The elders function as representative priests who hold golden incense bowls containing the prayers of the saints, who themselves are priests (Rev 5:8, 10).[117] These elders later give thanks for the vindication of the saints (11:16–18). The twenty-four elders are last seen in 19:4. After the rider on the white horse appears, the elders disappear.

The imagery of the four living creatures is clearly adapted from Ezekiel chapters 1 and 10. But what about the twenty-four elders? In chapters 8 and 11 Ezekiel is taken by the Spirit to the temple in Jerusalem. In 8:11–13 the prophet sees a group of seventy leaders called elders (πρεσβύτεροι). These elders have censers in hand from which incense is emanating. In 8:16 he sees another group of about twenty-five men, who are most probably priests.[118] The elders and the priests are both engaged in idolatrous worship. Another group of twenty-five men is seen in chapter 11:1ff. Craigie identifies them as princes of the people, "in effect ministers of state, and their meeting is thus an assembly of the national council ruling Judah and Jerusalem, under delegated authority."[119] These leaders have acted wickedly and have now fallen under divine judgment. It is these groups of elders, priests, and leaders after which John has probably patterned his heavenly council of elders, who in contrast are godly. He has rounded off the number to twenty-four to conform with his symbolic use of twelve and its multiples, since the characteristic number of the heavenly city is twelve.

In 21:12–14 the twelve tribes and the twelve apostles represent the collective people of God. John's elders probably symbolize a similar reality of the twelve Old Testament patriarchs and the twelve apostles. Wall, however, takes the view that heavenly elders exemplify the community of true Israel that has remained faithful to the apostolic witness of Christ: "the elders are not specifically the risen apostles, long since martyred; rather, they represent the community they founded and continue to nourish through their memories and teachings."[120] This perspective is unlikely; rather Jesus'

---

117. The saints are likewise seen holding harps and singing the song of Moses (Israel) and the Lamb (the church) in 15:3 (cf. 14:1–2).

118. The Hebrew text says about (-כ) twenty-five in 8:16 but drops the 'about' in 11:1. The Septuagint reads twenty men in 8:16 and about (ὡς) twenty-five men in 11:1. Alexander, "Ezekiel," 6:784, makes a likely suggestion that this number is "representative of each of the twenty-four courses of the priests plus the high priest (cf. 1 Chron 23)."

119. Craigie, *Ezekiel*, 74.

120. Wall, *Revelation*, 93.

promise (Matt 19:28) of thrones to his apostles in the eschaton is here seen fulfilled. If John the Revelator is John the apostle, his inclusion among the Twelve on the foundations of the new Jerusalem is a proleptic one.[121]

In 6:11 the martyrs are each given white robes as they rest, awaiting other martyrs to join them. These white robes indicate the group's blessedness as they patiently await the consummation. Charles suggests that because the martyrs have already reached the stage of perfection, here and in 7:9, 13 they are shown clothed in heavenly bodies. However, "from the rest of the faithful this gift was withheld till the end of the world, as they were still in a state of imperfection, even though redeemed."[122] This conclusion is based on his distinction between the saints and the martyrs. However, as argued earlier in the chapter, this group in white robes includes all believers. The white robes depict that "the honours of victory have already been conferred upon them individually (ἑκάστῳ), though the general and public award is reserved for the Day of the Lord."[123]

In 7:9–14 a great multitude dressed in white robes and holding palm branches is seen by John standing before the throne of God and the Lamb. "These are marks of festal rejoicing, especially in victory."[124] One of the elders asks John to identify this multitude dressed in white robes. When John is unable to respond, the elder answers that this multitude has come out of the great tribulation.[125] "This group seems to complete the full circle of participants before the throne begun in chapter 4."[126] Mealy's suggestion that this vision is a representation of the parousia is probably correct.[127]

This group has washed (ἔπλυναν) their robes and whitened (ἐλεύκαναν) them in the blood of the Lamb (7:14), hence the imagery seems paradoxical—clothing is reddened, not whitened, when dipped

---

121. Trebilco, *Early Christians in Ephesus*, 292n. 1, writes, "That the author of Revelation speaks of the twelve apostles as figures of the past in 21:14 means its is very unlikely that he was the son of Zebedee." This argument ignores the symbolic features of Revelation's apocalyptic genre. Also, John himself was undoubtedly tested as an apostle but found true (Rev 2:2).

122. Charles, *Revelation*, 1:97; cf. 1:187.

123. Swete, *Apocalypse of St. John*, 91.

124. Beckwith, *Apocalypse of John*, 544.

125. Whether ἔρχομαι should be translated as a present or a perfect is often discussed. A present indicates an ongoing process, while a perfect suggests the victory of the multitude is accomplished. The two aorists that follow lend certainty to the latter view. The vision is thus proleptic and anticipatory.

126. Johnson, "Revelation," 12:486.

127. Mealy, *After the Thousand Years*, 217.

The Fulfillment of the Victor Sayings

in blood. The symbolism is clearly spiritual and not literal.[128] Two Old Testament allusions are possible. In Genesis 49:11 (LXX) Judah "will wash (πλυνεῖ) his robe (στολὴν) in wine, and his garment in the blood of the grape." When the law was given at Mount Sinai, the Israelites consecrated themselves by washing their clothes and abstaining from sexual relations (Exod 19:14-15). In 7:14 the two aorist verbs "look back to the life on earth when the cleansing was effected."[129] This is the positive aspect of those said not to have defiled their garments (cf. 3:4). Kraft believes the explanation of these white garments relates to baptism, "daß sie ihre Gewänder gebleicht haben; die weißen Taufegewänder sind ein Bild für die verklärten Leiber."[130] Because first-century liturgical practices are obscure, it is difficult to make such a positive correlation. The final beatitude (22:14) likewise pronounces a blessing on those who wash (πλύνοντες) their robes. This picture continues to show the victors as active, not passive, participants in their salvation.

In 14:4 the followers of the Lamb who have not defiled themselves with women (γυναικῶν) are called virgins. Yarbro Collins interprets this sexual imagery literally, suggesting that continence is advocated for those men ("John's patriarchal point of view") engaged in the holy war.[131] Schüssler Fiorenza prefers a metaphorical interpretation: the virgins are God's people of either sex who have not committed spiritual fornication with the woman (γυναῖκα/γυνὴ 17:3, 4, 6, 7, 9, 18) Babylon/Rome, the mother of all harlots.[132] Neither Yarbro Collins nor Schüssler Fiorenza links this verse to the Sardian letter where the only other use of μολύνω is found. In 3:4 the verb describes those in the church who have not defiled their white garments. The awareness of approaching God in a ritually impure way is found even among unbelievers. In a confessional inscription from Kula in Asia a woman acknowledges she is being punished for entering the temple area of Apollo Bozenos in "a dirty garment" (ῥυπαρῷ ἐπενδύτῃ; cf. Rev 22:11).[133] For the Asian churches a defiling association with the imperial cult was a signal temptation (cf. 2:14). However, in Thyatira the γυνὴ Jezebel also threatened the churches with her false

---

128. In the ancient world fullers used old urine, rich in ammonia, to wash and whiten garments.

129. Swete, *Apocalypse of St. John*, 103.

130. "that their garments have been bleached; the white baptismal garments are a picture of the glorified bodies"; Kraft, *Offenbarung des Johannes*, 130.

131. Yarbro Collins, *Crisis and Catharsis*, 129-31.

132. Schüssler Fiorenza, *Book of Revelation*, 88.

133. "A Confessional Inscription," *New Docs* 8:171.

prophecy. Contact with either woman, Babylon or Jezebel, would soil their garments or, to change metaphors, lose their virginity. Nakedness and shame would be the result.

With the arrival of the wedding of the Lamb (19:7–8), the bride receives a gift of a clean shining linen garment (βύσσινον λαμπρὸν καθαρόν) to wear. The bride's apparel contrasts with the purple and scarlet linen in which the harlot is dressed (Rev 17:4; 18:16). Both here and in 3:5 the verb περιβάλλω occurs, which "can possibly be understood as a direct middle and accords with the idea of worthiness in the last phrase of 3:4."[134] The nature of this fine linen is finally defined: it is the δικαιώματα of the saints. This explanatory note was apparently added by John. Because Charles believes such garments are spiritual bodies, he considers 8b a gloss.[135] Charles's attempts to manipulate the text around his presuppositions has been rightly criticized by later commentators. The plural form here, according to Mounce, "may indicate that the bride's garment is woven of the innumerable acts of faithful obedience by those who endure to the end."[136]

Δικαιώματα is understood by commentators either as an existential or a forensic reality. Benedict affirms the former interpretation, "Therefore the garments of Revelation 3:5 and 19:8 are not a reference to justification nor to character, but to the deeds or acts which flow out of these two."[137] Mealy, however, claims that the translation "righteous deeds" found in most English versions obscures the point of this verse, since the word normally means "valid legal claims" or "just decrees." Hence, he states, "the meaning is that the saints display the credential recognized by God himself as those which make one worthy of acquittal in his court: faith in Christ's atonement, and a life lived in consistent profession of that faith, even to the point of death (cf. 3.4–5; 7.14)."[138]

Δικαιώματα is used one other time in Revelation—15:4. Here the victors over the beast sing the song of Moses and of the Lamb. The song opens, "Great and marvelous are your deeds" (ἔργα; v. 3) and closes, "for your δικαιώματα were revealed." A relationship between these two words is evident. As Swete states, "a δικαίωμα is a concrete expression of righteousness, whether in the form of a just decree . . . or a just act, as here

---

134. Benedict, "Use of NIKAΩ in the Letters," 30.
135. Charles, *Revelation*, 2:128.
136. Mounce, *Book of Revelation*, 340.
137. Benedict, "Use of NIKAΩ in the Letters," 31.
138. Mealy, *After the Thousand Years*, 79–80.

The Fulfillment of the Victor Sayings

and in xix. 8."[139] The antonym of δικαιώματα is used in 18:5. The sins of Babylon's residents are piled up to heaven, and God has remembered her unrighteous acts (ἀδικήματα). A cry is then heard to repay them double for their deeds (ἔργα; v. 6). Again deeds is found in the immediate context. Mealy fails to discuss 18:5, which essentially nullifies his point. Thus it is problematic to translate 19:8 as "fine linen is the valid legal claims of the saints."[140] These claims, these credentials, are in fact the worthy deeds that flow out of justification.[141] Indeed, as Revelation 22:11 declares, the righteous (i. e., the justified) are to practice righteousness (δικαιοσύνη) manifested in righteous deeds (δικαιώματα).

In 19:14 the armies of heaven riding white horses follow the rider on a white horse. They are dressed in clean white linen garments. The vision clearly has a thematic and verbal relationship with 19:8. Here λευκόν is substituted for λαμπρόν, indicating that the terms are synonymous. Likewise, in 17:14 when the Lamb triumphs over the beast and the ten kings, he is accompanied by his called, chosen, and faithful followers. The army is thus to be identified as the bride, the saints, and not as an angelic host.[142] That the victors will rule with Christ as his co-adjudicators is suggested throughout Revelation. Mealy rightly observes that "this ongoing process of confirmation and extension serves to prepare the reader to recognize the theme's presence when it appears for the first time in imagery in chapter 19."[143]

The final beatitude in 22:14 commends those who are washing (οἱ πλύνοντες) their robes."[144] Charles appropriately calls this phrase the spiritual equivalent of οἱ νικῶντες: "Each class alike has endured and overcome, and as access to the tree of life is here promised to those who have cleansed their robes, so in ii.7 the right to eat of the tree of life is given to those who have overcome."[145] Swete suggests this is another version

---

139. Swete, *Apocalypse of St. John*, 197.

140. Cf. Ladd, *Commentary on the Revelation of John*, 249.

141. As Wall, *Revelation*, 222, aptly says, "The church is given the garment to wear, but it must still put it on!"

142. Contra Swete, *Apocalypse of St. John*, 253–54.

143. Mealy, *After the Thousand Years*, 80.

144. Benedict, "Use of ΝΙΚΑΩ in the Letters," 8n. 4, adopts the reading: ποιοῦντες τὰς ἐντολὰς αὐτοῦ citing the support of a majority of manuscripts. Apart from manuscript evidence and on stylistic grounds alone, such a reading is unlikely. In the two earlier uses of ἐντολή, John uses the verb τηρέω both times (12:17; 14:12). Since this beatitude relates to the Ephesian promise, for the variant to work the object should have been ἔργα to conform to its use with ποιέω in the letter (2:5).

145. Charles, *Revelation*, 2:177.

"interpreted in the light of the Cross," of the beatitude of Jesus, "Blessed are the pure in heart, for they will see God" (Matt 5:8).[146] This is the positive aspect of those said not to have defiled their garments (3:4; 14:4). Meeting this condition is a prerequisite for realizing two other promises—partaking of the tree of life and entering the holy city, new Jerusalem.

The blessed are again contrasted with individuals outside who are practicing certain sins, the first of which is called "dogs." The baseness of this group who roll in the filth of their sins is juxtaposed with the victors who wash their garments in the blood of the Lamb. In Matthew 7:6 (cf. 15:26–27) Jesus compares people to unclean dogs; in Revelation it sounds "like apostolic exposition of this mysterious saying."[147]

The Book of Life

The Sardian promise has a negative side, and this perspective is presented in several of the later uses of the book of life in Revelation. The appearance of the first beast (13:1ff.) induces deception upon the earthdwellers and provokes persecution on the saints. Those earthdwellers who worship the beast do not have their names written in the Lamb's book of life. In 13:8 and 21:27 the book of life is specifically called the Lamb's book. Mention of the book of life is somewhat incongruous in 13:8, where "the purpose may be to minimize the significance of the general acceptance of the Caesar-cult, or possibly to call attention to the individual responsibility of the worshippers."[148]

This passage forms a remarkable doublet with 17:8. The two passages are presented next, and it is clear that 17:8 condenses elements of the same vision presented in chapter 13.

---

146. Swete, *Apocalypse of St. John*, 307.
147. Michel, "κύων, κυνάριον," *TDNT* 5:1104.
148. Swete, *Apocalypse of St. John*, 166.

The Fulfillment of the Victor Sayings

13:1, 3, 8	17:8
1 Καὶ εἶδον ἐκ τῆς θαλάσσης θηρίον ἀναβαῖνον, 3 καὶ ἐθαυμάσθη ὅλη ἡ γῆ ὀπίσω τοῦ θηρίου 8 καὶ προσκυνήσουσιν αὐτὸν πάντες οἱ κατοικοῦντες ἐπὶ τῆς γῆς, οὗ οὐ γέγραπται τὸ ὄνομα αὐτοῦ ἐν τῷ βιβλίῳ τῆς ζωῆς τοῦ ἀρνίου τοῦ ἐσφαγμένου ἀπὸ καταβολῆς κόσμου	8 τὸ θηρίον ὃ εἶδες ἦν καὶ οὐκ ἔστιν καὶ μέλλει ἀναβαίνειν ἐκ τῆς ἀβύσσου καὶ θαυμασθήσονται οἱ κατοικοῦντες ἐπὶ τῆς γῆς, ὧν οὐ γέγραπται τὸ ὄνομα ἐπὶ τὸ βιβλίον τῆς ζωῆς ἀπὸ καταβολῆς κόσμου, βλεπόντων τὸ θηρίον ὅτι ἦν καὶ οὐκ ἔστιν καὶ παρέσται

The unusual prepositional phrase ἀπὸ καταβολῆς κόσμου is found in several other New Testament texts. Jesus' teaching in Matthew 25:31ff has already provided a background for the images of shepherd and judgment by fire. Verse 34 provides another verbal parallel—at the last judgment the king will invite the blessed at his right hand to inherit the kingdom prepared for them ἀπὸ καταβολῆς κόσμου. Carson elaborates, "This glorious inheritance, the consummated kingdom, was the Father's plan for them from the beginning."[149]

The kingdom is the reward for being written in the book of life; the choice of being written therein relates to the doctrine of election. Ephesians 1:4 addresses this, stating that Jesus chose us to be holy and blameless before him πρὸ καταβολῆς κόσμου. Lincoln notes that "This phrase indicates an element in the thinking about election which cannot be found in the OT and occurs only later in Jewish literature." The language of this verse, he continues, "by making the pretemporal aspect of election explicit, sets salvation in protological perspective."[150] In Ephesians the Jewish and Gentile audience is assured of God's eternal elective plan for them. In Revelation assurance is also given, perhaps to same audience.[151] However, that assurance is presented in a negative form.

A final related verse is found in 1 Peter 1:20. The readers are assured that their redemption was secured by the precious blood of Christ the lamb chosen πρὸ καταβολῆς κόσμου. Michaels cautions, "Rev 13:8, despite its reference to Jesus as the Lamb, is a doubtful parallel: the phrase

---

149. Carson, "Matthew," 8:521.

150. Lincoln, *Ephesians*, 23.

151. This suggestion is based on the premise that Ephesians was circulated among the churches of Asia, among which were the seven churches.

ἀπὸ καταβολῆς κόσμου ('ever since [not "before"] the beginning of the world') refers not to the death of the Lamb (or to God's knowledge of it), but simply strengthens 'not' to 'never' . . . in asserting the nonelection of those not inscribed in the Lamb's book of life (cf. Rev 17:8)."[152] Michaels overstates the force of ἀπό, since the prepositions ἀπό and πρό are interchangeable in these texts (cf. Luke 11:50; John 17:24), therefore Petrine use may be a background for the phrase's appearance in Revelation.

An interpretive problem in 13:8 concerns the referent of this prepositional phrase. Is it the "Lamb slain" or the verb "written"? If the latter, twelve words separate the modifier from its antecedent. Johnson sets forth the conundrum, "In the former instance, the emphasis would rest on the decree in eternity to elect the Son as the redeeming agent for mankind's salvation (13:8; 1 Peter 1:20); in the latter, stress lies on God's eternal foreknowledge of a company of people who would participate in the elect Son's redeeming work (17:8)."[153]

Regarding the sentence's structure, Swete notes that "the order suggests that the words should be taken with τοῦ ἐσφαγμένου, in the sense indicated by I Pet. i.18f. . . . but the close parallel in xvii. 8 . . . seems to be decisive in favour of connecting ἀπὸ καταβ. κόσμου with γέγραπται in this context also."[154] Caird, adopting the other view, believes that John is speaking here about the means of the elect's redemption, a thought complementary to 17:8.[155] Besides the change of placement of the prepositional phrase, in 13:8 the relative pronoun is the singular οὗ[156] while in 17:8 it is the plural ὧν. Another difference is that the Lamb slain is mentioned only in 13:8.[157] Perhaps the ambiguity in meaning is intentional. John knows his Asian audience is familiar with the Ephesian and Petrine passages and allows both the elective and redemptive purposes to be suggested. In the end it seems best to adopt the most natural grammatical reading—it is Lamb who is slain from the foundation of the world.

---

152. Michaels, *1 Peter*, 67.

153. Johnson, "Revelation," 12:528. He provides this further theological reflection, "the words 'from the creation of the world' cannot be pressed to prove eternal individual election to salvation or damnation since 3:5 implies that failure of appropriate human response may remove one's name from the book of life."

154. Swete, *Apocalypse of St. John*, 167.

155. Caird, *Revelation of St. John the Divine*, 168; cf. Charles, *Revelation*, 1:354.

156. Mounce, *Book of Revelation*, 256, suggests that the unexpected shift in the Greek text from the plural to the singular "is perhaps intended to emphasize the individual responsibility of each one who worships the beast."

157. Contra the comment of Beckwith, *Apocalypse of John*, 638, concerning "precisely parallel words in 17:8."

The Fulfillment of the Victor Sayings

The relationship between 17:8 and 13:8 has already been noted. The earthdwellers marvel at the revivified beast. Again this group consists of those whose names are not written in the book of life. Whereas in 13:8 it was the Lamb's sacrificial mission which was recorded from the foundation of the world, here it is the name of the victor recorded ἀπὸ καταβολῆς κόσμου. Because election is from the beginning, Charles observes that "the presupposition is that only the elect can withstand the claims of the imperial cult backed by the might of the empire itself."[158] John, however, never presents a deterministic doctrine of election wherein passivity may result; obedience, here resulting in martyrdom at the hands of the beast, is continually advocated.

John sees a vision of the great white throne judgment with all the dead standing before the throne (20:12). As they await their fate, books are opened and they are judged according to their individual deeds, both good and evil, recorded in the books. "The sentence of the Judge is not arbitrary; it rests upon written evidence."[159] 2 Baruch 24:1 similarly speaks of books that will be opened "in which are written the sins of all those who have sinned." Salvation is never presented as based on good works in Revelation, but is always related to the blood of the Lamb. In the Testament of Abraham 13:9–14, however, two angels weigh the righteous deeds against the sins of each individual. Those whose deeds are burned up by fire are consigned to punishment with other sinners, while those whose works survive are placed with the other righteous.[160]

Another book—the book of life—is likewise opened.[161] Nothing more is said of this book until verse 15. Here is stated the factor to avoid being cast into the lake of fire: εἴ τις οὐχ εὑρέθη ἐν τῇ βίβλῳ τῆς ζωῆς γεγραμμένος . . . . The co-text for this reference is Daniel 12:1 where God's people will be delivered, those εὑρεθῇ ἐγγεγραμμένος ἐν τῷ βιβλίῳ. Daniel 12:3 was likewise found to be a source of the morning star imagery found in the Thyatiran promise. The risen Jesus suggests in Revelation 3:5 that a person's name could be erased from the book of life. The consequence of that erasure—the lake of fire—is starkly

---

158. Charles, *Revelation*, 1:354.

159. Swete, *Apocalypse of St. John*, 272.

160. Smith, "Book of Life," 220, rightly distinguishes this type of record of deeds from similar biblical references to a list of persons.

161. Beasley-Murray, *Revelation*, 302, gives this theological comment regarding the testimony of the two books: "In the judgment God's justice and grace are neither divorced from one another, nor set in conflict with each other, but are harmonious, uniting in a single voice in their declaration of the destiny of every child of man."

portrayed here. "For such people the presence of God could be nothing but a horror from which they, like the earth they made their home, must flee, leaving not a trace behind."[162]

The English translation of 20:15, "If anyone is not found written in the book of life," might suggest doubt whether anyone will be thrown into the lake of fire. Johnson asserts that the Greek construction is not so indefinite: "John uses a first-class condition, which assumes the reality of the first clause and shows the consequences of the second class." He paraphrases, "If anyone's name was not found written in the book of life, and I assume there were such . . . ."[163]

The vision of the new heaven and new earth immediately follows in chapter 21. John's purpose is clearly to juxtapose the punishment of those not written in the book of life with the reward of those whose names are written in the book of life. In the book of life "are the names of those who have reserved space in the new Jerusalem because of their faith in and faithfulness towards God and God's Lamb."[164] This insight is assured through this final reference to the book of life in the midst of this vision.

John in his vision of the heavenly city sees the nations walking by the light of the glory of God (21:24). "The community of overcomers exists in harmony with the character of a holy God, disclosed in the life of God's Lamb."[165] No one, especially the abominators and liars, can enter the city, except those whose names are written in the Lamb's book of life (21:27). Isaiah's vision (Isa 65:8–25) of the new Jerusalem likewise contrasts the sinners who are judged with the servants who inherit the blessings of the new heaven and new earth.

John's brief list of those excluded is a condensation of the longer vice list in 21:8. There the destiny of the sinners is the second death in the lake of fire. "The phrase 'except those who are inscribed' implies that it is possible for those of the first category to become part of the second group. This is consistent with the vision's portrayal of the redeemed as those who have been purchased from 'every nation, tribe, tongue, and people.'"[166] To the end, John's portrait of the redeemed is one of inclusive exclusivity.

---

162. Caird, *Revelation of St. John the Divine*, 260.
163. Johnson, "Revelation," 12:590.
164. Wall, *Revelation*, 241.
165. Ibid., 255.
166. Mulholland, *Revelation*, 331.

The Fulfillment of the Victor Sayings

The Confession of a Name

The verb ὁμολογέω found in the promise (3:5) is never again used in Revelation. The only text in the fulfillment section that uses the preposition ἐνώπιον is found in 20:12. Here the reference is not to the Father, but to the One sitting on the great white throne. The dead, great and small, are standing before him awaiting their judgment. The link in the promise between the confession of the victor's name and the book of life suggests that fulfillment is probably found in a text which likewise speaks of the book of life. The book of life is mentioned both in 20:12 and 20:15. While the consequences of the opening of the book of life are left unstated, perhaps a roll call of the names of the victors is conducted. Jesus confesses each name found in the book of life before his Father and the angels.

Sardian Fulfillment Conclusion

The image of white garments is closely linked with the future resurrection body. Garber concludes that "the white garments or robes in the Apocalypse are to be understood as spiritual bodies, in the tradition of the Jewish apocalypses."[167] But again, would the Sardians have understood any literal sense to the image? Adam and Eve were naked in paradise before the Fall, so perhaps the Edenic restoration would bring back the innocence of nakedness. However, the shame connected to nakedness throughout the book suggests that the audience would not view nakedness as a virtue. The white garments seen on the elders and martyrs would indicate that a spiritual and glorious garb is found in heaven. Jesus was seen in a dazzling white robe at his transfiguration and appeared in clothing following his resurrection. The immortal, imperishable body was certainly expected at the first resurrection, but that this resurrection body would be clothed in pure white linen was probably also anticipated.

The book of life seems a needless reminder for a God who is omniscient. Yet the book is not to refresh his memory at the last assize, but to demonstrate his justice to saint and sinner alike. The victors are assured that they are enrolled in the heavenly register. They probably have an expectation that their names will be confessed publicly at the final roll call. Contrarily, another book contains the names of those who resisted God and persecuted his people. Their deeds are likewise made public, they are judged for what they have done (and have not done), and they receive the lake of fire as their final allotment.

---

167. Garber, "Symbolism of Heavenly Robes in the New Testament," 274.

The Philadelphian Fulfillment

The Pillar in the Temple

There no further mention of the victors as pillars in Revelation. Prigent notes a small difficulty for this promise to be fulfilled: "en effet la Jérusalem céleste qui descend du ciel et que mentionne la fin du verset (3:)12, ne comporte pas de temple (Ap. 21, 22 . . .)." The answer, he believes, is that the temple is simply the sign of Christ's presence among his people. The fulfillment is that "C'est pourquoi les hommes qui vivent en étroite communion avec le Christ peuvent être regardés comme étant dès à présent et à jamais dans le temple."[168] The heavenly temple of God is associated with the people of God in 15:2ff. Mealy likewise asserts that "to overcome so as to be made part of God's temple is thus to be a member of the eschatological community of God, the intimacy of whose experience of his presence can only be suggested by the way in which God's glory used to fill his tabernacle/temple in times past."[169] The verb λατρεύω is used twice in Revelation. A proleptic view is given in 7:13ff. of the victors—those out of the great tribulation—in the heavenly city, who are worshiping (v. 15) day and night in the temple. In 22:3 the slaves of God worship before his throne which has supplanted the temple (21:22). The close relationship between this worshiping group and mention of the divine name written on their foreheads (as in the promise) suggests strongly that this understanding of the fulfillment is correct.

In the promise (3:12) the victors are affirmed ἔξω οὐ μὴ ἐξέλθῃ from the temple of God. In 21:27 whatever is unclean οὐ μὴ εἰσέλθῃ into the holy city, new Jerusalem. The final beatitude, which assures the victors that they will enter the gates of the city, is juxtaposed with the types of sinners who will be outside (ἔξω; 22:14–15). "To enter the city is to help make it up—and there is nothing about leaving it once the glory and honor have been brought in."[170] These are the only two occurrences of the preposition ἔξω in Revelation.

---

168. "in fact the heavenly Jerusalem that descends from heaven and that is mentioned at the end of verse 3:12, does not comprise any temple (Rev 21, 22)"; "It is why the men who live in close communion with Christ can be regarded as being presently and forever in the temple"; Prigent, *L'Apocalypse de saint Jean*, 71.

169. Mealy, *After the Thousand Years*, 84.

170. Gundry, "New Jerusalem," 264.

Divine Names Written

Even as the victors are promised that the name of God and the new name of Jesus will be inscribed on them, the followers of the beast have his name written on them. In order to buy and sell, the earthdwellers are forced to have the mark of the beast—his name or the number of his name (as grammatical appositives)—inscribed on their right hand or forehead (13:16–17). J. Finnegan writes, "The position of these marks reflects the Jewish phylacteries . . . but the manner of the followers of the beast is a travesty of the Jewish custom, for here the one mark is on the right hand, not the left, and the other mark is on (ἐπί) the brow, not over the brow."[171] The purpose of the mark here is probably to parody the sealing of God's servants in chapter 7.

The saints are encouraged to calculate (ψηφίζω) his number—666 (13:18). Neron Caesar is the most likely solution of this gematria, and this name was inscribed on the coinage of Ephesus, Sardis, and Laodicea.[172] Some commentators have suggested that to buy and sell using such "marked" Roman coinage was to participate in the beast's system. This explanation is too facile, however, since Jesus sanctioned the use of Roman coinage that bore the emperor's image (Mt 22:18–21). Deissman's explanation seems most plausible: "χάραγμα is the name of the imperial seal, giving the year and the name of the reigning emperor (possibly also his effigy), and found on bills of sale and similar documents of the first and second centuries."[173]

The verbal relationship here with the Pergamene promise suggests that the new name written on the white stone (ψῆφος) is also perhaps some type of gematria. Examples of such gematria are known from antiquity. A graffiti from Pompeii (ca. AD 79) reads, "Amerimnus thought upon his lady Harmonia for good. The number of her honorable name is 45 (με)." Another example reads, "I love her whose number is 545 (φμε)." After mentioning these gematria, Johnson comments, "In these cases, the

---

171. Finnegan, *Archaeology of the New Testament*, 346. The *tefillah*, or phylacteries, worn during the first century were inscribed and knotted to form the letters of the divine name Shaddai (שדי), translated παντοκράτωρ in the Septuagint. "So the faithful Jew wore the divine name upon his forehead in the form of an abbreviation consisting of the first letter (shin) of that name or, if the knot be counted as making a daleth, an abbreviation consisting of the first two letters of the name, while the knot on the arm could be considered as completing the spelling of the name" (Ibid., 345).

172. Wilson, "Pie in a Very Bleak Sky?," 65; for calculating the number, see Wilson, *Charts on the Book of Revelation*, 86

173. Deissman, *Bible Studies*, 246.

number conceals a name, and the mystery is perhaps known for certain only by the two lovers themselves."[174]

There is further mention of the beast's mark. Ugly and painful sores break out on the bodies of those who receive his mark (16:2). Those so marked are said to be deceived by the beast and the false prophet (19:20). Finally, only those who did not receive the beast's mark on their hand or forehead reign during the thousand years (20:4). The followers of Jesus receive his mark on their foreheads to show they belong to him instead of the beast and to protect them from God's wrath.

John sees the Lamb standing on Mount Zion accompanied by the 144,000 who have his name and his Father's name written on their foreheads (14:1). A stark contrast is presented between those who take the name of the beast and those who take the name of God and the Lamb. "The Divine name on the forehead suggests at once the imparting of a character which corresponds with the Mind of God, and the consecration of life to His service."[175] Reference to the two divine names is reminiscent of the language of the promise in 3:12. Whereas the third name given there is the new Jerusalem, here the name of Jerusalem as Mount Zion is realized. Mount Zion, according to Ladd, "stands for the eschatological victory which, according to the Revelation, is in the new Jerusalem . . . ."[176]

These names are evidently the content of the seal (σφραγίς) which this group received earlier on their foreheads (7:2–8; 9:4). The nature of this seal has long been debated. Its Old Testament background is probably to be found in Ezekiel 9:1–11 where an angel is told to put a mark on the foreheads of Jerusalem's residents who grieve over evil. The angel is to slaughter those who do not receive the mark (תו; v. 5). Taw is the last letter of the Hebrew alphabet and in the Old Hebrew script was written in the form of a form of a cross (X) during Ezekiel's day until the New Testament period. The Greek letter chi was recognized as an equivalent to taw. "This was the more readily possible because, on the one hand, in early Greek the chi was often written as an erect cross mark, and because, on the other hand, the taw itself was often written in the sideways position, so that it was already like the later more usual form of the chi (χ) and like the Latin x."[177] The Damascus Document (19.12) states that at the time of the

---

174. Johnson, "Revelation," 12:533.
175. Swete, *Apocalypse of St. John*, 177.
176. Ladd, *Commentary on the Revelation of John*, 189.
177. Finnegan, *Archaeology of the New Testament*, 343.

Messiah's coming, quoting Ezekiel, the only ones to be spared the sword are those marked by the taw (התו; adding the article).[178]

Craigie likewise suggests a relationship between Ezekiel's vision and John's vision in 14:1: "The names of the Lamb and his Father were written on the foreheads of the faithful, and the sign X, in Greek script, is the first letter of the name *Christ*. Without delving into the complexities of St John's vision, there is clearly continuity with that of Ezekiel."[179] Interestingly, John does not use the Septuagint reading of σημεῖον for "mark" (Ezek 9:4; cf. *T. Sol.* 15:7), but instead uses σημεῖον for supernatural signs as does the Fourth Gospel (cf. Rev 12:1; 13:13, etc).[180] Rather John uses χάραγμα, a word not used in the Septuagint and only in Acts 17:29, apart from its seven uses in Revelation. Perhaps this is because chi is its first letter, also the first letter of Χριστός, and another clue to the identification of the mark and of the name. A Jewish Christian told Origen that "the form of the Taw in the old [Hebrew] script resembles the cross, and it predicts the mark which is to be placed on the foreheads of the Christians" (*Sel. Ezek.* 9.13.801).

The group on Mount Zion is likewise represented as the virgins who have not defiled themselves (14:1–5), who are contrasted with those who take the mark of the beast's name (13:16–17). These idolatrous worshippers will receive no rest from their torments (cf. 9:4; *Pss. Sol.* 15:9), unlike the saints who will receive rest (14:11–13).

At the last battle Jesus, described as Faithful and True (19:11), appears astride a white horse followed by the armies of heaven. Both names are given as epithets in 1:5 and 3:7, 14 so they are not secret or unknown. The mention of Faithful and True seems to contradict the claim they are known only to Jesus. Symbolically this is fitting, however, because "The unknown name of the Christ comports with the fact that his nature, his relationships to the Father, and even his relationship to humanity, tran-

---

178. Finnegan, ibid., 344, explains, "While the statement may be only figurative, it is at least possible that the taw mark was literally put upon the foreheads of the members of this community, perhaps at the time of their initiatory baptism, as a sign to guarantee their salvation in the final Judgment."

179. Craigie, *Ezekiel*, 68.

180. Origen (*Sel. Ezech.* 9.13.800) tells us that Aquila and Theodotion translated the Hebrew *taw* in Ezekiel 9:4 as τοῦ θαῦ. Tertullian (*Marc.* 3.22) likewise refers to the mark Tau when quoting the Ezekiel text. These other renderings of Ezekiel's text understand the mark (*taw*) as "nothing other than the alphabetic character, taw, a mark in the form of a cross, standing for protection, deliverance, and salvation" (Finnegan, *Archaeology of the New Testament*, 344).

scend all human understanding."[181] However, upon him is written a new name known only to himself (v. 12). We should probably rule out the suggestion of Alford that John saw the name but did not reveal it because he did not know its import—"some new and glorious name, indicative, as appears from the context there, of the completed union between Him and His people, and of His final triumph."[182] Jesus names himself the Alpha and the Omega in 22:13, the same name the Lord God gave himself in 1:8. As Wall observes, "Perhaps this is the unknown name disclosed only after the 'Day of the Lord' is completed and Christ's full equality with God is disclosed in the new Jerusalem."[183]

According to 19:13, the secret name is the "Word (λόγος) of God" (cf. John 1:1, 14). Earlier commentators suggested that this name was interpolated because of the inconsistency of a secret name being named.[184] Kiddle, however, rightly asserts, "Such misunderstandings arise out of a failure to do full justice to John's cryptic and subtle style. He has told us the name is secret, but he wishes also to indicate the extent of the power which is implied by this secret name."[185] Although this expression is found earlier in the book (e.g., 1:2, 9), it is not found as a personal name until here. Mounce points out that Word as the title used in Revelation "emphasizes not so much the self-revelation of God as it does the authoritative declaration by which the nations of the world are destroyed."[186] Schüssler Fiorenza postulates that Wisdom of Solomon 18:15–16 may be the source for John's image here.[187] Clarke defines the meaning of "Word" here in the Wisdom of Solomon: "The concept of both idea and action being inseparable in *Word* is Hebraic. Here *Word* is linked with action; the *Word leapt* and is personified as *a relentless warrior*."[188] The convergence of similar imagery is striking, but use of the Wisdom of Solomon as a co-text cannot be proven.

In 19:16 another picture is presented. Upon the garment and thigh (μηρὸν) of Jesus is written another name—*King of kings and Lord of lords*. This image is perplexing. That this name is literally tattooed on his

---

181. Beasley-Murray, *Revelation*, 280; cf. Matt. 11:27.
182. Alford, "Apocalypse of John," 4:727.
183. Wall, *Revelation*, 231.
184. Cf. Charles, *Revelation*, 2:132–33.
185. Kiddle, *Revelation of St. John*, 385.
186. Mounce, *Book of Revelation*, 345.
187. Schüssler Fiorenza, *Revelation*, 105.
188. Clarke, *Wisdom of Solomon*, 121.

thigh must be ruled out,[189] given the Jewish aversion to marking the body permanently (cf. Lev 19:28). It might possibly signify a sword sheath.[190] Cicero (*Verr.* 4.43) mentions a statue of Apollo that had a name written on it in small silver letters.

This picture contrasts with that of the beast covered with blasphemous names and the woman who sat upon it, having the following titles on her forehead—Babylon the Great, the mother of prostitutes and of the abominations of the earth (17:3–5).[191]

In the heavenly city the slaves of God and the Lamb will see his face, and his name will be on their foreheads (22:4). Du Rand suggests: "This probably alludes to the name of God on the forehead of the high priest (cf. Ex 28:36). Now all the righteous are priests in the presence of God in the heavenly Jerusalem."[192] It is remarkable that this mark continues into the eschaton, apparently marking the victors for eternity. The pronoun is singular here—"his name"—yet refers both to God and the Lamb. Beasley-Murray errs when he says "in 22:4 only the Father's name is mentioned."[193] Finnegan believes that, since the taw sign stood for the name of God in Jewish thought, it probably also came to stand for the name of Christ in Jewish Christian thought. Speaking of 22:4 where God's name is upon their foreheads, Finnegan notes that "the reference in the immediately preceding verse was not only to God but also to the Lamb."[194]

The New Jerusalem Coming Down from Heaven

The promise of the new Jerusalem is fulfilled in a number of references to the heavenly city in Revelation 21. In 21:2 the "holy city" (cf. Isa 52:1), also called the "new Jerusalem," is revealed. In 21:10 (cf. 22:19) this city is called "the holy city Jerusalem." An alternate name in 3:12 is "the city of my God." Another variation is "the city" (21:14, 15, 16 [2x], 19, 21, 23; 22:14).[195]

189. Contra Wall, *Revelation*, 232.

190. Cf. Charles, *Revelation*, 2:137 for this and other suggestions.

191. Translations differ as to whether "Mystery" should be included as a title. Grammatically "mystery" functions better as an appositive to "name" rather than as the first title of the series.

192. Du Rand, "Imagery of the Heavenly Jerusalem," 78.

193. Beasley-Murray, *Revelation*, 222.

194. Finnegan, *Archaeology of the New Testament*, 346.

195. Of all the promises and fulfillments more has probably been written on this one than all the others. The major perspectives are reviewed here. A complete overview of recent discussion on the new Jerusalem can be found in Park, "More than a Regained Eden."

Zion is used once in 14:1. Like the Old Testament and the book of Hebrews, Revelation links Zion with Jerusalem. "As the earthly Zion was the meeting point for the tribes of the old Israel [cf. Ps 122:3–4], so the heavenly Zion is the meeting point for the new Israel."[196] As indicated earlier, the promise of the threefold names of God, city, and Jesus are realized here. Beckwith encapsulates, "Mount Zion, synonymous with Jerusalem, is one of the standing terms to designate the central seat of the eschatological kingdom."[197]

In 21:1 John sees the new heaven and new earth, and from this new heaven the holy city, the new Jerusalem, descends (v. 2). Earlier in the book other things also came out of heaven. An angel was seen descending out of (ἐκ indicating direction, not source) heaven in 10:1; 18:1; and 20:1. The second beast causes fire to fall out of heaven (13:13), during the seventh bowl huge hailstones fall out of heaven (16:21), and fire falls out of heaven to devour God's enemies at the battle of Gog and Magog (20:9). Wall incisively notes, "Because it comes down out of heaven from God to earth, the reader assumes the realization of God's promised salvation will be historical and public rather than spiritual and private."[198]

As in 20:5–6 where the first resurrection and second death are mentioned, in 21:1 a first heaven (πρῶτος οὐρανὸς) and a first earth (πρώτη γῆ) pass away (ἀπῆλθαν) to reveal a new heaven and new earth, that is, a second heaven and a second earth. The coming of a new, second Jerusalem thus implies the passing away of an old, first Jerusalem (cf. v. 4, τὰ πρῶτα ἀπῆλθαν). The threefold use of καίνος in verses 1–2 (cf. v. 5, ἰδοὺ καινὰ ποιῶ πάντα) shows an emphasis on newness, "new" being an eschatological catchword. This newness suggests not only renewal and renovation, but also replacement. Irenaeus (*Haer.* 5.36.1) likens the new order to the resurrection body, an apt analogy since John dealt with it first in 20:5–6. The spiritual body has both continuity and discontinuity with the natural body, according to Paul (1 Cor 15:42–44). The spiritual body necessarily follows the natural body (v. 46), but they are of two different worlds—the first heavenly, the second earthly (v. 48). A similar concept of the new pervades the realities of which John is speaking here. "Revelation . . . makes it clear that the NJ [New Jerusalem] is present in heaven and is being

---

196. Bruce, *Epistle to the Hebrews*, 373.
197. Beckwith, *Apocalypse of John*, 647.
198. Wall, *Revelation*, 245.

prepared through the sole creation of God, and awaiting the moment of manifestation at the consummation of God's *Helisgeschichte* [sic]."[199]

The descent of the new Jerusalem to the new earth brings an end to the former division between heaven and earth. God was formerly in heaven and humanity on earth, with the cosmic heaven in between. With the descent of the new heaven, the sun and moon are no longer needed to give their light (Rev 22:5), for God and the Lamb through their glory illuminate the new creation.

Bridal imagery is first presented in 19:7 where the great multitude in heaven rejoices because the marriage of the Lamb has come and "his bride has prepared herself." Because this preparation has resulted from her righteous deeds (v. 8), her wedding garment is given to her. Garber suggests, "The meaning is that the wedding garment will be in keeping with, resultant upon, and conditioned by the character or righteous deeds of the saints, which are an expression of their faith, their watching, and God working in them through his Spirit."[200]

This proleptic announcement leads into the fourth beatitude,[201] which speaks blessing on those invited to the wedding supper of the Lamb (19:9). Who is the bride? The text itself supplies the answer: she is the great multitude drawn from every nation. Beasley-Murray further clarifies, "The Bride is the Church viewed in the light of her destiny to share life with her divine Bridegroom in the city of God . . . already essentially that which she is destined to be in the day of Christ."[202]

In 21:2 the new Jerusalem which John sees descending from heaven is "prepared as a bride adorned for her husband." This bridal imagery is probably drawn from Isaiah 61:10. There the writer rejoices that he has been clothed with salvation and joy and adorned with ornaments like a bride (ὡς νύμφην κατεκόσμησέν LXX). In Isaiah and here in Revelation a simile is used—"as (ὡς) a bride," while in 21:9–10 the city is called "the bride," a metaphor.

The imagery is repeated again in 21:9 where John is again shown "the bride, the wife of the Lamb." Here an explicit link is made between the bride and the wife.[203] A duplicate vision of the holy city descending

---

199. Park, "More than a Regained Eden," 165.

200. Garber, "Symbolism of Heavenly Robes," 271.

201. Giblin. *Book of Revelation*, 217 n. 164, writes concerning this beatitude: "It is the only beatitude in which *no explanation* is stated—either negatively or positively, either in a causal clause or in a purpose clause, or in helpfully explanatory *adjuncta*."

202. Beasley-Murray, *Revelation*, 345.

203. A similar connection between city, bride, and wife is found in Joseph and Aseneth.

from heaven is seen by John.²⁰⁴ Note, however, that the order of the images seen by John is reversed. In 21:2 John first sees the new Jerusalem, then the bride; here John is shown the bride first (v. 9) before he sees the holy city descending from God. Park initially attributes no significance to this reversal, pointing to a similar reversal in the presentation of the wall and the gates. Yet he later suggests that "by way of introducing the NJ by means of the Bride, John may hint that his concern for the NJ is more as people rather than as place."²⁰⁵ However, where the bride is first linked with city imagery (21:2) a reference to the holy city comes first. Such a reversal of images indicates for John that the new Jerusalem is both a people *and* a place.

This vision is contrasted deliberately with the vision of the woman, the mother of harlots, in chapter 17. Both visions are introduced by εἷς ἐκ τῶν ἑπτὰ ἀγγέλων τῶ ἐξόντων τὰς ἑπτὰ φιάλας (17:1; 21:9). The angel ἀπήνεγκέν . . . ἐν πνεύματι John to see the visions (17:3; 21:10). Park rightly points out that these peculiar structural markers "should be seen as an indication of the presence of an antithetical relationship between Babylon and the NJ as 'whore' and 'bride.'"²⁰⁶ Beasley-Murray suggests that the section 21:9–22:5 is an extended exposition of the paragraph in 21:1–8. However, he properly acknowledges its affinities with other texts, particularly chapter 17. "He [John] could not but believe that the overthrow of the harlot-city and the Antichrist would be followed by the establishment of the bride-city in the rule of Christ."²⁰⁷

The contrast between two women—the harlot and the bride—was noted in the previous section. Here we note the contrast between two cities—Babylon and the new Jerusalem. While the fall of adulterous Babylon is depicted in chapter 18, the establishment of the new Jerusalem is described in chapters 21–22. The alternate name of the new Jerusalem is

---

Aseneth is renamed the City of Refuge because many nations will find refuge in her (*Jos. Asen.* 15:7). She is promised as a bride for Joseph (15:9; 18:11) and later becomes his wife after Pharaoh blesses their union and stages a seven-day wedding feast in their behalf (21:4–9). "The tradition of Sion, the City of God, also described under the figure of a woman, lies behind this concept" (Burchard, "Joseph and Aseneth," 2:189).

204. This illustrates the weakness of the proposed structuration of Revelation around four main visions marked by the phrase ἐν πνεύματι. In this view the fourth and final vision is thus found in 21:9–22:5. However, 22:9ff is a re-vision of 21:1–8, with both sections ending with inclusios of vice lists (cf. Turner, "The New Jerusalem in Revelation 21:1–22:5," 281–83).

205. Park, "More than a Regained Eden," 191; cf. 187n. 109.

206. Ibid., 56.

207. Beasley-Murray, *Revelation*, 315.

the holy city (21:2, 10). Following the second vision of the descent from heaven, imagery related to a city predominates. The city has walls, gates, foundations, and a street (21:12–25; 22:2). It is lit by the glory of God and the lamp of the Lamb (21:23; 22:5). People are walking in it (21:24). A paradisiacal park boasts a river of living water and the tree of life (22:1–2). And the throne of God and the Lamb sits within its boundaries (22:3). These detailed features of the city seem to contradict Park's view that John is describing an enormous Holy of Holies.[208] Further examination of these features is beyond the scope of this study.

Charles believes the twin descriptions of the heavenly Jerusalem are due to the inept efforts of John's literary executor. He claims the heavenly city depicted in 21:9—22:2, 14–15, 17 is the seat of the millennial kingdom on the present earth. "It is manifest that since sin, and therefore death, prevail outside the gates of the Heavenly City, the present order of things still prevails, the first heaven and the first earth are still in being."[209] He asserts that another heavenly city is depicted in 21:1–4; 22:3–5. "This second Heavenly City does not appear *till the first heaven and the first earth have vanished and their place been taken by the new heaven and the new earth.*"[210] Charles's distinction between the heavenly and the new Jerusalem, according to du Rand, "is based on the influence of a theological reading of chapter 20."[211] Likewise, his preoccupation with redaction overwhelms any attempt to understand how John has structured the dual visions for his own purposes. Beasley-Murray believes this second vision has primarily a pastoral purpose: "It guarantees the truth of the prophecy contained in the first paragraph, promising participation in the blessings of the new world to all who exercise faith and maintain it in face of discouragements, and warning of the doom which will overtake all who apostatise and persist in the ways of Antichrist."[212]

This picture of a renewed city fulfills numerous Old Testament prophecies. Jesus himself declares in the Fourth Gospel that his Father's house has many rooms. He promised to prepare a place (τόπος) for his disciples and to return to bring them to that place (John 14:2–4). Gundry has also asked the important question whether the new Jerusalem is a "place for people" or "people as place." He disclaims that "the city even partly sym-

---

208. Park, "More than a Regained Eden," 191.
209. Charles, *Revelation*, 2:151.
210. Ibid.
211. Du Rand, "Imagery of the Heavenly Jerusalem," 67.
212. Beasley-Murray, *Revelation*, 305.

bolizes the place where the saints will dwell forever"; rather it exclusively symbolizes the saints.[213] This assertion is not tenable given John's presentation of both dimensions of the new Jerusalem. We agree with Dumbrell that the imagery oscillates between city and community.[214]

Philadelphian Fulfillment Conclusion

The promise that the victors would become a pillar in the heavenly temple, never to leave, would suggest safety and security to the Philadelphians. The divine names written on them confirm their role as priests. As priests they would enjoy close fellowship with God and the Lamb who are the temple in the new Jerusalem. As the image of the pillar is both an object and a person, so is the heavenly city both a people and a place. As a people she is a glorious bride betrothed for marriage. As a place she is the domicile both for God and his people for eternity. In this city of people and place is found the fulfillment of every other promise. It is the all-encompassing reality that is the sum of existence in the eschaton following the coming of Jesus.

The Laodicean Fulfillment

The Divine Throne

Schmitz denies any fulfillment of the promise in 3:21: "But this participation of the company of overcomers in the throne of Christ is not depicted in the visions of Rev."[215] Apart from the victor saying, three other texts relate thrones to individuals connected to God and the Lamb. These texts—4:4, 11:16, and 20:4—are short and undeveloped, but the persons on the thrones seem to represent all the redeemed. We proceed with an examination of these texts plus several others that mention the related theme of kingdom.

In John's initial vision of heaven (4:1ff.) the divine throne in heaven is central.[216] Encircling it are twenty-four other thrones upon which are sitting the twenty-four elders (v. 4). Earlier we identified these elders as representatives of the total people of God—the twelve tribes of Israel and the twelve apostles of the church (cf. 21:12–14). This text suggests that the old covenant people of Israel are part of the heavenly community.

---

213. Gundry, "New Jerusalem," 255.

214. Dumbrell, *End of the Beginning*, 3.

215. Schmitz, "θρόνος," *TDNT* 3:166.

216. Beale, *Use of Daniel*, 189, sees the *Vorbild* of Daniel 7 behind the repeated references to "throne" in chapters 3–5.

The Fulfillment of the Victor Sayings

These elders are distinguished by two other features of the victors—white garments and golden crowns. They function as "a heavenly chorus that continually sings God's praises on behalf of God's people."[217] When the elders lay down their golden crowns before the throne, they exclaim, "Worthy are you, O Lord" (4:11).

The elders sing a song in 5:10 extolling Christ for purchasing individuals from every tribe, tongue, people, and nation with his blood. He has made them a kingdom and priests, and they will reign on earth, a statement clearly proleptic.[218] This recalls 1:6 where Christ's beloved, whom he has loosed from their sins with his blood, are made a kingdom. The elders exercise priestly duties holding the golden incense bowls, which are the prayers of the saints (5:8). In 11:16 the twenty-four elders seated on thrones again are portrayed worshiping God. They give thanks because the time of judging the unrighteous and rewarding the redeemed has come.

Schüssler Fiorenza likens these elders to angelic vassal-kings who mimic the court ceremony of Hellenistic-Oriental kingship rituals. She cites the account of Tacitus concerning the Armenian king, the Parthian Tiridates (*Ann.* 15.28).[219] Following his defeat by Corbulo, Tiridates was forced to lay down his diadem before the image of Nero that rested on the official Roman "throne." Later he journeyed to Rome to receive his crown back from Nero in person (*Ann.* 16.22). This account suggests an interesting correlation; however, the careful distinction John makes between crown and diadem in Revelation, discussed earlier in the chapter, undermines such an interpretation.

This heavenly scene in 20:4–6 shows a marked dependence on Daniel 7:9ff. Williamson questions whether the location of this scene is heaven or earth: "Since 20:4 follows Dan 7:9 . . . the likelihood that this is an earthly scene is enhanced."[220] This group is part of the heavenly church, and they have continuity with the martyrs of the fifth seal. Those seated on thrones are given authority to judge. Botha aptly catches the irony here: "The power to judge has now shifted from the champions of the imperial cult and power into the hands of the martyrs."[221] In 20:6 those participating in

---

217. Wall, *Revelation*, 92.

218. Jeremias ("παράδεισος," *TDNT* 5:770n. 42) comments that Revelation "uses eschatological ideas proleptically to depict the intermediate state of the martyrs (e.g., 6:11), so that intermediate and eschatological statements are intermingled in what is said about the martyrs."

219. Schüssler Fiorenza, *Revelation*, 59.

220. Williamson, "Thrones in the Book of Revelation," 142.

221. J. E. Botha, "Authorship; Final Judgment and Ultimate Salvation," 139.

the first resurrection lived again (cf. Rev 2:8) and reigned (ἐβασίλευσαν) with Christ for a thousand years. While they are given authority to judge, the martyrs are never shown to be judging. No judgment actually occurs until that of the great white throne; then the dead are judged (vv. 11–12). Schüssler Fiorenza rightly notes that "the image of the great white throne in the universal judgment scene of 20:11–15 parallels the throne image in 20:4 and recalls the throne room of chapters 4–5."[222]

Those seated on thrones are said to reign a thousand years. The interpretation of the thousand years is a notorious *crux interpretum* of the book. In the earlier discussion of the crown of life it was determined that all the victors, martyrs and otherwise, will participate in the first resurrection (20:5). Thus the vision portrays all the saints reigning during this period. Yet, as Mealy observes, "it is noteworthy that in terms of concrete pictures the promises of the good anticipated for the parousia remain absent. In preference to this, the essence of the promised role and status of the overcomers is expressed: they are blessed, they are holy, they are resurrected to life, they are invulnerable to the second death, they are priests and kings, and they are together with Christ."[223] The time periods mentioned in Revelation 19–20 are co-terminus, and these chapters rehearse the same story from differing perspectives.[224] Instead of being seated on horses (19:14), the victors are now seated on thrones (20:4). As Mealy remarks, "If they have seen themselves pictured as coming back to *judge* with Christ, they will be open to seeing a picture of themselves *reigning* as well. Both roles are promised equally in the letters (2.26–27; 3.11, 21), and the second has been prophesied in 5.10."[225] The two scenes thus fulfill John's purpose of showing the saints judging the rebellious nations and reigning with Christ.

Ulfgard denies a future eschatological sense to the fulfillment here, arguing that John's emphasis is on the present royal dignity of the Christian. To bolster his case, he adopts a variant reading not found in NA26/UBS5.[226] Park takes issue with this: "Although the present tense βασιλεύουσιν is attested by the best textual witness, codex Alexandrinus, the future tense βασιλεύσουσιν is found in most of the manuscripts and

---

222. Schüssler Fiorenza, *Revelation*, 108.

223. Mealy, *After the Thousand Years*, 116.

224. For other examples in Revelation see 12:1–6 with 7–17 and 21:1–8 with 9–21. For a discussion of this literary feature in biblical literature, see Anderson, "Double and Triple Stories," 71–89.

225. Mealy, *After the Thousand Years*, 108.

226. Ulfgard, *Feast and Future*, 44.

is preferred by the majority of the commentators of Revelation."[227] The beatitude abruptly moves the time frame from a visionary future reign to a present reminder to the victors. The use of the future is appropriate here, and it functions like the future περιπατήσουσιν in 3:5.

Johnson believes the καὶ οἵτινες clause here introduces a special class of the beheaded—those who did not worship the beast.[228] Ladd, however, suggests another identification—all the saints to whom judgment is given and a smaller group of martyrs.[229] Such suggestions attempt to alleviate the problem of why only the martyrs should live and reign with Christ. Although Johnson admits that in Revelation the relative pronoun οἵτινες usually refers to the preceding group and adds some further detail, he appeals to 1:7 as an exception. Yet this echo of Zechariah 12:10 scarcely singles out a special group or class either in 1:7 or in its source context. In 20:4 the reason for the beheading of the saints is stated positively and negatively: they bore testimony about Jesus and the word of God, while refusing to worship the beast or to receive his mark. It *is* possible that a second group is spoken of here. Such an interpretation is not problematic, since we earlier concluded that not everyone will be martyred. However, it seems best to view this as one group, the beheaded, who by metonymy represent all the saints who potentially must be prepared to follow Christ by giving up their lives.

In Revelation's final chapters the throne appears as the central object in the new Jerusalem and is twice said to be shared by God and the Lamb. In 22:1 the river of the water of life is seen flowing from the throne of God and the Lamb. And in 22:3 the slaves of God serve around the throne of God and the Lamb located in the midst of the holy city. Because Jesus himself triumphed (3:21), he was able to join his Father on the throne. Therefore it is now announced that the victors will be part of this regnal state, likewise promised to the Laodiceans, and will reign forever (22:5).

Laodicean Fulfillment Conclusion

The reference to thrones during the thousand years fulfills the promise to the Laodicean church. It is a proleptic reality realized at Christ's coming with his heavenly army and with the final binding of Satan. Divine rule is finally established when the enemies of God are defeated. The promise of kingship in a heavenly kingdom is finally realized. Giblin writes: "The victory

---

227. Park, "More than a Regained Eden," 304n. 100.
228. Johnson, "Revelation," 12:583; cf. Ulfgard, *Feast and Future*, 61.
229. Ladd, *Revelation of John*, 263.

promised the lax Laodiceans if they change their ways should astound any reader: they will share the *same throne* as God and the Lord Jesus! The underlying notion, of course, is the regal status of those in heaven (20:6) and in the New Jerusalem (22:3–5)."[230] The throne they share is the white throne from which God dispenses his judgment.

Chapter Summary

Yarbro Collins denies that such images as the new creation and the new Jerusalem describe the way things will be at some future time; "Rather, they say that, in a way we cannot fully understand, creation and life do, in the present, have the victory over chaos and death."[231] We have proposed just the opposite. Her conclusion presupposes a realized eschatology characteristic of other Johannine literature. However, such a perspective does not predominate in Revelation. Questions regarding the function of the promises will be addressed in the next chapter.

In chapter 1 it was suggested that the promises and their fulfillments are an important evidence that the structure of Revelation is chiastic. This chart, first presented there, is now completed with all the promises and their fulfillments.

B Seven Churches (1:4—4:2)	B′ New Jerusalem (19:6—22:9)
Promises	*Fulfillment*
1. Tree of life in paradise of God (2:7)	Tree of life (22:2, 14, 19)
2. Crown of life (2:10); second death (2:11)	First resurrection (20:5–6); second death (20:6, 14; 21:4, 8)
3. Hidden manna; white stone; new name (2:17)	River of living water (22:1, 17); wedding supper (19:7–9); precious stone? (21:19); new name (22:4)
4. Authority over the nations; rod of iron (2:26); Morning Star (2:27);	Conquers and judges nations with Christ who holds iron scepter (19:15; 20:4); Morning Star (22:16)
5. White garments; book of life; confession of name (3:5)	Dressed in white, as a bride (19:7–8; 21:2; cf. 7:9, 13), names in book of life (20:12, 15; 21:27; cf. 13:8)

230. Giblin, *Book of Revelation*, 226n. 183.
231. Yarbro Collins, *Apocalypse*, 144.

The Fulfillment of the Victor Sayings

B Seven Churches (1:4—4:2)	B′ New Jerusalem (19:6—22:9)
Promises	*Fulfillment*
6. Pillar in the temple; divine names written; new Jerusalem descending from heaven (3:12)	Divine names written (22:4; cf. 14:1); new Jerusalem descending from heaven (21:2, 10)
7. Divine throne (3:21)	Martyrs judge seated on thrones (20:4)

Minear rightly exclaims, "Not a single promise in this list is missing from the rest of the Apocalypse!"[232] These relationships, according to Ulfgard, demonstrate "how the promises to the conquerors in the letters to the seven churches refer to concepts in chs 21–22, another way of showing how the faithful confessor shares Christ's victory."[233]

Other commentators have suggested additional fulfillments. Schüssler Fiorenza suggests these—2:17 by 22:2; 2:26 transformed in 21:24; and 3:21 by 22:5.[234] Wall suggests these further relationships—the image of "name" (2:17) is parallel to 21:27 and the subjection of the "nations" (2:26–27) is parallel to the salvation of the "nations" (21:24).[235] We remain unconvinced regarding the applicability of these suggestions, however.

Two of the promises find their initial fulfillment outside the final new Jerusalem section (19:6—22:9) in the proleptic appearances of the heavenly saints. The image of white garments is seen in two passages—6:11 and 7:9, 13. The image of the divine name written, through the sealing of the saints, is most obviously seen in 14:1. These early iterations of two promises act as a downpayment, in a sense, that all the rest of the promises will be given in the new Jerusalem.

---

232. Minear, *I Saw a New Earth*, 61.

233. Ulfgard, *Feast and Future*, 103n. 442.

234. Schüssler Fiorenza, *Book of Revelation*, 65n. 129. An editorial error has made senseless the sequence between several of the scriptures she cites. 3:5 is not fulfilled by 21:10 but by 3:12 which is accidentally omitted, thus no fulfillment for 3:5 is given.

235. Wall, *Revelation*, 45n. 10.

6

The Appropriation of the Victor Sayings

Introduction

THIS FINAL chapter examines possible ways that the promises could have been appropriated by the Asian believers in their distinctive churches and communities. What kinds of messages would the Asian audience derive from the book, particularly the seven letters and their victor sayings? Thompson declares astutely, "Most of the key words and root metaphors used throughout the book are introduced in the letters to the seven churches."[1] It is therefore appropriate to examine the seven letters, particularly the promises, regarding macrodynamic theme development. Three proposed themes for the book will be discussed—persecution, the coming of Jesus, and victory. We then look at the function of the promises within the book. This discussion is an outgrowth of chapter 2 with its review of proposed forms for the seven letters. Discovering their function will lead to the likely appropriation of the promises.

Theme of Revelation

Persecution

Caird asks what it was that John expected to happen soon. He rejects the answer that it was the return of Christ in victory and judgment; rather "he expected persecution of the church by the Roman Empire." All the book's imagery including that of the promises has only one purpose—"to disclose to the prospective martyrs the real nature of their suffering and its place in the eternal purposes of God."[2] Likewise, the purpose of the seven prophetic letters is not to investigate whether the churches are ready to meet Jesus; instead Jesus is seeing "whether they are strong enough to

---

1. Thompson, *Book of Revelation*, 6; cf. 179ff.
2. Caird, *Revelation of St. John*, 12.

survive a thorough-going persecution."³ Caird gives four reasons why he chooses persecution.

1. Christ, who knows the churches' strengths and weaknesses, conducts the examination himself. They are being prepared by him, not for him.
2. Four letters contain a conditional threat that Christ will come in judgment unless there is repentance. This seems out of keeping with a belief in an imminent parousia.
3. The virtues most frequently praised are patience, endurance, constancy, and loyalty, not love or joy, which are virtues for normal times. These stern virtues, important when the church is struggling for survival, will not be the only ones that matter at the last assize.
4. The climactic promises to the conquerors determine the character of the letters. But the conqueror is the martyred Christian who testifies concerning Christ and thus wins the victory over temptation and death.

Caird thus sees the promises as directed to believers destined to give up their lives in the coming tribulation. Trites concurs with this assessment, that "basically the Revelation is a prophetic book for prophets, which is another way of saying that it is written to prepare Christians for martyrdom."⁴

A response to each of Caird's points is called for. First, the bridal imagery found in chapters 19–20 is negated if point 1 is true. 19:7 states clearly that the bride, through her righteous deeds, has made herself ready for the wedding of the Lamb.

Second, our outline of the coming sayings presented in chapter 2 indicates localized comings to five churches—Ephesus (2:5); Pergamum (2:16); Thyatira (2:22–23); Sardis (3:3), and Laodicea (3:20). However, such local comings for judgment of the unrepentant are easily distinguished from references to the final parousia (2:25; 3:11). Holman suggests rightly that "it is likely that some of the 'comings' are *anticipatory* of the parousia at the end . . . . Such preliminary 'parousias' are specifically directed to individual churches and are conditional upon failure to rectify some deficiency."⁵

3. Ibid., 27.
4. Trites, *New Testament Concept of Witness*, 167.
5. Holman, "Eschatological Delay," 340.

Third, it is true that such stern virtues as endurance and loyalty are repeatedly praised. But the Thyatirans are commended for their love (2:19), while the Ephesians are specifically chastised for loss of their love (2:4). And by implicit contrast other virtues are indeed commended in light of the last judgment. The vice lists (21:8; 22:11, 15) comprise unrighteous acts that will exclude their perpetrators from the heavenly city. Contrarily, those who are pure, loving, chaste, devout, honest, etc. will become citizens of the new Jerusalem. As we will see next, not all believers were destined to become martyrs, hence more "normal" virtues are likewise important for Jesus and John.

We will elaborate a bit more on the fourth and final point. Roberts critiques Caird's viewpoint, stating that "when he sets up the eschatological perspective and his own understanding of the impending crisis as mutually excluding viewpoints, he is, I believe, in the wrong."[6] With Caird, Roberts identifies the crisis as one of Roman persecution, not of the coming end. But Roberts adds this qualifier, "However, the reality of the coming end and the return of Christ in victory was the perspective by means of which the author was trying to consolidate the endurance of his readers so that they would experience his victorious reign in the moments of their deepest despair."[7]

As noted before, persecution had already been experienced in Pergamum and was at hand in Smyrna; indeed John's own penal situation on Patmos was possibly precarious. In his visions of the martyrs in heaven John sees a great multitude drawn from every nationality on earth. Yet it is doubtful if universal martyrdom is ever implied here. Some churches, like the Thyatirans and the Sardians, would be little affected by persecution. Within a given rhetorical situation, Bitzer states that "there will be at least one controlling exigence which functions as the organizing principle: it specifies the audience to be addressed and the change to be effected."[8] While persecution is certainly the historical exigence that gives rise to Revelation, there are other more important themes, which are discussed in the next sections.[9]

---

6. Roberts, "Letter to Seven Churches," 18.

7. Ibid.

8. Bitzer, "Rhetorical Situation," 7.

9. Bitzer, "Rhetorical Situation,"13, speaks about rhetorical situations that persist, "which are in some measure universal." That is why Revelation is still relevant today. The persecution of Christians remains prevalent in many countries, and Christ's parousia still lies ahead.

The Coming of Jesus

Regarding the coming of Jesus, Holman asserts, "The hope of the imminent return of Christ is presented more forcefully in the New Testament Apocalypse than in any other canonical document."[10] While the development of a delay motif in the Pauline and Synoptic apocalypses was in part prompted by a false eschatological enthusiasm, John apparently addresses no comparable problem in Revelation.[11] Rather, Holman continues, "John seems to desire to *rekindle* expectation which has grown lax and cold (over the years?) and in the face of worldly pressures."[12]

Revelation's opening words, Ἀποκάλυψις of Jesus Christ (understood as "coming"), and the closing invitation, "Amen. Come, Lord Jesus," frame the book and focus the audience on this theme. The phrases ἃ δεῖ γενέσθαι ἐν τάχει (1:1) and ὁ γὰρ καιρὸς ἐγγύς (1:3) found in the opening verses are repeated in 22:6 and 22:10 respectively. "Such balance makes prominent the 'imminence' motif, while the climactic conclusion serves to underscore the idea further."[13] In 22:10 the book is not to be sealed because the time is near. Here, Kümmel explains, ὁ γὰρ καιρὸς ἐγγύς "is used unambiguously to denote the nearness of the end of the world."[14] The beatitude in 1:3 is likewise paired with the beatitude in 22:7, which is linked with the threefold declaration, "I am coming soon" (22:7, 12, 20). Mazzaferri writes, "Jesus' promise, ἔρχομαι ταχύ is scarcely intelligible, let alone a motivation for perseverance, except in the sense of imminence."[15] Other references to Christ's coming are found throughout the book—1:7–8; 2:25; 3:11; and 16:15. All this leads Gager to claim: "The one undeniable fact is that the attention of the community . . . was entirely on the imminent End."[16]

---

10. Holman, "Eschatological Delay," 338.

11. While divine judgment fell on Jerusalem in AD 70 and perhaps unknown localized judgments on some of the Asian churches, the expected parousia did not occur. How was this disappointment handled in the late first century? Westcott believes the Gospel (and the epistles) of John provide the answer. "In the Apocalypse that 'coming' of Christ was expected, and painted in figures: in the Gospel the 'coming' is interpreted" (*Gospel According to St. John*, lxxxvii). Thus the Fourth Gospel is the spiritual interpretation of the Apocalypse.

12. Holman, "Eschatological Delay," 378.

13. Ibid., 339–40.

14. Kümmel, *Promise and Fulfilment*, 20.

15. Mazzaferri, *Genre of the Book of Revelation*, 237.

16. Gager, *Kingdom and Community*, 153.

The Appropriation of the Victor Sayings

The historical situation in the Roman Empire surrounding Nero's demise probably evoked an expectant response among the Asian Christians. Robinson describes it this way:[17]

> [A]ll the evidence suggests that the latter 60s of the first century (not unnaturally in the light of what was happening both in Rome and Jerusalem) saw a quickening of the expectation that the end could not now be long delayed (I Peter 4.7) but that Christ would come very soon to his waiting church (Rev 1.7; 3.3; 22.7, 20), in fulfilment of the promise that the first, apostolic generation would live to see it all (Mark 9.1; 13.30; etc.). When therefore all the other 'pillars' (Gal 2.9) had been removed by death (James in 62, Peter and Paul in 65+) and John only 'remained,' a supposed promise of Jesus that he would not die, but that the end would come first, must have fed fervid expectations of an imminent consummation.

Mazzaferri likewise claims, "There is sufficient unequivocal, explicit evidence firmly to establish that Rev stresses an eschaton imminent in John's very day."[18]

Within the seven letters the use of the present tense in Jesus' instructions to the churches implies imminence. The coming sayings that refer to the parousia (2:25; 3:11) immediately precede the victor sayings. "In hearing the seven letters, therefore, the reader will naturally find him- or herself being trained to associate promised rewards with the parousia."[19] After the Asian audience had read the opening vision and the seven letters, what might they know about the parousia? Mealy responds:[20]

> They know that the parousia is the public revelation of Jesus from heaven as king and judge of all humankind. They also know that, if they remain true to him, it will be: the time of their reunion with him, the time of their participation with him in his kingly rule, the time of their confirmation as royal priests and citizens of his kingdom, and the time of their confirmation as people of the New Jerusalem, which comes down from heaven.

Earlier we concluded that persecution was the historical exigence that gave rise to Revelation; now we suggest that the soon coming of Jesus was the spiritual exigence behind the book. Without repentance, many of the Asian churches were to receive a localized coming with judgment, which

---

17. Robinson, *Redating the New Testament*, 281.
18. Mazzaferri, *Genre of the Book of Revelation*, 236.
19. Mealy, *After the Thousand Years*, 215.
20. Ibid., 215–16.

was to purify and prepare them for the eschatological coming that loomed in the not-too-distant future.

Victory

By this time it is evident that the theme of victory is significant in Revelation. Its importance has been observed by a number of commentators. Swete notes that "the book is a record and a prophecy of victories won by Christ and the Church."[21] Parez adds, "And it is then this victory of the Church that is foreshadowed in, and forms the subject of, the whole book . . . . Christ's victory is to be achieved through His Church."[22] And Bauckham sees a movement in Revelation's later chapters "from Christ's victory on the cross towards the fulfilment of that victory at the *parousia*, and he structures that movement in the series of sevens."[23] We will next look at the observations of P. Minear and K. Strand.

In the chapter titles of his commentary *I Saw a New Earth*, Minear proposes that victory is the theme of Revelation's six visions.[24] These titles are: (1) The Promise of Victory, (2) The Lamb as Victor, (3) The Prophets as Victors, (4) The Faithful as Victors, (5) Victory over Babylon, and (6) Victory over the Devil. Unfortunately Minear provides no explanation regarding why he chose victory as the overriding theme for the book's divisions.

Acknowledging his debt to Minear, K. Strand has proposed that victor, or overcomer, is the macrodynamic theme developed in Revelation. Strand builds upon his earlier study wherein he structures the book chiastically (cf. chapter 1). The following charts show two charts supplied by Strang—the first illustrates the development of the overcomer theme and the second the book's chiastic structure, which Strand has modified slightly from its initial presentation.[25]

---

21. Swete, *Apocalypse of St. John*, 29.
22. Parez, "Seven Letters and the Rest of the Apocalypse," 285.
23. Bauckham, "Delay of the Parousia," 29.
24. Minear, *I Saw a New Earth*, xvii.
25. Strand, "'Overcomer,'" 239, 240.

The Appropriation of the Victor Sayings

	Vision 4		Vision 8
Visions 1–3 ↗		Visions 5–7 ↗	
Process of overcoming during the historical era	Overcomers in the present age	Judgment and doom of the hierarchy of evildoers during eschatological judgment era	Overcomers in the eternal age

		Vision 3	Vision 4	Vision 5	Vision 6		
	Vision 2	8:2—11:18	11:19—14:20	15:1—16:17	16:18—18:24	Vision 7	
Vision 1	4:1—8:1	Trumpet warnings	Evil powers opposing God and his saints	Bowl plagues	Evil powers judged by God	19:21—21:4	Vision 8
1:10b—3:22	God's ongoing work of salvation					God's judgment finale	21:4—22:5
Church militant							Church triumphant

Strand divides the two major parts of Revelation into "historical-era visions" (Visions 1–4) and "eschatological-judgment visions" (Visions 5–8). In the first group Vision 1 gives the requisites for becoming a victor in the victor sayings of the seven letters.[26] The seals septet in Vision 2 emphasizes victory through the blood of the Lamb; the trumpets septet in Vision 3 emphasizes victory through the prophetic word of the two witnesses.[27] The blood of the Lamb and the word of their testimony are set out in Vision 4 as the two elements by which the saints triumph over

26. Ibid., 241.
27. Ibid., 244.

the dragon and the two beasts. These two elements, basic to the process of conquering, establish a connection with the central elements in visions 2 and 3.[28] However, like Vision 8, Vision 4 "also indicates results of overcoming, albeit in a different way and context."[29] This concession is the first indication that this schema has problems.

The second half of eschatological-judgment visions begins with the vindication of the victors from the wrongful verdicts and punishments they have suffered.[30] In Vision 5 the plagues of the six bowls fall upon the earthdwellers who have taken the beast's mark; Vision 6 describes the judgment of Babylon wherein she is rewarded for her evil deeds, and in Vision 7 the beast, false prophet, and finally the dragon are thrown into the lake of fire.[31] Strand's chiastic diagram of the rise and demise of this evil hierarchy does not accord with his division of the visions, another weakness of his hypothesis.[32] In Vision 8 "Revelation's 'overcomer' theme reaches its ultimate climax and conclusion in the granting to the overcomers all the things promised to them in the letter to the churches in the introductory vision of the book."[33]

Strand's observation concerning the importance of the victor theme to Revelation is significant; however, we disagree with his methodology. We have already proposed an alternative chiastic structure in chapter 1. Strand's arbitrary division between the two eras in the book—the historical and the eschatological-judgment—also does not hold up, because considerable overlap exists between the two. For example, the judgments of the seals and trumpets are likewise eschatological. The fifth trumpet in Vision 3, like the bowl judgments, brings suffering on the earthdwellers who do not have the seal of God but instead possess the mark of the beast. Such hortatory elements as the *hode* sayings and the beatitudes inject a present emphasis to the visions of his supposedly future era in Section 2.

The following outline, based upon the chiastic structure proposed in chapter 1, shows the victor theme in present and future time as presented in the book. It also presents the past victory of Jesus, which is the basis for the present and future triumph of the saints. References to blood and piercing in Section A, the prologue (1:5, 7), anticipate fuller explications of Jesus'

---

28. Ibid., 245.
29. Ibid., 241.
30. Ibid., 246–47.
31. Ibid., 248.
32. Ibid., 254; cf. his outline presented in chapter 1.
33. Ibid., 249.

The Appropriation of the Victor Sayings

	A	B	C	D	E	D′	C′	B′	A′
					12:1–17				
				8:2—11:19	Present 12:11	*13:1—16:21*			
			3:21—8:5	Present 11:3-6		Present (Beast) 13:7	*16:18—19:10*		
		1:4—4:2	Past (Lamb) 5:5-6	Present (Beast) 11:7		Present 13:9-10, 18; 14:1-5, 12-13; 16:15	Future 19:1-2, 6-8	*19:6—22:9*	
		1:1-8	Past (Lamb) 1:18; 3:21	Future 11:11-12, 18		Present (Lamb) 14:1, 4	Present 19:9	Future 20:4-6; 21:2-4	*22:6-21*
		Present 1:3	Present (Beast) 6:2			Future 15:2-4	Future (Lamb) 19:11-16	Present 21:6-7	Future (Lamb) 22:7a, 12, 20
	Past (Lamb) 1:5	Present 2:2-3, 9-10, 13, 19, 24-25; 3:4, 8-10	Future 6:9-11; 7:9-10, 13-17						Present 22:7b
	Future (Lamb) 1:7	Future 2:7, 10-11, 17, 26-28; 3:5, 12, 21							Future 22:14, 17

propiatory role. Note that explicit reference to his victory is found only in Sections B and C. Every use of the title "Lamb" after that implicitly refers to Christ's victory at the cross. The beast's present victory is also pointed out as a minor theme. But his victory is transient and quickly fades.

Each section has an overt reference to victory. Those texts marked present, except for the references to the beast, refer to the believers' ongoing witness before martyrdom. Those texts marked future show the heavenly victors and their rewards after death. The praise sayings in the seven letters describe the deeds, past and present, that produce victory. The victor sayings show the rewards of the victorious life. A constant interplay between the present and future aspects of victory is seen throughout the book. Such a diagram betters accords with the literary development of victory as a macrodynamic theme. Victory is therefore a prophetic theme that reverberates throughout Revelation.

When does the victory of the saints begin? Mealy claims that the victory is future: the saints receive their promised rewards during the thousand years. Beale rather observes: "If the saints conclude their 'overcoming' at death (so 12.11), it makes much sense that their reward for overcoming . . . would begin to be given in their exalted state at the time of death."[34]

Theme Conclusion

Several themes have been proposed for Revelation. Persecution, past and future, is an important historical exigence for the writing of Revelation, yet it fails as an encompassing theme. While persecution generated by the dragon, the beast, and the false prophet is a real threat, it is transitory in the face of overwhelming heavenly realities. From the apocalyptic situation of Jesus it is his coming that is all important. At his parousia heaven will be on the earth. To ensure that the saints will be a part of this new heaven and earth, they must be victorious over the temptations and persecution perpetrated by the unholy trinity. From John's prophetic situation exhortations toward that victory are necessary to ensure readiness for Christ's parousia. Thus we conclude that the coming of Jesus and the victory of the saints are the two macrodynamic themes of Revelation.

The Function of the Seven Letters and the Promise Sayings

What is the function of the seven letters, particularly the victor sayings, in Revelation? Various functions have been suggested. White concludes,

---

34. Beale, *John's Use of the Old Testament in Revelation*, 159.

following his examination of ancient epistles generally, that the longer length of Christian letters is "directly related to their function as letters of instruction."[35] And Hartman believes the seven letters have a double function: "[O]n the one hand they engage the readers/listeners, so that they become directly and explicitly involved in the prophecy; their own and their neighbors' virtues and vices are mustered. On the other hand, the messages correspond to a common phenomenon in revelatory literature, viz., that the divine revelation usually responds to problems and situations presented before or brought forward during the visions."[36]

Although the rhetorical situation of each of the seven churches was unique (e.g., persecution, indifference, accommodation), a collective situation was likewise shared among the churches. According to Goguel, "The Letters to the Seven Churches . . . show that the Churches of Asia felt that they were members of an organic group which could be addressed as a single body."[37] From the mutuality of the problems faced, it is clear that the churches interacted with each other (cf. Rev 2:23). Park believes "the book as a whole may be understood as being written to challenge the Christian of the seven churches to enter the NJ [New Jerusalem]."[38] Hence the promises are given generally to all the Asian believers, yet the letters also have elements particularized to each church.

Scobie suggests that the local references employed in the letters serve as a collective reinforcement of John's message: "The various churches would immediately note the advice and warnings, reinforced by local references, given to the other communities. John seeks in a sense to shame each church into complying with his demands by creating a situation in which the various churches will be closely watching each other. In this way he reinforced his appeal to each individual community."[39] While Scobie's language about shaming is too strong, nevertheless his point is well taken. In his absence John calls the churches and their prophets to be mutually accountable to one another, so that the challenges facing them individually and collectively might be faced and overcome.

Building upon these general suggestions, we will now examine twelve functions proposed for the promises. While some proposed functions are demonstrated to be unlikely, several appear equally plausible and in fact

---

35. White, *Light from Ancient Letters*, 19.
36. Hartman, "Form and Message," 143–44.
37. Goguel, *Primitive Church*, 167.
38. Park, "More than a Regained Eden," 258.
39. Scobie, "Local References," 623.

complement each other. Hermeneutically this concept of multiple functions is valid. Such a perspective does justice to the exegetical procedure of a pluralism of methods. Using such a methodology pays high heuristic dividends as we try to understand the probable spiritual outcomes in the Asian churches.

A Rhetorical Function: Argumentative/Persuasive Nature of Revelation 2–3

In chapter 2 we evaluated Kirby's suggestions regarding the rhetorical form of the seven letters; here we discuss his suggestions related to their rhetorical function. Kirby, after identifying Aristotle's three *species* of oratory—judicial, epideictic, and deliberative, opts for deliberative as the overall rhetorical species of Revelation "since it is concerned with events in the future (Rev 1.1, 3) and with a course of action expedient to the audience (22.11–12)."[40] He argues that, although the seven letters may at first seem to have a judicial aspect because of their juridical evaluation of past action, "finally their thrust is deliberative, for each letter purports to stir its audience to a course of action."[41]

The praise and blame sayings in the letters, however, are typical of epideictic rhetoric. Stowers explains, "Moralists argued that praise and blame were harmful unless employed as a kind of exhortation."[42] The praise given to every church but Laodicea was therefore viewed as a type of exhortation.

Regarding the promises, Kirby believes they "function rhetorically as epilogues to each letter, and consequently it is not surprising to find the argument from *pathos* developed in them."[43] Aune criticizes Kirby for failing to see that "the 'epilogue' section has no typical rhetorical function at all."[44] However, Kennedy claims that, according to most rhetoricians, "An epilogue has two functions: it recapitulates the major point or points of the speech, and it seeks to stir the audience to action."[45] While not speaking specifically of the epilogue, Bitzer states that a work of rhetoric "functions ultimately to produce action or change in the world; it per-

---

40. Kirby, "Rhetorical Situations," 200.
41. Ibid.
42. Stowers, *Letter Writing*, 77.
43. Kirby, "Rhetorical Situations," 201.
44. Aune, "Form and Function," 183n. 5.
45. Kennedy, *New Testament Interpretation*, 62.

forms some task. In short, rhetoric is a mode of altering reality."[46] This is an apt description as to how the promises function rhetorically in the letters and in the book.

A Covenant Renewal Function

Shea's suggestion that the form of the seven letters followed ancient Near East covenants was evaluated in chapter 2. Based on his analysis, Shea concludes that the letters of chapters 2–3 function as New Testament covenant renewal messages for each of the seven churches.[47] However, the covenant in Revelation is the new one prophesied by Jeremiah, which is not like the covenant made with Israel. This covenant is based on relationship, "I will be their God and they will be my people" (Jer 31:33), language echoed in the final victor saying in Revelation 21:7.

This new covenant was initiated through the Lamb who triumphed through the shedding of his blood. It is not centered in the earthly temple in Jerusalem but in the heavenly temple. We therefore do not accept Shea's contention that Revelation 2–3 shows a "function of the ancient suzerainty covenant . . . carried out on a rather sweeping scale in a major block of material from the last book of the NT."[48] The blessings of the promises are not fulfilled by command as in law but through persuasion and exhortation as in grace.

A Liturgical Function

In chapter 2 we examined Prigent's proposal that the form of the seven letters follows that of early liturgical practices. Sweet summarizes Prigent's view of their function: they evoke "the message of Christian worship, i.e., that the final coming of Christ and the blessedness of the heavenly banquet are anticipated here and now in his eucharistic presence."[49] We find little evidence of explicit eucharistic imagery in the victor sayings and therefore must reject attempts to give a liturgical function to the letters.

A Warfare Function

A number of recent commentators have found evidence of the holy war theme in Revelation. For the Asian believers Yarbro Collins sees the story about combat functioning as a model "for understanding and coming to

---

46. Bitzer, "The Rhetorical Situation," 3–4.
47. Shea, "Covenantal Form," 83.
48. Ibid., 83–84.
49. Sweet, *Revelation*, 42.

terms with powerlessness, suffering and death."[50] While the bulk of the Holy War imagery is usually found in chapters 4–22, Giblin observes that such imagery is somewhat discernible in the victor sayings of chapters 2–3: "These promises, most of which John later depicts as verified in a heavenly state after death and/or in the new creation . . . serve to predict the 'promised land,' which is the positive result or fruit of the term and goal (*telos*) of the Holy War."[51]

Bauckham sees a much more explicit linkage between the promises and Holy War: "They function to invite the readers to participate in the eschatological war which is described in the central part of the book, where the vocabulary of conquest (νικᾶν) is frequent, and so gain their place in the new Jerusalem."[52] We agree that John is calling his audience not to be spectators, but to participate actively in the struggle which some may seek to ignore or evade. Bauckham likens John's use of the Holy War tradition to that found in the War Scroll from Qumran (1QM), although John makes the warfare metaphorical rather than literal. He concludes: "But in religious function there is a certain parallel between the two works."[53]

In chapter 3 we interpreted the ὁ νικῶν motif in terms of athletic games rather than military conquest, preferring the translation "victor" rather than "conqueror." Although warfare imagery is explicitly used in the Pergamene letter (e.g., "sword," "war" [2:16]), it is absent in the rest. Therefore, while acknowledging that Holy War plays a thematic role in such chapters as 12, 16, and 19, it does not function as a significant theme in the victor sayings.

A Salvation History Function

An older interpretive approach with few adherents today sees the promises functioning as a type of God's historical dealings with humanity in the Old Testament. Poirier represents this view: "Les promesses entre elles offrent le phénomène singulier d'un dévelopement historique basé sur l'Ancient Testament, depuis Adam jusqu'au Christ."[54] A progressive development is seen in the Old Testament allusions and quotations in the seven promises.

---

50. Yarbro Collins, *Apocalypse*, xiv.
51. Giblin, *Book of Revelation*, 29n. 29.
52. Bauckham, *Climax of Prophecy*, 213.
53. Ibid.
54. "The promises among themselves offer the singular phenomenon of historical development based on the Old Testament, from Adam to Christ"; Poirier, *Les sept églises*, 43.

The Appropriation of the Victor Sayings

The following chart gives three outlines of this development suggested by Bullinger,[55] Crosthwaite, and Poirier.[56]

Church	Bullinger	Crosthwaite	Poirier
Ephesus	Eden	Creation and fall	Paradis et chute
Smyrna	Fall	Capitivity in Egypt	Captivité en Egypte
Pergamum	Wilderness	Wilderness	Exode et conquête de Canaan
Thyatira	Wilderness/Davidic reign	Conquest (Joshua)	Royaume uni
Sardis	End of Davidic reign	Judges	Royaume divisé
Philadelphia	Temple of Solomon	Kings	Exil et retour
Laodicea	Throne of Solomon	Exile and restoration	Restauration

The lack of agreement among these three interpreters exemplifies the difficulty of typological interpretation. Even Poirier acknowledges regarding the Laodicean promise, "le rapprochement avec l'Ancien Testament ne peut être très parfait."[57]

A further refinement of this approach is advanced by Trench, who sees "an order parallel to that of the unfolding of the kingdom of God from its first beginnings on earth to its glorious consummation in heaven."[58] The 4 + 3 plan he sees is this: E—creation, S—fall, P—wilderness, T—united kingdom, Sa—judgment day, Ph—new Jerusalem, L—eternal reign. A glaring omission in this scheme is the church age, which is totally absent.

---

55. According to Bullinger, *Commentary on Revelation*, 73–86, the references to the Old Testament in the seven letters likewise follow the historical order of events, yet are different than those in the promises: E—Israel's espousal (Ex); S—Israel's wanderings (Nm); P—wilderness (Nm); T—Israel's kings (1 and 2 Ki); Sa—Israel's removal (1 and 2 Chr); Ph—Judah's king's (2 Chr); L—Judah's removal (Minor prophets).

56. Bullinger, *Commentary on Revelation*, 86–102; Crosthwaite, "Symbolism of the Letters to the Seven Churches," 397–99; and Poirier, *Les sept églises*, 49–50. The translation of Poirier's categories is: Paradise and fall, Captivity in Egypt, Exodus and conquest of Canaan, United kingdom, Divided kingdom, Exile and return, Restoration

57. "the comparison with the Old Testament cannot be very perfect"; Poirier, *Les sept églises*, 49.

58. Trench, *Epistles to the Seven Churches*, 229; for the 4 + 3 plan see pp. 229–31.

Such approaches are the antithesis of the historical-prophetical interpretations first popularized by Joachim of Fiore (ca. 1135–1202), who used a principle of recapitulation arguing that the different prophecies in Revelation referred to the same event. His successor Alexander the Minorite (d. 1271) abandoned Joachim's method and sought to link the prophecies with events in chronological order. Wainwright explains, "The letters to the seven churches, he explained, represent the life of the early church, and their angels were bishops."[59] Numerous permutations of this interpretation evolved, and are found in Trench's excursus.[60] John's use of Old Testament imagery in the victor sayings was demonstrated in chapter 4. However, that he consciously constructed the letters and their promises around the history of Israel (or of the church!) is doubtful; neither would his audience have read such an intent in them.

A Juridical Function

Käsemann likens the victor sayings to sentences of holy law (*Sätze heiligen Rechtes*) found in the Old Testament and in the Synoptics: "It is therefore prophecy's function of leadership in the community which finds expression in the sentences of holy law."[61] Citing Matthew 10:32, he writes that "confession of Christ is estimated to be the standard of judgment at the Last Day, and also in the form of the sentence. Prophecy proclaims blessing and curse on those members of the community who confess and those who deny by establishing within it the eschatological *jus talionis*."[62]

Bauckham thinks the Sardian saying (3:5) wherein Jesus promises to confess the victor's name before his Father and the angels is "just such a sentence of eschatological divine law as Käsemann has identified as characteristic of early Christian prophetic pronouncements."[63] However, Bauckham believes that the stylistic form of holy war sentences and the idea of eschatological *jus talionis* can be found in purer forms than in the promises (e.g., 11:18; 16:6; 22:18–19). Schüssler Fiorenza characterizes the additional victor saying in 21:6–7 as "a 'Sentence of Holy Law' similar

---

59. Wainwright, *Mysterious Apocalypse*, 53–54.

60. Trench, *Epistles to the Seven Churches*, 232–45.

61. Käsemann, *New Testament Questions of Today*, 77. Such sentences of holy law are typically structured in the form of a chiasmus (a, b. b, a) [cf. Aune, *Prophecy in Early Christianity*, 237].

62. Käsemann, *New Testament Questions of Today*, 77.

63. Bauckham, *Climax of Prophecy*, 95; cf. Aune, *Prophecy in Early Christianity*, 239.

to that found in Paul."[64] Beasley-Murray likewise finds juridical language in the last beatitude (22:14), which mentions the tree of life.[65] He accordingly believes that John's purpose in writing the book was "to inspire in his readers the faith that the empire of the Antichrist and his minions is destined to be replaced by the rule of the Christ and his saints."[66]

Regarding John's use of supposed sentences of holy law, Hill notes that "at best it is only a hypothesis, but one which has been elevated to the level of assumed fact by reason of its frequent reiteration."[67] Aune cites several weaknesses with the holy law proposal. The origin of holy law is in Wisdom literature, not prophetic literature; its features are fluid, not stable; and its use is found in Greco-Roman prophetic speech also.[68] That the Sardian promise alone functions as a sentence of holy law seems unlikely, given the interrelatedness of the promises. This perspective is thus unsatisfactory as an approach to all the promises.

A Therapeutic Function

Pointing to a sociological solution, Gager suggests that Revelation had a therapeutic function for the community. He states that "a simple message of consolation, encouraging believers to stand firm and reiterating earlier promises, would have been inadequate to the needs of the occasion. Indeed, these traditional hopes and promises were very much a part of the crisis, for their credibility had been called into question by the fact of persecution, and simply to repeat them would have been to compound the agony."[69] John's answer, according to Gager, is to construct a Christian myth. A rhythmic contrast between victory and oppression oscillates throughout the book. Gager believes this pattern commences in the seven letters before its main development in seven visions from 4:1—22:5. He depicts this oscillation in the following chart:[70]

---

64. Schüssler Fiorenza, *Book of Revelation*, 101.
65. Beasley-Murray, *Revelation*, 339.
66. Beasley-Murray, *Revelation*, 315.
67. Hill, "On the Evidence for the Creative Role of Christian Prophets," 271–73.
68. Aune, *Prophecy in Early Christianity*, 238–39.
69. Gager, *Kingdom and Community*, 52; cf. 56.
70. Ibid., 53.

Victory/Hope	Oppresion/Despair
4:1—5:14 Throne and the Lamb	
	6:1–17 First six seals
7:1—8:4 Multitude of the faithful and the seventh seal	
	8:5—9:21 First six trumpets
10:1—11:1 Dramatic interlude in heaven	
	11:2–14 Attack of the beasts
11:15–19 Seventh trumpet	
	12:1–17 Dragon assaults the woman 13:1–18 Beast with horns
14:1–7 Mount Zion and the Lamb	
	14:8—15:1 Destruction and judgment
15:2–8 Martyrs worship God	
	16:1–20 Seven bowls of wrath 17:1—18:24 Fall of Babylon
19:1–16 Worship in heaven	
	19:17—20:15 Final judgment
21:1—22:5 New heaven, new earth, new Jerusalem	

By depicting such an oscillation, Gager clearly captures the importance of the victory theme in Revelation, something we have likewise pointed out. Gager is also to be commended for understanding that the persecution against the Asian Christians is real and not perceived.

That Jesus would speak to the churches individually and declare his personal knowledge of their situations must have provided spiritual and psychological therapy to them. Yet, as we have demonstrated, this so-called "myth" that has been constructed is little more, in one sense, than an updating and recycling of traditional apocalyptic and prophetic motifs. John, in fact, reiterates earlier Old Testament promises by re-presenting them through the risen Christ as applicable for the Asian churches in their situation. Persecution was one thing Jesus promised repeatedly to his disciples (e.g., Matt 5:10–12; 10:33; 23:34). So the Asian believers should not have been surprised at their present trouble. Jesus was seeking to shake their spiritual lethargy and to stimulate them toward action and repentance, not to mollify them.

The Appropriation of the Victor Sayings

Du Rand likewise points to the cathartic value of the divine victory over evil depicted repeatedly in Revelation: "The readers' actual emotions of fear and humiliation are psycho-therapeutically released through the theological content of the literary enactments."[71] Du Rand wisely grounds the catharsis of the audience, not in myth, but in their faith in Jesus' victorious death and resurrection. Hence, "[t]he Christian's perspective of his destination of the heavenly Jerusalem, however, is not merely psychological compensation but divine fulfillment."[72] We agree that the promises with their fulfillments have a therapeutic aspect, which seeks to transform the readers in their socio-historical situation in first-century Asia.

An Ethical Function

The nature of Jesus' eschatological teaching in the Gospels has been discussed by New Testament scholars for many years. The particular link between eschatology and ethics has been developed by Wilder. Ethics were important, he noted, because "pressing problems of social ethics and public order, and of the proper message of the church with regard to them, create a responsibility for biblical scholarship in this field."[73] Wilder found it difficult to deny "that Jesus' whole call to repentance and his urgent summons to the righteousness he preached were set against a background of vivid eschatological rewards and punishments which he saw as imminent."[74] However, he believed that the relationship between eschatology and ethics in Jesus' teaching is best illustrated in the immediate connection established between the coming event and the ethical reform involved in repentance.[75] This is demonstrated in five of the seven letters where the word μετανόεω occurs (2:5 [2x]; 2:16; 2:21 [2x], 22; 3:3 [2x]; 3:19). Only the churches of Smyrna and Philadelphia are excluded because they receive no words of blame. For a prophet/apocalyptist like John, the kingdom of God always had a double aspect of promise and warning. Wilder adds, "It was a supreme good whose coming meant reward and vindication for the righteous, and it was therefore a threat to all unrighteousness."[76]

---

71. Du Rand, *Johannine Perspectives*, 286.

72. Ibid.

73. Wilder, *Eschatology and Ethics*, 1. If Wilder's statement were true in 1950 when he penned those words, how much more true is it today with the moral declension of home and society a universal phenomenon!

74. Ibid., 11.

75. Ibid., 74.

76. Ibid., 81.

The importance of virtuous deeds is emphasized repeatedly in Revelation both by Jesus and John. The praise/blame sayings of five of the letters begin with the phrase, "I know your deeds . . . ." Only the letters to Smyrna and Pergamum—churches which have suffered persecution—fail to mention their deeds. Such deeds "are regarded by our author simply as the manifestation of the inner life and character."[77] Boring likewise affirms: "This insistence on the importance of Christian action shows that even in his situation of persecution, threat, and expectation of the near End John does not understand the Christian life to be simply passive waiting . . . . John calls his churches to do more than endure; there is a ministry to be performed in the meantime."[78] This view is consistent with our perspective that the victors were not just the martyrs, but all the saints. Surely ethical concerns were important, given the emphasis on deeds in Revelation and the vice lists at the end of the book. Righteous deeds though were a means to an end for the victor, that of preparing for the coming of Jesus and receiving the promised reward.

A Character Development Function

Closely related to the ethical function is that of character development. Neall has analyzed the concept of character in the Apocalypse against the background of Platonic and Aristotelian philosophies. In Revelation's typical dualistic style, two types of character are presented—likeness to God, personified in Christ the Lamb, and likeness to Satan, personified in the dragon, the beast, and the false prophet. In the Pergamene and Thyatiran churches believers were indulging in practices that compromised their character. Neall writes, "This perverse doctrine that advocated the most debasing sins—idolatrous feasting and immorality—called forth the divine wrath (Rev 2:16, 22–23)."[79] Likewise, spiritual declension was evident in the Ephesian, Sardian, and Laodicean churches: "All three churches had suffered a decline in the commitment, love, and earnestness that mark the true Christian."[80]

According to Neall, John employed exhortations in the seven letters to discourage actions that brought spiritual declension and to encourage deeds that resulted in virtuous character.[81] These exhortations are ampli-

---

77. Charles, *Revelation*, 1:cxv.
78. Boring, *Revelation*, 95.
79. Neall, *Concept of Character in the Apocalypse*, 70.
80. Ibid., 75.
81. Apollonius of Tyana likewise addressed letters to several Asian cities, including

The Appropriation of the Victor Sayings

fied and reinforced throughout the rest of the book. One of the most prominent is the promise or victor sayings, which show that "Righteous character is developed through conquering."[82] Four foes are to be conquered: (1) sin, with apostasy being the most prominent, (2) the fear of death, (3) the accusations of Satan, and (4) the beast, its image, and the number of its name. The victory of the saints rests on Christ's prior victory at the cross and his future victory in the eschaton. Conquering these four foes of the saints comes "by participating in and appropriating Christ's victory to themselves through connection with Him (3:21; 17:14)."[83] Just as Christ's death was not a defeat but a victory, so will be the death of the saints. Working from her educational perspective, Neall presents an effective argument that the promises played a role in developing the Christian character of the Asian audience. Nevertheless, we do not believe that character development was the primary function of the promises.

An Eschatological Function

Commentators are divided over the eschatological import of the promises. Feuillet writes: "Some such as Gelin, Loisy, Boismard, see them as referring exclusively to the future life. Others (Allo, Bonsirven) are aware that, in Johannine thought, eternal life begins here on earth. Thus they think that these promises are directed at the same time to the life of Christians as it is here on earth."[84] Jeremias concludes that "all the victor sayings in the seven letters of Rev. have an eschatological character,"[85] even as Leivestad suggests that "eternal life is the reward for which the victor has qualified himself, and there is in fact no victory at all if the reward is missing."[86]

The imminent coming of Jesus Christ is a predominant theme in the book, as we have seen. The Asian churches, like the Corinthians, seem to have had a diminished expectation of that coming (cf. 1 Cor 15:1ff; 2 Pet 3:3ff). Most of the churches had so accommodated themselves to the surrounding culture that they had lost the proper eternal perspective. Yarbro Collins believes "the visions concern the future, but they were written down in order to illuminate the present experience of the author and the

---

Ephesus (*Ep.* 37, 65) and Sardis (*Ep.* 38–41, 56, 75–76), which criticized their perceived character faults and moral failures.

82. Neall, *Concept of Character in the Apocalypse*, 126.
83. Ibid., 127.
84. Feuillet, *The Apocalypse*, 38.
85. Jeremias, "παράδεισος," *TDNT* 5:768.
86. Leivestad, *Christ the Conqueror*, 216–17.

first readers and to evoke a particular response to that experience."[87] It is this tension between present and future that Revelation seeks to maintain. John thus speaks of a future "whose prolepsis is already at work in the present."[88] The eschatological rewards are therefore promised to those victorious in their present circumstances.

A Parenetic Function

Parenetic, pastoral, hortatorical—such words describe the particular function considered in this section. Parenesis is a distinctive feature of Revelation, and one that distinguishes it from other apocalyptic literature.[89] Minear accounts for at least eight literary forms in Revelation that fit this description, including the victor sayings.[90] Goldingay points to the revelatory material in Daniel as the background for the parenesis in Revelation 2–3: "Revelation incorporates parenesis in its visions; Daniel presents its parenesis in story form, in keeping with OT precedents."[91] Schüssler Fiorenza believes that John's choice of the concentric, or chiastic, pattern of structuring his visions emphasizes the hortatorical element: "The basic movement of the narrative represents the prophetic movement from promise to fulfillment."[92]

But what is the focus of the parenesis and exhortation both in the letters and specifically in the promises? Endurance is suggested by Holman—"there is a strong parenetic emphasis upon endurance, with the encouragement of future rewards and with warnings to avoid any compromise which held out hope of circumventing suffering."[93] Rogers believes that the readers are assured "that God's justice will be done on behalf of the faithful, who suffered because of their faithfulness.... Even those who suffered unto death are promised eventual resurrection in the last days when the new city of God is established."[94] The parousia is another proposed parenetic focus. The prophet John, writing as a pastor, is not interested in calculating the time of Jesus' return, according to Wall; "[r]ather he is interested to motivate his audience to respond to Christ immediately

---

87. Yarbro Collins, *The Apocalypse*, x.
88. Stuckenbruck, *Angel Veneration and Christology*, 37.
89. Wilson, "A Pie in a Very Bleak Sky?" 78–79.
90. Minear, *I Saw a New Earth*, 215–21.
91. Goldingay, *Daniel*, 320.
92. Schüssler Fiorenza, *Book of Revelation*, 176.
93. Holman, "Eschatological Delay," 362.
94. Rogers, "Images of Christian Victory," 73.

and properly in the light of his soon and sudden return."[95] Persecution is another suggestion. Aune believes that the basic purpose of the exhortation to conquer "is to encourage Christians to meet the challenges which face them in circumstances of religious and political oppression."[96] Finally, du Rand concludes that the function "is to provide consolation and to suppress the distinction between the flawed present and the ideal future . . . . The imagery of the heavenly Jerusalem is in that sense a persuasive expression for the readers to identify with."[97] All of these suggested parenetic functions are credible and provide insight on the text.

The use of local backgrounds fulfills a particular pastoral function. Because Jesus has knowledge of the personal situations in each of the seven cities, he can be trusted to know the future with certainty. While the believers may not know what is going on in Rome or the empire at large, they can rely upon the omniscient and omnipotent Lord to look out for their best interests. Jesus likewise presents himself as the Shepherd in Revelation who will lead and guide his people to security and safety.

A Prophetic Function

Closely related to the parenetic function is the prophetic function. John regarded himself as a prophet to the seven churches, prophesying during a volatile and unstable period.[98] In our discussion of Revelation's chiastic structure we agreed with the assessment of Schüssler Fiorenza that "the structure of the book underscores that the main function of Rev. is the prophetic interpretation of the situation of the community."[99] It follows logically that the seven letters with their victor sayings should serve a prophetic function.

Mazzaferri thinks that John's central purpose is not just to strengthen the saints; instead "he delivers a forceful, prophetic message in typical conditional style to both the righteous and the wicked, urging the first to remain steadfast and the second to repent."[100] Mealy likewise affirms, "The promises contained in the seven letters are thus intended to spur the Christian readers on toward becoming overcomers at any cost, and toward seeing themselves throughout the text as those who stand to re-

95. Wall, *Revelation*, 263.
96. Aune, *Prophecy in Early Christianity*, 278.
97. Du Rand, "Imagery of the Heavenly Jerusalem," 70.
98. Wilson, "A Pie in a Very Bleak Sky," 95–97.
99. Schüssler Fiorenza, *Book of Revelation*, 175.
100. Mazzaferri, *Genre of the Book of Revelation*, 170.

ceive the blessings promised to the overcomer alone."[101] Fekkes doubts if John merely borrows such Old Testament texts as Psalm 2:8–9 found in the Thyatiran promise for their poetic effect or metaphorical force: "It seems more likely that John highlights these particular OT consolations because he wants the readers to appreciate the prophetic foundation of his statements."[102] We concur that the letters with their promises function as prophetic statements to the Asian congregations.

Function Conclusion

The multiplicity of functions suggested for the seven letters and their victor sayings belie the various interpretive perspectives brought to Revelation. We have found that many of these suggestions have little or no validity. Minear warns with justification that when the interpreter attempts to reconstruct the full scale of the conflict seen in Revelation, "he is almost bound to exaggerate one thesis concerning John's purpose in writing."[103] Hopefully we can avoid exaggeration by suggesting not one, but three purposes. The three final functions reviewed—eschatological, parenentic, and prophetic—are most consistent with our earlier analysis of the form of the letters in chapter 2 and our subsequent discussion of the book's themes earlier in this chapter. Because the seven letters are a *mixtum compositum*, we should expect several functions to be apparent. Du Rand concurs with such an assessment, stating that Revelation combines "a prophetic eschatological aim and a pastoral touch presented in the framework of a letter."[104]

Chapter Summary

Revelation was written in response to a crisis, but one that was not unexpected. The crisis had been predicted by Jesus in the Synoptic apocalypses (Matt 24, Mark 13, Luke 21). Revelation then is a reiteration, an update, a contemporization of that prophetic word to "this generation" that received the initial prophecy.[105]

Were the Asian churches successful in appropriating the promises given by Jesus through the prophet John? An immediate historical answer comes in the form of other letters written to the Asian churches by Ignatius,

---

101. Mealy, *After the Thousand Years*, 84.
102. Fekkes, *Isaiah and Prophetic Traditions*, 69.
103. Minear, *I Saw a New Earth*, 213.
104. Du Rand, "Imagery of the Heavenly Jerusalem," 70.
105. Wilson, "A Pie in a Very Bleak Sky?," 83–89.

The Appropriation of the Victor Sayings

bishop of Antioch (ca. AD 110). Three of the seven churches are addressed by Ignatius—Ephesus, Philadelphia, and Smyrna—as well as two other churches that lay between Ephesus and Laodicea—Magnesia and Tralles. Polycarp, a contemporary of Igatius, served as bishop of Smyrna for over four decades (ca. AD 110–156). Indeed the Asian churches had endured! John's audience had apparently repented and was spared Christ's coming in temporal judgment. The believers had resisted the beast and his mark and survived the ensuing persecution.

As seen in chapter 5, some of the promises have a proleptic fulfillment as the persecuted church waits in heaven. However, most of the promises await fulfillment at the parousia and the concomitant arrival of the new Jerusalem. Hence, the cry of the church remains, "Come, Lord Jesus" (Rev 22:20). In summation, the promises to the victors prove to be more than just "pies in a very bleak sky!" They are dynamic spiritual incentives that have motivated believers not only in the first century but throughout church history.

Appendix

Letter Sayings Analysis

Address Sayings

Ephesus	Smyrna	Pergamum	Thyatira	Sardis	Philadelphia	Laodicea
2:1 Τῷ ἀγγέλῳ τῆς ἐν Ἐφέσῳ ἐκκλησίας γράψον·	2:8 Καὶ τῷ ἀγγέλῳ τῆς ἐν Σμύρνῃ ἐκκλησίας γράψον·	2:12 Καὶ τῷ ἀγγέλῳ τῆς ἐν Περγάμῳ ἐκκλησίας γράψον·	2:18 Καὶ τῷ ἀγγέλῳ τῆς ἐν Θυατείροις ἐκκλησίας γράψον·	3:1 Καὶ τῷ ἀγγέλῳ τῆς ἐν Σάρδεσιν ἐκκλησίας γράψον·	3:7 Καὶ τῷ ἀγγέλῳ τῆς ἐν Φιλαδελφείᾳ ἐκκλησίας γράψον·	3:14 Καὶ τῷ ἀγγέλῳ τῆς ἐν Λαοδικείᾳ ἐκκλησίας γράψον·

Epithet Sayings

1 Τάδε λέγει ὁ κρατῶν τοὺς ἑπτὰ ἀστέρας ἐν τῇ δεξιᾷ αὐτοῦ, ὁ περιπατῶν ἐν μέσῳ τῶν ἑπτὰ λυχνιῶν τῶν χρυσῶν·	8 Τάδε λέγει ὁ πρῶτος καὶ ὁ ἔσχατος, ὃς ἐγένετο νεκρὸς καὶ ἔζησεν·	12 Τάδε λέγει ὁ ἔχων τὴν ῥομφαίαν τὴν δίστομον τὴν ὀξεῖαν·	18 Τάδε λέγει ὁ υἱὸς τοῦ θεοῦ, ὁ ἔχων τοὺς ὀφθαλμοὺς αὐτοῦ ὡς φλόγα πυρὸς καὶ οἱ πόδες αὐτοῦ ὅμοιοι χαλκολιβάνῳ·	1 Τάδε λέγει ὁ ἔχων τὰ ἑπτὰ πνεύματα τοῦ θεοῦ καὶ τοὺς ἑπτὰ ἀστέρας·	7 Τάδε λέγει ὁ ἅγιος, ὁ ἀληθινός, ὁ ἔχων τὴν κλεῖν Δαυίδ, ὁ ἀνοίγων καὶ οὐδεὶς κλείσει καὶ κλείων καὶ οὐδεὶς ἀνοίγει·	14 Τάδε λέγει ὁ Ἀμήν, ὁ μάρτυς ὁ πιστὸς καὶ ἀληθινός, ἡ ἀρχὴ τῆς κτίσεως τοῦ θεοῦ·

Appendix

Praise Sayings

Ephesus	Smyrna	Pergamum	Thyatira	Sardis	Philadelphia	Laodicea
2 Οἶδα τὰ ἔργα σου καὶ τὸν κόπον καὶ τὴν ὑπομονήν σου καὶ ὅτι οὐ δύνῃ βαστάσαι κακούς, καὶ ἐπείρασας τοὺς λέγοντας ἑαυτοὺς ἀποστόλους καὶ οὐκ εἰσὶν καὶ εὗρες αὐτοὺς ψευδεῖς, 3καὶ ὑπομονὴν ἔχεις καὶ ἐβάστασας διὰ τὸ ὄνομά μου καὶ οὐ κεκοπίακες. 6ἀλλὰ τοῦτο ἔχεις, ὅτι μισεῖς τὰ ἔργα τῶν Νικολαϊτῶν ἃ κἀγὼ μισῶ.	9 Οἶδά σου τὴν θλῖψιν καὶ τὴν πτωχείαν, ἀλλὰ πλούσιος εἶ, καὶ τὴν βλασφημίαν ἐκ τῶν λεγόντων Ἰουδαίους εἶναι ἑαυτούς, καὶ οὐκ εἰσὶν ἀλλὰ συναγωγὴ τοῦ Σατανᾶ.	13 Οἶδα ποῦ κατοικεῖς, ὅπου ὁ θρόνος τοῦ Σατανᾶ, καὶ κρατεῖς τὸ ὄνομά μου καὶ οὐκ ἠρνήσω τὴν πίστιν μου καὶ ἐν ταῖς ἡμέραις Ἀντιπᾶς ὁ μάρτυς μου ὁ πιστός μου, ὃς ἀπεκτάνθη παρ' ὑμῖν, ὅπου ὁ Σατανᾶς κατοικεῖ.	19 Οἶδά σου τὰ ἔργα καὶ τὴν ἀγάπην καὶ τὴν πίστιν καὶ τὴν διακονίαν καὶ τὴν ὑπομονήν σου, καὶ τὰ ἔργα σου τὰ ἔσχατα πλείονα τῶν πρώτων. 24ὑμῖν δὲ λέγω τοῖς λοιποῖς τοῖς ἐν Θυατείροις ὅσοι οὐκ ἔχουσιν τὴν διδαχὴν ταύτην, οἵτινες οὐκ ἔγνωσαν τὰ βαθέα τοῦ Σατανᾶ ὡς λέγουσιν.	4 ἀλλὰ ἔχεις ὀλίγα ὀνόματα ἐν Σάρδεσιν ἃ οὐκ ἐμόλυναν τὰ ἱμάτια αὐτῶν, καὶ περιπατήσουσιν μετ' ἐμοῦ ἐν λευκοῖς, ὅτι ἄξιοί εἰσιν.	8 Οἶδά σου τὰ ἔργα, ἰδοὺ δέδωκα ἐνώπιόν σου θύραν ἠνεῳγμένην, ἣν οὐδεὶς δύναται κλεῖσαι αὐτήν, ὅτι μικρὰν ἔχεις δύναμιν καὶ ἐτήρησάς μου τὸν λόγον καὶ οὐκ ἠρνήσω τὸ ὄνομά μου. 9ἰδοὺ διδῶ ἐκ τῆς συναγωγῆς τοῦ Σατανᾶ, τῶν λεγόντων ἑαυτοὺς Ἰουδαίους εἶναι, καὶ οὐκ εἰσὶν ἀλλὰ ψεύδονται.	

Blame Sayings

Ephesus	Smyrna	Pergamum	Thyatira	Sardis	Philadelphia	Laodicea
2:4 ἀλλὰ ἔχω κατὰ σοῦ ὅτι τὴν ἀγάπην σου τὴν πρώτην ἀφῆκες.		2:14 ἀλλ' ἔχω κατὰ σοῦ ὀλίγα ὅτι ἔχεις ἐκεῖ κρατοῦντας τὴν διδαχὴν Βαλαάμ, ὃς ἐδίδασκεν τῷ Βαλὰκ βαλεῖν σκάνδαλον ἐνώπιον τῶν υἱῶν Ἰσραὴλ φαγεῖν εἰδωλόθυτα καὶ πορνεῦσαι. 15 οὕτως ἔχεις καὶ σὺ κρατοῦντας τὴν διδαχὴν [τῶν] Νικολαϊτῶν ὁμοίως.	2:20 ἀλλὰ ἔχω κατὰ σοῦ ὅτι ἀφεῖς τὴν γυναῖκα Ἰεζάβελ, ἡ λέγουσα ἑαυτὴν προφῆτιν καὶ διδάσκει καὶ πλανᾷ τοὺς ἐμοὺς δούλους πορνεῦσαι καὶ φαγεῖν εἰδωλόθυτα. 21 καὶ ἔδωκα αὐτῇ χρόνον ἵνα μετανοήσῃ, καὶ οὐ θέλει μετανοῆσαι ἐκ τῆς πορνείας αὐτῆς.	3:1 Οἶδά σου τὰ ἔργα ὅτι ὄνομα ἔχεις ὅτι ζῇς, καὶ νεκρὸς εἶ.		3:15 Οἶδά σου τὰ ἔργα ὅτι οὔτε ψυχρὸς εἶ οὔτε ζεστός. ὄφελον ψυχρὸς ἦς ἢ ζεστός. 16 οὕτως ὅτι χλιαρὸς εἶ καὶ οὔτε ζεστὸς οὔτε ψυχρός, μέλλω σε ἐμέσαι ἐκ τοῦ στόματός μου. 17 ὅτι λέγεις ὅτι Πλούσιός εἰμι καὶ πεπλούτηκα καὶ οὐδὲν χρείαν ἔχω, καὶ οὐκ οἶδας ὅτι σὺ εἶ ὁ ταλαίπωρος καὶ ἐλεεινὸς καὶ πτωχὸς καὶ τυφλὸς καὶ γυμνός,

Appendix
Coming Sayings

Ephesus	Smyrna	Pergamum	Thyatira	Sardis	Philadelphia	Laodicea
1:5 μνημόνευε οὖν πόθεν πέπτωκας καὶ μετανόησον καὶ τὰ πρῶτα ἔργα ποίησον· εἰ δὲ μή, ἔρχομαί σοι καὶ κινήσω τὴν λυχνίαν σου ἐκ τοῦ τόπου αὐτῆς, ἐὰν μὴ μετανοήσῃς.	1:10 μηδὲν φοβοῦ ἃ μέλλεις πάσχειν. ἰδοὺ μέλλει βάλλειν ὁ διάβολος ἐξ ὑμῶν εἰς φυλακὴν ἵνα πειρασθῆτε καὶ ἕξετε θλῖψιν ἡμερῶν δέκα. γίνου πιστὸς ἄχρι θανάτου,	1:16 μετανόησον οὖν· εἰ δὲ μή, ἔρχομαί σοι ταχὺ καὶ πολεμήσω μετ᾽ αὐτῶν ἐν τῇ ῥομφαίᾳ τοῦ στόματός μου.	1:22 ἰδοὺ βάλλω αὐτὴν εἰς κλίνην καὶ τοὺς μοιχεύοντας μετ᾽ αὐτῆς εἰς θλῖψιν μεγάλην, ἐὰν μὴ μετανοήσουσιν ἐκ τῶν ἔργων αὐτῆς, 23 καὶ τὰ τέκνα αὐτῆς ἀποκτενῶ ἐν θανάτῳ. καὶ γνώσονται πᾶσαι αἱ ἐκκλησίαι ὅτι ἐγώ εἰμι ὁ ἐραυνῶν νεφροὺς καὶ καρδίας, καὶ δώσω ὑμῖν ἑκάστῳ κατὰ τὰ ἔργα ὑμῶν. 24 βοῦ βάλλω ἐφ᾽ ὑμᾶς ἄλλο βάρος, 25 πλὴν ὃ ἔχετε κρατήσατε ἄχρι[ς] οὗ ἂν ἥξω.	2:2 γίνου γρηγορῶν καὶ στήρισον τὰ λοιπὰ ἃ ἔμελλον ἀποθανεῖν, οὐ γὰρ εὕρηκά σου τὰ ἔργα πεπληρωμένα ἐνώπιον τοῦ θεοῦ μου. 3 μνημόνευε οὖν πῶς εἴληφας καὶ ἤκουσας καὶ τήρει καὶ μετανόησον. ἐὰν οὖν μὴ γρηγορήσῃς, ἥξω ὡς κλέπτης, καὶ οὐ μὴ γνῷς ποίαν ὥραν ἥξω ἐπὶ σέ.	2:9 ἰδοὺ ποιήσω αὐτοὺς ἵνα ἥξουσιν καὶ προσκυνήσουσιν ἐνώπιον τῶν ποδῶν σου καὶ γνῶσιν ὅτι ἐγὼ ἠγάπησά σε. 10 ὅτι ἐτήρησας τὸν λόγον τῆς ὑπομονῆς μου, κἀγώ σε τηρήσω ἐκ τῆς ὥρας τοῦ πειρασμοῦ τῆς μελλούσης ἔρχεσθαι ἐπὶ τῆς οἰκουμένης ὅλης πειράσαι τοὺς κατοικοῦντας ἐπὶ τῆς γῆς. 11 ἔρχομαι ταχύ· κράτει ὃ ἔχεις, ἵνα μηδεὶς λάβῃ τὸν στέφανόν σου.	2:18 συμβουλεύω σοι ἀγοράσαι παρ᾽ ἐμοῦ χρυσίον πεπυρωμένον ἐκ πυρὸς ἵνα πλουτήσῃς, καὶ ἱμάτια λευκὰ ἵνα περιβάλῃ καὶ μὴ φανερωθῇ ἡ αἰσχύνη τῆς γυμνότητός σου, καὶ κολλ[ο]ύριον ἐγχρῖσαι τοὺς ὀφθαλμούς σου ἵνα βλέπῃς. 19 ἐγὼ ὅσους ἐὰν φιλῶ ἐλέγχω καὶ παιδεύω· ζήλευε οὖν καὶ μετανόησον. 20 ἰδοὺ ἕστηκα ἐπὶ τὴν θύραν καὶ κρούω· ἐάν τις ἀκούσῃ τῆς φωνῆς μου καὶ ἀνοίξῃ τὴν θύραν, [καὶ] εἰσελεύσομαι πρὸς αὐτὸν καὶ δειπνήσω μετ᾽ αὐτοῦ καὶ αὐτὸς μετ᾽ ἐμοῦ.

Letter Sayings Analysis

Hearing Sayings

Ephesus	Smyrna	Pergamum	Thyatira	Sardis	Philadelphia	Laodicea
1:7 ὁ ἔχων οὖς ἀκουσάτω τί τὸ πνεῦμα λέγει ταῖς ἐκκλησίαις.	2:11 ὁ ἔχων οὖς ἀκουσάτω τί τὸ πνεῦμα λέγει ταῖς ἐκκλησίαις.	2:17 ὁ ἔχων οὖς ἀκουσάτω τί τὸ πνεῦμα λέγει ταῖς ἐκκλησίαις.	2:29 ὁ ἔχων οὖς ἀκουσάτω τί τὸ πνεῦμα λέγει ταῖς ἐκκλησίαις.	3:6 ὁ ἔχων οὖς ἀκουσάτω τί τὸ πνεῦμα λέγει ταῖς ἐκκλησίαις.	3:13 ὁ ἔχων οὖς ἀκουσάτω τί τὸ πνεῦμα λέγει ταῖς ἐκκλησίαις.	3:22 ὁ ἔχων οὖς ἀκουσάτω τί τὸ πνεῦμα λέγει ταῖς ἐκκλησίαις.

Victor Sayings

Ephesus	Smyrna	Pergamum	Thyatira	Sardis	Philadelphia	Laodicea
7 τῷ νικῶντι δώσω αὐτῷ φαγεῖν ἐκ τοῦ ξύλου τῆς ζωῆς, ὅ ἐστιν ἐν τῷ παραδείσῳ τοῦ θεοῦ.	10 καὶ δώσω σοι τὸν στέφανον τῆς ζωῆς. 11 ὁ νικῶν οὐ μὴ ἀδικηθῇ ἐκ τοῦ θανάτου τοῦ δευτέρου.	17 τῷ νικῶντι δώσω αὐτῷ τοῦ μάννα τοῦ κεκρυμμένου καὶ δώσω αὐτῷ ψῆφον λευκήν, καὶ ἐπὶ τὴν ψῆφον ὄνομα καινὸν γεγραμμένον ὃ οὐδεὶς οἶδεν εἰ μὴ ὁ λαμβάνων.	26 καὶ ὁ νικῶν καὶ ὁ τηρῶν ἄχρι τέλους τὰ ἔργα μου, δώσω αὐτῷ ἐξουσίαν ἐπὶ τῶν ἐθνῶν 27 καὶ ποιμανεῖ αὐτοὺς ἐν ῥάβδῳ σιδηρᾷ ὡς τὰ σκεύη τὰ κεραμικὰ συντρίβεται, 28 ὡς κἀγὼ εἴληφα παρὰ τοῦ πατρός μου, καὶ δώσω αὐτῷ τὸν ἀστέρα τὸν πρωϊνόν.	5 ὁ νικῶν οὕτως περιβαλεῖται ἐν ἱματίοις λευκοῖς καὶ οὐ μὴ ἐξαλείψω τὸ ὄνομα αὐτοῦ ἐκ τῆς βίβλου τῆς ζωῆς καὶ ὁμολογήσω τὸ ὄνομα αὐτοῦ ἐνώπιον τοῦ πατρός μου καὶ ἐνώπιον τῶν ἀγγέλων αὐτοῦ.	12 ὁ νικῶν ποιήσω αὐτὸν στῦλον ἐν τῷ ναῷ τοῦ θεοῦ μου καὶ ἔξω οὐ μὴ ἐξέλθῃ ἔτι καὶ γράψω ἐπ' αὐτὸν τὸ ὄνομα τοῦ θεοῦ μου καὶ τὸ ὄνομα τῆς πόλεως τοῦ θεοῦ μου, τῆς καινῆς Ἰερουσαλὴμ ἡ καταβαίνουσα ἐκ τοῦ οὐρανοῦ ἀπὸ τοῦ θεοῦ μου, καὶ τὸ ὄνομά μου τὸ καινόν.	21 ὁ νικῶν δώσω αὐτῷ καθίσαι μετ' ἐμοῦ ἐν τῷ θρόνῳ μου, ὡς κἀγὼ ἐνίκησα καὶ ἐκάθισα μετὰ τοῦ πατρός μου ἐν τῷ θρόνῳ αὐτοῦ.

Bibliography

Akurgal, E. *Ancient Civilizations and Ruins of Turkey*. 8th ed. Istanbul: Net, 1993.
Alexander, R. H. "Ezekiel." In *The Expositor's Bible Commentary*, edited by F. E. Gaebelein, 6:737–996. Grand Rapids: Zondervan, 1986.
Alford, H. "Apocalypse of John." In *The Greek Testament*, 4:544–750, 1875. Repr., Grand Rapids: Guardian, 1985.
Allo, E. B. *Saint Jean, l'Apocalypse*. 3rd ed. Paris: Gabalda, 1933.
Andersen, F. I. "2 Enoch." In *The Old Testament Pseudepigrapha*, edited by J. H. Charlesworth, 1:91–213. Garden City, N.Y.: Doubleday, 1983.
Anderson, A. A. *2 Samuel*. Dallas: Word, 1989.
Anderson, H. "4 Maccabees." In *The Old Testament Pseudipigrapha*, edited by J. H. Charlesworth. 2:531–64. Garden City, N.Y.: Doubleday, 1985.
Anderson, F. I. *Job*. Downers Grove, Ill.: InterVarsity, 1976.
Anderson, J. C. "Double and Triple Stories, the Implied Reader, and Redundancy in Matthew." *Semeia* 31 (1985): 71–89.
Archer, G. L. and Chirichigno, G. C. *Old Testament Quotations in the New Testament: A Complete Survey*. Chicago: Moody, 1983.
Arnold, C. E. *Ephesians: Power and Magic*. Grand Rapids: Baker, 1992.
———. "Mediator Figures in Asia Minor: Epigraphic Evidence." Paper presented at the Society of Biblical Literature annual meeting. San Francisco, 1992.
Arnold, I. R. "Festivals of Ephesus." *American Journal of Archaeology* 76 (1972): 17–22.
Arslan, M. *Roman Coins*. Ankara: Museum of Anatolian Civilizations, 1992.
Ashmole, B. *Architect and Sculptor in Classical Greece*. New York: New York University Press, 1972.
Aune, D. E. "The Social Matrix of the Apocalypse of John." *Biblical Research* 24 (1981): 16–32.
———. "The Odes of Solomon and Early Christian Prophecy." *New Testament Studies* 28 (1982): 435–60.
———. "The Influence of Roman Imperial Court Ceremonial on the Apocalypse of John." *Biblical Research* 28 (1983): 5–26.
———. *Prophecy in Early Christianity and the Ancient Mediterranean World*. Grand Rapids: Eerdmans, 1983.
———. "The Apocalypse of John and the Problem of Genre." *Semeia* 36 (1986): 65–96.
———. "The Apocalypse of John and Graeco-Roman Revelatory Magic." *New Testament Studies* 33 (1987): 481–501.
———. "Revelation." In *The Harper's Bible Commentary*, edited by J. L. Mays, 1300–1319. San Francisco: Harper & Row, 1988.
———. "The Prophetic Circle of John of Patmos and the Exegesis of Revelation 22.16." *Journal for the Study of the New Testament* 37 (1989): 103–16.
———. "The Form and Function of the Proclamations to the Seven Churches (Revelation 2–3)," *New Testament Studies* 36 (1990): 182–204.
———. *Revelation*, 3 vols. Nashville: Thomas Nelson, 1997, 1998.

Bibliography

Avery, C. B., ed. *The New Century Classical Handbook*. New York: Appleton-Century-Crofts, 1962.

Bach, D. "La structure au service de la prédication: Les sept lettres d'Apocalypse 2–3." *Etudes théologiques et religieuses* 2 (1981): 294–305.

Bagnall, R. S. and P. Derow. *Greek Historical Documents: The Hellenistic Period*. Chico: Scholars Press, 1982.

Bailey, K. E. *Poet and Peasant: A Literary-Cultural Approach to the Parables of Luke*. Grand Rapids: Eerdmans, 1976.

Baldwin, J. G. *Haggai, Zechariah, Malachi*. Downers Grove, Ill.: Inter-Varsity, 1972.

———. *Daniel*. Downers Grove, Ill.: Inter-Varsity, 1978.

Barclay, W. *Letters to the Seven Churches*. Philadelphia: Westminster, 1957.

———. *The Revelation of John*, 2 vols. Rev. ed. Philadelphia: Westminster, 1976.

Barr, D. L. "The Apocalypse as a Symbolic Transformation of the World: A Literary Analysis." *Interpretation* 38 (1984): 39–50.

———. "The Apocalypse of John as Oral Enactment." *Interpretation* 40 (1986): 243–56.

———. "Plots and Echoes: Myth and Meaning in the Structure of the Apocalypse." Paper presented at the Society of Biblical Literature annual meeting. Chicago, 1994.

———. *Tales of the End*. Santa Rosa: Poleridge, 1998.

Barrett, C. K. *The Gospel According to St. John*. Rev. ed. Philadelphia: Westminster, 1978.

———. *The New Testament Background: Selected Documents*. 2nd ed. San Francisco: Harper & Row, 1987.

Barton, J. *Amos' Oracles against the Nations*. Cambridge: Cambridge University Press, 1980.

Bauckham, R. J. "The Delay of the Parousia." *Tyndale Bulletin* 31 (1980): 3–36.

———. *Jude, 2 Peter*. Waco: Word, 1983.

———. *The Climax of Prophecy*. Edinburgh: T. & T. Clark, 1993.

———. *The Theology of the Book of Revelation*. Cambridge: Cambridge University Press, 1993.

Bauer, W., W. F. Arndt, F. W. Gingrich, and F. W. Danker. *A Greek-English Lexicon of the New Testament and Other Early Christian Literature*. Chicago: University of Chicago Press, 1979.

Beagley, A. J. *The 'Sitz im Leben' of the Apocalypse with Particular Reference to the Role of the Church's Enemies*. Berlin/New York: De Gruyter, 1987.

Beale, G. K. *The Use of Daniel in Jewish Apocalyptic Literature and in the Revelation of St. John*. Lanham, Md.: University Press of America, 1984.

———. "The Interpretative Problem of Rev. 1:19." *Novum Testamentum* 34 (1992): 360–87.

———. *John's Use of the Old Testament in Revelation*. Sheffield: Sheffield Academic Press, 1998.

———. *The Book of Revelation*. Grand Rapids: Eerdmans, 1999.

Bean, G. *Turkey Beyond the Maeander*. London: John Murray, 1971.

———. *Aegean Turkey*. 2nd ed. London: John Murray, 1979.

Beasley-Murray, G. R. *Jesus and the Future*. London: Macmillan, 1954.

———. *Revelation*. Rev. ed. Grand Rapids: Eerdmans, 1978.

———. *John*. Dallas: Word, 1987.

———. *Jesus and the Last Days*. Peabody, Mass: Hendrickson, 1993.

Beckwith, I. T. *The Apocalypse of John*. New York: Macmillan, 1922.

Bell, A. A. "The Date of John's Apocalypse: The Evidence of Some Roman Historians Reconsidered." *New Testament Studies* 25 (1979): 93–102.

Bibliography

Benedict, R. R. "The Use of ΝΙΚΑΩ in the Letters to the Seven Churches of Revelation," ThM thesis, Dallas Theological Seminary, 1966.
Benner, M. *The Emperor Says: Studies in the Rhetorical Style in Edicts of the Early Empire.* Göteborg: Acts Universitatis Gothoburgensis, 1975.
Bieder, W. "Die sieben Seligpreisungen in der Offenbarung des Johannes." *Theologische Zeitschrift* 10 (1954): 13–30.
Bitzer, L. F. "The Rhetorical Situation," *Philosophy and Rhetoric* 1 (1968): 1–14.
Black, M. "Some Greek Words with 'Hebrew' Meanings in the Epistles and Apocalypse." In *Biblical Studies: Essays in Honour of William Barclay*, edited by J. R. McKay and J. F. Miller, 135–46. London: Collins, 1976.
Blaiklock, E. M. *The Seven Churches.* London: Marshall, Morgan & Scott, 1951.
Blass, F., A. Debrunner, and R. W. Funk. *A Greek Grammar of the New Testament and Other Early Christian Literature.* Chicago: University of Chicago Press, 1961.
Blevins, J. L. *Revelation as Drama.* Nashville: Broadman, 1984.
Blomberg, C. A. "The Structure of 2 Corinthians 1–7." *Criswell Theological Review* 4 (1989): 3–20.
———. *Matthew.* Nashville: Broadman, 1992.
Boardman, J., J. Griffin, and O. Murray. *The Oxford History of the Classical World.* Oxford/New York: Oxford University Press, 1986.
Bonfante, L. and E. Jaunzems. "Clothing and Ornament." In *Civilization of the Ancient Mediterranean: Greece and Rome*, edited by M. Grant and R. Kitzinger, 3:1385–1413. New York: Charles Scribner's Sons, 1988.
Boring, M. E. "The Theology of Revelation." *Interpretation* 40 (1986): 257–69.
———. *Revelation.* Louisville: John Knox, 1989.
Boring, M. E., K. Berger, and C. Colpe. *Hellenistic Commentary to the New Testament.* Nashville: Abingdon, 1995.
Botha, J. E., P. G. R. de Villiers, and J. Engelbrecht, eds. *Reading Revelation.* Pretoria: van Schaik, 1988.
Botha, J. E. "Authorship; Final Judgment and Ultimate Salvation (19:11–22:5)." In *Reading Revelation*, edited by J. E. Botha et al., 1–2, 134–50. Pretoria: van Schaik, 1988.
———. "The Potential of Speech Act Theory for New Testament Exegesis: Some Basic Concepts." *Hervormde Teologiese Studies* 47 (1991): 277–93.
Botha, P. J. J. "God, Emperor Worship and Society: Contemporary Experiences and the Book of Revelation." *Neotestamentica* 22 (1988): 87–102.
———. "Greco-Roman Literacy as Setting for New Testament Writings." *Neotestamentica* 26 (1992): 195–215.
———. "Living Voice and Lifeless Letters: Reserve towards Writing in the Graeco-Roman World." *Hervormde Teologiese Studies* 49 (1993): 742–59.
Bousset, W. *Die Offenbarung Johannis.* Göttingen: Vandenhoeck & Ruprecht, 1906.
Bowie, E. "The Readership of Greek Novels in the Ancient World." In *The Search for the Ancient Novel*, edited by J. Tatum, 435–59. Baltimore: Johns Hopkins University Press, 1994.
Bowman, J. W. "Revelation, Book of." In *The Interpreter's Dictionary of the Bible*, edited by G. A. Buttrick, 58–71. Nashville: Abingdon, 1962.
Brandon, S. G. F. *The Fall of Jerusalem and the Christian Church.* London: SPCK, 1951.
Breck, J. "Biblical Chiasmus: Exploring Structure for Meaning." *Biblical Theology Bulletin* (1987): 17, 70–74.
———. *The Shape of Biblical Language: Chiasmus in the Scriptures and Beyond.* Crestwood, N.J.: St. Vladimir's Seminary Press, 1994.

Brewer, R. "The Influence of Greek Drama on the Apocalypse of John." *Anglican Theological Review* 18 (1936): 74–92.
Bromiley, G. W., ed. *International Standard Bible Encyclopedia*. 4 vols. Rev. ed. Grand Rapids: Eerdmans, 1979–1988.
Brouwer, W. *The Literary Development of John 13–17: A Chiastic Reading*. Atlanta: Society of Biblical Literature, 2000.
Brown, C., ed. *New International Dictionary of New Testament Theology*. 4 vols. Grand Rapids: Zondervan, 1975–86.
Brown, F., S. R. Driver, and C. A. Briggs. *The New Brown-Driver-Briggs-Gesenius Hebrew-Aramaic Lexicon*. 1906. Repr., Peabody, Mass: Hendrickson, 1979.
Brown, S. "The Hour of Trial (Rev. 3:10)." *Journal of Biblical Literature* 85 (1966): 308–14.
Bruce, F. F. *The Epistle to the Hebrews*. Grand Rapids: Eerdmans, 1964.
———. "The Spirit in the Apocalypse." In *Christ and Spirit in the New Testament*, edited by B. Lindars and S. S. Smalley, 333–44. London: Cambridge University Press, 1973.
———. *Peter, Stephen, James and John*. Grand Rapids: Eerdmans, 1979.
———. *Commentary on Galatians*. Grand Rapids: Eerdmans, 1982.
———. "Revelation." In *The International Bible Commentary*, edited by F. F. Bruce, 1593–1629. Rev. ed. Grand Rapids: Zondervan, 1986.
———. *The Canon of Scripture*. Downers Grover, Ill.: InterVarsity, 1988.
Bullinger, E. W. *Figures of Speech Used in the Bible*. 1898. Repr., Grand Rapids: Baker, 1968.
———*Commentary on Revelation*. 1902. Repr., Grand Rapids: Kregel, 1984.
Burchard, C. "Joseph and Aseneth." In *The Old Testament Pseudipigrapha*, edited by J. H. Charlesworth, 2:177–247. New York: Doubleday, 1985.
Burnett, A., M. Amandry, and P. P. Ripollès. *Roman Provincial Coinage*. 2 vols. London: British Museum Press/Paris: Bibliothèque Nationale, 1992.
Cadoux, C. J. *Ancient Smyrna*. Oxford: Blackwell, 1938.
Caird, G. B. *The Revelation of St. John the Divine*. New York: Harper & Row, 1966.
Carson, D. A. "Matthew." In *The Expositor's Bible Commentary*, edited by F. E. Gaebelein, 8:3–594. Grand Rapids: Zondervan, 1984.
Carson, D. A., Moo, D. J. and Morris, L. *An Introduction to the New Testament*. Grand Rapids: Zondervan, 1992.
Casson, L. *Travel in the Ancient World*. 2nd ed. Baltimore: Johns Hopkins University Press, 1994.
Chambers, R. R. "Greek Athletics and the Jews: 165 b.c.–a.d. 70." PhD diss., Miami University, 1980.
Charles, R. H. *Studies in the Apocalypse*. 2nd ed. Edinburgh: T. & T. Clark, 1915.
———. *The Revelation of St. John*. 2 vols. Edinburgh: T. & T. Clark, 1920.
Charlesworth, J. H., ed. *The Old Testament Pseudepigrapha*. 2 vols. Garden City, N.Y.: Doubleday, 1983.
Christenson, D. *Deuteronomy*. Waco: Word, 1991.
Clark, D. J. "Criteria for Identifying Chiasm." *Linguistica Biblica* 35 (1975): 63–72.
Clarke, E. G. *The Wisdom of Solomon*. Cambridge: Cambridge University Press, 1973.
Clines, D. J. A. *Job 1–20*. Waco: Word, 1989.
Collins, J. J. "The Jewish Apocalypses." *Semeia* 14 (1979): 21–59.
———. *The Scepter and the Star: The Messiahs of the Dead Sea Scrolls and Other Ancient Literature*. New York: Doubleday, 1995.
Comblin, J. *Le Christ dans l'Apocalypse*. Tournai: Desclée, 1965.

Combrink, H. J. B. "The Structure of the Gospel of Matthew as Narrative. *Tyndale Bulletin* 34 (1983): 61–90.
Corsini, E. *The Apocalypse*. Wilmington, Del.: Michael Glazier, 1983.
Court, J. M. *Myth and History in the Book of Revelation*. London: SPCK, 1979.
———. *Revelation*. Sheffield: JSOT Press, 1994.
Craigie, P. *Ezekiel*. Philadelphia: Westminister, 1983.
———. *Psalms 1–50*. Waco: Word, 1983.
Crawford, J. S. "Multiculturalism at Sardis." *Biblical Archaeology Review* 22.5 (1996): 38–47.
Crosthwaite, A. "The Symbolism of the Letters to the Seven Churches." *Expository Times* 22 (1910–11): 307–9.
Culpepper, R. A. "The Pivot of John's Prologue." *New Testament Studies* 27 (1980–81): 1–31.
Davids, P. H. *The Epistle of James*. Grand Rapids: Eerdmans, 1982.
Deismann, G. A.. *Bible Studies*. 1901. Repr., Peabody, Mass: Hendrickson, 1988.
———. *Light from the Ancient East*. New York: Doran, 1927.
Delebecque, É. "Où situer l'arbre de vie dans la Jérusalem céleste?" *Revue Thomiste* 88 (1988): 124–30.
De Smidt, J. C. "The Holy Spirit in the Book of Revelation—Nomenclature." *Neotestamentica* 28 (1994): 229–44.
Dewey, J. "The Literary Structure of the Controversy Stories in Mark 2:1—3:6." *Journal of Biblical Literature* 92 (1973): 394–401.
———. *Markan Public Debate: Literary Technique, Concentric Structure, and Theology in Mark 2:1—3:6*. Chico: Scholars Press, 1980.
De Young, J. C. *Jerusalem in the New Testament*. Kampen: Kok, 1960.
Dibelius, M. "The Isis Initiation at Apuleius." In *Conflict at Colossae*, edited by F. O. Francis and W. A. Meeks, 61–121. Rev. ed. Missoula: Scholars, 1975.
Diefenbach, M. "Die 'Offenbarung des Johannes' offenbart, daß der Seher Johannes die antike Rhetoriklehre kennt." *Biblische Notizen* 73 (1994): 50–57.
Dillard, R. B. and T. Longman III. *An Introduction to the Old Testament*. Grand Rapids: Zondervan, 1994.
Dittenberger, W. *Orientis Graeci Inscriptiones Selectae*. Vol. 2. 1905. Repr., Hildesheim: George Olms, 1960.
Dumbrell, W. J. *The End of the Beginning: Revelation 21–22 and the Old Testament*. Grand Rapids: Baker, 1985.
Dunn, J. D. G. *The Epistles to the Colossians and to Philemon*. Grand Rapids: Eerdmans, 1996.
Du Rand, J. A. "The Imagery of the Heavenly Jerusalem (Revelation 21:9–22:5)." *Neotestamentica* 22 (1988): 65–86.
———. *Johannine Perspectives. Part 1: Introduction to the Johannine Writings*. Midrand: Orion, 1991.
———. "A 'basso ostinato' in the Structuring of the Apocalypse of John?" *Neotestamentica* 27 (1993): 299–311.
———. "'Now the salvation of our God has come. . . .' A Narrative Perspective on the Hymns in Revelation 12–15." *Neotestamentica* 27 (1993): 313–30.
———. "The Transcendent God-view: Depicting Structure in the Theological Message of the Apocalypse of John." *Neotestamentica* 28 (1994): 557–73.
Edelstein, E. J. and L. *Asclepius*. 2 vols. Baltimore: Johns Hopkins, 1945.
Efird, J. M. *Revelation for Today*. Nashville: Abingdon, 1989.

Bibliography

Ehrman, B. D. *The New Testament: A Historical Introduction to the Early Christian Writings.* New York/Oxford: Oxford University Press, 1997.
Ellingworth, P. *Commentary on Hebrews.* Grand Rapids: Eerdmans, 1993.
Elliott, J. E. "Sorcery and Magic in the Revelation of John." *Listening* 28 (1993): 261–76.
Elliott, J. K. *The Apocryphal New Testament.* Oxford: Clarendon, 1993.
Ellul, J. *Apocalypse: The Book of Revelation.* New York: Seabury, 1977.
Enroth, A-M. "The Hearing Formula in the Book of Revelation." *NTS* 36 (1990): 609–13.
Erdemgil, S. *Ephesus: Ruins and Museum.* 4th ed. Istanbul: Net, 1994.
Erim, K. *Aphrodisias.* New York: Facts on File, 1986.
Farrer, A. M. *The Rebirth of Images: The Making of St. John's Apocalypse.* Philadelphia: Westminster, 1949.
———. *The Revelation of St. John the Divine.* Oxford: Oxford University Press, 1964.
Fee, G. D. *The First Epistle to the Corinthians.* Grand Rapids: Eerdmans, 1987.
———. *1 and 2 Timothy, Titus.* Peabody, Mass: Hendrickson, 1988.
———. *Paul's Letter to the Philippians.* Grand Rapids: Eerdmans, 1995.
Fekkes, J. *Isaiah and Prophetic Traditions in the Book of Revelation.* Sheffield: JSOT Press, 1994.
Feuillet, A. *The Apocalypse.* New York: Alba House, 1965.
Filson, F. V. "Ephesus and the New Testament." In *The Biblical Archaelogist Reader* 2, edited by D. N. Freedman and E. F. Campbell, Jr., 323–52. Garden City, N.Y.: Doubleday Anchor, 1964.
Finnegan, J. *The Archaeology of the New Testament.* Princeton: Princeton University Press, 1992.
Fitzmeyer, J. A. *The Gospel According to Luke.* Garden City, N.Y.: Doubleday, 1982.
Ford, J. M. *Revelation.* Garden City, N.Y.: Doubleday, 1975.
Fox, R. L. *Pagans and Christians.* New York: Knopf, 1987.
Fredericks, D. G. "Chiasm and Parallel Structure in Qoheleth 5:6—6:9." *Journal of Biblical Literature* 108 (1989): 17–35.
Freedman, D. N., ed. *The Anchor Bible Dictionary.* 6 vols. New York: Doubleday, 1992.
Freely, J. *Classical Turkey.* San Francisco: Chronicle Books, 1990.
Friesen, S. J. *Twice Neokoros: Ephesus, Asia, and the Cult of the Flavian Imperial Family.* Leiden: Brill, 1993.
———. "Ephesus: Key to a Vision in Revelation." *Biblical Archaeology Review* 19.3 (1994): 24–37.
———. *Imperial Cults and the Apocalyse of John.* Oxford: Oxford University Press, 2001.
Furnish, V. P. *II Corinthians.* Garden City, N.Y.: Doubleday, 1984.
Gaechter, P. "Semitic Literary Forms in the Apocalypse and their Import." *Theological Studies* 8 (1947): 547–73.
Gager, J. *Kingdom and Community: The Social World of Early Christianity.* Englewood Cliffs, N.J.: Prentice-Hall, 1975.
Garber, S. D. "Symbolism of Heavenly Robes in the New Testament in Comparison with Gnostic Thought." PhD diss., Princeton Theological Seminary, 1974.
Giblin, C. H. *The Book of Revelation.* Collegeville, Minn.: Michael Glazier/Liturgical Press, 1991.
Giet, S. *L'Apocalypse et l'histoire.* Paris: Presses Universitaires de France, 1957.
Glasson, T. F. *The Revelation of John.* Cambridge: Cambridge University Press, 1965.
Goguel, M. *The Primitive Church.* London: George Allen & Unwin, 1963.
Goldingay, J. G. *Daniel.* Waco: Word, 1989.

Bibliography

Goodspeed, E. J. *New Solutions of New Testament Problems.* Chicago: University of Chicago Press, 1927.
Goulder, M. D. "The Chiastic Structure of the Lucan Journey." *Texte und Untersuchungen* 87 (1964): 195–202.
———. "The Apocalypse as an Annual Cycle of Prophecies." *New Testament Studies* 27 (1981): 342–67.
Grant, M. *Roman History from Coins.* Cambridge: Cambridge University Press, 1968.
———. *Greek and Latin Authors 800 BC–AD 1000.* New York: H. W. Wilson, 1980.
———. *Atlas of Ancient History: 1700 BC to 565 AD.* New York: Dorset, 1984.
Gundry, R. L. "The New Jerusalem: People as Place, not Place for People." *Novum Testamentum* 29 (1987): 254–64.
———. *A Survey of the New Testament.* 3rd ed. Grand Rapids: Zondervan, 1994.
Guthrie, D. *The Relevance of John's Apocalypse.* Grand Rapids: Eerdmans, 1987.
———. *New Testament Introduction.* 4th ed. Downers Grove, Ill.: InterVarsity, 1990.
Hadorn, W. *Die Offenbarung des Johannes.* Leipzig: Werner Scholl, 1928.
Hahn, F. "Die Sendschreiben der Johannesapokalypse. Ein Beitrag zur Bestimmung prophetischer Redeformen." In *Tradition und Glaube,* edited by G. Jeremias, H-W. Kuhn, and H. Stegemann, 357–94. Göttingen: Vandenhoeck & Ruprecht, 1971.
Hamilton, R. *The Architecture of Hesiodic Poetry.* Baltimore: Penguin, 1989.
Hammond, N. G. L. and H. H. Scullard, eds. *Oxford Classical Dictionary.* 2nd ed. Oxford: Clarendon, 1970.
Hanfmann, G. M. A., ed. *Sardis from Prehistoric to Roman Times.* Cambridge, Mass.: Harvard University Press, 1983.
Hanfmann, G. M. A., F. K. Yegül and J. S. Crawford. "The Roman and Late Antique Period." In *Sardis from Prehistoric to Roman Times,* edited by G. M. A. Hanfmann, 139–67. Cambridge, Mass.: Harvard University Press, 1983.
Hansen, E. V. *The Attalids of Pergamon.* 2nd ed. Ithaca: Cornell University Press, 1971.
Harrington, W. *Mark.* Wilmington, Del.: Michael Glazier, 1979.
Harris, H. A. *Greek Athletics and the Jews.* Cardiff: University of Wales Press, 1976.
Harris, M. A., "The Literary Function of Hymns in the Apocalypse of John." PhD diss., The Southern Baptist Theological Seminary, 1988.
Harris, W. V. *Ancient Literacy.* Cambridge, Mass: Harvard University Press, 1989.
Hartman, L. "Form and Message. A Preliminary Discussion of 'Partial Texts' in Rev 1–3 and 22.6ff." In *L'Apocalypse johannique et l'apocalyptique dans le Nouveau Testament,* edited by J. Lambrecht. Gembloux: Duculot/Leuven: University Press, 1980.
Hastings, J. *A Dictionary of the Bible.* 5 vols. New York: Charles Scribner's Sons, 1923.
Hatfield, D. E. "The Function of the Seven Beatitudes in Revelation." PhD diss., The Southern Baptist Theological Seminary, 1987.
Hawthorne, G. F. *Philippians.* Waco: Word, 1983.
Hayes, D. A. *John and his Writings.* New York/Cincinnati: Methodist Book Concern, 1917.
Hellholm, D., ed. *Apocalypticism in the Mediterranean World and the Near East.* Tübingen: J. C. B. Mohr, 1983.
Hellholm, D. "The Problem of Apocalyptic Genre and the Apocalypse of John." *Semeia* 36 (1986): 13–64.
Hemer, C. J. "The Cities of the Revelation." In *New Documents Illustrating Early Christianity,* edited by G. H. R. Horsley, 3:51–58. North Hyde: Macquarie University, 1983.
———. *The Letters to the Seven Churches of Asia in their Local Setting.* Sheffield: JSOT Press, 1986.

Hendrickson, W. *More than Conquerors*. Grand Rapids: Baker, 1940.
Hengel, M. *Judaism and Hellenism*. 2 vols. London: SCM, 1974.
———. *Poverty and Riches in the Early Church*. London: SCM, 1974.
———. *The Johannine Question*. Philadelphia: Trinity Press International, 1989.
Hepper, F. N. *Baker Encyclopedia of Bible Plants*. Grand Rapids: Baker, 1992.
Hill, D. "Prophecy and Prophets in the Revelation of St. John," *New Testament Studies* 18 (1971–72): 401–18.
———. "On the Evidence for the Creative Role of Christian Prophets," *New Testament Studies* 20 (1974): 262–74.
———. *New Testament Prophecy*. Atlanta: John Knox, 1979.
Holman. C. L. "Eschatological Delay in Jewish and Early Christian Literature. PhD thesis, University of Nottingham, 1982.
Holtsmark, E. B. 1970. "Ring Composition and the *Persae* of Aeschylus." *Symbolae Osloenses* 45, 5–23.
Homcy, S. L. 1995. "'To him who overcomes': A Fresh Look at What 'Victory' Means for the Believer according to the Book of Revelation." *Journal of the Evangelical Theological Society* 38, 193–201.
Hornblower, S. and A. Spawforth. *The Oxford Classical Dictionary*. 3rd ed. Oxford/New York: Oxford University Press, 1996.
Hort, F. J. A. "The Apocalypse of St John I–III." In *Expository and Exegetical Studies*., i–42. 1908. Repr., Minneapolis: Klock & Klock, 1980.
Hubbard, D. A. *Joel and Amos*. Downers Grove, Ill.: InterVarsity, 1989.
Hubert, M. "L'architecture des lettres aux Sept Églises (Apoc, ch II–III)." *Revue biblique* 3 (1960): 349–53.
Jart, U. "The Precious Stones in the Revelation of St. John xxi. 18–21." *Studia Theologica* 24 (1970): 150–81.
Jeremias, J. "ΙΕΡΟΥΣΑΛΗΜ/ΙΕΡΟΣΟΛΥΜΑ." *Zeitschrift für die neutestament-liche Wissenschaft* 65 (1974): 273–76.
Johnson, A. C., P. R. Coleman-Norton, and F. C. Bourne. *Ancient Roman Statutes*. Austin: University of Texas Press, 1961.
Johnson, A. F. 1981. "Revelation." In *The Expositor's Bible Commentary*, edited by F. E. Gaebelein, 12:399–603. Grand Rapids: Zondervan, 1981.
———. *Revelation*. Grand Rapids: Zondervan, 1983.
Johnston, A. W. "*IG* II2 2311 and the Number of Panathenaic Amphorae." *Annual of the British School at Athens* 82 (1987): 125–29.
Jones, A. H. M. *Cities of the Eastern Roman Provinces*. Rev. ed. Oxford: Clarendon, 1971.
Jones, B. W. *The Emperor Domitian*. London: Routledge, 1992.
Judge, E. A. "The Regional *kanon* for Requisitioned Transport." In *New Documents Illustrating Early Christianity*, edited by G. H. R. Horsley, 1:36–45. North Ryde: Macquarie University, 1981.
Käsemann, E. *New Testament Questions of Today*. London: SCM, 1969.
Kee, H. C. "Testaments of the Twelve Patriarchs." In *The Old Testament Pseudipigrapha*, edited by J. H. Charlesworth 1:775–828. New York: Doubleday, 1983.
Kennedy, G. A . *New Testament Interpretation through Rhetorical Criticism*. Chapel Hill: University of North Carolina Press, 1984.
Kerkeslager, A. "Apollo, Greco-Roman Prophecy, and the Rider on the White Horse in Rev 6:2." *Journal of Biblical Literature* 112 (1993): 116–21.
Kernell, N. J. "Ordering Principles and Principles of Order: Chiasmus and Related Patterns in Euripides' *Bacchae*." PhD diss., University of Iowa, 1992.

Bibliography

Kiddle, M. *The Revelation of St. John*. London: Hodder & Stoughton, 1940.
Kidner, D. *Psalms 73–150*. Downers Grove, Ill.: InterVarsity, 1973.
Kirby, J. T. "The Rhetorical Situations of Revelation 1–3." *New Testament Studies* 34 (1988): 197–207.
Kittel, G., G. Friedrich, and G. W. Bromiley, eds. *Theological Dictionary of the New Testament*. 10 vols. Grand Rapids: Eerdmans, 1964–74.
Kline, M. "The First Resurrection." *Westminster Theological Journal* 37 (1974–75): 366–75.
Knibb, M. A. 1985. "Martyrdom and Ascension of Isaiah." In *The Old Testament Pseudepigrapha*, edited by J. H. Charlesworth, 2:142–76. Garden City, N.Y.: Doubleday, 1983.
Knibbe, D. "Ephesos—Nicht nur die Stadt der Artemis: Die ‚Anderen' ephisischen Götter." In *Studien zur Religion und Kultur Kleinasiens*, edited by S. Şahin, E. Schwertheim, and J. Wagner, 489–503. Leiden: Brill, 1978.
Koester, C. R. *Revelation and the End of All Things*. Grand Rapids: Eerdmans, 2001.
Koester, H., ed. *Ephesos: Metropolis of Asia*. Valley Forge: Trinity Press International, 1995.
Koester, H. "Ephesos in Early Christian Literature." In *Ephesos: Metropolis of Asia*, edited by H. Koester, 119–40. Valley Forge: Trinity Press International, 1995.
Kraft, H. *Die Offenbarung des Johannes*. Tübingen: J. C. B. Mohr, 1974.
Kümmel, W. G. *Promise and Fulfilment*. 3rd ed. London: SCM, 1961.
Kunze, M. *The Pergamon Altar*. Mainz: Philipp von Zabern, 1995.
Laaton, A. "The Composition of Isaiah 40–55." *Journal of Biblical Literature* 109 (1990): 207–28.
Ladd, G. E. *A Commentary on the Revelation of John*. Grand Rapids: Eerdmans, 1972.
Lambrecht, J. "A Structuration of Revelation 4, 1–22, 5." In *L'Apocalypse johannique et l'apocalyptique dans le Nouveau Testament*, edited by J. Lambrecht, 77–104. Gembloux: Duculot/Leuven: University Press, 1980.
Lane, W. L. *The Gospel of Mark*. Grand Rapids: Eerdmans, 1974.
Lawrence, D. H. *Apocalypse*. 1931. Repr., New York: Penguin, 1976.
Laws, S. *In the Light of the Lamb*. Wilmington, Del.: Michael Glazier, 1988.
Lebram, J. C. H. "The Piety of the Jewish Apocalyptists." In *Apocalypticism in the Mediterranean World and the Near East*, edited by D. Hellholm, 171–210. Tübingen: J. C. B. Mohr, 1983.
Le Déaut, R. *The Message of the New Testament and the Aramaic Bible (Targum)*. Rome: Biblical Institute Press, 1982.
Lee, M. V. "A Call to Martyrdom: The Significance of the Chiastic Structure of Revelation." Paper presented at the Evangelical Theological Society annual meeting. Philadelphia, 1995.
Leivestad, R. *Christ the Conqueror*. London: SPCK, 1954.
Lenski, R. C. H. *The Interpretation of St. John's Revelation*. Minneapolis: Augsburg, 1943.
Levi, P. *Atlas of the Greek World*. New York: Facts on File, 1984.
Liddell, H. G. and R. Scott. *An Intermediate Greek-English Lexicon*. Oxford: Clarendon, 1889.
Lightfoot, J. B. *St. Paul's Epistle to the Galatians*. 1865. Repr., Peabody, Mass: Hendrickson, 1993.
———. *St. Paul's Epistle to the Philippians*. 1868. Repr., Peabody, Mass.: Hendrickson, 1993.
———. *St Paul's Epistles to the Colossians and Philemon*. 1875. Repr., Peabody, Mass.: Hendrickson, 1993.

Bibliography

———. *The Apostolic Fathers*. 5 vols. 1889–90. Repr., Peabody, Mass: Hendrickson, 1977.

Lightfoot, J. B., J. R. Harmer, and M. W. Holmes. *The Apostolic Fathers*. 2nd ed. Grand Rapids: Baker, 1992.

Lilje, H. *The Last Book of the Bible*. Philadelphia: Muhlenberg, 1957.

Lincoln, A. T. *Ephesians*. Dallas: Word, 1990.

Llewelyn, S. R., ed. *New Documents Illustrating Early Christianity*, vol. 8. Grand Rapids: Eerdmans, 1998.

Loenertz, R. J. *The Apocalypse of Saint John*. London: Catholic Book Club, 1948.

Lohmeyer, E. *Die Offenbarung des Johannes*. 2nd ed. Tübingen: J. C. B. Mohr, 1953.

Lohse, E. *Die Offenbarung des Johannes*. Göttingen: Vandenhoeck & Ruprecht, 1960.

Lombard, H. A. "Charisma and Church Office." *Neotestamentica* 10 (1976): 31–52.

———. "The Character, Epoch (Period), Origins (Motives) and Methods of Jewish Apocalyptic." *Neotestamentica* 12 (1981): 20–40.

———. "The Structure of Revelation." In *Reading Revelation*. Edited by J. E. Botha et al., 154–57. Pretoria: van Schaik, 1988.

Long, T. M. S. "A Real Reader Reading Revelation." *Neotestamentica* 28 (1994): 395–411.

Longnecker, R. N. *Galatians*. Dallas: Word, 1990.

Louw J. P. and E. A. Nida, eds. *Greek–English Lexicon*. 2nd ed. New York: United Bible Societies, 1989.

Lund, N. W. *Chiasmus in the New Testament*. 1942. Repr., Peabody, Mass: Hendrickson, 1992.

———. *Studies in the Book of Revelation*. Chicago: Covenant Press, 1955.

Luter, A. B. "Twin Peaks: The Complementary Chiasms in Revelation 13, 14–15." Paper presented at the Evangelical Theological Society annual meeting. Chicago, 1994.

Luter, A. B. and M. V. Lee. "Phillippians as Chiasmus: Key to the Structure, Unity and Theme Questions," *New Testament Studies* 41 (1995): 89–101.

Luter, A. B. and R. O. Rigsby. "An Adjusted Symmetrical Structuring of Ruth." *Journal of the Evangelical Theological Society* 39 (1996): 15–28.

McLean, B. H. *An Introduction to Greek Epigraphy of the Hellenistic and Roman Periods from Alexander the Great down to the Reign of Constantine (323 BC–AD 337)*. Ann Arbor: University of Michigan Press, 2002.

McComiskey, T. E. "Alteration of OT Imagery in the Book of Revelation: Its Hermeneutical and Theological Significance." *Journal of the Evangelical Theological Society* 36 (1993): 307–16.

McRay, J. *Archaeology and the New Testament*. Grand Rapids: Baker, 1991.

McVann, M., ed. "The Apocalypse of John in Social-Scientific Perspective." *Listening* 28.3 (1993).

Magie, D. *Roman Rule in Asia Minor*. 2 vols. Princeton: Princeton University Press, 1950.

Malay, H. *Greek and Latin inscriptions in the Manisa Museum*. Wien: Verlag der Österreichischen Akademie der Wissenschaften, 1994.

Malina, B. *On the Genre and Message of Revelation*. Peabody, Mass.: Hendrickson, 1995.

Mann, R. E. "Chiasm in the New Testament." Th.M. thesis, Dallas Theological Seminary, 1982.

———. "The Value of Chiasm for New Testament Interpretation." *Bibliotheca Sacra* 141 (1984): 146–57.

Marrou, H. I. *A History of Education in Antiquity*. New York: Sheed & Ward, 1956.

Marshall, I. H. *Commentary on Luke*. Grand Rapids: Eerdmans, 1978.

Bibliography

Martin, A. and J. Martin. *Isaiah: The Glory of the Messiah*. Chicago: Moody, 1983.
Martin R. P. *James*. Waco: Word, 1988.
———. "Worship." In *Dictionary of Paul and His Letters*, edited by G. F. Hawthorne, R. P. Martin, and D. G. Reid, 982–91. Downers Grove, Ill.: InterVarsity, 1993.
Martínez, F. G. *The Dead Sea Scrolls Translated*. 2nd ed. Grand Rapids: Eerdmans, 1996.
Mason, H. J. *Greek Terms for Roman Institutions*. Toronto: Hakkert, 1974.
Mazzaferri, F. D. *Genre of the Book of Revelation from a Source-Critical Perspective*. Berlin/New York: De Gruyter, 1989.
Mealy, J. W. *After the Thousand Years: Resurrection and Judgment in Revelation*. Sheffield: JSOT Press, 1992.
Meeks, W. *The First Urban Christians*. New Haven: Yale University Press.
Mellor, R. ΘΕΑ ΡΩΜΗ: *The Worship of the Goddess Roma in the Greek World*. Göttingen: Vandenhoeck & Ruprecht, 1975.
Meinardus, O. F. A. *St. John of Patmos and the Seven Churches of the Apocalypse*. New Rochelle, N.Y.: Caratzas Brothers, 1979.
Merrill, E. T. *Essays in Early Christian History*. London: Macmillan, 1924.
Metzger, B. *The Text of the New Testament*. 3rd ed. New York: Oxford, 1992.
Michaels, J. R. *1 Peter*. Waco: Word, 1988.
———. *Interpreting the Book of Revelation*. Grand Rapids: Baker, 1992.
———. *Revelation*. Downers Grove, Ill.: InterVarsity, 1997.
Miller, A. M. "Apolline Ethics and Olympian Victory in Pindar's Eighty *Pythian* 67–78." *Greek, Roman, and Byzantine Studies* 30 (1989): 461–84.
Millar, F. *The Emperor in the Roman World*. London: Duckworth, 1977.
Miller, S. G. *Arete: Greek Sports from Ancient Sources*. 2nd ed. Berkeley: University of California Press, 1991.
Minear, P. S. *Images of the Church in the New Testament*. Philadelphia: Westminster, 1960.
———. *I Saw a New Earth*. Washington, DC: Corpus Books, 1968.
Mitchell, S. *Anatolia*. 2 vols. Oxford: Clarendon, 1993.
Moffatt, J. "Revelation of St. John the Divine." In *The Expositor's Greek Testament*, edited by W. R. Nicoll, 279–494. New York: Doran, 1910.
Mommsen, T. *Res gestae divi Augusti*. Berlin: np, 1883.
Morris, L. *Revelation*. Rev. ed. Grand Rapids: Eerdmans, 1987.
Mounce, R. H. *The Book of Revelation*. Grand Rapids: Eerdmans, 1977.
Moyise, S. *The Old Testament in the Book of Revelation*. Sheffield: Sheffield Academic Press, 1995.
Mulholland, Jr., M. R. *Revelation*. Grand Rapids: Zondervan, 1990.
Müller, U. B. *Die Offenbarung des Johannes*. Gütersloh: Gerd Mohn/Würzburg: Echter-Verlag, 1984.
Munck, J. *Petrus und Paulus in der Offenbarung Johannis*. Copenhagen: n.p., 1950.
Musurillo, H. *The Acts of the Christian Martyrs*. Oxford: Clarendon, 1972.
Neall, B. S. *The Concept of Character in the Apocalypse, with Implications for Character Education*. Washington, D.C.: University Press of America, 1983.
Nicol, G. G. "The Threat and the Promise." *Expository Times* 94 (1983): 136–39.
O'Brien, P. T. *Colossians, Philemon*. Waco: Word, 1982.
Osbourne, G. R. *Revelation*. Grand Rapids: Baker, 2002.
Oster R. "The Ephesian Artemis as an Opponent of Early Christianity." *Jahrbuch für Antike und Christentum* 19 (1976): 24–44.
———. "Numismatic Windows into the Social World of Early Christianity: A Methodological Inquiry." *Journal of Biblical Literature* 101 (1982): 195–223.

Bibliography

———. "Ephesus as a Religious Center under the Principate, I. Paganism before Constantine." *Aufstieg und Niedergang der römischen Welt* 2.18.3 (1990): 1661–1728.

Parez, C. H. "The Seven Letters and the Rest of the Apocalypse." *Journal of Theological Studies* 12 (1911): 284–86.

Park, Sung-Min. "More than a Regained Eden: The New Jerusalem as the Ultimate Portrayal of Eschatological Blessedness and its Implication for the Understanding of the Book of Revelation." PhD diss., Trinity Evangelical Divinity School, 1995.

Parunak, H. V. D. "Oral Typesetting: Some Uses of Biblical Structure." *Biblica* 62 (1981): 153–68.

Peake, A. S. *The Revelation of John*. London: Holborn, 1920.

Petersen, D. L. *Haggai and Zechariah 1–8*. Philadelphia: Westminster, 1984.

Pfitzner, V. C. *Paul and the Agon Motif*. Leiden: Brill, 1967.

Philo. *The Works of Philo*. Translated by C. D. Yonge. Peabody, Mass.: Hendrickson, 1993.

Pilch, J. J. "Lying and Deceit in the Letters to the Seven Churches: Perspectives from Cultural Anthropology." *Biblical Theology Bulletin* 22 (1992): 126–35.

Pohl, A. *Die Offenbarung des Johannes*. 2 vols. Wuppertal: R. Brockhaus, 1969, 1971.

Poirier, L. *Les sept églises ou le premier septénaire prophétique de l'Apocalypse*. Washington, D.C.: Catholic University of America Press, 1943.

Porter, S. E. "Why the Laodiceans Received Lukewarm Water (Revelation 3:15–18)." *Tyndale Bulletin* 38 (1987): 143–49.

———. "ἴστε γινώσκοντες in Ephesians 5,5: Does Chiasmus Solve a Problem?" *Zeitschrift für die neutestamentliche Wissenschaft* 81 (1990): 270–76.

Porter, S. E. and J. T. Reed. "Philippians As a Macro-Chiasm and Its Exegetical Significance," *New Testament Studies* 44 (1998): 213–31.

Pretorius, E. A. C. "The Seventh Bowl (16:17—19:10)." In *Reading Revelation*. Edited by J. E. Botha et al., 120–33. Pretoria: van Schaik, 1988.

Price, S. R. F. *Rituals and Power: The Roman Imperial Cult in Asia Minor*. Cambridge: Cambridge University Press, 1984.

Prigent, P. *Apocalypse et liturgie*. Neuchatel: Delachaux et Niestlé, 1964.

———. "Au temps de l'Apocalypse." *Revue d'histoire et de philosophie religieuses* 54 (1974): 455–83; 55 (1975): 215–35, 341–63.

———. *L'Apocalypse de saint Jean*. 2nd ed. Geneva: Labor et Fides, 1988.

Radt, W. *Pergamon: Archaeological Guide*. 3rd ed. Istanbul: Türkiye Turing ve Otomobil Kurumu, 1984.

Rajak, T. *Josephus: The Historian and His Society*. Philadelphia: Fortress, 1984.

Ramsay, W. M. *The Church in the Roman Empire Before AD 170*. 5th ed. London: Hodder & Stoughton, 1893.

———. *St. Paul the Traveller and the Roman Citizen*. London: Hodder & Stoughton, 1895.

———. *The Letters to the Seven Churches*. 1904. Edited by M. W. Wilson. Peabody, Mass: Hendrickson, 1994.

———. *Historical Commentary on the Pastoral Epistles*. 1909–1911. Edited by M. W. Wilson. Grand Rapids: Kregel, 1996.

———. *Historical Commentary on First Corinthians*. 1900–1901. Edited by M. W. Wilson. Grand Rapids: Kregel, 1996.

Rapske, B. *The Book of Acts in its First Century Setting: Paul in Roman Custody*. Grand Rapids: Eerdmans, 1994.

Reardon, B. P., ed. *Collected Ancient Greek Novels*. Berkeley/Los Angeles/London: University of California Press, 1989.
Rickman, G. *The Corn Supply of Ancient Rome*. Oxford: Clarendon, 1980.
Rife, J. M. "The Literary Background of Revelation II–III." *Journal of Biblical Literature* 60 (1941):179–82.
Ringwood, I. C. *Agonistic Features of Local Greek Festivals Chiefly from Inscriptional Evidence*. Poughkeepsie, N.Y.: Ringwood, 1927.
Rissi, M. *Time and History*. Richmond: John Knox, 1966.
———. *The Future of the World*. London: SCM, 1972.
Robert, L. "Le cult de Caligula à Milet et la province d'Asie." *Hellenica* 7 (1949): 206–38.
Roberts, J. H. "A Letter to Seven Churches in the Roman Province of Asia." In *Reading Revelation*, edited by J. E. Botha et al., 17–35. Pretoria: van Schaik, 1988.
Roberts, R. "The Tree of Life (Rev ii.7)." *Expository Times* 25 (1913–14): 332.
Robinson, J. A. T. *Redating the New Testament*. London: SCM, 1976.
Rogers, C. "Images of Christian Victory: Notes for Preaching from the Book of Revelation." *Quarterly Review* 10.3 (1990): 69–78.
Roloff, J. *Revelation*. Minneapolis: Fortress, 1993.
Rosscup, J. "The Overcomer of the Apocalypse," *Grace Theological Journal* 3 (1982): 261–86.
Rostovtzeff, M. *The Social and Economic History of the Roman Empire*. 2 vols. 2nd ed. Oxford: Clarendon, 1957.
Rowland, C. *The Open Heaven*. New York: Crossroad, 1982.
———. *Revelation*. London: Epworth, 1993.
Rowley, H. H. *The Relevance of Apocalyptic*. London: Lutterworth, 1963.
Rudberg, G. "Zu den Sendschreiben der Johannes-Apokalypse." *Eranos* 11 (1911): 170–79.
Rudwick, M. J. S. and E. M. B. Green. "The Laodicean Lukewarmness." *Expository Times* 69 (1957–58): 176–78.
Russell, D. S. *The Method and Message of Jewish Apocalyptic*. Philadelphia: Westminster, 1964.
Ryken, L. "Revelation." In *The New Testament in Literary Criticism*, edited by L. Ryken, 302–8. New York: Ungar, 1984.
Saffrey, H. D. "Relire L'apocalypse à Patmos." *Revue biblique* 82 (1975): 385–417.
Scarre, C. *Chronicle of the Roman Emperors*. New York: Thames and Hudson, 1995.
Schoedel, W. R. *Ignatius of Antioch*. Philadelphia: Fortress, 1985.
Scholer, D. M. and K. R. Snodgrass. "Preface." In N. W. Lund, *Chiasmus in the New Testament*, vii–xxi. Peabody, Mass.: Hendrickson, 1992.
Scobie, C. H. H. "Local References in the Letters to the Seven Churches." *New Testament Studies* 39 (1993): 606–24.
Scott, P. M. "Chiastic Structure: A Key to the Interpretation of Mark's Gospel." *Biblical Theology Bulletin* 15 (1985): 17–26.
Scherrer, P., ed., *Ephesus: The New Guide*. Istanbul: Ege Yayınları, 2000.
Schüssler Fiorenza, E. *The Book of Revelation: Justice and Judgment*. Philadelphia: Fortress, 1985.
———. "Revelation." In *The New Testament and its Modern Interpreters*, edited by E. J. Epp and G. W. MacRae, 407–27. Philadelphia: Fortress/Atlanta: Scholars, 1989.
———. *Revelation: Vision of a Just World*. Philadelphia: Fortress, 1991.

Bibliography

Seager, A. R. and A. T. Kraabel. "The Synagogue and the Jewish Community." In *Sardis from Prehistoric to Roman Times*, 168–90, edited by G. M. A. Hanfmann, 168–90. Cambridge, Mass.: Harvard University Press, 1983.

Seiss, J. A. *The Apocalypse: Lectures on the Book of Revelation*. 1975. Repr., Grand Rapids: Zondervan, 1975.

Shea, W. H. "Chiasm in Theme and by Form in Revelation 18." *Andrews University Seminary Studies* 20 (1982): 249–56.

———. "The Covenantal Form of the Letters to the Seven Churches." *Andrews University Seminary Studies* 21 (1983): 71–84.

———. "Revelation 5 and 19 as Literary Reciprocals." *Andrews University Seminary Studies* 22, (1984): 249–57.

Shepherd, H. H. *The Paschal Liturgy and the Apocalypse*. London: Butterworth, 1960.

Sherk, R. K. *Roman Documents from the Greek East: Senatus Consulta and Epistulae to the Age of Augustus*. Baltimore: Johns Hopkins University Press, 1969.

Siew, Antonius King Wai. *The War between the Two Beasts and the Two Witnesses: A Chiastic Reading of Revelation 11.1—14.5*. London: T. & T. Clark, 2005.

Skehan, P. W. *Studies in Israelite Poetry and Wisdom*. Washington, D.C.: Catholic Biblical Association of America, 1971.

Smalley, S. S. *Thunder and Love: John's Revelation and John's Community*. Dallas: Word, 1994.

———. *The Revelation to John: A Commentary on the Greek Text of the Apocalypse*. Downers Grove, Ill.: InterVarsity, 2005.

Smith, C. R. "The Book of Life." *Grace Theological Journal* 6 (1985): 219–30.

Smith, G. V. *Amos*. Grand Rapids: Zondervan, 1989.

Snyder, B. W. "Combat Myth in the Apocalypse: The Liturgy of the Day of the Lord and the Dedication of the Heavenly Temple." PhD diss., Graduate Theological Union/University of California, Berkeley, 1991.

Stauffer, E. *Christ and the Caesars*. London: SCM, 1965.

Stephens, S. A. "Who Read Ancient Novels?" In *The Search for the Ancient Novel*, edited by J. Tatum, 405–18. Baltimore: Johns Hopkins University Press, 1994.

Stendahl, K. 1962. "The Apocalypse of John and the Epistles of Paul in the Muratorian Fragment." In *Current Issues in New Testament Interpretation*, edited by W. Klassen and G. F. Snyder, 239–45. New York: Harper & Row, 1962.

Stillwell, R., ed. *The Princeton Encyclopedia of Classical Sites*. Princeton: Princeton University Press, 1976.

Stock, A. "Chiastic Awareness and Education in Antiquity." *Biblical Theology Bulletin* 14 (1984): 23–27.

Stowers, S. K. *Letter Writing in Greco-Roman Antiquity*. Philadelphia: Westminster, 1986.

———. "4 Maccabees." In *Harper's Bible Commentary*, edited by J. L. May, 922–34. San Francisco: Harper & Row, 1988.

Strack, H. L. and P. Billerbeck. *Kommentar zum Neuen Testament aus Talmud und Midrasch*. 1926. Repr., Munich: C H Beck'sche, 1982.

Strand, K. A. "Chiastic Structure and Some Motifs in the Book of Revelation." *Andrews University Seminary Studies* 16 (1978): 401–8.

———. *Interpreting the Book of Revelation*. Naples, Fl.: Ann Arbor, 1979.

———. "The Eight Basic Visions in the Book of Revelation." *Andrews University Seminary Studies* 25 (1987): 107–21.

———. "The Victorious-Introduction Scenes in the Visions in the Book of Revelation." *Andrews University Seminary Studies* 25 (1987): 267–88.

———. "'Overcomer': A Study in the Macrodynamic of Theme Development in the Book of Revelation." *Andrews University Seminary Studies* 28 (1990): 237–54.
Strelan, R. *Paul, Artemis, and the Jews in Ephesus.* Berlin/New York: de Gruyter, 1996.
Strobel, A. "Abfassung und Geschichtstheolgie der Apokalypse nach Kp. 17, 9–12." *New Testament Studies* 10 (1963–64): 433–45.
Stuart, D. *Hosea-Jonah.* Waco: Word, 1987.
———. *Ezekiel.* Dallas: Word, 1989.
Stuart, M. "The White Stone of the Apocalypse." *Bibliotheca Sacra* 1 (1843): 461–77.
Stuckenbruck, L. T. *Angel Veneration and Christology: A Study in Early Judaism and in the Christology of the Apocalypse of John.* Tübingen: Mohr/Paul Siebeck, 1995.
Sweet, J. *Revelation.* Philadelphia: Trinity Press International, 1979.
Swete, H. B. *The Apocalypse of St. John.* 3rd ed. London: Macmillan, 1909.
Talbert, C. H. "Artistry and Theology: An Analysis of the Architecture of Jn 1, 19–5, 47," *Catholic Biblical Quarterly* 32 (1970), 341–66.
———. *Literary Patterns, Theological Themes and the Genre of Luke-Acts.* Missoula: Scholars Press, 1973.
———. *The Apocalypse.* Louisville: Westminster John Knox, 1994.
Tate, M. E. *Psalms 51–100.* Dallas: Word, 1990.
Taylor, J. B. *Ezekiel: An Introduction and Commentary.* Downers Grove, Ill.: InterVarsity, 1969.
Tenney, M. C. *Interpreting Revelation.* Grand Rapids: Eerdmans, 1957.
Tenney, M. C., ed. *Zondervan Pictorial Encyclopedia of the Bible.* 5 vols. Grand Rapids: Zondervan, 1976.
Thomas, C. M. "At Home in the City of Artemis." In *Ephesos:Metropolis of Asia*, edited by H. Koester, 81–117. Valley Forge: Trinity Press International, 1995.
Thompson, L. L. *The Book of Revelation: Apocalypse and Empire.* New York: Oxford, 1990.
Thompson, S. *The Apocalypse and Semitic Syntax.* Cambridge: Cambridge University Press, 1985.
Thomason, I. H. *Chiasmus in the Pauline Letters.* Sheffield: Sheffield Academic Press, 1995.
Torrey, C. C. *The Apocalypse of John.* New Haven: Yale University Press, 1958.
Trebilco, P. R. *Jewish Communities in Asia Minor.* Cambridge: Cambridge University Press, 1991.
———. "Asia." In *The Book of Acts in its First Century Setting:Graeco-Roman Setting*, edited by D. W. J. Gill and C. Gempf, 291–362. Grand Rapids: Eerdmans, 1994.
———. *The Early Christians in Ephesus from Paul to Ignatius.* Tübingen: Mohr Siebeck, 2004.
Trell, B. L. "The Temple of Artemis at Ephesos." In *The Seven Wonders of the Ancient World*, edited by P. Clayton and M. Price, 78–99. New York: Routledge, 1989.
Trench, R. C. *Commentary on the Epistles to the Seven Churches in Asia.* London: Macmillan, 1883.
Trevett, C. "The Other Letters to the Churches of Asia: Apocalypse and Ignatius of Antioch." *Journal for the Study of the New Testament* 37 (1989): 117–35.
Trites, A. A. *The New Testament Concept of Witness.* Cambridge: Cambridge University Press, 1977.
Trudinger, L. P. "Some Observations Concerning the Text of the Old Testament in the Book of Revelation." *Journal of Theological Studies* 17 (1966): 82–88.
Turner, C. H. *Studies in Early Church History.* Oxford: Clarendon, 1913.

Turner, D. L. "The New Jerusalem in Revelation 21:1—22:5: Consummation of a Biblical Continuum." In *Dispensationalism, Israel and the Church*, edited by C. A. Blaising and D. L. Bock, 264–92. Grand Rapids: Zondervan, 1992.
Ulfgard, H. *Feast and Future: Revelation 7:9–17 and the Feast of Tabernacles*. Stockholm: Almqvist & Wiksell, 1989.
Van Hartingsveld, L. *Revelation*. Grand Rapids: Eerdmans, 1985.
Van Nijf, O. M. *The Civic World of Professional Associations in the Roman East*. Amsterdam: J. C. Gieben, 1997.
Vanhoye, A. "L'utilisation du Livre d'Ezechiel dans l'Apocalypse." *Biblica* 43 (1962): 436–76.
Vanni, U. *L'Apocalisse: Ermeneutica, Esegesi, Teologia*. Bologna: Dehoniane, 1988.
Van Tilborg, S. *Reading John in Ephesus*. Leiden/New York/Köln: Brill, 1996.
Veyne, P. "The Roman Empire." In *A History of Private Life: From Pagan Rome to Byzantium*, edited by P. Veyne, 5–234. Cambridge, Mass.: Belknap Harvard, 1987.
Vos, L. A. *The Synoptic Traditions in the Apocalypse*. Kampen: Kok, 1965.
Wainwright, A. W. *Mysterious Apocalypse*. Nashville: Abingdon, 1993.
Wall, R. W. *Revelation*. Peabody, Mass: Hendrickson, 1991.
Walter, J. C. "Egyptian Religions in Ephesos." In *Ephesos: Metropolis of Asia*, edited by H. Koester, 281–309. Philadelphia: Trinity Press International, 1995.
Walvoord, J. F. *The Revelation of Jesus Christ*. Chicago: Moody, 1966.
Waters, K. "The Character of Domitian." *Phoenix* 18 (1964): 49–77.
Welch, J. W. "Chiasmus in the New Testament." In *Chiasmus in Antiquity: Structures, Analyses, Exegesis*, edited by J. W. Welch, 211–49. Hildesheim: Gerstenberg, 1981.
Welles, C. B. *Royal Correspondence in the Hellenistic Period*. New Haven: Yale University Press, 1934.
Wendland, E. R. "A Comparative Study of 'Rhetorical Criticism,' Ancient and Modern—with Special Reference to the Larger Structure and Function of the Epistle of Jude." *Neotestamentica* 28 (1994):193–228.
Wenham, D. *The Rediscovery of Jesus' Eschatological Discourse*. Sheffield: JSOT Press, 1984.
———. "Acts and the Pauline Corpus: II. Pauline Parallels." In *The Book of Acts in its Ancient Literary Setting*, edited by B. W. Winter and A. D. Clarke, 215–58. Grand Rapids: Eerdmans, 1993.
Wenham, G. J. *Numbers*. Downers Grove, Ill.: InterVarsity, 1981.
Westcott, B. F. *The Gospel According to St. John*. 1881. Repr., Grand Rapids: Eerdmans, 1964.
White, J. L. *Light from Ancient Letters*. Philadelphia: Fortress, 1986.
Whitman, C. H. *Homer and the Heroic Tradition*. Cambridge: Harvard University Press, 1958.
Wilder, A. N. *Eschatology and Ethics*. New York: Harper & Row, 1950.
Wilkinson, R. H. "The STULOS of Revelation 3:12 and Ancient Coronation Rites." *Journal of Biblical Literature* 107 (1988): 498–501.
Williams, J. R. *Renewal Theology: Salvation, the Holy Spirit and Christian Living*. Grand Rapids: Zondervan, 1990.
———. *Renewal Theology: The Church, the Kingdom, and Last Things*. Grand Rapids: Zondervan, 1992.
Williamson, R. L. "Thrones in the Book of Revelation." PhD diss., The Southern Baptist Theological Seminary, 1993.
Wilson, J. C. "The Problem of the Domitianic Date of Revelation." *Journal of Theological Studies* (1993): 587–605.

Bibliography

Wilson, M. "Revelation 19:10 and Contemporary interpretation." In *Spirit and Renewal: Essays in Honor of J. Rodman Williams*, edited by M. W. Wilson, 191–202. Sheffield: Sheffield Academic Press, 1994.

———. "Chiasmus as a Tool for Interpreting the Book of Revelation." Paper presented at the Evangelical Theological Studies annual meeting. Chicago, 1994.

———. "Seven Wonders, Seven Churches." Paper presented at the Evangelical Theological Society Northeast Regional Meeting. Valley Forge, Penn., 1995.

———. "A Pie in a Very Bleak Sky? Analysis and Appropriation of the Promise Sayings in the Seven Letters to the Churches in Revelation 2–3." D.Litt. et Phil. thesis, The University of South Africa, 1996.

———. "The Book of Revelation" in the *Zondervan Illustrated Bible Backgrounds Commentary*, edited by Clinton E. Arnold, 4:244–383. Grand Rapids: Zondervan, 2002.

———. "The Early Christians in Ephesus and the Date of Revelation, Again," *Neotestamentica* 39.1 (2005): 163–93.

———. *Charts on the Book of Revelation: Literary, Historical, and Theological Perspectives*. Grand Rapids: Kregel, 2007.

Witherington III, B. *Conflict and Community in Corinth*. Grand Rapids: Eerdmans, 1995.

———. *Revelation*. Cambridge: Cambridge University Press, 2003.

Wojciechowski, M. "Seven Churches and Seven Celestial Bodies (Rev 1.16; Rev 2–3)." *Biblische Notizen* 45 (1988): 48–50.

Wolf, H. M. *Interpreting Isaiah*. Grand Rapids: Zondervan, 1985.

Wolfe, K. R. "The Chiastic Structure of Luke-Acts and Some Implications for Worship." *Southwestern Journal of Theology* 22 (1980): 60–71.

Wood, P. "Local Knowledge in the Letters of the Apocalypse," *Expository Times* 73 (1961–62): 263–64.

Yamauchi, E. M. *New Testament Cities in Western Asia Minor*. Grand Rapids: Baker, 1980.

Yarbro Collins, A. *"The Combat Myth in the Book of Revelation."* Missoula: Scholars Press, 1976.

———. *The Apocalypse*. Collegeville, Minn.: Michael Glazier/Liturgical Press, 1979.

———. "The Early Christian Apocalypses." *Semeia* 14 (1979): 61–121.

———. "Revelation 18: Taunt-song or Dirge?" In *L'Apocalypse johannique et l'apocalyptique dans le Nouveau Testament*, edited by J. Lambrecht, 185–204. Gembloux: Duculot/Leuven: University Press, 1980.

———. *Crisis and Catharsis: The Power of the Apocalypse*. Louisville: Westminster John Knox, 1984.

Yarbro Collins, A., ed. *Early Christian Apocalypticism: Genre and Social Setting*. Semeia 36 (1986).

Young, D. C. "Athletics." In *Civilization of the Ancient Mediterranean: Greece and Rome*, edited by M. Grant and R. Kitzinger, 2:1131–42. New York: Charles Scribner's Sons, 1988.

Young, E. J. *The Prophecy of Daniel*. Grand Rapids: Eerdmans, 1949.

———. *The Book of Isaiah*. 3 vols. Grand Rapids: Eerdmans, 1969.

Youngblood, R. F. "2 Samuel." In *The Expositor's Bible Commentary*, edited by F. E. Gaebelein, 3:802–1104: Grand Rapids: Zondervan, 1992.

Zahn, T. *Acta Joannis*. 1880. Repr., Hildesheim: Gerstenberg,1975.

Zerwick, M. *Biblical Greek*. Rome: Editrice Pontificio Istituto Biblico, 1963.

www.ingramcontent.com/pod-product-compliance
Lightning Source LLC
Chambersburg PA
CBHW071239230426
43668CB00011B/1511